D1607798

Jews in Minnesota Politics

Jews in Minnesota Politics

The Inside Stories

Robert (Bob) Latz

NODIN PRESS

ISBN 10: 1-932472-65-7
ISBN 13: 978-1-932472-65-3

Library of Congress Control Number: 2007935576

design and layout: John Toren

Nodin Press LLC
530 North Third Street
Suite 120
Minneapolis, MN 55401

Dedication

Public figures in the political world receive recognition in this book and elsewhere. Too often overlooked are those volunteers who labor in the vineyards of politics. These "grassroots" politicians are the keys to success for those who seek public office. Without their efforts, few candidates would prevail.

I therefore dedicate this book to those unsung and critically important participants in the political process – the volunteers.

Acknowledgements

I owe a debt of gratitude to family members and others for their help in the publication of this book.

I am profoundly grateful for the love and support of my wife, Carolyn, and our children Ron, Marty, Mickey and Shari and their spouses.

University of Minnesota Professor Emeritus Hyman Berman provided invaluable insight into the history and political process. Professor Berman is truly 'Minnesota's historian.'

My thanks to Teresa Fane, and Wayne, Sandy and Greg Freeman of the Executive Suites, who made her services available. Teresa displayed patience, skill and insight throughout my many drafts and redrafts.

I have been fortunate over the last sixty years to have been associated with dedicated politicians and community volunteers in and out of the Jewish community. They have all written the history on which this book is based. Without them, this book would not have been possible.

Contents

Foreword

Since the early 1930's, Jews have played an influential role in Minnesota government and politics. Despite religious intolerance and discrimination they have succeeded as advisors, leaders, appointed and elected officials. Both major political parties have had "stars" who have been Jewish. The Jewish people have a historical commitment to social justice. This ethic is at the core of the involvement of the Minnesota Jews described in this book. The Jewish community of this state has reason to be proud of the contributions made by its sons and daughters. Their leadership and involvement has made Minnesota a better place for all of us.

The Minnesota Jewish community, measured in numbers, is miniscule. Yet, I still remain amazed at the strength and power of Jewish influence in almost every aspect of our civic life. My story is not unique. I began as a little known young Minnesotan trying to build a public life. Long before I had become known or accepted by the general public, Jewish leaders like Burton and Geri Joseph, and Bob and Carolyn Latz—and so many others described in this book—helped build and shape my public career and together we helped shape progressive policies for our community and nation. The friendship and kindness I felt then remain with me as among the warmest and most fulfilling memories of my public career.

Bob Latz is a perfect example. He and Carolyn are old friends of ours, brilliant, positive and engaged in our civic life. Bob Latz has lived a long and exciting life in politics, the law and wherever people and ideas are important. Just as his Dad before him, it is wonderful to see their son, Ron Latz, serve with such distinction in the Minnesota Legislature.

I will never cease to be grateful for what this community meant to me and to our state and nation. In this new book, Bob Latz helps us better understand this wonderful history. You can tell that he had a great time writing it and I can tell you, I had a great time reading it.

This book covers some of the most interesting and controversial events in the history of Minnesota politics and government. It takes us behind the scenes and inside the world of politics and the people who make and influence public policy that affects all Minnesotans. The people and events portrayed in this book have shaped the political landscape and made our state unique. Bob Latz's experience in and out of public office makes this truly an "insider's story."

Bob Latz covers over 70 years of history of those who have been intimately involved in the political process. He explores the important role played by public-spirited citizens who, working with elected officials, have succeeded in passing significant legislation that affects us all. Included are biographical profiles of Jewish leaders in political and community organizations, at the state and national level, and in both political parties, who have made Minnesota a state recognized nationally far out of proportion to its population size and location.

"Jews in Minnesota Politics" offers comprehensive and valuable information about our public institutions and leaders found in no other book. While some of the opinions offered may be controversial, they are sure to stimulate thought and debate. This book is a welcome addition to what has been written about the history of our state.

– Walter F. Mondale

About the Author

From the indelible experience of attending the funeral of Governor Floyd B. Olson at age 6 to his retirement as a lobbyist on the election of his eldest son, Ron, to the Minnesota House of Representatives almost 70 years later, former state representative and University of Minnesota Regent, Robert (Bob) Latz has had a unique opportunity to observe, live and now write about Minnesota's Jews and their participation in Minnesota's political and public life. Bob grew up and lived on Minneapolis' northside. He has had an "insider's" insight into the people and institutions that made a significant impact on the Jewish and general communities. These Jews survived and prospered in what was an alien, and even hostile, political, economic and religious environment. Grass roots participation in Farmer Labor, DFL and Republican politics provided ambitious Minnesota Jews an opportunity to achieve an impact in party politics, appointive and elective office, and on Minnesota's cultural, economic and political scene. It was almost unmatched for the small numbers of Jews in this predominantly German and Scandinavian state.

Bob Latz's life provides a living history of experiences, successes and failures in community life and public office. It is a chronicle of one person's efforts to serve and lead in the continuing struggle for recognition and acceptance for Jews throughout Minnesota. This book is not just one person's community and political testament. The years covered involve many Jewish political and community leaders whose participation and leadership in the Twin Cities and other areas throughout Minnesota have enriched the Jewish and non-Jewish communities in which they have lived and served. They have provided a roadmap and benchmarks for participation and leadership in Minnesota's and in our nation's political and community life. The stories and events depicted are about Jews and non-Jews who have helped, and sometimes impeded, progress. They are the stories of the Hubert Humphrey's and Orville Freeman, Walter (Fritz) Mondale as well as those of Paul Wellstone, Rudy Boschwitz, Norm Coleman's, Larry Cohen, Arthur Naftalin, and Geri Joseph, to name a few. They have all climbed the political ladder and achieved election or appointment to high national, state, and local office. But those who have achieved the spotlight of significant office are just a few of those whose individual and collective efforts have influenced and helped shape the political and economic landscape of our state. Individually and collectively they have all served not just as Jews, but more importantly as Minnesotans and Americans. They have preserved their rich religious traditions, cultural and economic identities and experiences. Then they used them as building blocks to help shape the destinies of their fellow Jews and of their communities. This then is their story – Minnesota Jews in politics and public life: their history, contributions, successes and failures. It is a story well worth telling.

Introduction

The History and Life of Jews in Minnesota

In "Jews in Minnesota – A People of Minnesota"[1], Professor Hyman Berman and Linda Mack Schloff capture the rich history and contributions of Minnesota Jews from the 1800's to the present. Here I expand on the writings of Berman and Schloff by capturing the spirit and accomplishments of those who have lived their personal, professional and organizational lives in a way that has affected public policies at all levels, local, state, and nationally. These people, and their successes and failures, have shaped the fabric of Minnesota politics in the last century, and particularly in the last 70 years.

I focus specifically on the role and the contributions of the many Jews who have been involved in Minnesota politics, government and community institutions. I attempt to captures the spirit and accomplishments of those who have played significant roles in the Jewish community and in the community-at-large; in both major political parties; in community and business institutions and organizations and in religious and secular environments.

Portrayed are the lives of many who have contributed to building the foundations of Minnesota, national and international organizations. They are described from my unique perspective through my insights and my experiences gained from over 55 years in politics, government and community organizations. These include never told stories of people and events that have helped shape the course of Minnesota history. They will help us understand where we are today and where we are going as we embark into the third century of Minnesota politics.

The participation of Minnesota Jews in politics has not occurred in a vacuum. Their stories, and the records of their accomplishments and defeats, are intertwined with those of other faiths who have contributed and participated in Minnesota government and politics. They are individuals and organizations of both major political parties, as well as the separate political parties and movements that preceded them. Socialists, Communists, Democrats, Farmer Laborites, Non-partisan Leaguers, independents and their adherents have all been involved in the political history of Minnesota. They range from the far left to the far right. They encompass liberals, social moderates, and economic and social conservatives.

Explored are the changes, many of them profound, that have occurred in both major political parties together with fringe groups. Centered around individual personalities, such as Jesse Ventura and Ralph Nader, they have become forces that can decide elections in Minnesota and nationally. The role of Jews and others involved in Minnesota government and politics does not occur in a vacuum. Political party organizations, the nature and composition of the Minnesota Legislature, the public policy and special interest groups that influence them, and their members and leaders need to be identified and their roles explored.

Finally, we will look forward into the new century. Significant changes have occurred in the political orientation of the Minnesota Jewish community. They mirror, in part, the changes that have occurred in Minnesota's two major political parties. Both the character and missions of the DFL and the Republicans have changed. Lastly, I explore the future of Minnesota Jews of both major parties who may aspire to careers in elective office. "Is anti-Semitism dead?" Is "Liberal" a dirty word in politics? Is there a place for "moderates" in the Republican Party? In raising and discussing these issues and others, I hope to stimulate thought, discussion and debate.

Here I define "politicians" in a broader sense than simply persons who have been elected or appointed to public office. Formation of public policy is the end result of the political process at all levels. But to reach this end result requires the participation and influence of many persons and organizations involving men and women who have neither sought nor been elected or appointed to public office. Nonetheless, they have often made remarkable contributions to the formation of public policies and laws which affect each and every one of us. Ideas that result in legislation or public policy decisions very often emanate from participants and leaders who believe that they have a responsibility to participate in the processes that leads to decision-making at every level of government and politics. I discuss competition between interest groups and individuals for power and leadership in the political process. Governance and lawmaking by elected and appointed officials of local, state, and federal government are only the end result of the participation of special interest and public interest groups. I analyze how these various groups and individuals seek to influence government through lobbying activities.

Money has been described as the "mother's milk of politics" by former U.S. House Speaker "Tip" O'Neill. In the chapter on "Shaking the Money Tree," I draw portraits of those prominent Minnesota Jews who have influenced the election of candidates and the political process through their ability to raise significant dollars to finance candidates for public office.

To many, the term "politics" and "politicians" are labels used with derision. The terms have always been contentious. More recently the polarization of politics and politicians caused by such emotion-laden subjects as abortion rights and gay marriage has increased the negative connotations applied to those who are involved in the political process. Politics in its basic form has been defined as "the art of the possible." However, those who are pragmatic, and may be willing to settle for the proverbial "half-a-loaf," are often derided as "politicians" in the most negative sense. Those who seek elective office are often too busy raising money, speaking to groups, and ringing doorbells to try to make major efforts to soften or eliminate this negative image.

One observer, David Tibbles[2] has sought to define and categorize politicians. Tibbles' literal definition of a politician is "a person experienced in the art or science of government, especially one actively engaged in conducting the business of government." However, he states that politicians define themselves throughout their career, especially in an election." Tibbles places politicians in four categories. He cites specific examples of politicians he believes fit in each category. The first is the "spontaneous politician." The spontaneous person, such as Bill Clinton and Ronald Reagan, is defined by his willingness to meet people face-to-face. This gives him an impression of integrity. This Tibbles believes is a "must for winning an election." According to Tibbles, the person who is "very rarely seen in politics" is what he calls the "honest politi- cian." This is a person who is very noble, and often very outspoken. He lets his views reflect who he is and votes only because of his beliefs. Tibbles puts Minnesota's former Governor Jesse Ventura in this category.

The third category is the "letter politician. He is one whose views are always the same views of his or her party." Tibbles believes that they are "clearly the majority of Congress. They are also quick to approve their own party's position without question." Finally, Tibbles seeks to define the "ideal politician" as one who "stands for his or her ideas." This person admits when he made a mistake or is wrong and will work to help the true ideal succeed. The "ideal politician" never votes because of party lines, but stands with what he or she believes will work best, even if by doing so he puts at risk his own personal and political life."

I will leave to the reader what, if any, category fits the politicians who are referred to in this text. A politician may fit into a different category at different stages of his or her career. There are Minnesota Jews who are or have been affiliated with both major political par- ties. Their views may go from left to right. Thus, one may legitimate- ly inquire as to whether there is anything about being Jewish that influences the Jewish politician's views on public policy issues. There have been changes in attitude and political party affiliation of Min- nesota Jews as they have moved from the central cities to the suburbs and from near poverty to relative affluence. They have mirrored the changes which have taken place nationally and locally as described by Kramer and Leventman in *Children of the Gilded Ghetto*, Yale Uni- versity Press, 1961[3], and by Maisel and Forman in *Jews in American Politics*, Rowman and Littlefield Publishers, Inc., 2001.[4]

However, whatever the political party affiliation of Minnesota Jewish "politicians" may be, central to most is their philosophy and attitudes represented by the concept of "Tikkun Olam". (Literally "repair of the world.") Tikkun Olam represents the Jewish historical commitment to racial, social, and economic justice. It is the basic principle for Jewish involvement in the political process, public office and in community organizations. Such involvement serves as a means of translating the principle of Tikkun Olam into reality, such as through the enactment of social welfare legislation. Examples are the anti-discrimination laws passed in Minnesota in the 1950's and '60's outlawing discrimination in employment and housing opportunities based upon race, creed, color, religion, national origin, and sexual preference. There are community organizations, both Jewish and in the general community, that have pursued these goals and the implementation of this concept.

A prominent Jewish political scientist, the late Daniel Elazar, a Minnesota native, wrote of "Minnesota's special [political] culture."[5] Elazar refers to the intersection of "social action" and "political action" as an important characteristic of Minnesota's political culture. In the Jewish community of Minnesota the "social action" part of this equation is based on the concept of Tikkun Olam. Elazar's intersection of "social action" and "political action" has resulted in my broad definition of "politics." It also results in the inclusion of Jews of importance in the state in addition to those who have served in elective or appointive office.

The values and attitudes generated in the community and through community organizations are translated into efforts for social reform through political change. It involves personal involvement in partisan political activity by those who would not otherwise be involved in partisanship, because they realize the need to utilize the political system to meet the problems of the community.[6]

Thus, I write not only about the people, but also about the institutions, educational, religious, cultural and business, that have served as training grounds for those with political ambitions or interests in advancing social and political action. It is participation in these institutions that has helped shape the attitudes and opinions of these individuals.

Because of the exceptional success of Minnesotans who have been elected to national political office there has been much speculation about what is unique about "Minnesota's political culture". That "culture" has spawned success despite Minnesota's relatively small population and location in the heartland of the nation.

A "moralistic political culture" is present where a state's political order is sufficiently attuned to the kinds of issues which stimulate the participation of intellectuals, academics and the labor movement and generates intellectual and moral excitement. Elazar cites examples of Hubert Humphrey, Eugene McCarthy, Arthur Naftalin and Ambassador Max Kampelman as persons who have retained their standing as politicians while retaining their ties to the academic community. He referred to the DFL as a coalition of political "amateurs" who are interested in the party as a vehicle for implementing progressive liberal policy, as with the labor movement, and who had academic as well as ideological interests in politics.

Elazar states that the Independent Republican Party, by the early 1960's, also attracted academics and lawyers who rose from the grassroots to articulate new programs and who brought new blood to the party.[7] Both parties had a spirit of public concern with community problems that led to popular recognition of Minnesota as one of the nation's most progressive states. Elazar believed that political debate in Minnesota had been chiefly concerned with how large a role government should have in society, not whether government should play a part in the first place.[8]

At the time Elazar wrote his article issues were a central element in Minnesota politics. This resulted in the recruitment of new people and elements into the parties as issues changed. It also led to the domination of political parties by issue-conscious people, rather than by people interested in politics as a form of business.[9] Elazar died in 1999.

Elazar's description was reasonably accurate at the time it was written. It is very questionable as to whether it continues to be accurate today. There has been in recent years an injection of sharp partisanship in Minnesota politics on the part of both political parties. This has led to much less ability to compromise on issues. It has resulted in stalemates on such items as tax policy and social issues.

It remains to be seen whether this change is permanent or transitory. The partisanship that is evidenced at the national level, in an increasingly divided U.S. Congress, may have set the pattern for Minnesota, at least for the foreseeable future. International issues such as war, and domestic issues such as the economy and tax policy, remain imponderable. They can change the equation from election to election. We also have the shifting to the right of control of the Republican Party in Minnesota. This has resulted in the isolation of so-called "moderate" Republican politicians. This has marginalized their ability to be an effective voice within the Republican Party and within the halls of the Minnesota Legislature. I hope that this book will offer some insight into the changes which have resulted in the current political situation in Minnesota. This includes the increasingly conservative attitudes of Minnesota's Jews on social, economic and other political issues.

1959—House Speaker Ed Chilgren presenting the gavel to Bob Latz who presided as speaker pro tem.

Chapter One

Political Anti-Semitism
in Minnesota

Until the late 1940s, few Jews ran for or were elected to public office in Minnesota.[1] For the most part those that chose to run lived in small communities outside of the Twin Cities. They did not run for legislative or statewide office. Their efforts were limited to local offices such as city councils and school boards. As early as 1910, Benjamin Milavetz ran an unsuccessful race for the Virginia City Council.[2] In 1914, my father Rubin Latz ran an unsuccessful race for the Hibbing City Council. He was a self-described Eugene Debs "Socialist." For Debs, Socialism was as much about the dignity and humanity of the individual worker as it was about abstract questions of the proper organization of the American means of production or the distribution of wealth."[3]

Even those small town businessmen who were elected to local school boards kept a low profile on controversy.[4] Charles Upin, who was a successful merchant in Albert Lea, said, "I was chairman of the board of education for twelve years. I never campaigned. My neighbor went out and got up a petition to file my name. I always voted Democratic, but Albert Lea is a very strong Republican town. After one bad experience where I lost a customer, I never publicly went out and expressed my opinion again. I felt, I'm here to make a living. If I lose this store, nobody is going to put me back in business." From 1947 to 1951, Henry Bank served as an Alderman representing a North Minneapolis City Council ward. In the 1950's, Milton Rosen was a member of the St. Paul City Council.

It was not until 1934, during the era of Governor Floyd B. Olson, that the second Jew was elected to Minnesota constitutional office. Samuel Bellman was elected in 1934 to the Minnesota

House of Representatives. He was elected from a predominantly Jewish district in North Minneapolis. This was the same area
where Floyd B. Olson was born and raised. Bellman served one
two-year term. It was not until over a half century later, in 1958,
that the next Jewish member of the Legislature was elected. I was
elected from basically the same North Minneapolis district as
Bellman. My four legislative campaigns, resulting in eight years'
service in the Minnesota House, were remarkably free of overt
anti-Semitism. The same can be said for my 1966 campaign for
Minnesota attorney general.

The story of overt political anti-Semitism in Minnesota
emerges out of the social and economic turmoil of the 1930's. It
is intertwined with the rise to political prominence of Floyd B.
Olson, and the emergence of the Farmer Labor Party as a political force. In the 1930's, anti-Semitic attitudes were pervasive in
Minnesota. It was not simply benign anti-Semitism resulting in
exclusion from social and business organizations and institutions.
It was a period of overt anti-Semitic acts and attitudes fueled by
the economic turmoil of the Great Depression.

On the national level these attitudes and practices were promoted by such prominent businessmen as Henry Ford, one of
America's great automakers. Henry Ford has also been called "one
of America's great haters." With his immense financial resources,
Ford became famous around the country and in the world for his
rabid anti-Semitism. In the 1920's, he published a personal newspaper *The Dearborn Independent*. *The Dearborn Independent* featured
numerous anti-Semitic articles, such as "The International Jew:
The World's Problem."[5] Baldwin describes Henry Ford as "One of
the most obsessive anti-Semites of our time..." He also describes
how a splintered Jewish community attempted to cope with the
relentless anti-Semitic tirade conducted for 91 consecutive weeks.
The American Jewish community in the 1920's and 1930's had
difficulty in deciding how to deal with such prominent anti-Semites as Henry Ford. They generally reacted with silence. The most
prominent Minnesota Jewish Republican, Attorney Josiah Brill
Sr., failed to respond publicly to the anti-Semitic tactics employed

in the 1938 gubernatorial campaign in Minnesota.[6]

The rise of Adolf Hitler in the 1930's encouraged the organized anti-Semites and their supporters. Nationally, in addition to Henry Ford, there were Father Charles Coughlin, the "Radio Priest" in Detroit; Gerald L. K. Smith and his America First Party; and the German-American Bund and its Brown Shirts. There was William Dudley Pelley and his Silver Shirts. Pelley openly called for Jews to be driven from positions of responsibility and from the United States.

In Minneapolis, Pelley organized the Silver Shirt Legion to "rescue" America from an alleged Jewish-Communist conspiracy. Pelley intended that he and his Silver Shirts would save America from Jewish-Communists. One of the supposed leaders of this "Jewish Communist Conspiracy" was Maurice Rose. The Silver Shirts described Rose as an international banker in disguise. In fact, Rose worked as a chauffer to Governor Floyd B. Olson.

An expose' of the activities of the Silver Shirts was written in the Minneapolis Journal for September, 1936, by a young reporter named Arnold (Eric) Severeid. Severeid, a non-Jew, went on to become one of the nation's most respected journalists. Severeid's articles are described in a tribute to him posted on the homepage of the Minnesota News Council.

German-American Bund rallies in New York City posed a dilemma for mainstream Jewish leaders.[7] The Jewish leaders wanted the rallies stopped. However, they had no legal grounds on which to do so. A New York state Judge Nathan Perleman is reputed to have personally contacted gangster boss Meyer Lansky to ask him to disrupt the Bund rallies. Perleman cautioned Lansky to have his henchmen stop short of killing any Bundists. Reported enthusiastic for the assignment, and disappointed by the restraints, Lansky accepted all of the terms except one: he would take no money for the work.

In Minneapolis, a reputed gambling czar, David Berman, is said to have confronted Pelley's Silver Shirts on behalf of the Minneapolis Jewish community. It was reported that Berman learned that the Silver Shirts were mounting a rally at a nearby Elks Lodge.

When the Nazi leader called for all the "Jew-bastards" in the city to be expelled or worse, Berman and his associates burst into the room and started cracking heads. After 10 minutes they had emptied the hall. His suit covered in blood, Berman is reported to have taken the microphone and announced, "This is a warning. Anybody who says anything against Jews gets the same treatment, only next time it will be worse." After Berman broke up two more rallies, there were no more public Silver Shirt meetings in Minneapolis.[8]

Reverend Luke Rader was a prominent Christian evangelist who preached from a tabernacle on Lake Street in Minneapolis. Among his several anti-Semitic publications was a pamphlet entitled, "The Sinister Menace of Communism to Christianity." Rader called upon all Christians to support Hjalmer Petersen against Elmer Benson in the 1938 Farmer Labor Party Primary Election battle for governor. Rader described who he claimed to be Benson's Jewish Communist advisors.[9]

Jewish involvement in the Minnesota liberal political movements of the 1930's was intertwined with the career of Floyd B. Olson; the Farmer Labor and Communist parties; the emergence of an organized labor movement in Minneapolis; and the power of the Citizens Alliance. The Citizen's Alliance was an organization composed mainly of top executives in the banking, milling, mining, lumbering and utilities businesses in Minneapolis.[10] Floyd B. Olson grew up on Minneapolis' north- side. He developed strong ties to the northside Jewish community by performing the tasks that Judaism prohibited Jews from performing on the Sabbath. Olson, who could speak fluent Yiddish, was called by Jews a "Shabbos Goy". Olson's Jewish roots were stated best by Vince A. Day. Day was Governor Olson's private secretary. He later became a judge in Minneapolis. Day wrote, "Governor Olson was reared in Minneapolis, in a Jewish community, where he saw misery at its worst. He learned the language of the Jew and through it imbibed the spirit of resistance to poverty and injustice."[11]

The Farmer Labor Association was formed in 1923. It was an outgrowth of the Nonpartisan League, an agrarian movement that swept the Dakotas in the early part of the 20th century. The Farmer

Labor Association was an independent political and educational organization involving farmers and workers. The Farmer Labor Party was the election year vehicle for carrying on the campaigns for the candidates designated by the Farmer Labor Association.[12] Olson had achieved strong support from the Minneapolis Jewish community in his successful election as Hennepin County Attorney. This support carried over into his campaigns for governor.

Olson was first elected governor in 1930. He led a political coalition which included Farmer Laborites. As governor, Olson surrounded himself with a number of Jews. The organ of the Farmer Labor Party was the *Minnesota Leader*. Its editor was Abe Harris. The *Minnesota Leader* was the basic publication through which Governor Olson delivered his political messages. Olson selected Maurice Rose as his chauffer. George B. Leonard was a Minneapolis attorney. He founded the Leonard, Street, and Deinard law firm. Leonard was appointed by Olson to the University of Minnesota Board of Regents. He was the first Jew to serve on the university's governing body. Edward J. Pearlov was appointed by Olson as State Comptroller. Jean Spielman was selected as the State Printer. Harry Fiterman, a Minneapolis accountant, was appointed as Minnesota Tax Commissioner. Roger Rutchick was appointed as Assistant Attorney General. This was the first time in Minnesota history that a significant number of Jews had been appointed to state offices.[13]

Despite Olson's 1930 election as a Farmer Laborite governor, the Farmer Laborites won only a minority of members in the Minnesota State Senate and in the House of Representatives. Therefore, during his first term Olson did not have a legislative majority. Thus, he had tough sledding in pushing his liberal programs through the legislature. The 1932 election gave Olson not only a second-term as governor, but also gave him more substantial backing in the legislature. Olson then had a successful legislative session. He proposed a number of measures that became law. They included the landmark adoption of a state income tax. Also signed into law were measures strongly supported by the Minnesota labor movement. They outlawed "yellow dog contracts" and prohibited labor injunctions. A "yellow dog contract" is an employment contract that forbids membership in a labor union.

The Minnesota Farmer Labor Party was split into left wing and right wing groups. Basically, Olson supported the left wing of the party. There were continual allegations that the Farmer Labor Party and the Farmer Labor Association were infiltrated by avowed Communist Party members and their supporters.[14] The Minnesota Communist Party was particularly strong on the Iron Range with its large immigrant population. A Jew, Samuel Davis, was the unsuccessful Communist Party candidate for Minnesota Governor in 1934. Davis was the manager and editor of *Midwest Labor*, the statewide newspaper of the Congress of Industrial Organization (CIO). The CIO, basically comprised of industrial unions, was one of the two major umbrella organizations for organized labor in Minnesota. The other umbrella labor organization was the Minnesota Federation of Labor. It consisted primarily of craft unions in the building trades. It was affiliated with the American Federation of Labor (AF of L).

Irene Paull was called "The Guiding Spirit" of the publication *Midwest Labor*. Her pen name was "Calamity Jane". She learned about radical politics in working class life in Chicago. She then returned to Duluth and married a young attorney named Henry Paull. She became his office assistant. Together they defended the area's Communist Party members. Irene Paull left the law office to become the editor of *Midwest Labor*.[15]

The far left wing in organized labor was represented by the Minneapolis Teamsters Union. Avowed Communists, such as the Dunne brothers and Farrell Dobbs, led the Minneapolis Teamsters Local 544. The CIO unions in the 1930's were split between the leadership of persons with alleged Communist Party membership or those with allegiance to the more moderate CIO unions. The moderates were led by Sander Genis. Genis was the Business Manager of the Amalgamated Clothing Workers Union. Michael Finkelstein of the International Ladies Garment Workers Union, and Rubin Latz of the Laundry Workers and Dry Cleaners Union, were active Jewish leaders in the AF of L. The Minnesota AF of L unions were generally more politically conservative than the Minnesota CIO unions. At first the AF of L and CIO affiliates worked together. However, because of an ideological split in 1936, Sander Genis was sent by the Minneapolis AF of L Central Labor Union to Washington to argue the case for CIO-AF of L unity in Minnesota. At the AF of L National Convention, Genis was not permitted to speak on the floor. By the end of the year, the Minnesota Federation of Labor followed the orders of its national president William Green and expelled the Minnesota CIO unions from their organization.[16]

Sander Genis and Rubin Latz were key political and labor leaders during the 1930's and 1940's. Rubin Latz was a delegate to the 1944 Democratic National Convention. John Goldie of Minneapolis was the attorney for the Minnesota AF of L. Labor unions nationally and in Minnesota struggled in their organizational efforts in the Depression of the 1930's. In Minneapolis the organization of workers into labor unions was vehemently opposed by the Citizens Alliance. It was a highly organized group of leaders of business and industry. It hired many private detectives to conduct surveillance and foment dissension to keep union and left wing activity quiet. In 1934, the Teamsters Union local of truck drivers went on strike. Violence erupted. Armed supporters of the Citizens Alliance and the companies on strike deputized by local authorities tried to suppress the strike activities with violence. The essentially unarmed strikers responded with attacks of their own. There were many injuries and at least several deaths. The day of the most violence was called "Bloody Friday." Local law enforcement broke down. Governor Olson was required to bring in the Minnesota National Guard to restore order. The Teamsters ultimately were successful. They won the right to organize into labor unions which could bargain with the employers over wages, hours and other working conditions. Olson's intervention in the 1934 Teamsters strike led to the demise of the "open shop" in Minneapolis. An "open shop" is a place of employment where the workers are not represented by a labor union.

However, the elite of the Minneapolis business community, the bankers, industrialists and leading retailers, did not stop in their efforts to prevent the spread of unions in Minnesota and what they considered to be the growth of radicalism in Minnesota government. Putting their best economic resources in support of the Republican Party, the leaders of the Citizens Alliance waited for the opportunity to reassert their economic and political dominance. That opportunity came in the 1938 campaign for Minnesota Governor. The 1938 campaign was the most successful use of political anti-Semitism in the United States. It was the outgrowth of a significant split in the Farmer Labor Party resulting from the 1936 illness and death of Governor Olson.[17] Olson was immensely popular in Minnesota. He had successfully dealt with the Depression problems facing Minnesota and the unorganized workers. He had steered legislative initiatives into law. He had become a national figure. There was even talk that he might run for President.

In December 1935, the political landscape changed. U.S. Senator Thomas Schall was killed in an automobile accident. Olson had been looking at running against Schall for the U.S. Senate. Now with Schall's death, and with renewed vigor, he set his sights on that Senate seat. However, Olson's Senate ambitions created a struggle within the Farmer Labor Party for succession to the governorship. Olson and his supporters were faced with a dilemma. If he resigned as governor, and his successor Lieutenant Governor Hjlamer Petersen appointed Olson to Schall's unexpired term, Petersen would obviously have a leg up on election to a full term as governor. Those closely surrounding Governor Olson, including Roger Rutchick, convinced Olson to appoint Bank Commissioner Elmer A. Benson to the unexpired term of Senator Schall. There was an understanding that Benson would then run for governor, and Olson would run for the U.S. Senate seat the following year.[18] Olson's appointment of Benson to the senate foiled the political ambitions of Petersen. Petersen and his supporters then began a vicious campaign against Olson and Benson and what they called the "Mexican Generals." "Mexican Generals" were simply code words for the Jewish advisors and supporters of Governor Olson and Benson. Benson had formed a close personal and professional relationship with Roger Rutchick when Rutchick was an assistant attorney general advising Bank Commissioner Benson. This relationship grew even closer when Benson became governor. Benson named Rutchick as his private secretary. Rutchick became Benson's chief political advisor.[19]

"Petersen's secretary from November 1935 to February 1936 was Lillian Schwartz. Schwartz was a leading member of the Minneapolis Young Communists League. She subsequently married Carl Ross and then John Gates, two leading Communists of the next two decades."[20] Schwartz's short affiliation with Petersen did nothing to quell his blatant use of anti-Semitism and anti-Semitic stereotypes in his 1938 campaign against Elmer Benson.

Despite Petersen's campaign against the "Mexican Generals" during the 1936 Farmer Labor Party Convention, the convention endorsed Olson for the senate seat and Benson for governor.

In August 1936, Olson was diagnosed with and died of cancer. Benson continued his run for governor. The Farmer Labor Party State Committee selected Ernest Lundeen to replace Olson as the endorsed candidate for the senate.

The death of Olson caused an outpouring of grief in the northside Jewish community. While governor he had continued his close ties to the Jewish community. He had filled some patronage jobs in his administration with Jews, who along with the general population, were suffering economically during the Great Depression. My oldest sister, Bertha Arenson, worked in the Minnesota Agriculture Department to help the Latz family make it through the Depression. Even though Benson was Olson's anointed selection as governor, there was fear about the future. Those politically astute were reassured by Benson's close relationship with Rutchick. One of my earliest memories at age 6 was attending with my father the funeral for Olson. It was held at the Minneapolis Auditorium. We then joined the funeral procession to Olson's interment in Lakewood Cemetery.

The 1936 election resulted in a landslide reelection of President Franklin D. Roosevelt. The entire Farmer Labor ticket was overwhelmingly elected. Benson won with the largest majority given a gubernatorial candidate in Minnesota up to that time.[21] The Farmer Labor Party also gained control of the Minnesota House of Representatives, but not the state senate. Lundeen served as a U.S. Senator from 1937 until 1940, when he died in a plane crash. By 1940, the Republicans had seized control of state government. A Republican, Joseph Ball, succeeded Lundeen in the U.S. Senate. Ball, a newspaperman, had been a strong supporter of Harold Stassen in his run for governor in 1938. Ball served in the U.S. Senate until 1948, when he was defeated by Hubert H. Humphrey.

Shortly after Benson became governor, Hjalmer Petersen began his campaign of attacking Benson and his administration. The campaign featured the use of anti-Semitic innuendo with constant references to the "Mexican Generals." In a meeting held on February 2, 1938, Petersen was asked to name the "Mexican Generals." Petersen answered "…Abe Harris, Art Jacobs, and Roger Rutchick." Jacobs was Secretary to the Speaker of the Minnesota House of Representatives. Jacobs was also editor of the State House News, a weekly sheet of state news sold to rural newspapers.[22] Despite challenges to Petersen to repudiate these anti-Semitic statements and innuendoes, he never publicly disclaimed them. Petersen had an interesting coalition of supporters in that Farmer Labor Party Primary Election. They included not only leaders of the Citizens Alliance, but also Reverend Luke Rader. Rader published a pamphlet calling upon all Christians to support Petersen and defeat Benson and his Jewish Communist supporters.[23]

Both Rutchick and Harris were concerned about the success of these anti-Semitic attacks. They both offered to resign. To the credit of the leadership of the Farmer Labor Party, these resignation attempts were rejected. The leadership also rejected Petersen's anti-Semitic campaign. Benson himself attacked the use of anti-Semitism. He wrote a letter to Rabbi Stephen S. Wise of the American Jewish Congress. In that letter Benson equated the anti-Semitic campaign with campaigns for vigilantism and fascism which sought to make minority racial, religious, and political groups into objects of popular hate in order to give the people scapegoats for the present economic maladjustments.[24]

In 1938, Minnesota had an open primary law. That law has persisted to this date. Under the law voters are not limited to voting only for the candidates of the political party of their affiliation. No voter registration by party affiliation is required. Therefore, a Republican could cross over and vote in the Farmer Labor Party Primary and vice versa. Each could seek to nominate a candidate perceived to be the weaker and less likely to succeed in the General Election against the real candidate of their choice. Crossing over is not permitted in the General Election. The voter is limited to voting only for the candidates of the one party of his/her choice who prevailed in the Primary.

Despite what was described as a "massive Republican cross-over vote" in the 1936 Farmer Labor Primary, Benson won over Petersen with a margin of 16,000 votes out of a half million votes cast. This set up a contest in the General Election between Benson and the Republican candidate Harold E. Stassen. Professor Berman characterized the Republican Party and its supporters in 1938, as representing "the elite of Minnesota business." They launched a well-financed campaign on behalf of Stassen.[25] The campaign operated on two separate levels. While Stassen took the high road, Ray T. Chase orchestrated a virulent anti-Semitic campaign against Benson. Chase had run for and been elected to several offices. They included Minnesota State Auditor. He served for one term in the Congress. Chase ran unsuccessfully against Floyd Olson in the 1930 gubernatorial campaign. In that campaign, Chase was obsessed with attempting to establish a connection between Olson and what Chase called "Yiddish" gangsters, or Jew-Communists. He alleged underworld Jewish liquor interests were part of a conspiracy. Chase corresponded with William Dudley Pelley of the Silver Shirts, and the noted anti-Semite Gerald L. K. Smith. Chase received support from the University of Minnesota Dean of Student Affairs Edward E. Nicholson. Nicholson was especially concerned about what he termed "Jew Reds" on the university campus. Nicholson was particularly incensed that Governor Olson had appointed a Jew, George B. Leonard, as a regent of the university. He was obsessed by what he called "Jewish radicalism," and what he described as "Jew agitators." His targets included distinguished university faculty members, both Jew and non-Jew, who were moderate liberals. It was a classic case of attempted guilt by association.[26]

Stassen defeated an "old guard" Republican, Martin Nelson, in the 1938 Republican Primary. Chase supported Nelson. Despite Nelson's defeat, Chase continued the fight to defeat Elmer Benson. In the meantime, Stassen attempted to co-opt the liberal supporters of Olson and Benson. Stassen portrayed himself as the true heir of Olson. He made promises to reform the state civil service system. He claimed he could combine the best elements of the Roosevelt New Deal with the best elements of business efficiency.[27] A delegation of prominent Minnesotans, including some leading Jewish Republicans, sought to persuade Stassen to repudiate Chase's anti-Semitic campaign. Stassen did not do so. Chase disclaimed any anti-Semitic intent. He publicly announced that leading Republican Jews supported his activities. This put some leading Jewish Republicans in a difficult position within the Jewish community. However, no one among the Jewish Republicans publicly repudiated Chase or his allegations.[28]

Election Day 1938 was one of celebration for Chase and the Republican Party. Stassen overwhelmingly defeated Benson. Republicans were swept into every major state office. All but one Farmer Labor congressmen were defeated. Both houses of the legislature went overwhelmingly Republican. It was not until 1955, a decade after the merger of the Farmer Labor Party and Minnesota Democrats into the DFL Party, that the DFL was able to regain control of a single house of the legislature, the House of Representatives.

Despite Stassen's election as governor, the "old guard" Republicans remained in control of the Minnesota Republican Party and the major Minnesota constitutional offices. The dominance continued after Stassen's resignation as governor. J.A.A. Burnquist had served as governor from 1915 to 1921. He later was elected Minnesota attorney general and served in that post until 1954 when he decided not to seek reelection. Mike Holm served as secretary of state for 31 years. When he died in 1952, he was succeeded for 2 years by his wife. After first serving as Secretary of State for 14 years, Julius Schmahl was state treasurer for 28 years until his death in 1957. Stafford King occupied the position of State Auditor from 1931 until 1969.[29]

Only three other Jews have served in as close a role as a gubernatorial advisor since Roger Rutchick's service in the Floyd B. Olson era. They are Arthur Naftalin, Commissioner of Administration in the Orville Freeman administration; David Lebedoff with Governor Wendell Anderson; and Hyman Berman with Governor Rudy Perpich. Leonard Levine, a former St. Paul City Council member, served as head of the Human Services Department and as Transportation Commissioner under Rudy Perpich. There were no Jews serving in comparable positions as advisors or heading state departments under the Republican administrations of the 1940's and early 1950's, with one exception. That was Richard Golling. He was appointed Public Examiner by Governor Stassen in 1943. Golling served until DFL Governor Orville Freeman was elected in 1954. During the 1940's and early 1950's, there were no Jews serving in the Minnesota Legislature. There were few Jews prominent in GOP Party activities during those same years. The one notable exception was Alan "Buddy" Ruvelson, a St. Paul businessman who is profiled separately. It is not really surprising that those Minnesota Jews who were politically active during those years were all members of the DFL. This is true given the historic support of the Jewish community to more liberal political causes. The act of President Harry Truman in granting U.S. recognition to the fledgling State of Israel in 1948, served only to solidify that support.

It was not until after Luther Youngdahl became governor in 1946 that a new wind began to blow through the Minnesota Republican Party. Youngdahl, a Lutheran minister, had popular support even among some Democrats and many independents.

He exuded a law and order image. Youngdahl's term as governor lasted until he accepted an appointment as a federal judge in 1951. However, he did not bring new Republican blood into the Minnesota Legislature. It was not until the late 1950's and early 1960's, that a youthful group of moderate Republicans were elected to the Legislature. They began to change the Republican Party legislative ethos. It was not until 1978, that the first Jewish Republican, Harvard Law School graduate and attorney Elliot Rothenberg of St. Louis Park, was elected to the Minnesota House. He served for two two-year terms. In 1982, Rothenberg was the GOP candidate for attorney general. He was defeated in the General Election by Hubert H. "Skip" Humphrey. There has never been a Jewish Republican elected to the Minnesota State Senate.

Chapter Two

Social and Economic Anti-Semitism

As the Minnesota Jewish community entered the decade of the 1940's, there was much for the community to fear. The unexpected death of Governor Floyd B. Olson sent shock waves through the immigrant Jewish community on Minneapolis' north side. Many had pinned hopes on Olson's election to the U.S. Senate. He was one of their own – the "Shabbos Goy." Jews were among his closest friends and advisors. The Farmer Labor Party struggle between Elmer Benson and Hjalmer Petersen, with Petersen's anti-Semitic attacks, had caused more shock and despair. Their fears were somewhat assuaged by Stassen's and the Republican's sweep into office in 1938. Minnesota Jews, particularly on Minneapolis' north side, were still struggling to secure an economic and social foothold. The rise of Hitler and the Nazis in Germany, and their anti-Semitic supporters in the United States, also caused fear among Minnesota Jews. Hitler's campaign against the Jews raised images of the pogroms under the Russian czars which had caused their families to flee to America. Jewish supporters of the labor movement were concerned with the renewed efforts by the Minneapolis business elite, through the Citizen's Alliance, to crush Minneapolis' nascent union organizing efforts. They also feared renewed labor violence that had been abated by Olson's efforts during the 1934 Teamster's strike.

Jews were still excluded from employment in banks, business-oriented law firms, large business corporations, and in retailing. Jewish doctors were excluded from staff privileges at Minneapolis hospitals. Reverends Luke Rader and William Riley of the First Baptist Church were still stirring their parishioners with anti-Semitic sermons. The more militant Silver Shirts of William Dudley Pelley were continuing their activities.

Coupled with these fears was continuing social discrimination. Well into the 1950's, and even beyond, Jews were uniformly excluded from most community social organizations. These included Rotary, Kiwanis, Toastmasters, Lions, Masonic lodges, country clubs, the Minneapolis Athletic Club, the Minneapolis Club and the Minneapolis Auto Club. These anti-Semitic exclusions and attitudes were so pervasive that in 1946, author Cary McWilliams labeled Minneapolis as "the Capital of Anti-Semitism in America."[1] McWilliams wrote, "In almost every walk of life and within, the "Iron Curtain' separates Jews from non-Jews in Minneapolis. So far as I know, Minneapolis is the only city in America in which Jews as a matter of practice and custom, are ineligible for membership in the local Kiwanis, Rotary, Lions, or Toastmasters. Even the Automobile Club refuses to accept Jews."

Similar exclusion took place in Duluth, such as in the Northland Country Club. There is little evidence of such discrimination of Jews in the small towns outside of the Twin Cities metropolitan area. St. Paul was different from Minneapolis. McWilliams cites those differences, and what he believes to be the reasons for them. St. Paul was much more accepting of Jews in its community organizations. For example, in 1946, St. Paul City Council member Milton Rosen was elected President of the St. Paul Athletic Club. The reasons for the differences between the Twin Cities may be rooted in their respective ethnic backgrounds. St. Paul had a largely Irish and German Catholic population, compared to the Anglo-Saxon and predominantly Protestant Minneapolis. There was no reported evidence of religious rabble rousers from the Christian churches of St. Paul similar to Reverends Luke Rader and William Riley in Minneapolis. Overt anti-Semitism in St. Paul was unusual.

The Irish Catholic Church of North Minneapolis was more accepting of its Jewish neighbors. In the early 1940's, in the absence of a boxing program in the Jewish community, I was readily accepted into the Golden Gloves boxing program at the

Ascension Club at the Ascension Church. Another Jew in that Golden Gloves program was William Reimerman, a German Jewish refugee. Reimerman later became a valued staff member at the Minnesota Senate. When I boxed as part of the Ascension Club Golden Gloves team I wore kelly green trunks with a Star of David emblazoned thereon. That early relationship with the Ascension Church endured throughout my later political career on Minneapolis' northside.

The barriers to involvement and success in Minneapolis were not limited to employment, social and community organizations. There were also significant barriers to where Jews and other minorities could live. There were Jewish communities in both North and South Minneapolis. Jews were uniformly excluded from moving into the first tier suburbs adjoining the city. Real estate organizations strongly discouraged Jews seeking to purchase or build in Golden Valley, St. Louis Park and Edina. Edina was particularly noted for its religious and racial exclusionary policies. Areas in Edina, such as the Morningside area, had racial and religious exclusions written into the deeds to the property.

In 1948, that legal barrier was broken. The U.S. Supreme Court decided *Shelley v. Kraemer*, 334 U.S.1. *Shelley v. Kraemer* involved the validity of court enforcement of private agreements, generally described as "restrictive covenants." These covenants had as their purpose the exclusion of persons of a designated race, color or religion from the basic right to purchase and own real estate. The Supreme Court ruled that such restrictive covenants could not be enforced by the courts. This broke the back of the legal restrictions impeding the movement of Jews and Blacks to the suburbs.

However, the ruling did not stop unwritten agreements preventing such sales and movement. It took the threat of court action initiated by Jewish attorney Jonas Schwartz to allow Carl Rowan, a Black Minneapolis newspaper reporter, to purchase a home in Golden Valley. Rowan went on to have a distinguished career as a journalist, best selling author and official in the administration of John F. Kennedy. He served as Deputy Assistant Secretary of State and Ambassador to Finland.

The Minneapolis Jewish community responded to discrimination by supporting the efforts of Mayor Hubert H. Humphrey to effect a major change in citywide discriminatory attitudes toward Jews and other minorities. Humphrey, Minneapolis mayor from 1945 to 1948, initiated a citywide campaign to implement human rights reforms. In 1945, the Minneapolis City Council rebuffed his efforts to achieve passage of a fair employment practices ordinance. Humphrey then took a step back. He decided it was necessary to build a broader base of public support for his human rights initiatives. He established an advisory group known as the Mayor's Council on Human Relations. A prominent Minneapolis attorney Hyman Edelman served as Vice Chairman of the Council. Edelman was a partner in Maslon Kaplan Edelman Joseph Borman and Brand.

The Mayor's Council was assisted in its work by the Minnesota Jewish Council and its Executive Director Samuel Scheiner. The Mayor's Council initiated a landmark self-survey of human relations attitudes in Minneapolis. The effort was to determine the extent of racial and religious discrimination. However, Humphrey was impatient in seeking to reduce racial and religious bias in his city. Thus in 1947, a year before the Mayor's Council was to make its report, Humphrey successfully lobbied the Minneapolis City Council. He achieved passage of a Minneapolis Fair Employment Practices Ordinance. It is believed to have been the nation's first such ordinance. It outlawed exclusionary practices in employment. It served as a stepping stone to the passage eight years later of a Minnesota Fair Employment Practices Act.

Amos Deinard was a partner in another significant Jewish law firm Leonard Street and Deinard. He was appointed by Humphrey as a member of the newly established Minneapolis Fair Employment Practices Commission. In 1956, Deinard also served as chair of a 3-person tribunal named to hear and determine the first discrimination charges initiated under the newly enacted Minnesota Fair Employment Practices Act. This was in *Carl Carter v. McCarthy's Café*. As a Minnesota assistant attorney general, I prosecuted that case before the tribunal.

The passage of ordinances and laws in and of themselves do not change ingrained racial and religious attitudes and stereotypes. It was still some years before Jews were to gain equal employment opportunities in business, industry and the professions. It was not until the early 1960's, that the first Jewish lawyer, Mitchell Goldstein, was employed by Faegre and Benson. Faegre and Benson was and is one of the large Minneapolis law firms. It represented the elite of the business community, such as the Northwestern National Bank. In 1954, Arthur Weisberg had been hired by the other top firm Dorsey Coleman Scott and Barber. The Dorsey firm represented the First National Bank, another major Minneapolis bank.

The Minneapolis Fair Employment Practices Ordinance did not apply to membership in social, communal and business organizations. It was not until Jay Phillips, a very successful and prominent Minneapolis businessman and philanthropist, was elected chairman of the Chamber of Commerce, that the Minneapolis Club accepted him as its first Jewish member. This was only after Phillips indicated he would be very uncomfortable in holding meetings of the Chamber at the Minneapolis Club while not being accepted into membership. Several prominent Jewish community members soon followed Phillips into the Minneapolis Club. They included his longtime attorney Samuel Maslon and Temple Israel's Senior Rabbi Max Shapiro. Since that time several other leading Minneapolis Jews have been elected President of the Minneapolis Club. They include attorney Marvin Borman, and the publisher of *Minneapolis St. Paul* Magazine Burton Cohen.

The Minneapolis Club represented the epitome of success in business and social stature. Thus, the Phillips and subsequent admissions represented a substantial turnaround by the leading figures in Minneapolis' business and social life. It served as an indication of the beginning of success in the integration of Jews into the social structure of Minneapolis. In the Minneapolis labor community the Minneapolis Club is remembered as the bastion of the Citizen's Alliance. Some labor-oriented Jewish community members have had a hard time forgetting this history. In the mid and late 1960's, I was involved in working with the leadership of the Minneapolis business community in the Urban Coalition. The then President of the Coalition, Minneapolis banker Phillip Harder, invited me to lunch at the Minneapolis Club to discuss Coalition business. During the lunch Harder asked why I had such a serious look on my face. After pondering the response, I answered that my late father, labor leader Rubin Latz, must be spinning in his grave to see his son lunching at the Minneapolis Club. I recounted the history of involvement with the Citizen's Alliance and its anti-labor activities.

Into the 1960's, the Minneapolis Athletic Club remained the exclusive province of non-Jews. In the early 1960's, as a member of the Minnesota House of Representatives, I attended a Hennepin County Legislative Delegation meeting on the 14th floor of the Athletic Club. Embossed in parquet around the room was a symbol which duplicated the swastika of Nazi Germany. I was the only Jew in attendance. Profoundly angered and distressed by the symbol, I wrote a letter on my official legislative stationary to the president of the club. He was Maurice Hessian, the attorney for one of Minneapolis' large savings and loan associations. I requested an explanation for the presence of the symbol. Despite a follow-up letter and several phone calls requesting a response, I never received any explanation or apology.

The Minneapolis and St. Paul Jewish communities had a twofold response to the social and economic discrimination of these years. One response was the creation of separate Jewish social and fraternal organizations. The Gymal Doled Club, later known as the Standard Club, was a downtown Minneapolis social organization. It served as a Jewish alternative to the Minneapolis Club and the Minneapolis Athletic Club. Hillcrest Country Club in St. Paul, and Oakridge and Brookview Country Clubs in Minneapolis, served as alternatives to the exclusion from other country clubs. B'nai B'rith, a Jewish fraternal organization, also served as a social and fraternal alternative. A Jewish-oriented Masonic lodge, Sunset Lodge, was formed to include Jews who had been excluded from membership in other Masonic lodges.

The Minnesota Jewish Council served as a clearinghouse for

reports of anti-Semitic incidents and practices and for attempts to resolve them. The council was led by Executive Director Samuel Scheiner. Scheiner, an attorney, was a tireless and effective worker and leader. He spent his days working fulltime for the council while sustaining himself economically playing the piano in bars and nightclubs in the evening hours.

Through the years Scheiner was assisted by successful Jewish community leaders who served as presidents of the council. They included Louis Gross, a Minneapolis businessman and football star at the University of Minnesota; Jack Mackay, Associated Press reporter covering state government and politics, and father of prominent author, lecturer and businessman Harvey Mackay; and Benno Wolff, a partner in a St. Paul law firm. Many other prominent Jewish community members served on the board of the council. They included Rubin Latz who was also active in an affiliate organization the Jewish Labor Committee.

The activities of the council were concentrated in two principal areas. The first was responding to acts of overt anti-Semitism. The second was human relations education and efforts to attack the root causes of religious and racial discrimination. Dealing with acts of overt anti-Semitism was not simple. In the decades of the 1930's, '40's and mid-50's, the only civil rights law prohibiting discrimination in Minnesota outlawed discrimination based on race and religion in places of public accommodation. These included hotels, resorts, restaurants and bars. It was not until 1955, that the Legislature enacted the Minnesota Fair Employment Practices Act. In 1961, the Minnesota Fair Housing Act was passed. It took even longer, until 1964, for the U.S. Congress to enact the Civil Rights Act. This landmark law was primarily the result of efforts of Senator Hubert H. Humphrey and President Lyndon B. Johnson.

Working with few legal tools, Scheiner and the Minnesota Jewish Council used their limited financial and political resources to good effect. For example, many popular resorts in northern Minnesota routinely excluded Jews. If a person with a Jewish-sounding name called for reservations, the person was usually told that no accommodations were available. However, if a person with an anglo saxon name made the same call shortly thereafter, the person was greeted warmly and promptly afforded the accommodation. Sometimes, when confronted with such blatant discrimination, the resort owners showed flexibility. Occasionally, it took threats of publicity and legal action to accomplish the purpose. These discriminatory attitudes and practices were portrayed by Gregory Peck in the movie "Gentleman's Agreement."

In the mid-1950's, the B'nai B'rith, and its human relations arm the Anti-Defamation League (ADL), opened a regional office serving the Jewish communities of Minnesota, North Dakota and South Dakota. The ADL regional office was staffed by Monroe Schlactus. It had its separate board of directors. It coexisted with the Minnesota Jewish Council. I served on the boards of both organizations. I chaired the ADL board in the early 1970's. In 1975, I was elected to the ADL national governing body, the ADL National Commission. State Senator Ron Latz continues the family's commitment to human rights with his service on the ADL National Commission. Jack Mackay was the first Minnesotan elected to the ADL National Commission. Mackay was succeeded by Burton Joseph, a Minnesota political leader and successful grain merchant. In 1976, Joseph was elected National Chair of the ADL. He was the first and only Minnesotan to serve in that prestigious position. There was some overlapping of activities. The ADL regional office concentrated more on educational programs to combat bigotry in general and anti-Semitism in particular. Both the Minnesota Jewish Council and the ADL regional office were understaffed. Neither budget was sufficient to do an adequate job of combating overt anti-Semitism and conducting successful educational programs.

There was also a human relations committee of the Minneapolis Federation for Jewish Service, the principal fundraising arm of the Jewish community. That effort was staffed by Viola Hymes. Hymes had been elected a member of the Minneapolis School Board. She had also served as President of the National Council of Jewish Women.

In 1974, the Twin Cities Jewish communities and the national ADL both realized that supporting separate and overlapping organizations were a poor use of inadequate resources. After much negotiation, the national ADL and the Minneapolis and St. Paul Jewish Federations reached a merger agreement. They formed the Jewish Community Relations Council of Minnesota and the Dakotas (JCRC). The first executive director of the merged organization was Morton Ryweck. There has been a succession of successful executive directors of the organization. The current executive director is attorney Steven Hunegs. Hunegs gave up a successful law practice with his father Richard Hunegs to take the post succeeding Steve Silverfarb. The first president of the JCRC was Marcia Yugend. Yugend continued to be prominent in interfaith activities during and after her term as JCRC president. There have been a number of active DFLers who have served as President of the JCRC. They include Bill Aberman, Larry Gibson, Allen Saeks, Alan Weinblatt, the late Stanley Breen and Steven Hunegs. Weinblatt serves as legal advisor to the Minnesota DFL Party. Breen served as a staff member to Governor Wendell Anderson.

Not many Jews were prominent in the Minnesota Republican Party in the years before the 1980 election of Rudy Boschwitz to the U.S. Senate. Several who held public office included Richard Golling and Stuart Rothman. Golling served as Minnesota Public Examiner from 1943 until December 31, 1954. He was originally appointed by Governor Harold Stassen. He was reappointed by Republican governors Ed Thye and Luther Youngdahl. Stuart Rothman was a Minnesotan who supported Eisenhower for President. He was appointed as General Counsel to the National Labor Relations Board. He served in that post from 1959 to 1963. He also served as Solicitor for the U.S. Department of Labor. From public office he went on to a career as a lawyer in private practice and as a labor arbitrator. Minneapolis attorney Sidney Feinberg, a Willmar native, was an active Republican. In 1967, after earlier service as president of the Hennepin County Bar Association, Feinberg was elected president of the Minnesota State Bar Association. Feinberg was the first Jew to lead this influential organization of lawyers. At that time Feinberg was a partner in the Robins Davis and Lyons law firm which later became Robins Kaplan Miller and Ciresi. Feinberg worked with myself and Governor Elmer Andersen in a successful bipartisan effort that provided additional judges for the Hennepin County District Court.

The most prominent and still active Republican who never sought nor served in public office is 93 year-old Alan "Buddy" Ruvelson. Ruvelson's long and exceptional career as an active Republican and successful businessman is profiled separately. Ruvelson was and is a moderate Republican. For years he chaired the important platform committee at Republican state conventions. Ruvelson served with me on the ADL Regional Advisory Board. During activities which would shape the party platforms of the respective Republican and DFL Parties, Ruvelson and I would compare notes on platform proposals dealing with the State of Israel. In those years there were frequent battles by Israel's enemies seeking to insert anti-Israel planks in both political party platforms. It sometimes took battles on the floor of the conventions to amend or remove anti-Israel language or to include pro-Israel or more neutral language in the platform. In the DFL Party these efforts were often aided by other active DFL convention delegates such as Arnold "Bill" Aberman.

However, the work of fighting anti-Semitism and improving racial and religious relationships in our state, the United States and the world is far from over. In the fight for civil rights in Minnesota up through the mid-1960's, Black civil rights leaders such as Harry Davis, Cecil Newman, Matthew Little and Nellie Stone Johnson worked side-by-side with leaders of the Jewish community in efforts to eliminate discrimination in employment and housing opportunities. These two communities were united in their support of Hubert Humphrey in his anti-discrimination efforts in Minneapolis and nationally. Along with companion efforts by liberal and moderate Republicans and Democrats these efforts succeeded in the 1955 passage of the Minnesota Fair Employment Practices Act, and in the 1961 passage of the Minnesota Fair Housing Act.

These cooperative efforts extended into the grassroots political realm. In 1944, Nellie Stone Johnson, a Black labor leader and political activist, ran with Rubin Latz for two vacant seats on the Minneapolis Library Board. Rubin Latz was defeated in the Primary. Nellie Stone Johnson, who may have profited by her Scandinavian last name, was elected. Johnson became the first Black woman elected to public office in Minneapolis. She was also very active in the early efforts to merge the Farmer-Labor and Democratic parties into the DFL Party. Johnson later became a member of the Democratic National Committee. She served in that post for many years. My commitment to participate in the struggle for equal opportunity helped unify the diverse political elements in North Minneapolis. North Minneapolis Irish Catholics also had memories of ethnic and religious discrimination. The coalition of Black and Jewish voters in my behalf resulted in my receiving almost as great a margin of victory in the Black precincts as I did in my home precincts in North Minneapolis. I joined with Edward Gearty. We ran our campaigns together for the two seats in the north side legislative House races. This cooperation served to solidify the relationships between the Jewish, Black and Irish Catholic communities. The Minnesota Democratic Party was a predominantly Irish Catholic Party prior to the 1944 merger of the Democrats and the Farmer Laborites into the DFL.

By the mid-1960's, North Minneapolis was undergoing change. Blacks were moving westward into predominantly Jewish areas. North Minneapolis Jews were becoming more affluent. Housing opportunities in the suburbs were opening up. Some north side Jews began to move into first tier suburbs such as St. Louis Park. However, Plymouth Avenue remained the center of Jewish life on the north side. Many synagogues and small Jewish merchants such as grocers, shoemakers, barbers and clothing stores stayed to serve the still mainly Jewish community. But frustration and militancy was growing in the Black community. Job opportunities were still limited, particularly for young Blacks.

In the summer of 1966, the frustration erupted. Riots occurred on Plymouth Avenue. Burning and looting took place. Mayor Arthur Naftalin, the police, and social workers from the Wells Neighborhood House, Phyllis Wheatley Community Center, and Black leaders, such as Harry Davis, sought to quell the disturbances. Peace came only after the decimation of many businesses. The ensuing fear and animosity in the Jewish community resulted in the beginning of an exodus of North Minneapolis Jews to the suburbs. This exodus was enhanced by fears of violence toward young Jewish students in the longtime integrated North Minneapolis schools.

There were efforts to quell the fears of the Jewish community and to preserve a vibrant Jewish community with its many synagogues and small businesses. Leaders of the Jewish community, such as Rabbi Kassel Abelson of Beth El Synagogue, joined with Black community civic and business leaders. They formed the Minneapolis Urban Coalition. The riots served as a wake up call. They realized that their organizations must join together to address the issues that caused the riots. Joblessness among the city's Black youth was a major problem.

Leadership in the Minneapolis Urban Coalition was provided by a number of prominent Minneapolis businessmen. They included Phillip Harder, President of the First National Bank, Steve Keating, CEO of Honeywell, Dean McNeill, Executive Vice President of the Pillsbury Company and James Summers, CEO of General Mills. The leadership provided by the elite of the Minneapolis business community was proof of the long way that they had come from the days of the Citizen's Alliance and the 1934 suppression of the Teamster's strike. White church leaders of many denominations joined together with pastors of Black churches and rabbis, such as Rabbis Abelson and Max Shapiro, to throw the weight of the religious community behind the Urban Coalition's efforts.

I chaired the Urban Coalition Housing Task Force. Housing developer Ray Harris was an active member of the task force. I also served as ad hoc parliamentarian for coalition board meetings.

On one occasion a coalition board meeting was invaded by a group of militant American Indians led by Indian activist Clyde Bellecourt. They placed themselves in the front row of the meeting hall. They proceeded to unleash a full half hour of racist and anti-Semitic epithets directed toward Chairman Dean McNeill and myself seated at his side. One activist sat about three feet in front of me. He spewed his anti-Semitic tirade almost in my face. We all kept our cool. The meeting proceeded despite the interruptions. The disrupters were still present when the meeting adjourned. I can remember vividly Minneapolis City Council member Richard Erdahl, a coalition member and former football player, exiting the meeting hall with his fists clenched to protect himself from any potential assault. Fortunately, none occurred.

Providing job opportunities remained the primary focus of the Urban Coalition. However, the creation of better housing on the north side and throughout the city remained an important interest. The coalition formed the Greater Minneapolis Metropolitan Housing Corporation. The corporation was funded by grants of $100,000 per year from Minneapolis banks and major corporations. These grants were to provide seed money for the creation of multi-family housing projects and single family residences on the north side and throughout the Minneapolis metropolitan area. They were designed to assist not only racial minorities but all low and moderate income individuals and families with enhanced housing choices. I served as a board member of GMMHC from its inception for a period of 24 years. I served as President in 1981-1982.

The schism between the Jewish and Black communities resulting from the Plymouth Avenue riots never completely healed despite the efforts of the Urban Coalition and like-minded community and religious leaders. Fueling the Jewish move to the suburbs were fears, often well founded, that the absence of a potent Jewish political force on the north side would lead to a lessening of support for, and a subsequent decline in, the quality of the public schools in North Minneapolis. By 1966, I had left the legislature to run for the DFL nomination for attorney general. There were no other Jewish elected officials in the area. The school systems in Golden Valley, Edina and St. Louis Park were judged to be better funded and providing a higher quality of educational opportunities than those on the north side. Jewish political power at the Minneapolis city level was also absent. Henry Bank, the longtime and controversial city council member from North Minneapolis, had been voted out of office when Minneapolis charter reform reduced the number of city council positions from 26 to 13. He was replaced by Jerry Egan who had served alongside Bank in representing the 5th Ward. Joe "Pumpkin" Greenstein was 5th Ward alderman during that period. A northside grocer, he had a populist attitude. However, he was largely ineffectual at the city council level.

Part of the problems in the relationship between the Jewish, Black and American Indian communities was the fact that Jews were no longer considered to be "minorities" and therefore covered by affirmative action policies. These policies entitled those covered to the protections and opportunities available in the areas of employment and admission to colleges, universities and their professional schools. Jews were now more readily admitted into the dental and medical and other professional schools. The days of actual or benign "Jewish quotas" appeared over. But those opportunities were still limited as to the racial minorities. Affirmative action programs designed to increase educational opportunities for Black and other minority students could easily turn into the types of quotas that had excluded Jews. These fears of the return of quotas, and the exclusion of qualified Jewish students from these educational and employment opportunities, raised tensions and conflicts between the Jewish and Black communities nationwide. The Anti-Defamation League, after sometimes heated debates among the members of its National Commission, passed resolutions opposing affirmative action policies that might be quotas in disguise or implemented as quotas.

The decision by the U.S. Supreme Court in *Regents of the University of California v. Bakke*, 430 U.S. 265 (1978) upheld the general principle of affirmative action. Allan Bakke, a white man, had been denied admission to the University of California at Davis

Medical School. The school had admitted Black candidates with weaker academic credentials. Bakke contended that he was a victim of reverse racial discrimination. The Supreme Court ruled that Bakke had been illegally denied admission to the medical school. It also ruled that medical schools were entitled to consider race as a factor in admission. The special admissions program of the University of California Medical School was designed to assure the admission of a specified number of students from certain minority groups. The Supreme Court of California had held that the special admissions program was unlawful. It therefore had enjoined the university from considering the race of any applicant. It ordered Bakke's admission to the school. A divided U.S. Supreme Court held 5 to 4 that so much of the Judgment of the California Supreme Court that had held the special admissions program unlawful was correct. It directed the admission of Bakke to the Medical School. However, the Court also held that the portion of the California Supreme Court's Judgment that prevented the school from according any consideration to race in its admission's process must be reversed. Thus, the "affirmative action program," in that situation was considered legal.

The effects of the *Bakke* decision and its progeny are still subject to much debate and discussion among the Jewish community and those that the Court referred to as "underrepresented minorities." These include Blacks, Hispanic Americans and Native Americans. Justice Lewis Powell, who wrote the majority opinion for the divided U.S. Supreme Court, stated that diversity was an important enough goal – "a compelling interest" - to justify the use of affirmative action. Powell stated an admissions system that does this must be properly devised so that all candidates for admission compete against each other and race is only one of many factors.

In 2003, the U.S. Supreme Court agreed to consider two cases. One challenged the University of Michigan's undergraduate admissions policy. The other challenged the admissions policy of the University of Michigan Law School. In doing so the Court would decide whether the *Bakke* decision would continue to be the law. In the *Gratz v. Bollinger* and *Grutter v. Bollinger* decisions, June 2003, the U.S. Supreme Court, voting 5-4, upheld the policy at the University of Michigan Law School. In a 6 to 3 vote, the Court struck down the university's undergraduate admissions policy, which stated that its point system gave "specific weight" to minority applicants. This made it a quota system.

While the controversy over quotas versus affirmative action programs is far from settled, the Jewish and Black communities in Minnesota have come together in common efforts to improve relations between all races and religions. There have been a number of Jewish organizations that have focused on improving relationships between Minnesotans of all races, ethnic groups and religious faiths. Each, through educational programs and efforts to shape and influence the passage of human rights legislation, have contributed significantly to the improvement of these relationships. The organizations include the Jewish-Christian Learning Center at St. Thomas College. It was originally led by Rabbi Max Shapiro and now by Rabbi Barry Cytron. Others include the Joint Religious Legislative Council (JRLC); Jewish Community Action (JCA); the social action committees of several synagogues; the Minnesota Chapter of the National Council of Jewish Women; Hadassah, and the Leland Johnson Community Vision Program. The JRLC is an effort by the Catholic, Protestant, Jewish and Muslim communities to present a united front to the Minnesota Legislature on human rights legislation. According to the newsletter of Jewish Community Action, the organization "…is a membership organization bringing together Jews from different segments of the Jewish community to understand and take action on social and economic justice issues."[2] The JCA has been working with banks and faith-based institutions to increase socially responsible investments in the inner city. The JCA's Community Reinvestment Initiative has accounted for actual investments or pledges of more than $1 million.[3] State Representative Frank Hornstein has served as a leader since the organization's inception.

The Leland Johnson Community Vision Program is named after Patrice Johnson, the late daughter of Black community leader Josie Johnson. Patrice Johnson was the chief of staff to Congressman Mickey Leland of Texas. Leland and Johnson died in a plane crash in Ethiopia. Congressman Leland had worked for many years to bring together the Black and Jewish communities. He was a leader in the Black Congressional Caucus. The Leland Johnson Scholarship Fund provides scholarships to enable young Black student leaders to participate in a six-week summer program in Israel. It is an outgrowth of an interfaith dialogue group between members of Temple Israel of Minneapolis and the Pilgrim Baptist Church of St. Paul. The program provides young people with the skills and tools to become leaders in addressing racism and anti-Semitism.

Josie Johnson served as a Regent of the University of Minnesota. She was its first Black member. Johnson was also prominent in a bipartisan interfaith group that worked with me, then State Senator Donald Fraser and Governor Elmer Andersen, to achieve passage of the 1961 Minnesota Fair Housing Act. Among the prominent Minnesotans serving on the Leland Johnson Board are Max Fallek, a longtime civil rights advocate, and W. Matthew Little, former chairman of the Minneapolis Branch of the NAACP. Sherrill Borkon of Temple Israel has been a driving force in the organization. The cooperation between the Jewish and Black communities shown in the Leland Johnson Program is a welcome renewal of the fellowship between these communities.

Chapter Three

The 1950's

Despite Hubert Humphrey's election to the U.S. Senate in 1948 for a six-year term, the early 1950's saw the DFL Party and its candidates for statewide constitutional office in the political wilderness. Orville Freeman, the DFL-endorsed candidate for governor in 1952, lost to C. Elmer Anderson. J.A.A. Burnquist continued his long tenure as Minnesota attorney general. I continued to work at the grassroots of the DFL Party as Chairman of the 5th Ward DFL Club. Ward clubs were the unofficial DFL Party organization throughout Minneapolis. The official DFL organizations were at the county level both in the metropolitan area and outside. The official party organizations at the grassroots level were the party caucuses. They met every two years to select delegates to the county, congressional district and state DFL conventions and to endorse candidates for the Legislature.

While I continued as 5th Ward DFL Chair I was more preoccupied with completing my law school education at the University, working to pay for tuition, and engaging in campus organizational activities. Battles within the North Minneapolis political organization continued to play a role in my busy life. There were clashes between the 5th Ward's two city council members Henry Bank and Jerry Egan. When it became apparent that a citywide reorganization of the ward boundaries would reduce each ward to one rather than two city council members, the clash between Bank and Egan became very intense.

The Minneapolis ward clubs traditionally endorsed candidates for the city council. At endorsement time the struggle played itself out at a meeting of the 5th Ward Club. At the time one could join the club by simply declaring himself/herself to be a Democrat and paying the $1.00 annual dues. With membership came one vote on ward club matters including endorsements. There was no bylaw restriction requiring club membership for a particular length of time to secure the right to vote. Taking advantage of this omission, on endorsement night for the city council post, Bank scoured the bars on West Broadway. He brought a number of persons to the meeting. He obviously had given each of them the required $1.00 for membership dues. Bank brought sufficient numbers with him, along with his supporters among the regular club members, to have secured for himself the club endorsement.

I chaired the meeting. A point of order was raised as to whether the club should accept the membership payment and declare these persons eligible to vote on the endorsement. It was an unusual situation with no specific precedent. The point was made that allowing the newcomers to vote would destroy the purpose of the ward club. It was to be an organization where politically active Democrats could gather and make their influence felt on the party and political process. Everyone knew that those Bank brought in were there for that evening only. They would not return after they voted on the endorsement. I ruled that the newcomers were not allowed to vote on the endorsement. When an appeal was made by the Bank supporters from my ruling, I ruled only those who had previously been members of the club would be allowed to vote on the issue. A majority of the regular club members upheld the ruling. The new Bank supporters were not allowed to vote. When this happened they left en masse. While there were still significant Bank supporters among the regular club members, Egan prevailed over Bank and secured the 5th Ward club's endorsement.

The resulting campaign between Bank and Egan was a dirty one. There were assertions of impropriety by Bank who, in addition to his council membership, was an attorney in private practice. When Bank was defeated by Egan, Bank commenced a lawsuit. He charged Egan with violating the state corrupt election practices law. The end result was a decision by the Minnesota Supreme

Court in *Bank v. Egan*. Egan's claim to the 5th Ward City Council seat was confirmed.

The ward clubs in Minneapolis were an outgrowth of the Farmer-Labor clubs that began in 1932, the second year of Floyd B. Olson's administration. The ward clubs provided political bases for me and for others with political ambitions. The 5th Ward club, with its core of activists, provided the political base from which I later launched my campaign for the legislature.

I was elected a delegate to the Minnesota DFL Convention in Duluth when I was still under age 21 and thus ineligible to vote at the convention. This resulted in a challenge by Henry Bank at the Third Congressional District convention. The Third District convention was chaired by Reverend John Simmons. Simmons had known my father. Both were early allies of Hubert Humphrey. Simmons ruled the challenge out of order. I was confirmed as a delegate to the first of many DFL state conventions.

At the height of the cold war, with Senator Joseph McCarthy of Wisconsin pursuing his allegations of Communist influence in the government, I was faced with yet another serious challenge in the 5th Ward club. Nellie Stone Johnson applied for membership in the Club. Johnson was a well known and popular figure among the large Black community in North Minneapolis. In 1944, she had been elected to and served on the Minneapolis Library Board. Johnson's application for membership in the club was challenged by club member Ruth Ann Withrow. While we did not know it at the time, it turned out that Withrow was a former FBI infiltrator in the Communist Party. Withrow alleged that Johnson was a Communist Party member and was thus not eligible for membership in a DFL organization.

Previously there had never been any litmus test as to political philosophy for membership in the DFL ward clubs. It was assumed that anyone who sought to join a DFL organization was basically committed to the support of the party's principles and platform and to the candidates endorsed by the party. There were, however, no rules that proclaimed that if one publicly or privately objected to some plank in the party platform, or supported and voted for a non-endorsed candidate, they would lose their DFL Party membership.

However, actual *membership* in the Communist Party was not only illegal but contrary to the principles of the DFL. While there may have been Communist Party members, or "fellow travelers" who supported the Communists during the Farmer Labor days, the far left wing of the Farmer Labor Party had been defeated and read out of the party in 1944 after a bruising battle that led to the creation of the Minnesota DFL. Leading the charge for defeat of the far left members and supporters of the Communists were Hubert Humphrey, Orville Freeman, Dr. William Kubicek and Arthur Naftalin. A Macalaster College political science professor Dorothy Jacobsen and Eugenie Anderson were two of the women leaders in that anti-communist fight. After such a battle, the leadership of the DFL was not about to permit Communist Party members or their closet supporters to infiltrate back into the party ranks.

I was faced with a dilemma. I was not about to submit to the assertions of a "red-baiter" such as Withrow. Nor could I shrug off such a serious allegation. I also knew that the rejection of Johnson would send a racist and exclusionary message to the Black community that had been a bastion of support for DFL candidates at all levels. There was no doubt that Johnson espoused liberal principles which were quite close to mine. It was also true that Johnson had some relationships with persons with far left leanings in the Minneapolis labor movement. But guilt by association, particularly as practiced by Senator McCarthy and his right wing allies, was anathema to me and my supporters. I knew that I had sufficient support within the 5th Ward club to overcome any opposition and to admit Johnson to membership. I also was conscious of the precedent such a rejection would create, and the effect it would inevitably have on my own political ambitions. A reputation as a "red-baiter" was just something I was not prepared to accept. This was particularly when the allegations came from an acknowledged ex-Communist who had infiltrated the Communist Party at the request of a J. Edgar Hoover led FBI.

I decided to do whatever personal investigation I could to find out the validity of the allegations. I engaged in off the record talks with some in the labor movement and the DFL who were familiar with Johnson's background and activities. I found that while she was a believer in very liberal causes, such as the civil rights movement, no one believed that she adhered to Communist Party principles or had been a member of the Communist Party. Without more proof of Communist Party membership there was no way that we could or should reject Johnson's membership. After a heated battle with the some of the more conservative ward club members who had accepted Withrow's allegations, Nellie Stone Johnson was accepted into membership.

The events leading up to that acceptance were the beginning of a half-century long political and personal friendship between Johnson and I. Johnson went on to a formidable career in the DFL. It culminated in her election and longtime service as a member of the Democratic National Committee. Johnson was one of my strongest supporters in my quest for election to the legislature. She delivered huge margins for me in the Black community. She served as a mentor. She advised me on civil rights and other issues that came before the DFL and the legislature. That mentorship extended into the next generation. She offered sound counsel and advice to Ron Latz at the start of and during his political career.

Johnson's career as a "social activist, labor organizer, teamster, and "third-generation feminist"" is described in *Nellie Stone Johnson – The Life of an Activist*.[1] Johnson's relationship with the Latz family is described in this way:

> *For the bigger offices, I would get involved in campaigns. The next person I really went to work for was Bob Latz, the son of Rubin Latz, an attorney deciding to run for the legislature. I was shooting for a state Fair Employment Practices Act, to outlaw discrimination in hiring throughout Minnesota.*
>
> *Rubin was a business agent for the laundry workers on the north-east side, one of my labor mentors who was a member of the Central Labor Body. We ran for library board together, but I won the primary election, and he didn't. You have got to remember, I*

was still a new entity, young at that time, only 40.

During that election, he was very kind to me, walking me up and down the halls of labor temples that he knew better than I did. One thing I give him credit for is building a bridge between blacks and Jews in labor. After all, the Labor Lyceum, a Jewish labor group in the Jewish community, was the first group to endorse me. The Workman's Circle, an all-Jewish group, they raised some money for me from the Jewish business community.[2]

My political activities continued through my four-year studies in the law school. In my last year in law school, mutual political friends introduced me to Gerald Heaney. Heaney was a Duluth labor lawyer and DFL leader. He was part of the group that formed the DFL Party. He was aware of my family background in the labor movement and my interest in practicing labor law and representing labor unions when I graduated. Heaney suggested that he and I collaborate on an article to be published in the Minnesota Law Review. Law School Dean William Lockhart, who also taught labor law and constitutional law, agreed with the proposal. Heaney graciously suggested that I be named as a co-author of the article. This was an unusual offer. Rarely would an established attorney be willing to share authorship of such an article with a student not yet out of law school.

I spent the better part of my senior year in law school researching and writing drafts of the article. I would journey to Duluth to meet with Heaney to discuss, draft and redraft. The article was finally completed and was published in the June 1954 issue of the Minnesota Law Review. It was entitled *The Minnesota and National Labor Relations Acts – A Substantive and Procedural Comparison*[3] This article became a resource for attorneys practicing labor law, both for unions and employers. It dealt with the important similarities and differences between the two sets of laws that govern legal relationships between employers and the unions representing their employees.

The relationship with Heaney continued after my graduation. Heaney requested, and I instantly accepted, the opportunity to assist him in the trial of a labor injunction matter in Appleton,

Wisconsin. The time spent in Appleton also taught me another lesson. Appleton was the home of Senator Joseph McCarthy, the renowned red-baiter. While in an Appleton bar one evening during trial I made the mistake of making a negative comment about McCarthy. Unfortunately, the remark was overheard by some bystanders. They became indignant and physically threatening. I beat a hasty retreat.

The summer of 1954 saw not only my graduation from law school but my election as a delegate to the state DFL convention in Albert Lea. I had also been elected at the 3rd Congressional District DFL Convention to serve on the state party's endorsement committee. This was the committee that recommended for endorsement by the convention candidates for statewide office. There was little contest in the committee over the endorsement of the candidates for governor and lieutenant governor. At this time the governor and lieutenant governor ran together on the same ticket. Of necessity they would be jointly elected or defeated. Orville Freeman, who had been the losing DFL candidate for governor in 1952, again sought and gained the DFL endorsement. His running mate was state DFL Party chairman Karl Rolvaag. Rolvaag, like Freeman, had been a wounded and decorated veteran of WW II. C. Elmer Anderson, the Republican governor who had defeated Freeman in 1952 had a lackluster record. We all felt he was ripe for defeat.

However, the DFL faced an uphill battle for the attorney general's post. J.A.A. Burnquist, a former governor, had been the attorney general for many years. He was believed to be an unbeatable candidate for reelection. Thus, there was no prominent DFL lawyer who would put himself forward to be the expected sacrificial lamb in that contest. As the deliberations of the endorsement committee moved on, the chairman of the committee, labor leader Bob Hess of St. Paul, solicited suggestions from committee members as to who could be induced to be the DFL-endorsed candidate for attorney general. As he moved around the room he came to me and solicited my comments. Hess prefaced his remarks by saying, "Bob, if you were already a lawyer, we would endorse you for attorney general." (This was June 1954. I was slated to take the

July 1954 bar exam, successful completion of which was required to become an attorney.) The comment drew laughter, and Hess moved on to other members.

Finally, someone suggested that there was a young aggressive attorney from Crosby Ironton on the Range who might be willing to accept the endorsement. It was thought that the publicity occurring would help him develop his law practice. One of the members said that he knew Miles Lord and would call him. The committee continued on while the call was made to Lord. Lord accepted the challenge. The committee voted to recommend him for endorsement. That recommendation was ratified by the convention. Miles Lord became the DFL-endorsed candidate for attorney general in the 1954 election.

I thought I had a position set to work with a labor relations consultant in Washington, D.C. However, shortly after graduation, the prospective employer suffered a heart attack. The offer was withdrawn. While I continued to seek employment in the Twin Cities, I was offered an unpaid position to run the DFL campaign in Hennepin County. I accepted the offer. I shared an office in the party headquarters with Max Kampelman. Kampelman, an attorney and close associate of Hubert Humphrey, ran Senator Humphrey's reelection campaign. Kampelman was a brilliant political strategist. I learned much in listening to him develop much of the strategy around Humphrey's successful campaign for reelection. In later years Kampelman, after service as an assistant to Humphrey in Washington, became a prominent New York attorney. He later served as U.S. Ambassador to the United Nations and as U.S. Ambassador in disarmament negotiations.

Not long after the 1954 convention Burnquist decided not seek reelection as attorney general and to retire from public service. This left Lord with a clear shot at the attorney general's office. The entire DFL-endorsed ticket waged an aggressive campaign. In November the DFL-endorsed ticket swept every constitutional office from governor on with the exception of Republican Stafford King's return to office as State Auditor and Julius Schmahl as State Treasurer. For the first time since the era of Floyd

Olson in the mid-1930s, the DFL candidates – still labeled as Liberals – took control of the Minnesota House of Representatives. It was by only a one-vote margin. The Senate remained in Conservative-Republican-control.

Following the November election I was still unemployed. I interviewed with one law firm whose senior partner was a well known Twin Cities labor lawyer. However, one of the other partners interviewed me. He turned me off with a job offer of $200.00 per month. The going rate was $250.00. I was single and selective. Then Governor-elect Orville Freeman approached me with an offer I could not refuse. I would go to work in the attorney general's office under Miles Lord as a Special Assistant Attorney General. It was understood that I was in effect Freeman's man in the attorney general's office. I was thus given choice assignments in the areas of labor relations, education, workers compensation, election laws, and advising the then Industrial Commission on the enforcement of minimum wage laws. Given my interests in the labor area, it was a dream assignment. In addition, the position started at $5,500 a year salary. The position's demands gave me sufficient flexibility to continue my political activity in the DFL in my off-duty hours.

The main office of the attorney general where I worked was 102 State Capitol. It was immediately across the hall from the governor's office. At every opportunity I would go across the hall to the governor's office. It was primarily to speak with Governor Freeman's two main aides: Tom Hughes, Freeman's Executive Secretary, and Dorothy Jacobsen, his speech writer and political confidante. It gave me the opportunity to be an effective communication vehicle, in an informal way, between what was going on in the attorney general's office; the governor's office; and the DFL Party leadership. Jacobsen's husband, George Jacobsen, was one of the founders of Group Health Mutual which later evolved as Health Partners. My father had been an early supporter of the group health concept which was an outgrowth of the cooperative movement. Of course, my relationship with the governor's office created some tension between me and Attorney General Lord who demanded political and personal allegiance from his staff. My relationship with the governor and the governor's staff provided me with a degree of independence in my relationship with Lord. I knew that when push came to shove the governor had my back.

My relationship with the governor's office provided me with an opportunity to witness another side to Orville Freeman. There was a softer side to the wounded Marine veteran that was rarely revealed publicly. I was invited for several years to the governor's staff Christmas parties. They were held at the Jacobsen residence in Rosemount. In the conviviality of a holiday party I was able to see Jane and Orville Freeman in more relaxed circumstances. On one occasion I recall Governor Freeman in his t-shirt washing the dishes at the end of the party. These occasions served to solidify the personal relationships between me, the governor and his staff.

There is a common thread that runs through my political career and the careers of those I have observed over the years. This is the value of establishing personal relationships with those with whom the ambitious politician interacts on an otherwise professional level. It is not simply the relationship between the male politicians. Of equal importance are the relationships between the spouses. The insights that a spouse may offer to the other spouse can prove to be the key to the success of the ongoing relationship between the male politicians.

My relationship with a later governor, Karl Rolvaag, was solidified in the early years of Rolvaag's tenure by Carolyn Latz's relationship with Florence Rolvaag. I specifically recall one occasion at a political meeting at the Polish National Alliance Hall in northeast Minneapolis. During the evening Governor Rolvaag and Florence arrived. While Rolvaag worked the hall, shaking hands and conversing with the crowd, Florence stood by herself. People apparently were reluctant to approach her as the governor's spouse. Carolyn and I knew the Rolvaag's well enough so that Carolyn approached Florence Rolvaag and engaged her in conversation. Florence thanked Carolyn for coming over as she felt left out. Toward the end of the evening, the governor came over to Carolyn and also thanked her for helping bridge the gap while he did his politicking.

Among the significant appointments by Freeman to his administration team was his selection of Arthur Naftalin as Commission of Administration. This was a post that was critical to the effective functioning of state government. Naftalin was essentially the chief operating officer of the state. He proved worthy to the task.

Despite a divided legislature, Freeman was successful in his first two-year term. Several of his initiatives were signed into law. Among them were extending the terms of office of the state's constitutional officers from two to four years. This change, however, was not effective until 1962. Another important accomplishment was the passage by the 1955 Legislature of a bill outlawing discrimination in employment based on race, creed, color, religion and national origin. The proscriptions applied both to employers and labor unions. A Fair Employment Practices Commission was created to administer the law. In a compromise necessary to achieve passage, the final version of the bill provided that on an appeal from a finding of discrimination by the commission, the accused party would be entitled to a de novo hearing in the District Court. This meant that despite a complete hearing before a panel appointed by the commission an employer found to have discriminated against an employee, or an applicant for employment, was entitled to an entirely new hearing/retrial in the District Court. This so-called safety valve provision sought by employers proved to be fateful in the first prosecution under the new law.

Governor Freeman appointed Eugenie Anderson of Red Wing as the first chair of the Fair Employment Practices Commission. Anderson had served by appointment of President Truman as the first woman ambassador. She was posted to Denmark. Anderson was very successful in that post. Given my personal and family history in the civil rights movement, together with my labor background, I was a natural choice for selection as the first legal counsel to the commission. This assignment was added to my other assignments as a Special Assistant Attorney General. Wilfred Leland, Jr., who had served as the Director of the Minneapolis Fair Employment Practices Commission under Mayor Hubert

Humphrey, was appointed as the initial Executive Director of the state commission. Leland, who was Caucasian, was assisted by William Fox, a Black, as Assistant Director.

My first task was to draft and submit the rules to govern the conduct of the commission in its investigation and determination whether violations of the law had occurred. Thus I came into frequent contact with Anderson, Leland and Fox. Anderson was a mentor to me. I learned more from her intelligence, style and grace than from any other person with whom I worked in my early years in government. Anderson served as a role model for women in the political process and in government. In 1958, Eugenie Anderson was a candidate for the DFL endorsement for the United States Senate. Eugene McCarthy, a DFL congressman from St. Paul, was endorsed over Anderson. McCarthy went on to election as U.S. Senator. His career in the Senate and as a presidential candidate, particularly in 1968, when he refused to endorse Hubert Humphrey for the presidency, and his activities in opposition to the war in Viet Nam, have been described in many other publications. A conflict between the ambitions of McCarthy and Humphrey surfaced in 1964, at the Democratic National Convention in Atlantic City.

Carl Carter vs. McCarthy's Cafe

It did not take long for a major discrimination charge to come before the Fair Employment Practices Commission. Carl L. Carter filed a discrimination charge against McCarthy's Café located on Wayzata Boulevard in Golden Valley. McCarthy's Café was reputedly owned by Tommy Banks. Banks had been identified as the leader of one of the two liquor syndicates in the Minneapolis area. One was labeled the "syndicate." The other was labeled the "combination." Banks was Irish. He led one group claimed to control a number of bars, restaurants and liquor stores. The other, with similar interests, was headed by Isadore "Kid Cann" Blumenfeld who was Jewish. The manager of McCarthy's Café was Jerry Murphy.

Carter was employed as a bus boy at McCarthy's. He was the only Black who serviced the dining room where he was visible to patrons. Carter had worked as a dining car waiter on the railroads. He was tall, handsome and well-spoken. All of the servers/ waitresses were women. Carter sought to be upgraded to the position of waiter. Murphy and McCarthy's denied the request.

On July 4, 1955, Carter quit McCarthy's. He filed a Charge with the state's Fair Employment Practices Commission. He alleged race discrimination by McCarthy's because of its failure to upgrade him to the waiter's position.

On the day that Carter quit McCarthy's had 70 white employees and 22 Black employees. The Blacks held positions as porters, dishwashers, warehousemen, night watchmen, washroom attendants and bus boys. They had little contact with the public. If they did so it was only at a menial level of service. In addition to the primary charge of discrimination, Carter charged that McCarthy's had further violated the law by retaliating against him for his having filed the Charge of discrimination.

This was the first charge of employment discrimination against an employer that was filed after the passage of the law. It was thus a test case as to whether the steps to ensure equal employment opportunities for all citizens in Minnesota was to be accomplished. When conciliation efforts by the commission staff failed, a three-person panel to hear and determine the charges was appointed. The panel consisted of Amos S. Deinard, Minneapolis attorney; the Reverend Denzil A. Carty, a Black, and Rector of St. Philips Episcopal Church in St. Paul; and Barbara Stuhler, Assistant Director of the World Affairs Center at the University of Minnesota. I represented the commission and Carter, the charging party. McCarthy's was represented by the father and son team of Thomas O. Dougherty and Thomas O. Dougherty Jr.

The opening hearing was held on March 2, 1956. The Doughertys stated that they were challenging the law as a violation of both the federal and state constitutions. They also said they were likely to appeal to the District Court as provided by the law in the event that they lost before the panel. Director Bill Leland testified at the hearing that during the investigation of the charge he had found that after leaving McCarthy's Carter had worked successfully as a waiter at the Park Plaza Hotel. He testified that Murphy had responded that while it might work out alright at the Park Plaza with an all-Negro crew, that he didn't think it would work out in a situation where you would be mixing white waiters and waitresses with Negro waiters and waitresses. Carter testified that Murphy had said to him that he did not think that the people of Minnesota were ready to accept colored waiters.

A headwaiter at the café testified that on several occasions he spoke against firing Carter, because he sympathized with Carter's problem. However several of the café supervisors testified that Carter was an inadequate busboy, and that they would have liked to have fired him. A former busboy and now a parttime waiter at the café and another bus boy had been promoted over Carter. I argued that their experience and training were "not at all comparable to that of Carter, who had served as a busboy and waiter in high class establishments for almost nine years up to the time of his termination at McCarthy's." One of the two busboys promoted over Carter, Hartmuth Wegner, testified that on one occasion in the café about a year earlier, Carter had snatched up a knife and pointed it at him. Carter denied ever threatening Wegner or anyone else with a knife. Carter's testimony was borne out by another former Negro employee at the café who worked in the café kitchen at the time the alleged knifing incident took place. However, this witness on cross-examination gave varying testimony as to the knife allegation. The attorneys for McCarthy's produced evidence in which they alleged insolence and a lack of qualifications on the part of Carter in an incident at the Park Terrace Café where Carter had worked as a waiter. I then subpoenaed two women. They testified that Carter had been a very good waiter on the occasion in which it was alleged that he had acted improperly. Carter's present employer at the time of the hearing stated that Carter was a "very efficient" employee. He was always prompt, and he got along well with his fellow employees.

Murphy testified that the café had "no discriminatory attitude, that the color line was wide open." The chairman of the panel, Amos Deinard, suggested at one hearing that a compromise solution would be that McCarthy's rehire Carter as a busboy and give him training to qualify him as a waiter. It would be with the understanding that Carter would get the first opening for a position as waiter or, if Carter refused, that McCarthy's upgrade another Negro busboy to waiter. This suggestion was rejected by the attorneys for McCarthy's.

Carter testified that on the evening he quit, he tried to get Murphy to give him a reason why he could not become a waiter. Carter testified that Murphy told him that he did not set the policy at McCarthy's Café. That he was following orders, and that he had certain orders he has to take. Carter stated that on that same evening he asked his immediate supervisor why he could not become a waiter. The supervisor replied, "You don't have to ask me that. You know the reason, as well as I do." I argued to the panel that this testimony clearly inferred that Carter, as a Negro, should well understand the reason why he was not being promoted. It was his race. In response to Murphy's testimony that he was not personally prejudiced against Negroes, I stated in a memorandum submitted to the panel that: "An individual may be free of personal prejudice, but if that same individual, because of the fear of reaction of his employees or his customers against either himself or the particular employee involved, fails to grant that person equal employment opportunities, a violation of the Fair Employment Practices Act has occurred."

After he had filed the charge with the commission Carter had applied for reemployment at McCarthy's. That reemployment request had been denied. Therefore the charge against McCarthy's contained a second alleged violation of the law. It was retaliation against Carter because he had filed a charge with the commission. McCarthy's had hired a number of busboys, waiters and waitresses during the time that Carter's request for reemployment was refused.

The drama at the hearing was neatly summed up in a story in the *Minneapolis Tribune* by Bradley L. Morrison of the editorial page staff. Morrison described the members of the panel as presenting "…a perfect picture of gravity tempered by a warm human interest in the passing drama. The Reverend Denzil A. Carty of St. Paul was one of them, imperturbable, with just a trace of sadness in his sensitive face. Amos Deinard, Minneapolis attorney, was chairman, presiding with sureness, speaking with gentleness, ruling with firmness, always with the situation in complete control. The third member was Barbara Stuhler, Assistant Director of the University of Minnesota World Affairs Center. Sitting on Deinard's left she completed the picture, poised, serene, relaxed." Morrison summed up his observations by stating: "On the way home I couldn't shake the drama from my mind – or the actors. The performance, as a theater reviewer might remark, was low-keyed, dignified and honest."

After the attorneys submitted memoranda, the panel deliberated in private. They ruled unanimously that McCarthy's was guilty of an unfair employment practice under the law in refusing to upgrade Carter to a waiter's position. They found for McCarthy's on the second charge of violating the law by refusing to rehire Carter after he had quit his job. The panel ordered the café to remain under supervision of the commission, and that it show compliance with the law by "hiring at the first opportunity a qualified Negro waitress or waiter or by upgrading a Negro employee to the position of waitress or waiter." This act of compliance was to be done "on condition that such compliance is to be achieved without granting preference to any applicant because he is a Negro, but by hiring or upgrading on the basis of qualification only. Supervision by the commission is to continue after hiring of a qualified Negro as long as the commission considers it necessary to assure that the complaint has been satisfactorily adjusted." After the ruling Carter told *Minneapolis Tribune* staff writer Daniel J. Hafrey that he was no longer interested in a job at McCarthy's. Carter said that he was now working as a waiter at two restaurants. As part of its Findings of Fact the panel found that:

(1) Up until April 1957, McCarthy's never had employed a Negro as a waiter or waitress. (2) July 4, 1955 the date Carter quit, the café had 70 white employees and 22 Negro employees

and that all Negroes served in capacities of lesser rank." (3) Two white bus boys were upgraded to the position of waiter although they had much shorter experience in the food service business, although Carter had requested the promotion and although he was qualified to hold a waiter's position."[4]

As promised, following its defeat, McCarthy's appealed to the Hennepin County District Court. It sought a de novo hearing as provided by the law. While a de novo hearing would require a repetition of all of the testimony, evidence and argument provided to the three-person panel, Attorney General Miles Lord and I were prepared to go forward to vigorously represent and support the commission's findings and conclusions. However, out of all of the Hennepin County District Court judges to whom the appeal could have been assigned, the appeal was assigned to Judge Gerald Labelle. This was in the 1950's, when the case assignment system in the Hennepin County Municipal and District Courts was under suspicion. It was alleged around the courthouse and among attorneys and court observers that well connected attorneys and politicians could influence the judge selection process. The system then was unlike the now current and longstanding system of blind selection for judge assignments making such influence unlikely.

In any event, when we heard that Judge Labelle had been assigned to hear the appeal we knew that we faced an uphill battle to confirm the commission's and its panel's rulings. It was both an uphill and a probable losing battle. We were then faced on the appeal with an Irish owned and managed employer; a team of Irish lawyers; and an Irish judge. The reader can draw his/her own conclusions as to what kind of obstacles were presented. By that time I had completed my service in the attorney general's office. I had resigned to enter private law practice and run for the Legislature. Rather than hold a complete retrial de novo Judge Labelle dismissed the panel's findings and conclusions as not justified by the evidence. He ruled them contrary to law, and that there was no violation of the Fair Employment Practices Act. The appeal did not contest the constitutionality of the law. Therefore, the law remained in effect despite Judge Labelle's rulings on the individual charges by Carter.

Part of the duties of an assistant attorney general during the years I served were to both draft bills for introduction in the Legislature and to write Opinions of the attorney general interpreting laws that had previously been enacted. The bill drafting function in later years was assumed by the office of the Revisor of Statutes. The staff in the Revisor's office consisted of people who specialized in drafting legislation. Joseph Bright, with whom I had served on the attorney general's staff, later served as Revisor of Statutes. Bright, an Iron Range native, was a career member of the attorney general's staff. Joe Bright was one of the more experienced members of the attorney general's staff. His brother Myron Bright, a Fargo North Dakota native, has served for years as a judge of the U.S. Court of Appeals for the Eighth Circuit. Another person who became a career member of the attorney general's staff was William Serbine. Serbine was St. Paul City Attorney prior to his appointment to the attorney general's staff. Serbine was a specialist in municipal law. Another Jewish member of the attorney general's staff later served under Walter Mondale as the Chief Deputy Attorney General. He was St. Paul attorney Sydney Berde. I shared an office with Joe Bright and Bill Serbine. Since both were older and more experienced, I was able to use them as sources of advice and guidance on the varied areas of law covered by my portfolio in the office.

One of my assignments on the attorney general's staff was to provide advice on election law matters. This fit in quite nicely with my political interests. It also propelled me into one of the major controversies in the DFL Party in the mid-1950's. In 1956, Governor Adlai Stevenson and Senator Estes Kefauver of Tennessee were contesting for the Democratic Party nomination to oppose President Dwight David Eisenhower. Minnesota at the time had a Presidential Primary Election. The leadership of the Minnesota DFL was united behind Stevenson's candidacy. However, there were a number of maverick DFLers who were on the outside of the DFL party leadership. They included St. Paul State Representatives Peter Popovich and Donald Wozniak. Wozniak and

Popovich and their allies had several valid reasons for opposing the Stevenson candidacy. Among them was Stevenson's aloofness and inability to relate to the average person. Kefauver had a folksy manner. He was adept at reaching out to people during a grass-roots campaign. Kefauver's manner was appealing to rural Democrats. Stevenson was the favorite of the intellectuals in the party. The DFL party leadership lined up in support of Stevenson.

The state election laws relating to the presidential primary were complex. They provided, as do Minnesota's current primary election laws, that a voter need not provide any evidence of party affiliation to participate in a party's primary election. This provided opportunities for Republicans to cross over into the DFL Primary. It would be an effort to embarrass the governor and the DFL party leadership as well as to tarnish Stevenson's electability. DFL State Party chairman Ray Hemenway requested Attorney General Lord that I be assigned to accompany him on a tour of DFL county meetings throughout Minnesota. I was to serve as an election law resource while Hemenway sought to convince the DFL party faithful that they should support Stevenson over Kefauver. Hemenway and I toured by car. We attended many county and local meetings of DFL party leaders and workers throughout Minnesota's rural areas and small towns. The hostility to Hemenway expressed at some meetings was a surprise.

Ray Hemenway was a popular and very hardworking party chairman. The hostile reaction brought out his fighting instincts. He thus staunchly defended the party's support of the Stevenson candidacy. This was particularly on the issue of national electability over the little known senator from Tennessee. While Kefauver had made something of a name conducting investigations in the Senate, he was little known outside the Washington beltway.

Wozniak and Popovich and other Kefauver supporters had been successful in their arguments that the governor and the DFL leadership were trying to push the Stevenson candidacy down their throats. They appealed to the independence of DFLers. They argued that they should stand up to the party leadership. They should send them a message that they were independent enough to make their own choice as to who Minnesotans should support as the party presidential nominee. Kefauver's folksy manner was certainly more appealing to the average DFL supporter. The result was a Kefauver sweep of the 1956 Minnesota Presidential Primary.

The Kefauver victory was a rebuff to the party leadership. The Democratic National Convention that year roundly endorsed the Stevenson candidacy. Stevenson went on to suffer a crushing defeat in the November 1956 general election.

The Stevenson/Kefauver battle added yet another dimension to my experience about the likes and dislikes of Minnesotans and especially Democrats outside of the Twin Cities metropolitan area.

State of Minnesota vs. Gerald Connolly

One of the most interesting cases I participated in as an assistant attorney general involved a combination of alleged labor racketeering; violence; the national Teamsters union; Jimmy Hoffa; and two Twin Cities Jewish criminal defense attorneys. It all started with the takeover of a downtown Minneapolis department store, the John W. Thomas Company, located on Eighth Street off of what is now the Nicollet Mall. It turned out that the purchase of the retailer was with funds from the Central States Teamsters Pension Fund. A Chicagoan named Benjamin Dranow was installed as president of the store.

The next step toward extending Hoffa and his Teamster influence into the Twin Cities was Hoffa's sending Gerald Connolly, a reputed "tough guy," to the Twin Cities. Connolly's express mission turned out to be the takeover of two local teamsters unions. One was the Minneapolis liquor store drivers' teamster union run by Tony Felicetta. Felicetta was a flamboyant figure. He drove a yellow Lincoln convertible. Felicetta's counterpart in St. Paul was with a union local with the same type of membership. This was in the same period of time that much of the liquor traffic in the Twin Cities, particularly in Minneapolis, was divided between the "Banks' combination" and the "Kid Cann syndicate."

Both Felicetta and his St. Paul counterpart resisted Connolly's attempts to take over control of their union locals. They were both tough union leaders who had come up the hard way in organizing this industry. Connolly then tried what he believed to be a much more effective method. He sent a "signal" to the local union leaders as to what would occur if they did not relinquish their offices. One evening the backend of Felicetta's Lincoln was blown off. The back stoop of the St. Paul residence of the union leader was demolished by an explosion.

As might be expected, this caught everyone's attention, including George Scott, a former assistant attorney general, who was now Hennepin County attorney. As the attorney general's labor person, I was assigned to assist Scott in the prosecution.

A thorough investigation disclosed that Connolly had hired several derelicts off the bowery on Washington Avenue to set the explosions. The fuses were tested on a window sill in Connolly's office. The same persons had set off the explosions in Minneapolis and St. Paul. Under threat of more serious prosecution, they agreed to testify against Connolly.

Criminal proceedings against Connolly were instituted in both the Ramsey County and Hennepin County district courts. Connolly was indicted by a Hennepin County Grand Jury. I participated with Scott in presenting the case to the Grand Jury. Connolly was represented in the Hennepin County criminal proceedings by Irving Nemerov. It was later discovered that Nemerov's brother, Bernard Nemerov, a Chicago insurance broker, had close ties to the Hoffa-controlled Teamster's Central Conference Pension Fund.

In the Ramsey County prosecution Connolly retained a more well-known and successful criminal defense attorney Sydney Goff. Goff had been involved in DFL politics. He was once reportedly interested in running for governor. In Ramsey County the case was assigned to Judge Robert Rensch. After the presentation of the prosecution's case, Judge Rensch dismissed the charges based upon what we considered to be an unsupported technicality. He ruled that there was insufficient corroboration of the testimony of the people who had set the bombs. They had testified as to Connolly's having orchestrated the whole scenario.

Of course the prosecution was disappointed. However, we still had the prosecution in Minneapolis with which to nail Connolly. However, attorney Nemerov claimed that the grand jury indictment of Connolly should be dismissed. He asserted that I was an unauthorized person in the Grand Jury room while presenting the evidence leading to the indictment. There was ample precedent that the attorney general and his assistants had assisted prosecuting attorneys for many years throughout the state. This was particularly true in controversial crimes that may have been beyond the expertise or resources of a local county attorney. When Nemerov's challenge was denied in Hennepin County District Court, he took an appeal to the Minnesota Supreme Court. That court ruled that my presence and participation in the Grand Jury proceedings as an assistant attorney general was appropriate.

We then proceeded to trial. The trial in Hennepin County was presided over by Judge Rolf Fosseen. Judge Fosseen was an experienced and strict jurist. There was a no nonsense attitude that prevailed when appearing in his courtroom. The trial before Judge Fosseen went smoothly. He admitted the testimony of the co-conspirators despite the defense's objections. The case went to a twelve-person jury. It did not take long for the jury to come in with a guilty verdict. Gerald Connolly went to prison. Hoffa's attempts to take over the local teamsters unions failed. The attempts were not repeated during Hoffa's lifetime or thereafter.

The attorney general's office served as legal counsel to the State Labor Conciliator. He functioned at the state level in a comparable position to that of the regional office of the National Labor Relations Board. The Conciliator's job was basically to conduct elections or otherwise determine whether a petitioning union could be certified as exclusive representative for collective bargaining purposes as to both public employees and those in the private sector whose employers were not engaged in interstate commerce. It was in this assignment that I developed the rules governing collective bargaining elections for public employees. The position also gave me the opportunity to acquire appellate court experience. I appeared on behalf of the Labor Conciliator in the Minnesota Supreme Court. I learned from this experience in arguing a case before Minnesota's high court that a lawyer cannot always tell from the questioning by the justices how they approached their opinions on the final decision in the appeal. When I stumbled in answering a question from the Chief Justice, he commented, "Mr. Latz, we are like two trains passing in the night." My answer did not really respond to the question posed.

As I left the Supreme Court chamber following the conclusion of the argument I was dejected. I felt I had fumbled the opportunity in my first appellate argument. The opposing attorney, Robert Fenlon, was a very gracious lawyer with whom I subsequently had many engagements in private law practice. He put his arm around my shoulder and attempted to console me. Both of us thought he would prevail. To our surprise, when the Supreme Court decision was issued, the State Labor Conciliator prevailed. The lesson clearly was that you cannot tell from the questions asked what the judge is thinking. He/she may be simply a devil's advocate. The decision was in *State ex rel Dison vs. the State of Minnesota through Harry L. Hanson, State Labor Conciliator.* All of these experiences provided me with invaluable and unparalleled experience as a young lawyer. My political experience with Governor Freeman and other leaders of the DFL laid the groundwork for my entry into private law practice and a career in elective public office.

Private Law Practice and First Race for the Legislature

In 1958, after some three years in the attorney general's office I left the security of that office to enter private law practice in Minneapolis. I shared office space with other lawyers in downtown Minneapolis. Still unmarried, I had only one significant client. Norman Carle, an old friend of Rubin Latz in the labor movement, was head of the Hospital and Institutional Employees Union, Local 113. He retained me as the union attorney. Local 113 represented the same types of low paid workers as had my father's union, the Laundry Worker's and Dry Cleaners Union. Local 113 represented the nurse's aides and orderlies in Twin Cities area hospitals and nursing homes. Carle was an aggressive and outspoken labor leader and advocate for his members. His mercurial temperament made him a difficult client to represent. However, the $35.00 per hour fees paid the rent. The labor arbitration and court appearances provided me with a wealth of experience as well as many contacts in the labor movement. Representing labor unions has represented the core of my law practice for over 50 years.

The affiliation with the labor movement provided the base for my political support from a vital partner in the DFL Party. The endorsements by labor unions proved very helpful to my campaigns for and service in public office. In those bachelor days I continued to live with my mother in the 5th Ward. I maintained my political connections with North Minneapolis DFLers and DFL party activity throughout my years in the attorney general's office. I looked for an opportunity to make my first run for a seat in the Legislature.

That opportunity presented itself shortly before I resigned from the attorney general's staff. Gerald Mullin, the State Senator representing the then 35th District in North Minneapolis' 5th and 4th Wards, decided to not seek reelection. Mullin, a conservative Democrat, caucused with the Conservatives while they controlled the Minnesota Senate. During that period of service Mullin also rose to president of the Minneapolis Gas Company, now CenterPoint/Energy. As a State Senator Mullin had been a stalwart friend of the University. He safeguarded its interests in the Legislature. One of the two state representatives in the 35th District H. P. "Pat" Goodin decided to run for Mullin's senate seat. This left a vacancy to be filled in the House seat he vacated. The other 35th District Representative was DFLer Leo Mosier.

As I was preparing my resignation from the attorney general's office to enter private practice and run for the Legislature, I approached Governor Freeman for an endorsement. Freeman graciously agreed to endorse me in my quest. Freeman drafted and signed a letter warmly expressing the state's thanks for my service as an assistant attorney general. He praised my qualifications for service in the Legislature. I featured that letter and a picture of Governor Freeman on my major piece of campaign literature. The legend on the front of the piece was "See what Governor Freeman says about Bob Latz." That brochure and others I used throughout my four campaigns for the Legislature were designed by a very gifted artist and graphic designer Erwin Grossman. Grossman, a longtime friend, ran a very successful advertising agency. The agency is now continuing under the ownership of the Grossmans' sons. Arlis Grossman was a talented copywriter who assisted with the text of my campaign pieces.

The 5th Ward in North Minneapolis made up nearly half of the 35th Legislative District. It contained many Jews and Blacks. It also included the Ascension Parish which was predominantly Irish Catholic. I had developed close ties with the parish priest Father John Coates and Monsignor Dunphy. While a student at Lincoln Junior High I had been a member of the Ascension Club boxing team. The Emanuel Cohen Center, the Jewish community activity center, did not have a boxing program. I found myself in difficulty with some tough students in school, who were regularly punishing me in shop class and after school. At my mother's urging, I sought to learn how to defend myself. This was no mean task, since I was tall, skinny and vocal in expressing my opinions. I found a Golden Gloves boxing program at the Ascension Club.

The issue of endorsement by individuals and organizations is always a prime subject in any race for public office. In my first race for office I was initially faced with a mixed bag. Despite my labor background, the Minneapolis Central Labor Union Committee on Political Education (COPE) initially endorsed a union business representative Walter Bednarczyk for the seat I sought. Bednarczyk was a member of the 4th Ward DFL Club. A caucus of the DFLers in the 5th Ward ended in a stalemate. Two other Jewish candidates had surfaced vying for the seat. One was attorney Arnold Feinberg. The other was Samuel Bellman. Bellman's entry into the race was surprising. Bellman was a successful attorney in private practice. He had served one two-year term in the Legislature from 1934 to 1936. He was the Latz family attorney. Rubin Latz had helped Bellman, as a young attorney, build up a successful law practice. Bellman's wife was the sister of Bertha Aronson, the wife of Rabbi David Aronson of Beth El Synagogue on Penn Avenue. Both Bellman and I were Beth El members.

While the 35th District DFL Caucus did not produce a candidate with the required 60 percent of the votes necessary for an endorsement, I led the pack. The venue now shifted to the Hennepin County DFL Convention. There I won easily exceeding the required 60 percent. I received more than 3 ½ times the vote of my nearest competitor and better than twice as many votes as all other candidates combined. The other candidates were Bednarczyk, Bellman and George Swanson. Therefore, I became, along with Mosier, a DFL endorsed candidate for the legislature. That vote gave me the right to proclaim "DFL endorsed" in the primary election campaign.

Leo Mosier, the incumbent candidate for reelection to the other at-large 35th District seat, had no trouble being endorsed by both the Central Labor Union and the DFL. Endorsements by a powerful organization meant more than being able to list that endorsement on one's campaign literature. It also meant being listed on the sample ballots which were put out by the Central Labor Union and by the DFL Party. Thus, in the primary campaign Bednarczyk would be teamed with Mosier on the labor sample ballot. I would be teamed with Mosier on the DFL Party sample ballot. Then there was George Swanson who had been endorsed by the 4th Ward DFL Club, and Helen Santee Johnston, the Republican endorsed candidate. In the 1958 Primary Election for the 35th District there were a total of 15 candidates who filed for election for two seats. Among those 15 were Bellman and Feinberg, who also were from the 5th Ward, and Bednarczyk and Swanson from the 4th Ward.

During the primary campaign I was assisted by a strong campaign staff. They included Jay Paul and Phil Snyder. Paul had succeeded me as Chairman of the 5th Ward DFL Club and caucus.

Leroy McGowan and Nellie Stone Johnson were representatives of the Black community. Charles "Bud" Walsh was Irish Catholic. There were a number of others who filled important roles as campaign workers. Some, such as Jim Dehn and Alan Sherr, were campaign advisors. Others, such as Mary Ryan and Loretta Early, made many phone calls urging voters to register and to get out to vote and support me. I was endorsed by a strong group of Black voters in the 5th Ward as well as by William E. Cratic, a Black civic and human rights leader who lived outside the district. In endorsing me, Cratic made the following statement which was printed in the North Minneapolis Post, the community newspaper:

"I consider him, Robert Latz, a "chip off the block" for his father Rubin Latz the labor leader was a stalwart friend of the Negro and the common people. I urge the people of the 35th District to vote for Bob Latz for the Legislature."

The 35th District contained a population of about 75,000. It ran from Olson Highway on the south to the city limits, 53rd Avenue North, on the North, and from 3rd Street North on the east to Xerxes Avenue and Victory Memorial Drive on the west. It was thus a very large district to cover on foot. I then came upon a novel idea. I heard of a 1936 vintage Divco milk truck that was stored in a friend's garage. The truck was still in running order. I purchased the milk truck. I had it painted bright yellow with campaign posters and a large picture of myself on the side. We then had it outfitted with a loudspeaker system and record player. Throughout that initial campaign, and my three other successful legislative campaigns, Leroy McGowan drove the old floor shift milk truck up and down the entire 35th District. I or others would get on the loudspeaker urging people to get out and vote for Bob Latz, the DFL-endorsed candidate for State Representative. After the primary election, we also received the labor endorsement. The campaign truck attracted much attention. Most of the reception was favorable. Some objected to the noise generated. Since in my first campaign I was still unmarried, and with a just beginning law practice, much time was available. It was devoted to the most important type of campaigning – ringing doorbells; speaking directly with the prospective voter; and handing that person a piece of campaign literature to read and share with other household members. Nellie Stone Johnson literally took me by hand in a door-to-door campaign in the 9th Precinct where the bulk of the district's Black population lived. Nellie knew just about everyone there. She would repeat her personal endorsement of me; she would tell them about my background; and particularly about my service in prosecuting the McCarthy's Café case. She stated I had a strong commitment to the advancement of the civil rights movement.

I knew Friday night, the Jewish Sabbath, was no time to campaign in Jewish neighborhoods. But it was a time when other prospective voters received their paychecks and shopped at the area's supermarkets and banks. Thus, on most Friday nights, and in all kinds of inclement weather, I stationed myself on the southeast corner of Emerson and West Broadway. This was right in front of the entrance to a branch of the First National Bank. A supermarket was just down the street. I alternated my position between the front entrance to the bank and the entrance to the supermarket. The management of the supermarket was none to happy about my presence in their parking lot while patrons were entering or leaving the store. If patrons had their hands full leaving the store with groceries I would simply drop a piece of campaign literature in their grocery bag.

Name recognition is vital in any political campaign. I was blessed with a short last name. This allowed large letters on campaign signs. I also became known as "Robert (Bob) Latz." That is how the name was placed on the ballot. In my youth growing up in North Minneapolis I was commonly called "Bob" or "Bobby". Ronald Latz took the name shortening one step further by dropping the Ronald and simply appearing on the ballot as "Ron Latz." Picking a color for a lawn sign was no simple task. My team had observed many lawn signs that were of such a bland color that they were not easily visible. Therefore, we chose dayglow orange for the background with the Latz name superimposed in large black letters. Last name recognition was especially important, because no one knew the order in which a name would be placed on the ballot. While the law required a rotation of names in the printing of ballots, voters would need some assistance in recognizing their favorite candidate when marking their ballot. The repetition of my last name on lawn signs and in campaign literature would help voters remember and search for the name. This was especially important when, in my first campaign in 1958, the primary ballot for the two open house seats listed the names of 15 candidates.

Securing the best locations for the placement of campaign signs was also a very important part of the campaign strategy. I spent countless hours on the telephone, using synagogue, church and organizational membership lists to identify supporters, lawn sign locations, door-to-door workers, and sources of campaign contributions. Since I was still struggling to build a private law practice, the late afternoons were mostly filled with door-to-door campaigning and the evenings with campaign phone calls. The weekends were consumed with campaign activities. The first object in the lawn sign activity was to pick out as many locations as possible on major thoroughfares in the district and to secure the willingness of the resident to the placement of a campaign sign in his/her front yard. One of the major north/south thoroughfares running through the entire district was Penn Avenue. Therefore, I concentrated on placing as many lawn signs as possible on Penn. Penn stretched from Olson Highway (6th Avenue North) to 53rd Avenue North, the Minneapolis boundary. Intensive effort succeeded in placing several hundred lawn signs on Penn Avenue. Of course, the greatest number was concentrated in the 5th Ward, my base in the heavily populated Jewish community.

The signs were also located next to and across the street from Beth El Synagogue attended by both myself and Sam Bellman, my chief primary election opponent in the Jewish community. One evening I received a call from Rabbi David Aronson the spiritual leader of Beth El. The rabbi said that he thought it unseemly for both Bellman and I to have campaign signs along the competitive stretch of Penn Avenue that included the synagogue. Rabbi Aronson, for whom I had great respect, suggested that both I and

Bellman remove our campaign signs. My signs outnumbered Bellman's by a ratio of about 10-1. Rabbi Aronson was a strong-willed spiritual leader unafraid to voice his views on controversial issues. He had delivered a beautiful sermon at Rubin Latz's funeral. He had strongly criticized some in the political community for their lack of support in Rubin's quest for election to the Minneapolis Library Board and in his unsuccessful appointment to the Minneapolis Civil Service Commission. Showing all due respect to the rabbi, I politely declined the request. I told the rabbi that Bellman had had his shot at the Legislature some 25 years earlier. He had a successful law practice. He was middle aged; I was just embarking on my legal and political career. Bellman's parents had been my parents' best friends. It was just unexplainable why Bellman chose this time to attempt to thwart my first run for elective office. Rabbi Aronson understood and withdrew his request.

The saturation of Penn Avenue with Latz campaign signs also drew some more humorous comments. One evening I received a phone call. The caller related that she was driving down Penn Avenue with her daughter. Her daughter asked her, "Who is that Latz who is selling all of these homes on Penn Avenue?" We both had a good laugh. Perhaps I was embarking on the wrong career, and should have gone into the real estate business rather than the practice of law.

Sometimes residents had reasons why they did not want campaign signs in their front yard. Signs interfered with mowing the lawn. For others there was a bad experience with previous candidates who had failed to remove their signs after the election. Some prominent people in the community feared that identification with one candidate in a contested race would interfere with their business. Or it might put them at odds with their neighbors who supported another candidate. One Hennepin County District Judge with a DFL political background said that the Canons of Judicial Ethics prevented him from taking part in a political contest. However, he stated that their front yard was divided in half by a sidewalk down the middle. One half of the yard, he said, was his wife's. The other half was his. I could place my campaign sign on the wife's half of the yard. She was not a judge and not so restrained. That particular judge showed the same degree of astuteness in his rulings. He had grown up in a political household. His father was a longtime politician on the northside who became one of my supporters. While I do not recall having ever had the occasion to appear before Judge Donald Barbeau in Hennepin County District Court, his "lawn sign decision" was the type of "Solomon's baby" decision that showed the balance necessary for a successful jurist.

Rubin Latz passed away ten years prior to my first campaign in 1958. However, he had created a solid base of support for me in the Jewish and Black communities in the 5th Ward and among liberal-labor supporters in the 4th Ward. Thus, I was able to capitalize on my father's reputation among liberals and union members throughout the district. This helped in the primary election where Walter Bednarczyk had achieved the early pre-primary endorsement of the Central Labor Union (CLU). The importance of endorsements by the CLU and the DFL were underscored by the issuance by each group of "sample ballots." These were ballots that were mailed to voters in liberal areas listing the candidates who were endorsed by each group. Hopefully, a liberal candidate's name would appear on both ballots. However, in 1958, the pre-primary endorsements were split. Bednarczyk's name appeared on the labor sample ballot. My name appeared on the DFL sample ballot. Representative Leo Mosier appeared on both. In the general election campaign my name appeared on both. With many names running for office in a primary election it is difficult for many voters to keep track of which candidates for whom they wished to vote. The sample ballots were taken by the voter into the polling booth where they served as a checklist of those for whom they wished to vote.

The organizational endorsements, and the sample ballots, were particularly important in races for seats in the Legislature. At that time candidates for the Legislature ran on a non-partisan basis. They did not appear on the political party ballot as did candidates for statewide office. There a DFLer and a Republican would each be selected in the primary to run for governor or Congress as the party candidate to go forward in the general election. This lack of party labels in the primary election made this sample ballot even more important. Some legislative candidates in a number of districts throughout the state, including North Minneapolis, masked their true party affiliation by running as "liberals" or "conservatives" without a party identification. When they were elected, they would caucus either with the "liberals" or "conservatives" in the House or the Senate. Some rather conservative politicians, such as the then-retiring State Senator Gerald Mullin, campaigned as a Democrat in the district but caucused with the "conservatives" in the Senate. At the Legislature the "liberals" were DFLers while the "conservatives" were mostly Republicans. A candidate could have it both ways. Some, like Mullin, were truly conservative Democrats of the old school. They were part of the Irish Catholic base of the Minnesota Democratic Party before the 1944 merger of the Democrats and Farmer Laborites.

H. P. "Pat" Goodin ran as a DFLer and with labor endorsement as a state representative. He was elected with those endorsements to the state senate seat vacated by Mullin. He was elected only after a vigorous contest with Edward Gearty a former assistant attorney general. Gearty, an Ascension Church member, contested Goodin for the endorsements leading to the senate election. While Goodin triumphed over Gearty in that 1958 race, Goodin made a major political miscalculation when he became a state senator. Instead of caucusing with the liberals in the Senate, he chose to try to emulate Mullin. He caucused with the conservatives. This outraged the DFLers. In the next senate election Representative Leo Mosier moved up from his house seat challenging Goodin in the senate race. Gearty and I teamed up. We jointly campaigned for the two house seats. In the 1960 election, Mosier beat Goodin, and the Latz-Gearty team was elected. With Mosier's death several years later Gearty was elected to the state senate. He served many years with distinction including service as the presiding officer – President – of the Minnesota Senate.

In my campaigns I emphasized that the 5th Ward part of the district deserved to have separate representation in the Legisla-

ture. It had been at least ten years since a member of the Legislature had lived in the 5ᵗʰ Ward. The 5ᵗʰ Ward was more diverse
ethnically and religiously than the 4ᵗʰ Ward. There were heavy
concentrations of Blacks, Jews and Irish Catholics in the 5ᵗʰ Ward.
I also knew that the voting patterns of the 5ᵗʰ Ward showed higher
concentrations of votes for liberal candidates. Thus, I knew that I
needed to have a very strong turnout of my supporters from the 5ᵗʰ
Ward to overcome the more conservative voters in the 4ᵗʰ Ward.
The 4ᵗʰ Ward residents were also not as familiar with my name as
those in the 5ᵗʰ Ward where I had grown up.

There were many candidates in that first primary race. The
candidates ran at large in the district. Only four persons were to
be nominated in the primary to go on to the general election. I
knew that I had to devise a method to single myself out from the
other candidates almost all of whom were DFLers. The incumbent State Representative Leo Mosier had been endorsed by labor
and the DFL without opposition. He lived in the 4ᵗʰ Ward. He
was well-liked and had a good record. He was an overwhelming
favorite to lead the primary ticket and to go on to election. The
battle was really for the second spot. I and my supporters then
decided to use a technique called the "bullet ballot." This was a
perfectly legal and ethical concept. While the voter could vote for
two candidates on the ballot, since there were two legislative seats
open, they could also vote for only one. I feared that some Jewish
voters, familiar with Latz, Bellman and Feinberg, the three Jewish candidates in the Primary, would split their two votes between
the three Jewish candidates. For example, the voter could vote for
both Latz and Bellman. This would provide an avenue for other
and lesser known candidates to overtake me. I and my supporters
urged a vote for only one candidate – Bob Latz – in the primary.
This "bulleting" would assure that my principal opponents would
receive less votes.

The results of the primary election were that Mosier led the
ticket followed by Latz, Bednarczyk and Swanson in that order.
Four candidates were nominated for the two at-large seats. That
was also the order in the General Election results. I carried the

5th Ward precincts that contained the Jewish and Black voters by margins that varied from 9-1 to 7-1 over the non-incumbent candidates. I also ran strongly in the area covered by the Ascension Church. The further north in the district one went, the smaller were my margins. However, those margins were also respectable. This voting pattern in my first race for the Legislature carried over substantially in the following three successful elections.

Even as an incumbent, a state representative must run for reelection every two years. An incumbent must keep up his/her family and community activities while making a living and devoting time to attending legislative sessions and constituent services. Many voters fail to distinguish between the public offices held. Some just knew that he/she is a "politician." Problems relating to local matters, usually the province of a city council member, thus ended up with calls to my home, office or in the mail. At times I, like other members of the Legislature, would act as a "traffic cop" directing constituents to the appropriate local or state office or department where their questions could be answered or their requests addressed.

At times the appeals for help tugged at the heartstrings. On one such occasion the elderly man who picked up laundry and dry cleaning at our residence appeared one day very distraught. When I asked what the problem was, he replied that his driver's license had expired. He was required to take a written test to achieve the issuance of a new one. His job depended on his driver's license, as did his feeling of self-worth. He still needed to work for a living. The problem was that he was an immigrant to this country with very little formal education. His command of written English language was quite poor. He said that he had failed the written driver's test, because he did not really understand the questions. He had been driving for years. He considered himself a good driver. He had an accident-free record. I was touched by his economic needs and sincerity. My plea to the Minnesota Highway Department Driver's License Division achieved a compromise. He would be allowed to take an oral test to establish his qualifications, knowledge of the rules of the road, and so on. He was able to pass the test. He received a valid driver's license. He kept both his job and his self-respect. The lesson was not simply how one uses the powers of his office to assist a constituent. It also underscored the importance of driver's license privileges to seniors. Take away their "wheels" and you take away a large measure of their independence and self-respect. The lesson has not been lost on me as I too have become a senior citizen.

Moving into a seat in the Legislature did not mean that I could forego the community organizational activities and contacts that had helped strengthen my role as a community leader as well as a legislative candidate. I continued as a board member of the Minneapolis Federation for Jewish Service; the Minnesota Jewish Council; the B'nai B'rith; the Citizens League; the Minneapolis Joint Committee on Charter Review; and the Hillel Foundation at the University of Minnesota. I also continued on the boards of the Regional Office of the Anti-Defamation League and the Plymouth Avenue Business Association.

Each of these organizations also helped me to establish a base of financial support for my ongoing political activity. Political campaigns in the 1950's and 1960's were nowhere near as expensive as they are today. Much of the fundraising resulted in small contributions of under $100.00. Contributions from special interests with axes to grind at the Legislature were approached with caution if not rejection. Party endorsement did not carry with it money. It did help with volunteers and with the sample ballot. The largest expenditures were the costs of campaign literature and sign printing. Most of the expenses were self-financed. "Sweat equity" by volunteers was the key. Lawn signs were put together in a supporter's basement. The door-to-door campaigning and literature drops were all by the candidate or volunteers. The few print ads were confined to newspapers such as the North Minneapolis Post and the American Jewish World.

Governor Orville Freeman had been re-elected governor at the same 1958 November General Election. Hubert Humphrey continued as a U.S. Senator. The "liberals" had a majority in the House. The conservatives continued in control of the Senate. A

battle developed in the liberal caucus over who would serve as the
Speaker of the House. The Speaker was the presiding officer. He
was the person who named the committee chairs and assigned
members to committees. It was a key position. With my support,
Ed Chilgren was narrowly elected Speaker designate at a caucus of
the house liberals over Representative Fred Cina of Aurora. Chilgren was from Little Fork near the Canadian border. He was a
newspaper editor and publisher. Chilgren had the implicit support
of the DFL Party hierarchy. In return for my efforts, I began my
freshman year in the Legislature with a distinction unique in recent
state political history. Speaker Chilgren appointed me as a member
of the House Committee on Committees. This committee advised
the Speaker on the designation of membership and chairs of all
other committees. My appointment was the first time in history
that a first term legislator had been given this assignment. As part
of this twelve-member group I assured myself of favorable committee assignments. It also propelled me into political infighting
within the liberal-DFL caucus. The liberal members controlled the
House with 73 members to the conservatives 58.

The first fight within the Committee on Committees was
something of a replay of the 1956 Presidential Primary battle
between Kefauver and Stevenson. St. Paul Representative Peter
Popovich was a school bond attorney in his private law practice.
DFL Party leaders still remembered the scars that were inflicted
on them in Popovich's successful support of Kefauver in his Presidential Primary win over the DFL Party supported Governor of
Illinois. Popovich sought selection as Education Committee Chair.
Speaker Chilgren, with my support, sided with the DFL Party
leadership and rejected Popovich's request. Thus, I incurred the
enmity of Popovich and his supporters, who included Fred Cina.
Cina lost to Chilgren for Speaker. He became the House Majority
Leader.

The intra-caucus battles continued on when the 1959 legislative
session convened. There was what was described by Wallace Mitchell, a political reporter for the Minneapolis Star, as a "free-swing-
ing closed door session over their [house liberals] right to vote the

party line on (Freeman) administration-favored issues."[1] It was a floor fight over repeal of the Minnesota Presidential Primary law. The repeal was favored by DFL Party leaders including Governor Freeman. According to Mitchell, "feelings ran so high, according to reports, that at one point Rep. Peter S. Popovich, St. Paul, was challenged over his liberal bloc allegiance and he in turn offered to resign if that's what the group wished." Popovich did not resign.

Popovich and a devious lobbyist played a role in humiliating me in my first attempt to get a bill passed on the floor of the house. Minneapolis Police Inspector William Joyce, a constituent, induced me to sponsor a bill prohibiting the carrying of concealed handguns. I was told that it was a good government bill that had a substantial chance of success. What the lobbyist did not tell me was that the bill had been literally "shot down" in previous legislative sessions primarily through opposition from rural legislators. I got the bill passed through the House Crime Prevention Committee with little opposition. However, when the bill was brought up on the floor of the house a firestorm of opposition erupted. It was led by Popovich. The debate became quite emotional. Harsh words were traded between me and Popovich. Rural legislators who were farmers felt that the bill would prevent them from carrying weapons with them while they worked in the fields and were subject to animal attacks. The bill went down in flames. Only a handful of city legislators on the DFL side supported it. Conservative legislators saw it as a chance to defeat me early on in my career.

My successful selection to key house committees gave me a base for political prominence and participation in legislation that directly affected my varied constituency and the state. I sponsored a bill providing for a $ .75 per hour minimum wage for workers under 21, exempting workers in agriculture, domestic service and public employment. I argued on the floor of the Legislature that the present law simply was unworkable. However, even rural Liberals complained that establishing a $ .75 per hour minimum for retail employees would result in the loss of jobs for parttime workers in grocery stores and resorts. The increased minimum wage effort failed. The debate echoed the debate heard in the 2005 legislative session on increasing the state's minimum wage requirement.

Ethics in government was another subject with which I was involved. Governor Freeman had appointed an Ethics in Government Commission. The commission proposed a bill which would have imposed significant restraints on lobbyists. The bill was drafted by Sydney Berde an assistant attorney general. The bill was strongly supported by Governor Freeman. I was the chief house author. It was introduced with bipartisan support. Co-authors were conservative Representatives Clarence Langley of Red Wing and Donald Franke of Rochester. A liberal co-author was the one woman member of the Legislature at the time, Sally Luther of Minneapolis. Representative Franke was an outstanding example of a moderate Republican who caucused with the conservatives. Rochester, and Olmsted County, the home of the renowned Mayo Clinic, has through the years has been a political swing district. It could be as likely to elect a DFLer as a Republican so long as the person held moderate political views. Thus, it might have a DFL senator, such as Sandy Keith, and a conservative/Republican house member such as Don Franke. In succeeding years, with IBM supplanting the Mayo Clinic as the largest employer in the area, the political composition shifted to a more conservative representation. However, in something of a swing toward a more moderate stance, in 2004 the area elected a Jewish woman attorney, Tina Liebling, to a house seat.

Among the far-reaching restrictions in the ethics proposal was one that prohibited lawyer-legislators from practicing before state agencies. For example, a lawyer-legislator would be prohibited from taking claims for a client before a worker's compensation judge. The proposal engendered much controversy and opposition. More importantly, the bill would have set up a system of registration for lobbyists and their employers. Freeman's lobbyist registration bill would require lobbyists and their employers to register with the State Public Examiner.

The Governor's Commission on Ethics in Government was chaired by Rabbi W. Gunther Plaut of St. Paul's Mt. Zion Temple. In a presentation to the House General Legislation Committee

Rabbi Plaut summed up the proposal by stating, "Disclosure is the one word which sums up the philosophy of the committee report and of this legislation. Lobbying is a legitimate means of bringing the opinions of citizens to the public and to the legislature. We seek only to eliminate its negative or pernicious features."

Other individual ethics bills were introduced by DFLers and by conservatives. The differences were that under the bill proposed by the Governor's Commission, which I sponsored, the State Public Examiner would be required to file with legislative officers reports of money spent by lobbyists and their employers to influence legislation. It would also provide penalties for violations. The bill had to traverse several committees. In one committee amendments were adopted. Some of the sections were deleted. It was then referred to the House General Legislation Committee by a 10-4 vote. There it died.

Another controversial bill I sponsored provided for binding arbitration in labor disputes involving public employees. In 1959, Minnesota public employees were prohibited from striking. They were not given any adequate substitute. They could exercise their right to picket and perhaps have non-binding recommendations issued by fact-finding panels. However, their ultimate weapon – the strike – was prohibited. In this way Minnesota law at the time differed from private sector employment. In non-public employment the right to strike had been guaranteed since the passage of the Wagner Act in the mid-1930's. The bill I sponsored had widespread support from labor unions. It was vigorously opposed by municipal city councils throughout the state; by the Minneapolis/St. Paul Chambers of Commerce; and by the Minneapolis Taxpayers Association. The bill had a unique provision. It would allow a public body to levy taxes beyond normal limits to meet the costs of an arbitration award. The bill passed through the House Labor Committee late in the session. My effort to give the bill priority consideration by placing it on the Special Orders Calendar was defeated on a 75-33 vote.[2]

The House debate pitted me against many conservative legislators from throughout Minnesota. A challenging floor debate took place between me and Representative C. Donald Peterson, a conservative from Edina. Peterson and I were engaged in ongoing clashes as lawyers in the private sector. Peterson represented the Twin Cities Hospital Association. I was the attorney for the Hospital and Institutional Employees Union, Local 113. The law governing Minnesota hospitals, the Charitable Hospitals Act, provided for compulsory arbitration between a hospital and its employees when they could not agree on a contract. The Charitable Hospitals Act experience was essentially what I and the Minnesota labor movement wanted to extend to public employees.

In the floor debate Peterson leveled an accusation by questioning whether I had a conflict of interest in serving as the legal counsel for *public* employee unions while carrying the bill that affected their rights. Before I could answer the question in the negative, liberal majority leader Fred Cina termed the question "unfair." George French, a Minneapolis conservative, urged Peterson to withdraw the question. Peterson did so. I later told reporters that I did not represent any union affected by the bill.[3] What was quite interesting was that French had served as chairman of the house committee on insurance when the conservatives were in power. He had chaired the committee for a long period of time before and after 1959. At the same time French served as president and legal counsel to the Minnesota Insurance Federation. The federation was the statewide trade group for the Minnesota insurance industry. In the late '50's and 1960's the kinds of conflicts of interest evidenced by French's dual role were regarded benignly by many legislators on both sides of the aisle. Such subjects were not popular with many inside the legislative process. Those on the inside who had been around for a while knew of these conflicts of interest. This guided their actions in considering bills. But it was not a subject that one would raise in public debate.

Throughout my eight years in the legislature the sales tax, as an alternative to the statewide income tax and local property taxes, was a contentious issue between the DFL and the conservatives/Republicans. Governor Pawlenty's "no tax" pledge in 2005, and his labeling of a cigarette tax increase as a "fee," was the kind of playing with word games that goes back at least as far as 1959. In a House Tax Committee debate on the sales tax, Representative George French stated "if it takes money out of people's pockets, it's a tax."[4] The statement was made in reference to Governor Freeman's proposal for the implementation of a withholding system for the collection of income taxes. This was a proposal that was ultimately adopted. The sales tax was finally implemented in 1967, the session after I left the legislature. It was passed over Governor Harold Levander's veto.

Despite the other failures I was successful in passing a bill creating an Independent School District for the city of Minneapolis. While the bill on introduction received what was termed by a Minneapolis Star education reporter as "a fairly friendly reception...from the Hennepin County delegation of the house of representatives," it was openly opposed by the Minneapolis Taxpayers Association. The measure gave the Minneapolis School Board authority and responsibility "particularly in money-raising fields" but "always subject to voter approval."[5] The bill had been drafted by a bipartisan steering committee. It provided that the school board could authorize issuance of bonds raising property taxes subject to public approval. They would be issued separately from general bonds issued by the city. The Citizens League of Minneapolis and Hennepin County was a strong supporter of the bill. I headed a subcommittee of the Hennepin County Delegation which negotiated a compromise. It passed and became law.

During my legislative career there were county legislative delegations in both Hennepin and Ramsey counties. The Hennepin County Delegation involved legislators from both the House and the Senate from Minneapolis and suburban Hennepin County. If all of the members of a delegation, or at least a substantial majority, could agree on a bill it could become what was known as a "delegation bill." This usually assured its relatively easy passage in both houses of the legislature. Legislators from areas outside of that county would be reluctant to interfere with what they considered to be a "local bill." They too would have "local bills" that they would like to pass without interference from legislators from other parts of the state who, presumably, would have little or no interest in measures affecting a particular locale.

It is unfortunate that the delegation system fell out of favor in the 1970's and onward. It provided a bipartisan opportunity to negotiate legislation that affected only Minneapolis or Hennepin County. It showed that bipartisanship in the legislative process could work. At times the internal battles within the DFL or conservative/Republican members of the delegation could be fiercer than between the DFLers and the Republican groups in the delegation. There were DFLers in the delegation with more seniority in the Legislature. The same was true on the GOP side. George French led a group of more philosophically conservative members. There were those more recently elected, and more party-aligned, who were often at odds with their more senior and conservative delegation members. Sometimes there were conflicts that were based more on politics and personalities than on philosophy. For example, in 1963, the Republican "young turks," at an election that took place in our own home, defeated on a party line vote my spouse for reelection as President of the Rotunda Club. The Rotunda Club was a statewide non-partisan group of legislative wives. The conservative/Republican majority replaced her with Ruth Frenzel, the wife of Republican State Representative Bill Frenzel. At the time, Carolyn was the youngest person elected to preside over the Rotunda Club. The Club had been in existence for a number of years preceding my entry into the Legislature. It had never before been tainted by partisan politics. Previously, the leadership of the Rotunda Club was based strictly on the personal relationships and characteristics of the members. The Dome Club was the overall organization in which the wives of the Senators and State Representatives participated. At the time that Carolyn was elected, Arnold Rose was the only one other Jewish member of the House. I later led my group of Hennepin County liberals into a coalition with French and his conservative allies. This combination took control of the Hennepin County Delegation. It marginalized the Republican "young turks" who had for the first time involved the legislative wives in partisan politics.

The Republican "young turks" were more party-oriented than the "old guard" House and Senate Republicans epitomized by George French and Minneapolis Senator O. Donald Wright. Wright was the longtime Chair of the Tax Committee and one of a handful of "powerbrokers" in the Senate. These "powerbrokers" also included the Majority Leader Gordon Rosenmeier of Little Falls and Daniel Feidt of Minneapolis. These "conservative" leaders in both the senate and house held little allegiance to the Republican Party. They clashed within the Senate conservative caucus with more liberal and party-oriented Republicans such as Senators Elmer L. Andersen of St. Paul and Wayne Popham of Minneapolis.

With a divided legislature in the 1959 Session, and Freeman in the governor's office, the conservative-dominated senate presented a substantial obstacle to the passage of the Freeman and DFL legislative initiatives. From the 1959 Session and onwards through the subsequent years I served there were the respective liberal and conservative caucuses. Some senior liberal house members from Minneapolis were more conservative and followed George French on Delegation matters.

The "young turk" Republicans were an interesting group. They were closely aligned with the Republican Party. During the Freeman years they did as much as possible to thwart the Freeman and DFL legislative programs. They also clashed with my liberal/DFL oriented Minneapolis and Hennepin County group. This group included an Augsburg College graduate Minneapolis Representative Martin Olav Sabo. Sabo later became House Speaker and then Congressman from Minneapolis 5th District.

Others in my core group were Stanley Enebo, Richard Parish, Jim Adams and Arnold Rose. While I was the chair of the liberal group in the Hennepin County Delegation we were sometimes outnumbered by more senior House liberals and particularly those who represented northeast Minneapolis.

Several of the "young turk" GOP-oriented legislators from Minneapolis and Hennepin County went on to post legislative careers in public office. Representative Douglas Head became Minnesota Attorney General in the 1966 general election. Gary Flakne became Hennepin County Attorney. Bill Frenzel was elected to the U.S. Congress from the suburban 3rd District. After service in the legislature, John Yngve of Plymouth was elected to the University of Minnesota Board of Regents. In 1975, I replaced Yngve on the board.

While lobbying took place with special interest groups attempting to influence legislators in their votes, there was much more important and little understood "in-house lobbying" in the legislature in the 1950's and 1960's. This activity in the house was epitomized by George French. French was very skilled as a legislator. He developed personal and political relationships when his more conservative colleagues' interests were to be served. When a new legislator from Minneapolis or its suburbs of either political party entered the house, French would skillfully attempt to co-opt that person. He developed personal relationships by inviting the newcomer to dinner or to play pool at the St. Paul Athletic Club. When the conservatives were in control, he would assist the new DFL legislators and find them spots on the committees in which they were interested. No one ever knew whether French defrayed these expenses from funds from non-regulated lobbyists for special interests, or from his major client the Minnesota Insurance Federation. He simply picked up the bill for the gatherings of his invitees at the St. Paul Athletic Club, the Criterion Restaurant on University Avenue, or like establishments.

I was subject to these blandishments as were other newcomers. Because of the strong ties to the DFL Party and the Freeman administration these efforts at co-opting me, and others of my core group, were less successful. Astute observers of the statewide political scene knew that political party ascendancy, whether it be of the DFL or the GOP, spelled an erosion, if not the end, of the "Conservative" domination of the Legislature. However, every person in the legislative process was human. Each had his own weak spots. As strong and crafty as he was in his legislative activities, French was controlled by a higher force – his wife. One example proved the point. An evening out with French and other legislators after a day's legislative session was at the Criterion Restaurant, a well-known legislative gathering place. As the evening wore on and the hour of 10:30 p.m. approached, French looked at his watch and exclaimed; "My gosh. Look at the time. I was supposed to be home hours ago. My wife will really have it in for me." He turned to me and said, "Bob, would you please call my wife and tell her that I am tied up on some legislative matters and will be home as soon as possible." I agreed. I went to the pay phone, which, unfortunately, was located in an area subject to the conversation of the restaurant patrons. When I reached Mrs. French and tried George's explanation on her, she expressed, in strong and no nonsense terms, her disbelief. She simply said words to the effect that George better get his posterior home. The communication of that message to French quickly ended the evening's activities. The message to all of us was simple. No matter how powerful or skillful we thought we were in the halls of the Legislature, there were much more powerful forces to which we had to account on the outside, and they were not simply lobbyists for special interests or our constituents.

Chapter Four

The Media

L ittle has been recorded about the influence of individual members of the media on legislation and on the careers of public officials. In the days before the more widespread coverage of the Legislature and political campaigns by television, the focus of political coverage was on the daily newspapers in the Twin Cities. With the weeklies outside the metropolitan areas it was through reporters for the Associated Press and United Press. Each of the major newspapers and these networks had offices in the state capitol. In my earlier years the reporters' offices were in close proximity to the legislative chambers. In later years, and to this day, they have been relegated to offices in the basement of the state capitol. In my first political campaign I had quickly learned of the importance of the local community newspaper. The *North Minneapolis Post* was published weekly. Its political coverage was extensive. One of its reporters was Betty Wilson. Wilson went on to have a very successful career covering politics for the *Minneapolis Star Tribune*. The *North Minneapolis Post* was always looking for local political news. I took advantage of this opportunity in my first and successive campaigns. I put out press releases on bills that I intended to introduce if and when elected, as well as those I authored while in office. I was also very fortunate in being afforded the opportunity by the *North Minneapolis Post* editor H. O. "Sonny" Sonnesyn to write a weekly column on political and legislative matters. This column gave me the opportunity to expound on issues of interest on the local, state and national scene. Writing on such issues, many of them controversial, gave me increasing exposure to my constituents. It also provided an opportunity for my opponents to mount attacks on me. They frequently did so in the Letters to the

Editor column. When Ed Gearty was elected to the legislature, the Post afforded him the same opportunity to write a column.

At the state level I established professional relationships with the state capitol press corps. Key among that close knit fraternity was Jack Mackay. Mackay was the writer for the state bureau of the Associated Press. The AP wire carried news reports from the State Capitol to local newspapers and radio stations throughout Minnesota. Mackay was a very skillful journalist. Outside of the Capitol he was active in communal affairs. He was the first Minnesotan to serve on the National Commission of the Anti-Defamation League (ADL). Mackay was the father of Harvey Mackay, who became a noted Minnesota businessman, author and lecturer. My service on the board of the Minnesota-Dakota Regional Office of the ADL brought me into contact with Jack Mackay. Mackay, without in any way jeopardizing his journalistic independence, was very helpful to me as a young legislator in learning how to deal with the media. I also sought to cultivate professional relationships with the other members of the capitol press corps. They initially included John MacDonald of the *Minneapolis Tribune*; Wallace Mitchell of the *Minneapolis Star*; Karl Neumeir of the *St. Paul Dispatch Pioneer Press*; Gerry Nelson of the United Press (UP) and Arv Johnson of WCCO Radio. All the capitol reporters had quite open access to members of the Legislature as well as the governor's staff people who dealt with the media.

I learned early on in my career that information was a tool for political survival and advancement. Information is also an essential ingredient to the success of a reporter and his/her newspaper or other media outlet. Leaks and "off the record comments" were something of a "currency" shared between journalists and legislators. One hand rubbed the other. A political inside tidbit passed on to a reporter, resulting in an exclusive report from the capitol, could be expected to result in coverage when the public official said or did something in which the public might be interested. I never had a confidence breached by any media person with whom I dealt. However, the reporter would most often seek to confirm the information with a person who was willing to go on the record on the subject. This was simply good journalism. There was only one instance in my memory when an "off the record" statement was not honored. That was a situation involving Dan Cohen and an allegation that he leaked to the media negative information about DFL Lieutenant Governor candidate Marlene Johnson.

In my later years in office Frank Wright and Frank Premack were the political reporters for the *Minneapolis Star Tribune*. Reporters who covered politics were often present in circumstances that could prove embarrassing or destructive to a politician's career and ambition. Since reporters were present at political events that involved socializing and some drinking, they would be present when a legislator or other elected official might have over-indulged. The politician might have said or did something that while marginally newsworthy, could be destructive career-wise. Under such circumstances, the reporter would be faced with a dilemma as to whether to report such an observation. The reporter was on the frontline literally in determining what should or should not be written up and placed on an editor's desk. People in the media are only human. Personal likes and dislikes or personal opinions could, despite efforts to be independent, color a news story. When on the campaign trail a candidate and an accompanying reporter could occasionally have dinner or drinks together. If the politician was not careful he or she might be subject to the World War II adage of "loose lips sink ships."

One such occasion occurred when I was campaigning for the DFL nomination for attorney general. It was on a campaign tour of the Iron Range. After a rally in Hibbing covered by Frank Premack, I apparently had too much to drink. I made some comments to Premack that were negative about another candidate. It was about a Democrat running for another office. It was certainly not a comment that I would wish to be quoted on. But I didn't say the magic words - "this is off the record" - before making the comments. Of course, one could not unilaterally go off the record. It was an essential part of the protocol that the reporter agreed that the comment was off the record before the shield applied. In any event, when I awoke the next morning with a blazing headache and went to breakfast Premack asked me if I remembered what I had said the night before. I had no clue as to what I had uttered. When Premack told me, my headache and concern increased exponentially. I said, "Frank, I hope you don't intend to print that." Premack, to my relief, said he knew that it was a statement made in an unguarded moment, and that he would not take advantage of the situation. Of course, I owed Premack for his expressed journalistic judgment. I never forgot the situation. At an early age, Frank Premack died of a heart attack. He has been honored with the Frank Premack Award given each year to a person for outstanding journalistic achievement.

Besides Premack, there were other Jewish reporters for the Twin Cities newspapers who covered specialized areas. Among them was Richard Kleeman. Kleeman covered education matters for the Minneapolis Star Tribune. Sam Romer was the labor reporter for the same newspaper. In his earlier days Romer had been an active socialist. He had known Rubin Latz and reported on his activities in the labor movement. Since in my private law practice I represented labor unions, Romer had occasion to come in contact with me on a fairly frequent basis.

It was very hard to keep a political secret at the capitol. Each member of the capitol press corp had his "sources" that he could rely on to fill in on "background" from a leak of all or part of a story of political interest. This could be a story that was favorable to the legislator or his party or negative to the opposition. The caucuses of the factions at the Legislature were universally closed to the media so that political strategies could be openly discussed. However, there was no keeping of any secrets as to what took place. To try to preserve accuracy the caucus leadership would usually meet with the reporters who had been waiting outside the closed doors and brief them on what had occurred. The omitted details, which most often were what the media were really interested in, were later added in private conversations with a legislator who would "leak" the omitted details. There sometimes were meetings on strategy that were so confidential that legislators sought to hold them in remote locations in the capitol building or outside the capitol complex itself. There was one such meeting of House DFL conferees on a very controversial bill that we sought to keep away from the prying eyes and ears of the capitol press corp. A late arriving member saw St. Paul Dispatch Pioneer Press reporter Gene Newhall with his ear to the meeting room door. There was no way to evict Newhall from the hallway. The meeting broke up shortly thereafter. But Newhall apparently had heard enough, and confirmed enough other details, to write a story the following day. As can be expected, there was little love lost between those involved and this particular newsman.

Governor Freeman, as had governors before and after, had a press secretary. The key person in that role during his administration was former Minneapolis Star reporter Ted Smebakken. Governor Freeman also had media savvy people in his own close political circle. One of them, University of Minnesota Medical School Professor Dr. William Kubicek was author of the idea of developing a statewide radio network. This effort was very effective in spreading Freeman's views throughout the state. Radio in those days was a much less expensive medium for political advertising than running the traditional political ads in the daily and even weekly newspapers. Television as a political medium of communication was less used because of its expense. To attempt to saturate the viewing public was just too expensive. The one exception would be a concluding broadcast telecast on election eve featuring the party-endorsed candidates for office such as U.S. senator and governor.

During those years politicians did not develop the same personal contacts and relationships with television newspeople as they did with the print media. In part this was due to the fact that television reporters usually did not have the political background and experience as their counterparts with the newspapers. Some were selected primarily because of how articulate and presentable they would be on camera rather than having developed a journalistic or political background. This changed as time went on. Television became the more pervasive medium for political interviews on the evening news, and with public affairs and talk shows such as public television's *Almanac*.

In running a campaign for statewide office telegenic expertise was required. The same was true for a mayoral candidate in the markets served by local television. How to do an interview with a television reporter became important. This was particularly in how to speak in "sound bites" that would prove the candidate's point and not end up being cut in the editing process. Voice and personal appearance also counted. "Articulate your words carefully; keep your voice level measured; and look directly into the camera," were just a few of the words of advice that a television professional gave me and the other statewide DFL candidates when we rehearsed for television appearances in a rented television studio. Despite extensive public speaking experience one could initially not help but be nervous when he realized that what he said was being broadcast over the circuits to thousands of viewers watching the 6:00 p.m. or 10:00 p.m. newscast. My courtroom experience as a trial lawyer, literally on parade before a judge and a jury, helped ease my initial fears.

Chapter Five

Lessons Learned from
First Term in the Legislature

There were a number of practical and political lessons learned during my first two-year term in the Legislature. It was on the $2400 per year legislative salary. Making financial ends meet was difficult even as a single person living at home with my mother and with a start up law practice. I was sharing office space with other independent lawyers. There was no one to cover for me when I was away in St. Paul. Committee meetings and legislative sessions consumed most of the day. Often the only time in the law office was in the evening when I would respond to phone calls and answer correspondence. While legislative immunity prevented the courts from requiring my attendance in court during a legislative session, financial necessity dictated that I schedule court appearances at times when my committees did not meet or on Fridays. During the earlier days of the session, the house would not be in session or recessed early on Friday so that rural legislators could go home for the weekend. I worked out an agreement with the then Hennepin County District Court Judge Douglas K. Amdahl. Amdahl later served as a distinguished Chief Justice of the Minnesota Supreme Court. I tried one complicated case before Judge Amdahl for seven weeks. I was in court most mornings. The judge adjourned court in time for me to attend 12:00 noon meetings of the House Judiciary Committee.

Another lesson learned was the value of having someone close to you with whom one could share legislative experiences, frustrations and from whom you could secure advice. I lived at home with my widowed mother. Having lived a long married life with my father, who had been very active in the labor movement and in politics, my mother was able to provide not only love and affection, and substantial nourishment, but she rendered sound, and often profound, political advice on people, policy and tactics. Rose Latz never had had time while raising seven children during the Depression years to have a career of her own outside the home. In 1966, she shared with me her moment in the political sun. She made a moving speech to the assembled DFL Convention delegates when I was endorsed for attorney general.

Another profound lesson was "never forget who brought you to the dance." Put another way, never forget who your friends and allies are and particularly those who played a part in advancing your political career. I was fortunate to have essentially the same team working for my election and reelection throughout my eight years in the legislature. They worked long hard hours without any compensation other than knowing that I stood for and would fight for the principles we shared.

One also learned to distinguish between "friends" and "allies." "Allies" had a more transient relationship. They might work together to advance a party cause or a bill in the Legislature, but they lacked the personal and ongoing relationship and trust of "friends." Friends of this nature are like family. You may have disagreements from time to time, but you know that at the core they are with you when you need them. I was fortunate to have people I knew in the political process who fit in each category. A political friend may be someone with whom you may have had little or no contact over a period of years. But the shared relationship comes to the forefront when you need to call upon him/her. One who filled the category as a "friend" was and is Congressman Martin Olav Sabo. Marty Sabo was part of our core group of DFL Party-oriented liberals in the Minnesota House. Long after I left the legislature and was seeking election to the University Board of Regents, Sabo, then Speaker of the House of Representatives, played an important role in my election and return to public life.

What might be called the "care and feeding of constituents", or more rightly characterized as "constituent service," also remains a bedrock principle of a successful politician. One running for office for the first time has no idea how demanding constituents may be when pressing their views on a controversial subject or asking for help in navigating the confusing governmental process at any level. Voters most often do not really distinguish between the various offices a person may hold. They are not sure whether the person is a congressman, member of the Legislature, or a city ward councilmember. Responding to constituent's requests was no simple matter in those days. Legislators in the '50's and '60's had no private offices unless they were a committee chair. Of course, none of the minority members chaired committees. Therefore, our "offices" were at our desks in the House Chamber. When we had constituent's mail that required a written reply, we requested a secretary from the pool and dictated the response at our desks. Of course, there might be other legislators of both parties who were performing the same service at the same time. Therefore, confidential matters were not responded to with the use of a pool secretary. I was fortunate to have a secretary at my law office. The sensitive subjects were dealt with in the privacy of my law office in between or after committee or legislative sessions.

Another lesson learned was the value of establishing personal relationships with others of both political parties. Simply applying a party label of "DFLer," "Liberal," "Republican," or "Conservative" did not by any means go to the basic character or philosophy of the individual. This may sound trite. But it was true. When one reached across the political aisle, he sometimes found that the member of the other party really shared his goals and philosophy. This was sometimes more true than with my colleagues of the same political affiliation. I found that to be the case when I served as a coauthor of a bill with a Representative of the other party. If, in fact, the person did not become a "friend," he or she could become an "ally." The alliance may have been only for a particular bill on which each had a shared interest. Or it could have gone further in forming alliances that helped bridge the gap over several issues and over longer periods of time. The seating arrangements in those days helped foster the development of personal relationships with members of the other party. Seating location was drawn by lot according to seniority. Thus, a DFLer could be sitting next to or directly across the aisle from a Republican. It was, however, rare that they would be willing to sit side-by-side. But there was at least a close proximity that facilitated and fostered conversation and discussion.

Also, lobbyists often invited legislators out for lunch or dinner. More often than not legislators of both parties were brought together in social circumstances. These social sessions may have revolved around the interests of the sponsoring lobbyist. Or they would have also ranged into other subjects that were being processed in the Legislature. These discussions often resulted in several opposing legislators coming together and finding a common ground on which they could later act upon in passing or opposing a particular bill. We often found that we may have had more in common philosophically than we would have expected. We discussed the main differences that separated us in committee or on the floor of the legislature that were driven by political party dictates or personal ambition. The truth in this conclusion has been born out in my current experience. I belong to several luncheon groups of retired legislators. They meet periodically to discuss old times and how things were better then than they are now. What I and others have discovered is that there were less philosophic differences between the "young turk" Republicans of that era and our group of young Democrats. Since then we have both moved toward the middle politically while there has been a distinct polarization of legislators and political parties to the right with many Republicans and to the left with many Democrats. Now there is not as much searching for the middle ground on difficult policy issues as would serve to effect compromises and redound to the public interest.

Today political candidates and office holders from the top down are much more beholden to political benefactors who supply large sums of money for campaign purposes. They rely on those who represent powerful special interest groups that claim to control large blocs of hardcore persons who can certainly be expected to show up at party endorsement caucuses and conventions and on election day. In today's Legislature there is a stark division in seating arrangements. In the Minnesota House all of the DFLers are on one side of the center aisle and all of the Republicans on the other. This significantly limits political discussion and compromise efforts during the session. One may be viewed with suspicion if he/she moves over to the other side of the aisle to discuss matters. The legislation passed under the sponsorship of DFL Senator John Marty, placing strict limits on expenditures for meals and social events, has all but eliminated the socialization that has in prior years produced many positive results in the legislative process. The whole issue of campaign financing is a separate subject upon which much has been written. Substantial public financing of legislative campaigns, if one is willing to limit total campaign expenditures, has not eliminated the need for a candidate to expend significant time and personal resources to achieve election and reelection.

Every successful legislator needs a thorough understanding of the rules of parliamentary procedure. These rules govern the legislative and bill passing process. This is particularly true when one is in the minority. Then the recourse in protecting minority rights may be to require strict adherence to the rules. They may be invoked to prevent being steamrollered by the majority. There are two sets of rules that govern legislative procedure. The principal rules are set by the Rules Committee and adopted by a majority vote of the members. Mason's Manual of Legislative Procedure is known as the "Bible" of legislative procedure. When a matter is not specifically covered by the rules of the body, Mason's is the text relied on. The rules set forth in Mason's are similar but not quite the same as those set out in Robert's Rules of Order Revised. Robert's is the rule book governing most matters in political party organizations as well as in community settings.

My interest in the legislative and rule making process enabled me to conduct a semiannual orientation session for new DFL House members. We would go over the steps necessary to get a bill passed, and how to deal with various situations when a bill was being considered by a committee or on the house floor. It was most often the function of the caucus leadership, such as the House Minority Leader, to invoke rule challenges during floor debates. However, an individual legislator who was carrying or opposing a bill that did not have specific political overtones was left to his/her own devices when confronted with parliamentary tactics designed to advance or kill a bill in committee or on the floor.

Every first term legislator needs to realize that it is not simply enough to pilot a bill through the committee and even through passage on the house floor. The bill still needs to pass through the committee process in the other body – the senate. It must receive a majority vote on the floor. Then it must be signed into law by the governor. When there is divided control of the legislature, and particularly when there is a governor of the opposite party, this can be a very difficult process. The chief author must not only secure coauthors on the house file, hopefully with bipartisan support, he/she must also secure a chief author on the senate side. Usually the chief author in the other body will also attempt to sign on a bipartisan group of coauthors. The legislative sponsor must not only select wisely as to his/her coauthors. More importantly is the selection of the "right" chief author in the other body. The selection of a chief author in the other body who is not fully committed to the proposition may well result in failure.

Consideration and evaluation of the attitude of the leadership of the other body, especially when under control of the other political party, can prove to be a difficult proposition. When I was in my first term I found that passing a bill through the house with its DFL majority was not enough. When the bill languished in a Senate committee without a hearing, I was not sure what to do. When I approached a more experienced legislator, I was asked, "Have you been down to the bar at the St. Paul Hotel after the daily session concludes?" I most often returned to my law office immediately after the session concluded. I asked, "Why?"

The response was that this was where the senate conservative leadership held forth night after night. The senate conservative leadership, such as the Majority Leader Gordon Rosenmeier, could usually be found at the St. Paul Hotel or the Lowry Hotel. Experienced lobbyists for special interests groups could usually be found there also bending an elbow and establishing personal relationships with the leaders. While Twin Cities' legislators would be returning to their private pursuits or families after each day's session, legislators from outside the metropolitan area moved to St. Paul for the entire session. They were often without their spouses or families. Therefore, they had much open time in the evenings. I got the message and responded affirmatively. A semblance of a personal relationship was established with these leaders. These efforts were not successful in turning them into allies or friends. They did seem to succeed in taking some of the edge off my reputation as an outspoken, ambitious, and politically partisan young legislator. The personal contact at least seemed to move their opposition from a more personal level to a political and professional one.

This contact in the after hours also helped teach me a lesson as to the power and influence of lobbyists. In that first term I sponsored the Freeman administration bill to register and regulate lobbyists. As might be expected this did not make me popular with the community of lobbyists. Social contact with experienced professional lobbyists gave me a different perspective on the role of lobbyists.

The phrase "What have you done for me lately" is often the response when one returns to the well for political or financial support. Respect from friend and foe alike is the most for which one can hope. When asked for support, I developed my "go to the well" theory. That is, you have just so much water in the well or political capital available to spend for any given proposition. Each time the well is drawn upon you have less available on which to draw on in the future.

There is also the "Latz Elevator Rule." Never ever discuss anything of political or other consequence when riding on an elevator with others. I and a client learned that lesson the hard way. The client was seeking the presidency of a national trade organization. He was the favorite. Riding on an elevator before the election he continued the discussion of election strategy that had begun before the elevator arrived. As luck would have it one of the opponent's key supporters was on the elevator and overheard the conversation. The information was used to the client's detriment. He lost the election. Enough said.

Along with the several frustrations that accompanied my efforts to secure passage of proposals I sponsored, there were several notable successes. The most significant was sponsorship of a series of measures recommended by Governor Freeman and the Minnesota Office of Civil Defense Mobilization. They were to update state constitutional provisions to provide for continuity of state and local governments in event of nuclear attack. This was during the "cold war era." The fear of nuclear attack from the Soviet Union loomed very real. Two of my bills called for constitutional amendments. One would extend the line of succession to governor through the entire roster of top legislative and executive offices. At that time in the event of a vacancy in the governorship, the Constitution called for succession to the office through the lieutenant governor and then to the President Pro Tempore of the senate. A second proposed constitutional amendment provided for succession in the Legislature and local government offices. It provided for each legislator to designate no more than seven persons to fill his/her post in the case of a vacancy. Each designate would be named in priority of succession. The companion measures provided the legislation to carry out the provisions of the proposed constitutional amendments. These included procedures to fill vacancies in the supreme, district, and municipal courts and authorizing temporary relocation of seats of government.

The legislature approved the bill dealing with succession to the office of governor. The ballot question presented to the voters was "the adoption of a constitutional amendment to provide for succession to the office of governor: to provide for continuity of government in emergencies caused by enemy attack." It was adopted by the voters in the next statewide general election by over a 3-1 margin.

My nephew Norman Ornstein, Resident Scholar at the American Enterprise Institute for Public Policy Research in Washington, D.C., proposed a similar measure to provide for continuity in the federal government in the event of successful terrorists' attacks like those of September 11, 2001. Ornstein worked to form a blue-ribbon commission, The Continuity of Government Commission. It was "composed of a who's who of American politics, including such notables as Newt Gingrich, Donna Shalala, Kweisi Mfume, and Leon Panetta. In Spring 2003, the Commission issued its first report, which called for a constitutional amendment delegating to Congress the power to redress the issue of succession."[1] Unfortunately, congressional inertia and opposition has stalemated this proposal. Ornstein states, "I thought the biggest problem we'd face would be overcoming inertia and the same kind of reluctance people feel about writing a will – coming to grips with your own mortality. I've been taken aback by the strong opposition we've faced from some members of congress."[2]

It is interesting that there was never any discussion between Ornstein and I on the subject of continuity of government in the face of enemy attack. When in 2005, I raised the subject with Ornstein, he said he was unaware of the Minnesota constitutional provision. Political genes seem to work in mysterious ways. In commenting for the Broderick article on that subject Ornstein said:

"But even before that, my maternal grandfather, Rubin Latz was a major figure in the labor movement in Minneapolis and was part of Hubert Humphrey's Kitchen Cabinet that persuaded him to run for mayor and then later for the Senate. My grandfather died before I was born, but I grew up hearing about Humphrey (B.A., 39) and even got to know him a little so I guess you could say that an interest in politics runs in my family."[3]

The other significant successful proposal with which I was affiliated in my first session was a bill providing for Minneapolis to be converted from a special school district to an independent school district. The new district school board would have independent financial powers to provide education to the city's school children. I was named to head a subcommittee of the Hennepin County Delegation to work out a compromise that would be acceptable to the delegation, the school board and school administration, and other interested groups, such as the Citizen's League. The bill allowed the school board to issue, with voter approval, school bonds separately from the general Minneapolis city bonds. In the spirit of bipartisan compromise, the Hennepin County House Delegation approved the bill. After some pulling and tugging with the Senate conservatives from the city, a package was worked out that was acceptable to liberal and conservative legislators from Hennepin County in both bodies. The passage of time has proven the merits of that compromise proposal.

All things considered I had a most successful first term in the Legislature. Journalist Fred Neumeier, writing in the St. Paul Dispatch Pioneer Press, stated "Most outstanding freshman House member so far this session appears to be Rep. Robert Latz of Minneapolis. He'll bear watching…" At the end of the session a poll was taken of members of the legislature as to who were their picks as "most promising first-termer." In the senate, DFL Senator Paul Thuet was selected. In the house, it was Republican Representative C. Donald Peterson. I was "runner up" in the house. Runner up in the senate was A. M. "Sandy" Keith, DFLer from Rochester.

Chapter Six

Alan "Buddy" Ruvelson[1]

Until the 1970's, there were very few Jewish Minnesotans who achieved any degree of prominence in the Minnesota Republican Party. Then Rudy Boschwitz emerged to become Republican National Committeeman from Minnesota. For decades before Boschwitz, the Jewish Republican with the most prominence and activity within that party was Alan "Buddy" Ruvelson of St. Paul.

A businessman, Ruvelson had the distinction of being active in Jewish community organizations, while involved in activities related to the Catholic Church. Ruvelson first became a Republican in the late 1940's. There were few other Jewish Republicans at the time. One was Richard Golling. Golling was a graduate of St. Thomas College. He went on to become Minnesota's Public Examiner in a Republican administration. Another was Stuart Rothman who became an Assistant Secretary of Labor in the initial Eisenhower administration. Archie Gingold preceded Ruvelson at St. Thomas College. Gingold went on to become a respected judge in St. Paul. Ruvelson was not sure what Gingold's politics were. To Ruvelson he could have been either "mildly Republican" or "mildly Democratic." Ruvelson said he became involved with the Republican Party early on because of Harold Stassen. He believes Stassen was "a great governor." Stassen tried for the Republican presidential nomination in 1948.

He was beaten by New York Governor Thomas Dewey. Dewey lost to Harry Truman. Ruvelson states that Dewey, as New York Governor, had a staff which included some very "heavyweight" Jewish Republican activists. They came out here to Minnesota when Stassen lost to Dewey for the nomination. Ruvelson went to work for Dewey. Even after Dewey lost, Ruvelson continued to work in the Minnesota Republican organization at the precinct, district, Ramsey County, 4th congressional district and state levels. He became a Republican District Vice Chairman.

In 1956, he was elected as an alternate Republican National Convention Delegate. He was elected again in 1960, when Richard Nixon was nominated. Ruvelson expressed his disappointment that Nixon picked Henry Cabot Lodge instead of Minnesotan 5th congressional district congressman Walter Judd as his running mate. Ruvelson believes that had Nixon chosen Judd in 1960, as his vice presidential running mate, that Nixon "probably would have been elected."

Ruvelson states that "the Jewish people in Minnesota were never really heavily involved in the Republican Party. They became more involved as the Republicans were more successful in Minnesota and nationally." Ruvelson chaired the 1960 state Republican convention and the Republican platform committee in 1958, 1962 and 1964.

Ruvelson describes Elizabeth Peavey Heffelfinger as his "political godmother." In 1956, Heffelfinger recruited Ruvelson for Eisenhower's first presidential campaign. Ruvelson was a political realist. Despite his early allegiance to Stassen's campaign for the Republican presidential nomination, Ruvelson switched his support to General Dwight D. Eisenhower and Eisenhower's campaign for the presidency.

It is interesting that Elizabeth Heffelfinger, who was Republican National Committeewoman for Minnesota in the late 1940's and into the 1950's was also a close friend of my father, Rubin Latz, a staunch labor-oriented DFLer. Rubin Latz and Heffelfinger worked together in Minneapolis community affairs including the civil defense organization during World War II. In a letter to me dated September 15, 1955, Mrs. Heffelfinger stated in part: "I was interested to read in the paper that you had been appointed legal adviser to the newly created Minnesota Fair Employment Practices Commission. I am interested for two reasons – because you are the son of your darling father, whom I dearly loved, and because I believe so ardently in the job you are doing that I am glad to see a man of your caliber accepted."

My contact with Ruvelson began with our mutual involvement in the Minnesota Jewish Council and the Jewish Community Relations Council. There were also occasions when both the DFL and Republican parties held meetings at the Leamington Hotel in Minneapolis. On occasions when I served on the DFL platform committee, Ruvelson and I would meet to compare notes on platform planks that involved the State of Israel. Being one of the few Jews involved inside Republican Party politics, Ruvelson's influence on matters involving Israel and the Jewish community was important and persuasive.

I asked Ruvelson what caused him to become a Republican and a Republican activist rather than following a more traditional role of a Jew being active in Democratic Party politics. He responded, "I believed that I could do more as part of a minority within the Republican Party to advance the causes of our country and of our Jewish people, because there were a lot of Jewish folks associated with the Democrats and there were very few of us." Ruvelson believes that the role of Jews in the party is similar to that which is going on with respect to the Black community in the Democratic Party. Because they are both pretty much on one side of the fence, there is a tendency for other Democrats to take both communities for granted.

Ruvelson believes that there were some "privileges and rewards of being a Jewish member of the Republican Party in terms he would not have had otherwise." An example was in 1968, when he chaired the Republican state convention Middle East Policy Task Force. He states "it was a rare experience in my life." It is in his role as a fundraiser for various Republican presidential and Minnesota candidates that Ruvelson achieved his most prominence in the Republican Party. This was in a period before Rudy Boschwitz became one of the very prolific fundraisers for Republican candidates and presidents. Ruvelson never aspired to political office. He describes his role as "always been in the background."

Ruvelson believes that "Jews can not afford to be identified solely with one political party." As a successful businessman, he had the flexibility to support an important Democratic Party candidate when he so chose. Thus, he raised money with an "off the cuff dinner at the Minnesota Club" for Hubert Humphrey when Humphrey ran for Vice President with Lyndon Johnson. This was because Ruvelson was "not very much enamored with Barry Goldwater." The money raised went directly to Humphrey, because Ruvelson did not admire Lyndon Johnson then or now.

Ruvelson has supported George Bush the elder. He believes that the Republicans have had "our share of good ones and bad ones." However, he describes himself as "somewhat conservative." In retrospect, at the time he had his most prominent activity in the Republican Party, the Republican Party was "considerably more liberal than it is today." But the Republican Party has changed a lot in recent years, because of such issues as right-to-life and "some other things of a similar character."

Part of Ruvelson's Republican fundraising success came from more conservative Jewish businessmen in the Twin Cities. Ruvelson believes "many Jewish people are emotionally Democrats but economically Republicans."[2] These were individuals who for business reasons did not want to become prominently identified with the Republican Party or its candidates. However, they were willing to contribute to a fellow Jewish Republican businessman. Part of Ruvelson's fundraising story to them was his belief that Jews could not afford to become solely identified with the Democratic Party and its candidates.

Ruvelson's Republican Party activities made it possible for him to become a "Regional Field Adviser" with the Small Business Administration that was created during the Eisenhower administration. Ruvelson then became aware of legislation authorizing the creation of small business investment companies. He saw it as a potentially successful business opportunity. In March, 1959, he was awarded the first license in the country for a small business investment company. His company was named Midwest Capital Corporation. He became the first president of the National Association of Small Business Investment Companies. That involvement with the small business investment company made it possible for Ruvelson to achieve financial success as well as to make significant contacts in the business community.

Ruvelson has been called "a forefather of venture capital." He was described as "....one of the founding fathers of venture capitalism."[3] Professor Hayes, who had known Ruvelson for 35 years, said: "He's also someone everybody trusts; he's a down to earth guy, and that encourages people to talk and be honest. That is the essential aspect of any due diligence a venture capitalist has to do. When Buddy listens, people talk." The *New York Times* article stated that "his (Ruvelson's) ideas turned the small business lending universe upside down. Previously, loans were made in exchange for collateral; now investments are made in exchange for equity."

In 1994, Ruvelson was the recipient of an award from *Inc. Magazine* as the "supporter of entrepreneurship." The award was given to him as "an individual whose assistance or encouragement fosters the creation of entrepreneurial companies."[4] At the time of this award it was stated that "Ruvelson has spent more than three decades devising innovative techniques for financial entrepreneurial ventures....Ruvelson stuck to local deals that would help build a strong Twin Cities community. He has served on the Board of Economic Development for four Minnesota governors."[5] The *Inc. Magazine* article set forth an important insight into Buddy Ruvelson's character. It stated "the notion of money for entrepreneurs of every stripe appealed to the humanitarian in him too; his father had preached the value of a strong community conscience and taught him that while loyalty to the Jewish community was crucial, a broader embrace of society was also important."

Ruvelson provides a treasure trove of firsthand history of the St. Paul Jewish community; at the University of Minnesota; and in his relationship with the Catholic Church and its institutions. Ruvelson is a fourth generation St. Paulite. He is a Reform Jew. His great grandfather was the first Orthodox Rabbi in St. Paul. He served the Sons of Jacob Synagogue. Buddy Ruvelson grew up in Mount Zion Temple of St. Paul. He was one of the founding members of Northstar AZA, a fraternal group of Jewish men through high school age. At an early age he joined the B'nai

B'rith, the largest national Jewish fraternal organization. His sponsor there was Isidore Simon. He was close to Jack Mackay. Mackay was the Capitol Bureau Chief for the *Associated Press.* Ruvelson served as one of the founders of a division of the United Jewish Fund of St. Paul. He describes himself as having "continued (to be) very active in the Jewish community through my career." He served as a board member of Mount Zion Temple. He was co-chair of the committee that engaged Rabbi Gunther Plaut as Rabbi.

Ruvelson's membership in the B'nai B'rith led to his activity in the Anti-Defamation League of B'nai B'rith. He was active as well in the Minnesota Jewish Council and its successor the Jewish Community Relations Council. Both the ADL and the Minnesota Jewish Council were what could be called "Jewish defense organizations." Their activities were centered around efforts to combat anti-Semitism and discrimination against Jews in community, social and business organizations.

Ruvelson reflects on the admissions policies of organizations such as the St. Paul Automobile Club, the St. Paul Athletic Club, the Minnesota Club, the Minneapolis Club, and the various country clubs in the Twin Cities. Ruvelson describes the St. Paul community as "always a much more tolerant and accepting community than Minneapolis." This was probably because of the background of the residents of St. Paul whose origins and religious affiliations were basically Irish Catholic as compared to the Protestant religious affiliations of the Minneapolis community. At the time the St. Paul Athletic Club accepted the Rabbi of Mount Zion Temple as a member, they had only a limited number of Jewish members. There was an apparent quota or limitation on the number of Jewish members that would be accepted into the St. Paul Athletic Club. Unfortunately, there was a Jewish member who blackballed the applications of various members of the Jewish community. So far as the Minnesota Club was concerned, Ruvelson joined that club in the early 1960's without any problem. Jewish membership in the Minnesota Club went back to the territorial days when the Minnesota Club was first formed. As to the Minneapolis Club, Jay

Phillips became the first Jewish member after he was elected President of the Minneapolis Chamber of Commerce. Ruvelson said that he joined shortly thereafter when one of his corporate board members, Kenneth Dayton, said "Buddy, I want you to join." Buddy states that he "had the privilege of nominating the first female who was elected to membership in the Minneapolis Club. She was Geraldine Geltman, the wife of his cousin, Robert Geltman.

Golf club membership was described by Ruvelson as "another situation." He recalls that the "first Jewish club" was Northland Country Club in St. Paul. Northland consisted largely of early German Jewish members. Then there was the Oak Ridge Country Club in Minneapolis. This also was a "Jewish club." It was formed because at the time Jews were not admitted into membership at the other country clubs in the Minneapolis area. With the passage of time the membership of the Northland Country Club declined. It ceased to exist in 1945. Then a group headed by well known St. Paul attorney Samuel Lipschultz, which included Ruvelson, purchased the Hillcrest Country Club. In time, Ruvelson departed Hillcrest. He applied for membership in the Town and Country Club. Town and Country prior to that time "had not been very welcoming to Jewish people." The same was the case at the time with Minnikahda, Interlachen and Woodhill country clubs. None had Jewish members. Ruvelson believes that these clubs now have Jewish members.

In 1936, Ruvelson graduated first in his class with a bachelor's degree in business administration from the University of Minnesota. It was in "the depths of the depression." Ruvelson's father, a successful diamond merchant, wanted him to go to Harvard Law School. But his uncle, an attorney, said "I don't want him to go there and become a lawyer. All he will get are those lousy divorce and bootleggers...he can't get into a decent law firm because he is Jewish."[6]

At the time Ruvelson attended the university Jews were not members of any of the mainstream academic or professional fraternities or sororities. Therefore, they had to join what were at the time all Jewish fraternities and sororities. Ruvelson became a member of Sigma Alpha Mu. In addition to the social fraternities and sororities there were separate Jewish academic fraternities. There was a Jewish business fraternity; a Jewish dental fraternity; and a Jewish fraternity for medical students. As Ruvelson reflects "They didn't do that by choice, but because they could not get into any of the others."

At the age of 22, Ruvelson met and married Ethel Newberg whom he met at the university. Ethel grew up in a Jewish family in the small town of Ada in northwestern Minnesota. Ethel and Buddy had four children. Both Ethel and their daughter Mary Ellen died of ovarian cancer. These tragedies led to Ruvelson's establishment of the Ethel Anne Ruvelson Memorial Lecture Series at the University of Minnesota. It was "to provide continuing educational opportunity for members of the medical profession" in the areas of therapeutic radiology and radiation oncology.

Ruvelson became active in the University of Minnesota Alumni Association. His activities resulted in his election as treasurer of the organization. While there had been several Jewish predecessors in that treasurer's role, up to that time no Jew had been moved forward to the presidency of the organization. Ruvelson states that "because of the interest and sponsorship of a dear friend, Wally Salovith, I did go forward and in 1979 was elected President of the University of Minnesota Alumni Association." That was in the 75th year of the association. He reflects that there were several people, like Irene Kreidberg, who had done much work for the alumni association that had previously not been elevated to the presidency. Sometime after Ruvelson's presidency, Minneapolis attorney Ron Simon was elected president of the association. What was previously the business school at the university then became known as the Carlson School of Management. Ruvelson received an Outstanding Achievement Award from the school. He "had the pleasure and privilege" of receiving it from the Interim Dean of the school at the time, Dr. Larry Benvenisti. Benvenisti later became the Dean. He was the first Jew to achieve that position.

After Ethel Ruvelson died in 1965, Buddy met and married a widow who was Catholic. Ruvelson went to the rabbi of Mount

Zion Temple. He was told that he could not marry a Catholic at the temple without her conversion. Ruvelson had known then Monsignor John Roach when Roach had been Headmaster of St. Thomas Academy. Despite the fact that Ruvelson did not sign any vows of the Catholic Church and remained a committed Jew, he and his late second wife Louise Ruvelson were married in the sanctuary of her church, the Church of the Nativity. The marriage ceremony, with Buddy's son as his best man, and Louise's daughter as her maid of honor, "provided a religious experience for Ruvelson and his family."[7]

His services in Catholic related bodies included chairman of the Financial Advisory Board of St. Mary's Hospital (1970-71); trustee for the College of St. Benedict (1967-71); trustee of St. Thomas Academy (1976-82); the Convent of the Visitations School (1976-78); and the board of St. Catherine's College (1980-83). In 1997 St. Thomas Academy, from which Ruvelson had graduated, awarded him its *Opus Sancti Tomae* Award.[8]

Ruvelson's commitment to Catholic community institutions earned him a number of awards. The most significant was in 1983, by the Knights of the Holy Sepulcher of Jerusalem. The Knights of the Holy Sepulcher is the oldest order of the Catholic Church. The award was the Cross of Merit with Silver Star. Of course, Ruvelson as a Jew could not become a member of the organization. He was the first Jew in the history of the church to receive this decoration. It was awarded to him by a Bishop who came from the Middle East to their convention at a black tie dinner in Kansas City. The Bishop introduced Ruvelson as a Jew. There is an annual award - the Hanes Alumni Honors Award. It is awarded to graduates of St. Thomas Academy. Previous recipients had included the Reverend Michael O'Connell of the Basilica in Minneapolis and Archbishop John Roach. Ruvelson received that award in 1979.

In the mid-1980's, Ruvelson served on the task force on the principles of professionalism for the Minnesota State Bar Association. One of his children, Alan Ruvelson, Jr., is a practicing attorney. Buddy's "interest in and dedication to educational programs has been as extensive and far reaching as has his business involvement." Over the years he has been a member of the St. Paul School Superintendents Commission. He also served as vice chairman of the St. Paul Committee for School and Civic Improvement. In 1980, the business community made him the recipient of the Minnesota Business Hall of Fame Award.

Finally, Ruvelson reflected on his role in the Republican Party, and how he believes that party has changed over the years. He describes himself as a "middle of the roader." He believes that there has been a "big change…within the Minnesota Republican Party." The Minnesota Republican Party has "acquired a voting constituency" on the right-to-life issue. On a national scale the Republicans have "acquired the religious right." To many Jews this is quite a factor, because the "religious right" supports Israel. Along with many Democrats or liberals, Ruvelson is a member of the "Peace Now" movement on issues relating to the relationship between Israel and the Palestinians. Ruvelson prefers to be called both a "moderate and a liberal Republican." He just does not follow the party line, and he doesn't think that Jews should do so either. Every political issue should not be evaluated in terms of whether it is or is not good for the Jews. On September 5, 2005, Ruvelson celebrated his 90th birthday. In July, 2000, he told the *Twin Cities Business Monthly*, "Today, at an age when most of his contemporaries have retired, Ruvelson has no plans to quit. He says, 'I get a kick out of it, and I can't be out at the race track seven days a week.'" This engaging and very alert Jewish Minnesota Republican has continued to maintain an office in the Midway area of St. Paul and advise some clients in the business area. His fruitful, productive and varied career has been a credit to him, his family, the political process, and to the Jewish and Catholic communities of Minnesota.

Chapter Seven

The 1960's

The 1960's was a decade of conflict, turbulence and economic despair coupled with progress nationally and locally. The assassination of John F. Kennedy and Lyndon Johnson's accession to the presidency propelled Senator Hubert H. Humphrey to the vice presidency. It started the career in high public office of Walter F. (Fritz) Mondale. First it was as Minnesota Attorney General. Then as U.S. Senator succeeding Humphrey. The stories and the people who played vital roles in the 1960s are an important part of the history of Jews in Minnesota politics and public life. They helped lay the groundwork for the later emergence of Minnesota Jews who were elected and appointed to significant positions in state and local government and other bodies.

The 1960's also saw the deterioration in the once solid relationships between Jews and Blacks on Minneapolis' north side. This led to the Plymouth Avenue riots; destruction; and the beginning of an exodus of north side Jews, and their businesses and institutions, to the suburbs of St. Louis Park and Golden Valley. These events forever changed the dynamics of the once vibrant but somewhat insular north Minneapolis Jewish community centered around Plymouth Avenue.

1960 was a breakthrough year for Jewish candidates for public office in Minneapolis. The DFL ticket was headed by Arthur Naftalin as a candidate for mayor. There were four other Jewish candidates. They were Viola Hymes for the Minneapolis School Board (longterm), and Alan L. Sherr for the short term seat; Harry J. Lerner for the Library Board; and Beverly Smerling for Park Commissioner-at-Large. Viola Hymes played a prominent role as a member of the school board. She also served as national president of the National Council of Jewish Women. She was the first director of the human relations arm of the Minneapolis Federation for Jewish Service. Alan Sherr served as a campaign advisor in my legislative campaigns. Harry Lerner led a successful Minneapolis publishing company with its primary emphasis on children's books. Beverly Smerling and her husband Louis were prominent DFL fundraisers. Of these five candidates only Naftalin and Hymes were elected.

There is a side note to Naftalin's 1960 successful candidacy for mayor. Earlier in the year I was approached by 5th District DFL Chair Forrest Harris and prominent DFL activist Richard Moe about the possibility of my running for mayor. While I was flattered by the possibility, I had my sights on statewide office – attorney general. The attorney general's office was acknowledged by most observers as the second most powerful statewide elective office. It was second only to the governor. It was attractive to me. It combined my abilities as a lawyer with a powerful political and public service position. Another consideration was that I believed the post of Minneapolis mayor to be a political deadend for anyone other than a person with the tremendous abilities and personality of a Hubert H. Humphrey. Minneapolis had a weak mayor/strong city council form of government. This made the mayor's office more of a ribbon cutting operation than a political powerbase for anyone other than a person with the extraordinary skills of Humphrey.

I acknowledged to Harris and Moe that I did not consider myself possessing either the leadership skills of a Humphrey nor the administrative talent necessary to try to run city government with a strong city council. Naftalin, who had been a very successful Commissioner of Administration under Governor Orville Freeman, secured the DFL endorsement. He was elected mayor. Dick Moe later became state DFL chair. From there he became a key staff member to Vice President Walter Mondale. Moe was then elevated to an important post on the staff of President Jimmy Carter. After Carter and Mondale were defeated for reelection, Moe was elected President of the National Trust for Historic Preservation.

1960 saw me as a candidate for reelection to a second two-year term in the House. It was also a reelection year for Senator Humphrey. It was his third six-year senate race. In the 12 years since his first election in 1948, Humphrey had risen to a position of prominence and leadership in the Senate and on the national and world stages. He continued to be a champion of civil rights. However, his path to leadership in the senate was blocked by the "old guard" southern senators who still controlled the body.

Humphrey decided to campaign for the Democratic nomination for president. His major opponent was Massachusetts Senator John F. Kennedy. With my long history of personal and family relationships with Humphrey it was natural for me to actively participate in the Humphrey presidential campaign. This primarily involved campaigning for and with Humphrey in the key Wisconsin presidential primary election. Participation in a presidential primary contest was both arduous and exhilarating. It was shared with my colleague from the north side Ed Gearty.

There were several memorable events in that campaign. While on a bus tour of Wisconsin communities, we came upon a picket line at an automotive plant. The United Auto Workers were on strike. We all piled out of the bus. We joined arms with the strikers and sang the union anthem "Solidarity Forever." We later participated at a union rally in Milwaukee. We handed out campaign literature in all kinds of weather. During that primary week Ted Kennedy, Jack Kennedy's brother, pulled off a publicity stunt for the Kennedy campaign. He went off a very steep ski jump. It was featured on the front pages of the newspapers. Political lore had it that this was the first time that the Kennedy brother had participated in such a dangerous event. There was a message to all of us, including the large number of media that were traveling with us. It was that the Kennedy family would do anything and everything necessary to secure the nomination and election of their son and brother to the presidency.

This commitment was reinforced in the West Virginia primary which followed. There rumor had it that the Kennedy's spent substantial amounts of money to buy the support and votes of West Virginia politicians. This was apparently a common practice in West Virginia at that time. Humphrey lost both the Wisconsin and West Virginia primaries. These losses effectively sealed the fate of Humphrey's presidential ambitions that year. However, these two defeats did not cause Humphrey to withdraw from the race for the presidential nomination. The Humphrey campaign went on to the Democratic National Convention in Los Angeles.

I was elected a delegate to that convention. It was an exciting experience. The Minnesota DFL delegation was split between the Humphrey and Kennedy candidacies. While most knew that Humphrey's nomination was a forlorn hope, many of us continued to be upset at the way Kennedy had propelled himself into the favorite's role for the nomination. Particularly galling was the way in which he had prevailed in West Virginia. The Minnesota delegation was led by Governor Orville Freeman. Freeman and Lieutenant Governor, Karl Rolvaag were split between Kennedy, the assured winner, and loyalty to native son Humphrey. By the time the role call reached Minnesota, Kennedy had already garnered enough votes to secure the nomination. He was nominated by acclamation before the split Minnesota vote was announced. Orville Freeman, having acknowledged the futility of his good friend Humphrey's candidacy, had given a resounding nominating speech for Kennedy.

My selection as a delegate to the 1960 convention made me a second-generation delegate from Minnesota. My father, Rubin Latz, was a delegate to the 1944 convention in Chicago. It was at that convention that President Franklin Delano Roosevelt dumped Vice President Henry Wallace and selected Senator Harry Truman of Missouri as his vice presidential running mate. For the United States Jewish community that vice presidential selection proved fateful. In 1948 it was President Harry Truman who granted U.S. recognition to the new state of Israel. This was a difficult political decision for Truman. He had been advised against it by a number of leading figures in his cabinet including the Secretary of State. Truman's continued close friendship with Missouri

Bob Latz and Senator Huburt Humphrey campaigning for re-election on Plymouth Avenue.

small businessman Sam Jacobson played a role in his action. It once again underscored the importance of personal relationships in the political process.

Humphrey returned to Minnesota and campaigned for reelection to his senate seat. He and I went door-to-door campaigning along Plymouth Avenue. As expected we received a very warm reception. I continued my campaigning in my yellow milk truck. One afternoon we pulled up and parked the truck alongside a playground adjacent to a parochial school. The nuns and many school children were outside during noon recess. I got on a loudspeaker announcing "Vote for Jack Kennedy for president of the United States and Bob Latz for state representative." Hearing the Kennedy name caused a flood of youngsters and their teachers to our truck. They gathered around and shouted their support for Kennedy.

In the November 1960 election, I was elected for a second term. Humphrey was reelected to the Senate. Elmer Andersen, a Republican state senator from St. Paul, defeated Governor Orville Freeman. Kennedy carried Minnesota in the presidential race by 22,000 votes. Andersen beat Freeman by 23,800 votes.[1] It was evident that there was much crossing of party lines in that election. The rest of the DFL ticket for major statewide offices was reelected. They included Karl S. Rolvaag as Lieutenant Governor, Joseph Donovan as Secretary of State, and Miles Lord as Attorney General. After Kennedy's defeat of Richard Nixon in the November 1960 presidential election, Kennedy named Orville Freeman as Secretary of Agriculture. Kennedy, Humphrey and Freeman collaborated in sponsoring the historic Food For Peace program. This program sent American and Minnesota grain and foodstuffs to the starving populace of the Third World.

1960 also saw changes in my personal and professional life. I started dating St. Paulite Carolyn Spater. That relationship continued through the 1961 legislative session. I would stop and see Carolyn on my way home from legislative sessions. It culminated in marriage on August 6, 1961, at Mt. Zion Temple. 1960 also saw the formation of a new Minneapolis law firm. I formed a partnership with two University of Minnesota Law School classmates Richard F. Sachs and Mitchel I. Kirshbaum. The three, in association with Louis Sachs, formed the firm of Sachs, Latz and Kirshbaum. All three partners successfully practiced law together until Richard Sachs retired in 1982. Without the support of my law partners I would likely not have been able to continue my eight-year service in the Legislature.

The Fair Housing Law

The 1961 Session of the Minnesota Legislature was an eventful one. The DFL still controlled the House. The conservatives/GOP still controlled the Senate. Leaders of civil rights organizations determined that there was no reason to wait any longer for the passage of statewide legislation to prohibit discrimination in housing accommodations. It had been six years since the 1955 enactment of the Minnesota Fair Employment Practices Act. A coalition of civil rights groups and activists was formed to lobby for the passage of a fair housing act. This coalition included members of the Black community and its organizations. Mem-

1961 – Donald Lewis of NAACP presenting awards in recognition of enactment of fair housing law. From left to right, Rep. Bob Latz, Eleanor Andersen, Lewis, Senator Don Fraser.

bers included stalwarts such as W. Matthew Little of the National Association for the Advancement of Colored People (NAACP); Cecil Newman, owner and publisher of the Minneapolis Spokesman and St. Paul Recorder newspapers; and Josie Johnson. Johnson later became the first Black University of Minnesota Regent. Liberal Republicans and leaders of many religious denominations were also involved in the coalition. They included Ruth Gould, a liberal Republican, and Zeta Feder from the St. Paul Jewish community. The Minnesota Jewish Council and the Minnesota Dakotas Office of the Anti-Defamation League of B'nai B'rith, through their respective directors Sam Scheiner and Monroe Schlactus, offered wise counsel.

The bill was introduced with the full support of Republican Governor Elmer Andersen. The coalition devised a somewhat unusual strategy to secure increased support for the bill. In the conservative/GOP controlled state senate, Senator Donald Fraser, a DFLer, was the lead author. The second senate author was a conservative/Republican. In the House, we chose as lead author, Republican State Representative Donald Franke of Rochester. I was the second author. Among other of the five coauthors in the House was Representative L. J. Lee of Bagley in northwestern Minnesota. Lee was later to become involved in allegations of anti-Semitism involving the selection of a president for the University of Minnesota.

The fair housing law proposal ran into a number of obstacles as it worked its way through the legislative process. The most prominent impediment was the inclusion in the original bill of language that would have required non discrimination in the rental of duplexes which were in part owner-occupied. The opponents argued that resident owners should not be compelled to live in the same building with a minority member or family if they chose not to do so. While in principle this exception was abhorrent to the bill's supporters, prudence dictated that eliminating the inclusion of owner-occupied duplexes was a small price to pay if we could pass broad legislation notwithstanding the exclusion. This compromise proved to be effective. But this compromise in and of itself did not insure passage of the bill in the senate. The senate as a whole was a much more conservative body philosophically than the house. Were it not for the outstanding efforts of Governor Andersen the bill would have failed in the senate. Andersen was a senator before his election as governor. He maintained warm relationships with his former colleagues in the senate conservative/GOP caucus. He called in as many "due bills" with his former colleagues as were necessary to achieve the votes to pass the bill. After passing both houses of the legislature, the bill was signed into law by Governor Andersen. Don Fraser, Governor Andersen and I were later honored by the NAACP for our efforts on behalf of this landmark legislation. (See appendix for photo of the award presented by Don Lewis, the president of the local branch of the NAACP.)

The enactment of this fair housing act was my signal accomplishment during my eight-year legislative service. On a local level the act enabled Jews in Minneapolis and elsewhere to select housing opportunities in the suburbs. Many of these residents took advantage of these enhanced housing options particularly following the mid-1960's riots on Plymouth Avenue. Other members of the Jewish community who were active in the civil rights movement in the 1960's included Max Fallek of Temple Israel; Marvin Davidov, Matthew Stark and Jack Mogelson. Mogelson, a teamster union organizer, and Stark were also active in the leadership of the Minnesota Civil Liberties Union.

The Battle Over Congressional Redistricting

The law requires a census to be held every ten years. Thereafter the state legislature is required to redistrict the congressional and legislative districts of the state. Redistricting is a particularly volatile issue. Politics permeates most every judgment. When the issue of congressional redistricting came before the 1961 session of the legislature, an impasse occurred between the DFL-controlled house and the conservative/Republican-controlled senate. A conference committee consisting of five members from each body was appointed by the Speaker of the House and the Senate Committee on Committees respectively. The conference committee's responsibility was to attempt to reconcile the differences between the two bodies and come up with a measure that would satisfy the respective majorities. I was selected by the Speaker as one of the five house conferees. I was the one DFLer selected from the city of Minneapolis and the Hennepin County suburban areas. Therefore, I was particularly involved in redistricting as it affected the 3rd and 5th congressional districts which comprised these two areas. My counterpart on the senate side was Senator Alf Bergerud. Bergerud represented suburban Hennepin County. He was an active Republican and, at that time, president of Red Owl grocery stores.

Reverend Walter Judd, a Republican, had represented the 5th congressional district of Minneapolis for many years. Judd was a conservative with close ties to the then Chiang Kaishek government in China. Judd had been a missionary to China before his election to Congress. Minneapolis, however, was increasingly a stronghold of the DFL. Arthur Naftalin was mayor. The DFL held a majority of the seats on the Minneapolis City Council and other city elective offices. DFL legislators and the DFL party strongly felt that if the 5th congressional district could be confined primarily to the city of Minneapolis, rather than also including more conservative Hennepin County suburbs, the DFL could defeat Judd and elect a Democrat to that seat. The 3rd Congressional District comprised basically the balance of Hennepin County. It was represented by Republican congressman Clark MacGregor. The battle lines were drawn with the Republicans focusing on preserving the suburban Hennepin County 3rd District as a Republican enclave. I and the DFLers sought to shape the 5th District so that Judd could be defeated.

Senator Bergerud and I went head to head in the negotiations over drawing the lines for these two districts. The party organizations, DFL and GOP, were deeply involved in the background of these negotiations. A stalemate resulted over the drawing of the 3rd and 5th District lines. Both I and Senator Bergerud held stubbornly to our respective party positions. The stalemate prevented the passage of the redistricting bill. There had been essential agreement in the conference committee on the shape of the other congressional districts. This deadlock caused pressure on both Bergerud and me to withdraw as members of the conference committee. Acceding to the pressure, we both withdrew.

Following the appointment of our successors, and under pressure from legislative and party leaders, an acceptable compromise still did not initially occur. The Republicans could preserve the suburban 3rd District with its very strong Republican voting history. But to do so they would be compelled to sacrifice Congressman Judd in the 5th District. Finally, a compromise resulted. The Legislature enacted a redistricting bill that created a 5th Congressional District which would basically comprise the city of Minneapolis. The resulting 3rd Congressional District involved basically suburban Hennepin County with parts of Anoka County included.

In the following congressional election State Senator Donald Fraser, who represented northeast and southeast Minneapolis, defeated congressman Judd. Fraser had been a law partner of Orville Freeman. He was a leader of the DFL group in the Senate. Ever since that election, the 5th Congressional District has remained in the DFL column. The 3rd Congressional District seat has continued to held by a liberal Republican. Fraser, who later became Mayor of Minneapolis, was succeeded in congress by former Speaker of the House Martin Olav Sabo. Sabo represented the 5th District for 27 years before his retirement in 2006. With his seniority in the Congress, Sabo was very influential member of the key Budget and Appropriations committees. Former State Representative William Frenzel succeeded Clark MacGregor in the 3rd District. That seat is now held by former State Senator Jim Ramstad.

Chapter Eight

Esther Fieldman

Esther Fieldman[1] is one of the most fascinating women I have met in politics. The 93-year-old was the first Jewish woman to be elected to and serve in the Minnesota House of Representatives. She lived in Park Rapids, Hubbard County, in northwestern Minnesota's resort country. Fieldman's late husband Max ran dry cleaning establishments. Max courted and married Esther who lived with her parents in Coney Island, New York. Esther's family was involved in several businesses including real estate. Max's uncle Ben Glantz was an active Republican in the Park Rapids area. Glantz was a generous man and well-known in the community. He brought over many members of the family from Europe. Most of them eventually left the Park Rapids area and settled in the Twin Cities.

After World War II the store became Fieldman's army and navy store. Max Fieldman was a veteran of that war. He returned to Park Rapids after his military service. Max and Esther Fieldman raised their four children in Park Rapids. One of them, Ardis Wexler, is active in the DFL Party. To keep their religious commitments Esther and Max would pile their children into the family station wagon and go to an orthodox synagogue in Fargo, North Dakota.

There was little overt anti-Semitism directed toward the Fieldman family in Park Rapids. What their children may have experienced as they grew up and went through the school system was never brought to their parents' attention. One explanation was that the children lived through it while growing up. They knew that it was just part of being Jewish in a small town. Esther describes it thusly about her son Stephen: "Long after Stephen was a grown man and in various businesses for himself, I one day asked him about coming back to a school reunion. He said, "Why would I want to come back, mom, when I didn't like it then?" Esther said, "You didn't tell me you didn't like it." Stephen then named what he called "one little creep from a creepy family who had made some kind of attack." Esther states, "But he never told me. He lived through it."

As Esther describes it, "Max and I had a wonderful relation-ship with the community. We were Jewish, and they knew we were Jewish. In fact, when a letter was addressed to the chief rabbi of Park Rapids, Minnesota, the mayor of the community brought the letter and said, "I think it is for you, Max." Years later, when Esther ran for the legislature, she says, "it felt like I had a very healthy chance, then there was a little sneakiness. Maybe even a little bit. They didn't know what a Jew was. So far as the legislature, it got a little nasty. Before that, when I ran for the school board, which was my first venture into politics, I mean professional politics, the man I ran against was heard to say, "You aren't going to vote for that Jew, are you?"" As Esther describes it, "…they did because I really creamed him when I ran for the school board."

Esther was elected and reelected to the school board both before and after she served in the legislature. When I asked her why they did so, she repeated the one quote that she heard about herself. It was, "You may not have agreed with her, but you at least knew where she stood." Esther Fieldman was known not only as to her opinions and stands on the issues, but she was outspoken about them. She was fortunate to have had a husband who gave her the latitude to do so despite the fact that he was in business. Esther pointed out to Max that some people had said that because of her opinions, "We aren't going to treat with Max," or words to that effect. Max's response was, "Hey, I am minding my business, you mind your business. That is my business. You go do your busi-ness." Esther to this day tells her children that they have a right to say something. If they have something to say, say it. Esther's prin-ciples when she was on the local school board were that: "They had the school board, they had to let the school board operate."

Max Fieldman ended up being chairman of the DFL party in Hubbard County. Max would chair the meeting and Esther would be the secretary. There were only a small group of Democrats in the county. She says they used to say, "In which phone booth are we meeting tonight?" Esther used to make sure that they had coffee and donuts for the attendees. And then she did the serving herself. In 1958, they needed to have a DFL candidate to run for the legislature. There was no incumbent. There were five Republicans running for the seat. Max ran and came in third. She got to stay in the store. He got to run for the legislature. Shortly after that loss in the primary Max said to Esther, "You are going to run the next time." She said, "Oh, no, I am not." He responded, "Well, I say you are." As Esther describes it, as time went on they talked a little bit, and she came on to the idea of running for the legislature.

In 1960, they put her name on the ballot. Esther still believes that they didn't vote just for her. They voted against her opponent. He was, as she describes it, "an arrogant Republican." He was a resort owner who drove his Cadillac while campaigning. He had a "magnificent resort with a fly-in airport." The Fieldmans found an old broken-down pickup truck and put a big sign on it, "The poor man's candidate." It was the biggest turnout up to that date in a legislative race in Hubbard County. Approximately 5,000 people voted. Esther won by about 100 votes. Esther described Hubbard County then and now as a Republican county. She said, "If there were Democrats voting they must have come out of the woodwork for it to be a 100 vote plurality."

Esther Fieldman was the first woman ever elected to the legislature from Hubbard County. There hasn't been a woman elected from that county since. In her 1960 campaign for the legislature she and Max heard little snippets about Jews, "You don't need Jews." "But they were snippets. It never really came to us."

In the 1961 session, there was only one other woman member of the house. Sally Luther represented the Kenwood Area in Minneapolis. During the legislative week Esther lived in St. Paul at the Lowry Hotel. There was little to do in the evenings for legislators from outside the metropolitan area. They frequently socialized at the Lowry or St. Paul Hotels. They were often wined and dined by lobbyists. Esther was the only woman legislator present at these social events. She describes her treatment by the male legislators as, "the men really treated me like a sister, a sister that they really liked." Esther is an outgoing person. She fit in well with the out-state legislators of both political parties. On most Friday nights Esther would take the train back to Wadena which was the train stop closest to Park Rapids. Max would come and pick her up.

At that time, the two youngest children were in elementary school. They had a mature woman as a housekeeper while Esther was at the legislature and Max was running the store. Esther describes the raising of the children this way: "…one of my first letters at the legislature in my box came from my son Stephen (who was in elementary school). I will never forget 'cuz I really laughed every time I reread it." Stephen wrote: "Mom, is Francine allowed to wear your winter boots, because she is, you know." Esther told him that daddy was looking out for things and to take his complaints to his father. She imagined that he did. Esther states that "Max took very good care of those kids. He made sure that the housekeeper, she wasn't a live-in, lived down the block, kind of made sure she was there before he left in the morning and made sure she was there until he got home at night. It was very carefully taken care of. Those children did not suffer."

Esther Fieldman is very proud of how her children were raised. She recalls how when she was defeated for reelection to the school board by a school teacher, her son Stephen, who was in the teacher's class, due to his mother's prompting, walked up to the teacher and said, "Mr. Johnson, congratulations." He then returned to his seat. The father of one of the other little boys in that class met Esther on the street a few days later and said, "My God, I could never have done that. My kid would never do that." Esther said, "That is the way the Fieldman children are raised."

With her prior service on the school board Esther's natural interest at the legislature was on education issues. Because of the nature of Hubbard County, with its lakes, resorts and forests, conservation was of special interest to Esther and her constituents.

One might have expected that DFL Rep Sally Luther would provide some mentorship to Fieldman. But that was not the case. Fieldman describes her relationship with Luther as "polite but very distant."

Constituent service is always an important part of a legislator's job. This is particularly the case during the legislative session when constituents of all types may bombard the legislator with their views on pending legislation or with their ideas about what should be done. This also includes the constituent's problems with state departments and agencies. Constituent service is particularly important when a legislator represents a district which has traditional ties to the opposing political party. This was the case with Fieldman. Since she was elected by that very narrow margin of 100 votes in a traditionally Republican district, she could be expected to lean over backwards to assist those who may have opposed her in the previous election. This is particularly true in a non metropolitan community where most everyone knows the political affiliation of their neighbor.

The services provided by the then titled Minnesota Conservation Department were particularly important in the northwestern area Fieldman represented. Fieldman describes how she had to act to replace a conservation department employee whose drinking problems caused him to perform poorly. She was successful in resolving the problem with the department. She believes that thereafter the people affected by the employee's deficits supported her politically. Esther strived to provide services to the business community in Park Rapids. Most all of them had opposed her in her first campaign. They had spent money on newspaper ads about how awful a representative she would be if elected. Her services did not seem to change their traditional support for the Republicans. In the next election they continued to oppose her.

Max Fieldman filled a political role for Esther while she was in St. Paul during the session. Constituents would call or go see Max during the day at his store. Max would then call Esther in St. Paul. He would tell her what they wanted. He also offered suggestions as to what he thought she should do. She and Max had a "very agreeable" relationship on these political matters. If she agreed with his suggestions, she would say so. Likewise, she would tell him if she disagreed.

The 1960's were a difficult time for women in politics. It was still not widely accepted that however qualified women, particularly from the areas outside the Twin Cities, would be able to withstand rumors and allegations of misconduct that went with being away from their spouses and families for the long legislative sessions. When Esther stood for reelection for another two-year term she was subject to many of the same comments made in her first election campaign. They were, "She is a woman. ...She is a woman who the lobbyists will eat alive." Then there was "...a word spread through the women's organization of the Republican Party in Hubbard County, that 'she sleeps with every man in St. Paul.'" Fieldman remembers that particular slur hit her very hard. She recalls later having gone on a visit to New York. She was sitting beside her mother. Esther suddenly burst into tears. Her mother asked, "What is the matter with you?" Esther replied, "Do you know what they said? They were saying that I slept with every man in St. Paul." Esther's mother, who was almost 70 at the time, was a puritan, if there ever was one. She looked at Esther for a moment and said with a straight face, 'What a pity you didn't know. You could have had such a good time.'

A sense of humor is obviously an important refuge in times like that. In that race for reelection Hubbard County retreated to its Republican roots. Esther was defeated. Thus the feisty female voice from northwestern Minnesota was removed from the Legislature. Even in retrospect it is rather amazing that a New York born Jewish woman engaged in business in a small town in northwestern Minnesota could be elected and serve many years on the local school board and then get elected to the legislature. This is especially true in a Republican area. Max and Esther Fieldman were the only Jews in Hubbard County. There were a small number of other Jews in northwestern Minnesota at the time. There were the Hartmans in Detroit Lakes. They were in the hide and fur business. There was a Jewish family in the scrap metal business in Wadena. There were the Patterson's, Saeks' and the Gill brothers who were mainstreet retail merchants in Bemidji. Bemidji native Allen Saeks became a prominent Minneapolis attorney and Jewish community leader. It was some years later that St. Cloud merchant Jack Kleinbaum was elected to the Legislature. Stearns County, where St. Cloud is located, is a heavily German Catholic area with few Jews other than those who are faculty members at St. Cloud State University.

Even after Esther lost in her race for reelection, she continued to be active in the community. She passed several civil service exams and obtained a position with the state at Itasca State Park. She was there for 16 years before retiring. After Max's death Esther stayed in Park Rapids for at least 6 or 7 years before moving to the Twin Cities to be closer to family. When Esther decided to move, her friends in Park Rapids threw a party for her. Esther recalls that the nicest thing said about how they all felt about her was one's statement, "With Esther it was so easy because she would talk to Republicans and she would talk to Democrats and they both listened to her."

Part of the legacy that Esther and Max Fieldman leave is the lesson about how important it is for any person with political ambitions to have the support of their spouse. Max's role as the chairman of the Hubbard County DFL, with Esther running for the legislature, was perhaps an unexpected role reversal. However, it was understandable, since Max had to remain home to run the family business. The other part of the legacy is part of the history of women and the importance of their role in the DFL Party and in Minnesota politics. Both Esther Fieldman and her daughter Ardis Wexler have been recognized as "Women of Distinction" by the Minnesota DFL Party and appropriately so. Fieldman received the DFL's Hubert H. Humphrey award. Fieldman died on June 29, 2007.

Chapter Nine

The 1962 Campaign
The Andersen-Rolvaag Recount

The 1962 election pitted incumbent Governor Elmer Andersen, a liberal Republican, and Karl Rolvaag, the incumbent
lieutenant governor. In the 1960 election Andersen defeated Freeman for governor. However, Rolvaag, Freeman's lieutenant governor, won reelection. This was at a time when the governor and
lieutenant governor ran for office separately. Since a constitutional
amendment adopted in 1972, the governor and lieutenant governor of each party run together. They are either elected or defeated
jointly.

In 1962, it was expected that Rolvaag would have a clear path for
the DFL-endorsement for governor. However, despite Rolvaag's long
history of service to the DFL Party, he had to overcome opposition at
the DFL state convention from a group of younger and more ener-
getic party hopefuls. They felt that it was time for them to take over
from the DFL "old guard" who had succeeded in the merger which
formed the DFL. The so-called "old guard" included Humphrey and
Rolvaag.

These younger party leaders and workers favored endorsing
Attorney General Walter Mondale for governor. State Senator
Sandy Keith was one of those younger leaders. In a compromise
move, the convention endorsed Rolvaag for governor and Keith for
lieutenant governor. Going into the final weeks of the campaign
the polls showed that there was no more than a three point difference between Andersen and Rolvaag. The Minnesota Poll taken
the last weekend in October showed Andersen with 50 percent and
Rolvaag with 47 percent.[1] Charges were made in the final week

before the election "by a highway construction worker" (brother of a Rolvaag campaign aide) that there were deviations from federal standards in the construction of Interstate Highway 35. Rolvaag claimed that the Andersen administration had exerted pressure to speed up the highway construction schedule so that a special ribbon cutting ceremony might focus attention on the governor just before the election. Andersen emphatically denied the charges. Whatever the merits of the claims, an investigation by the Federal Bureau of Roads, completed after the election, verified some defects but of a relatively minor nature.[2] Senator Hubert Humphrey and Congressman John Blatnik of the 8th District campaigned on the Highway 35 issue on the Iron Range and adjoining areas. An election analysis showed that support for Andersen in these areas was significantly below his 1960 vote total. According to Mitau and other observers, the Highway 35 allegations clearly proved to be "a critical factor" in Rolvaag's defeat of Andersen.[3]

The election was so close that a recount ensued. A panel of three District Court Judges was convened to oversee the recount. The saga of the unprecedented recount battle is the subject of an entire volume. "*Recount*" was written by Ronald F. Stinnett, a Humphrey staffer, and University of Minnesota political science professor Charles H. Backstrom.[4] The final result of the recount was that Rolvaag defeated Andersen by 91 votes out of 1,267,502 votes cast. This was .007 percent. This was the closest election for governor in Minnesota history. Rolvaag was elected to a 4 year term. In 1958 the voters had approved a state constitutional amendment lengthening the term of the governor from two years to four years. It was not until March 25, 1963, after 139 days of "battling for ballots by the Republican and DFL parties," that Karl Rolvaag was sworn in as Minnesota Governor.[5]

Stinnett and Backstrom's analysis of voter preferences taken from the Minnesota Poll of January 12, 1962, revealed that Catholics who considered themselves DFLers outnumbered Catholic Republicans by a ratio of five to one. Only 18 percent called themselves independents.[6] This was in a year long before abortion politics changed the political allegiances of many Minnesota Catholics. The

1962 – Rabbi Moishe Feller presenting memoirs of Lubovitcher Rabbi to Governor Karl Rolvaag and Bob Latz

Attorney General Walter "Fritz" Mondale and Bob Latz at the 5th District DFL Convention

extreme closeness of the Andersen-Rolvaag race also revealed electability problems for Rolvaag. As Stinnett and Backstrom described it, "Lack of full support from his own party, lack of appeal to the independent voter, and inability to produce a positive image of himself were the real problems Rolvaag had to solve."[7] Even though Rolvaag won this extremely close race for governor the problems reflected in Stinnett and Backstrom's comments indicated that Rolvaag had problems within the DFL and with the voting public. He had to overcome them to serve successfully as governor for the forthcoming four years. Unfortunately, these problems were compounded by Rolvaag himself. They led to the party insurrection in 1966, and the Keith-Rolvaag battle for the DFL endorsement and nomination for governor.

Since the Minnesota Constitution provides that the incumbent governor continues to serve until his successor is elected and qualified, Andersen continued to serve as governor during the lengthy recount. Rolvaag as the incumbent lieutenant governor had a small office in the Capitol during the recount. The results of the election were that the conservatives/Republicans continued in control of the senate. They also took control from the DFL of the house. Thus, despite having been easily reelected in the November 1962 election, I was now relegated to serving in the minority. I lost my seats on the key committees on which I had served during DFL control of the house. I was relegated to relatively minor committees dealing with such issues as conservation of water resources. Even in that role I tried to effect a change in public policy. I made an effort, ultimately unsuccessful, to eliminate the wasting of water in the air conditioning units of large office buildings. Rather than being recycled, the water was discharged into the sewer systems and ultimately flushed into the Mississippi River.

In the recount itself there were a number of Jewish attorneys who participated in the process. Foremost was Sydney Berde, deputy attorney general, and a key staff person for Attorney General Walter Mondale. Berde was Rolvaag's legal counsel and recount director.[8] Among the DFLers who were Rolvaag inspectors in carrying out the physical recount of more than 770,000 paper ballots were

Max Fieldman of Park Rapids; Alan Sherr, attorneys Sam Bellman, Richard Hunegs and Irving Nemerov of Minneapolis and Jerome Kaner of Eveleth. Another DFL inspector ultimately appointed by Rolvaag as a judge was Mitchell Dubow, a Jewish attorney from Virginia. There were no Jewish names among those selected as inspectors for Governor Andersen. As neutral inspectors appointed by the court were Rabbi Sheldon Gordon of Duluth, Rabbi Bernard Raskas of St. Paul and Mrs. Phillip N. Stern of Minneapolis.[9]

Among those active in the recount on behalf of Rolvaag was James Rice of North Minneapolis. Rice was a leader of a group which had opposed the DFL leadership in Hennepin County and the 5th Congressional District. This same group was on opposite sides from me in Minneapolis and district DFL contests. Rice later became the Executive Secretary to Governor Rolvaag. He was a key person in blocking access to Rolvaag by the DFL House-Senate Legislative Coordinating Committee of which I was a member. It was frustration caused in large measure by the inability of the DFL legislative leaders to consult with the governor, and plan a common legislative strategy, that led to the opposition of these legislators to Governor Rolvaag at the Sugar Hills Conference in 1966.

Sydney Berde was the head of all DFL recount organizational matters.[10] Berde had most of the legal responsibilities ceded to the Minneapolis law firm of Fine, Simon and Schneider. The Minneapolis Jewish lawyers who participated with that firm were William Fine, Ronald Simon, and Ralph Schneider. Ronald Simon is the father of now State Representative Steve Simon of St. Louis Park and Hopkins. State Senator Jack Davies worked with Fine, Simon and Schneider in initiating "most of the recount procedures prior to the actual recounting of the ballots."[11] Davies later was appointed to the Minnesota Court of Appeals where he served with distinction. The Republican legal team was headed by the law firm of Briggs and Morgan.

The recount jockeying continued in the courts. Each party sought tactical advantages and tried to bring the matter before a judge who would be favorable to their side. The issue of the

District Court's jurisdiction over the recount found its way to the Minnesota Supreme Court. There the Court, with a three to two Republican majority, continued to favor Andersen and the Republicans. As Stinnett and Backstrom observed, the Minnesota Supreme Court began to field the questions that were being raised as to whether the Court was "perfectly free of political taint or not," and whether the "common citizen's confidence in justice and the courts was shaken by the continued one-sidedness of the [Supreme Court's] decisions."[12] The two teams of lawyers representing Andersen and Rolvaag arrived independently with the idea of the Supreme Court appointing a three judge panel to hear and determine the recount practices and procedures. They finally agreed on three District Court judges to serve on the panel with one alternate. One of the three judges agreed upon, and appointed by the Supreme Court, was Judge Sidney Kaner of Duluth. Kaner was one of the few Jewish District Court Judges at the time. One of the others was Judge Irving Brand who had been appointed to the Hennepin County District Court by Governor Orville Freeman. Kaner had also been appointed by Freeman. Judge J. H. Sylvestre of Crookston, a Luther W. Youngdahl appointee; and Judge Leonard J. Keyes were the other two judges approved. Keyes had first been appointed a Municipal Court Judge by Freeman and elevated to District Court Judge by Elmer L. Andersen.[13]

While the recount was pending the conservatives/Republicans controlled the legislature. Governor Andersen still served as a "lame duck governor." Andersen submitted to the senate for approval 119 appointments to state boards and commissions. Later on, when it was evident to both the DFL and Republican recount directors that Rolvaag was going to win, Andersen sent another 28 names to the senate for confirmation.[14] The result of the recount trial was that Rolvaag prevailed by 91 votes. The recount trial could be extended another month or two if Andersen decided to appeal the ruling of the three judge panel to the Minnesota Supreme Court. Andersen decided not to appeal.[15] On March 25, 1963, 139 days after the election, Karl Rolvaag was sworn in as Minnesota's 31st Governor. Significantly, every decision by the three judge panel was unanimous.

The recount struggle showed both the good and the bad sides of the Minnesota judiciary and particularly the Minnesota Supreme Court. Despite some obviously partisan decisions in a court led by Chief Justice Oscar Knutson, the court, in a series of unanimous decisions, clarified Minnesota election laws. These decisions, together with the appointment of an outstanding trio of District Court judges to hear the recount proceedings, restored the public and political party confidence in Minnesota's judicial system. The dignity with which the three judge panel performed its tasks, coupled with the skill and professionalism of lawyers for both Andersen and Rolvaag, also showed that Minnesota had a judicial and political system that worked.

Governor Elmer Andersen came out of the long struggle with a mixed bag of personal and political successes and failures as a holdover lame duck governor. His successful efforts in combination with the senate conservative/Republican majority to appoint and confirm his choices to positions in state government were simply political power plays. This was particularly true when it became increasingly evident that Rolvaag was the likely victor in the recount struggle. On the other hand, Andersen, after losing the recount battle and the decision of the three judge panel against him, decided against appealing that decision to the Minnesota Supreme Court. An appeal would have continued him in the governorship for probably another two months. He conducted himself with dignity after being declared the loser in the recount. Elmer Andersen's stature with Minnesotans of all political persuasions, except the right wing of the Republican Party, improved substantially in the years following his single term as governor. He became a leader of moderate forces in the Republican Party along with former Governor Arne Carlson. He conducted a successful publishing business. He wrote perceptive editorials for his chain of weekly newspapers. He authored a number of books. He was an elder statesman respected by political observers of both parties.

Elmer Andersen was a true friend of the Jewish community. His close relationship with Rabbi Bernard Raskas brought him closer to Minnesota Jews. He dedicated a portion of the Andersen

Library on the University West Bank to a collection in collaboration with the Jewish Historical Society of the Upper Midwest. I was honored with the opportunity to introduce Governor Andersen at the dedication of the Andersen Library. I aptly referred to Andersen as a "renaissance man." Rabbi Raskas delivered an eloquent eulogy at Andersen's funeral. He was mourned by Minnesotans of all religious persuasions and political affiliations.

The 1965 Legislative Redistricting

The U.S. District Court ruled that a 1959 legislative apportionment was invalid. A bipartisan reapportionment commission recommendation resulted in the passage in the 1965 session of a reapportionment bill. Another court challenge followed. Then after a second Rolvaag veto on May 18, 1965, a third reapportionment bill was passed by the legislature and signed into law. The conservatives/Republicans benefited most from the reapportionment. It shifted votes from rural areas to the metropolitan areas. The seats in the suburban areas that were added were Republican in composition. Those new suburban seats were won by conservative/Republican candidates. They have remained basically Republican in the 42 years since that election. Despite the DFL gains in the 2004 and 2006 legislative races, the DFL still has failed to find a winning combination of issues that will break a Republican stranglehold on voters in the suburban areas. However, the polarization of the parties based on religious and socially conservative issues may effect change in the attitudes of suburban voters. Moderate Republicans who populate such heretofore Republican bastions as Edina and Minnetonka may have started a trend toward election of more moderate-middle-of-the road candidates. In 2004, a majority of Edina residents voted for Democrat John Kerry for President. In that same year Minnetonka resident Maria Ruud, a DFLer, was elected State Representative. In a 2005 special election, Terri Bonoff, a Jew from Minnetonka, was elected to the Minnesota Senate. Both were reelected in 2006.

Chapter Ten

1964 – A Time of Change in Minnesota Politics

In 1964, I continued my active role in DFL politics at the Minneapolis and state levels. I was fortunate to chair 5th District and the state DFL conventions. I enjoyed a reputation as an efficient chair and knowledgeable parliamentarian. I was elected a delegate to my second Democratic National Convention. This was after a bruising battle at the 5th District convention with the forces led by Jim Rice. Rice led the forces which sought to depose Forrest Harris as 5th District DFL chair. This was also as Rice was serving as executive secretary to Governor Rolvaag. The Harris forces were successful in continuing to control the DFL in the 5th District which comprised the city of Minneapolis. This battle exacerbated the tensions between the DFL leadership and Governor Rolvaag.

The 1964 Democratic National Convention was held in Atlantic City, New Jersey. I was accompanied by my spouse Carolyn. We plunged into the social and political maelstrom of a national political convention. At the time Carolyn was pregnant with our second son. There must have been some political gene that influenced Marty in utero in his presence at that convention. Many years later, during his own activity in the ill-fated campaign for president of Massachusetts Governor Michael Dukakis, Marty was the guardian of the entrance to the "green room" at the 1988 Democratic National Convention. It was his duty to assure that only those with the proper credentials gained access to the area immediately behind the rostrum where the speakers to the convention assembled before their appearances. Marty went on to

1964 – Carolyn Latz, Senator Eugene McCarthy, and Bob Latz at 1964 National Democratic Convention at Atlantic City

serve at the national headquarters of the Dukakis campaign in Washington, D.C. The many contacts and friendships he developed during that campaign made it possible for him to serve on the White House Advance Teams for presidential visits during the Clinton administration.

Those attending as delegates and alternates to the 1964 national convention were the leaders of the Minnesota DFL Party from throughout the state. The times on the floor of the convention as well as during the convention social events gave me an opportunity to renew friendships and develop new ones with the delegates who would likely be choosing the party's endorsed candidates at the 1966 DFL state convention. The Atlantic City convention was exciting in many respects for the Minnesota delegation. Foremost was the controversy surrounding who President Lyndon Johnson would select as his vice presidential running mate. Senator Humphrey had been a close ally of President Johnson in pushing for the successful passage of the landmark 1964 Civil Rights Act. Humphrey was the favorite of most of the Minnesota delegation which included a number of civil rights activists. But it was not simply a matter of Minnesotans supporting their favorite son Humphrey as they had in his ill-fated 1960 quest for the presidency. The other Senator from Minnesota, Eugene McCarthy, felt that he, rather than Humphrey, was entitled to, and slated to be, Johnson's running mate. Johnson, in his inimitable manipulative manner, had held out the prospect of the vice presidential nomination to both Humphrey and McCarthy. When Johnson finally selected Humphrey as his running mate it was rather obvious that McCarthy was bitter toward President Johnson for not having been selected. That bitterness carried over to Humphrey. While close observers never felt that there previously was anything more than a politically correct relationship between Humphrey and McCarthy, the second place finish of McCarthy in the vice presidential selection process carried over into their relationship in the Senate and in politics generally.

It was widely felt that McCarthy's failure to endorse Humphrey for the presidency in 1968 until very late in the campaign was one reason why Humphrey lost the presidency. Others felt that in 1968 McCarthy was a true hero in galvanizing the opposition to the Viet Nam war and President Johnson's continuation of the American involvement in Viet Nam. However, there were a number of other factors leading to Humphrey's close defeat in 1968.

Humphrey's election as Vice President in the November 1964 election created a vacant U.S. Senator spot from Minnesota. Governor Rolvaag's appointment of Attorney General Walter F. Mondale to the Humphrey seat was widely applauded within the DFL. Rolvaag had good political reasons for selecting Mondale besides Mondale's obvious qualifications. It removed Mondale as a potential candidate for Rolvaag's endorsement and reelection as governor. In the 1962 DFL convention, Senator Sandy Keith and others would have preferred Mondale rather than Rolvaag to be the party's candidate for governor. Rolvaag won the endorsement in the convention. In a unity effort he endorsed Keith for lieutenant governor.

The Mondale record as attorney general was stellar. He coined the term "the people's lawyer." He had an outstanding record for enforcement of consumer's rights. Rolvaag's choice to replace Mondale as attorney general was surprising to many including me. I had maintained a close political relationship with Governor Rolvaag both before and after his ascension to the governor's office. Before making the appointment of a replacement for Mondale, the governor called me on the telephone. Rolvaag knew I had served with Robert Mattson in the attorney general's office. Mattson had continued in the attorney general's office serving under Mondale while I had gone on to election to the legislature. I had shared an office with Mattson and had gotten to know him quite well. When Governor Rolvaag asked me for my candid and off-the-record assessment of Mattson as a potential attorney general, I, fully expecting that my honest and candid advice and opinion would be held in strict confidence, gave just such an opinion. It was not favorable to Mattson. Rolvaag thanked me for my opinion without making any other response. A short time later, and prior to the time that any appointment was made, I had occasion to ride from a political function with my former boss Miles Lord. Lord asked me why I had spoken negatively about Bob Mattson to Governor Rolvaag. I was completely taken aback by the question. I had assumed that my comments about Mattson were to be held in complete confidence. Obviously they were not.

I responded just as candidly with Lord as I had to the governor. Miles Lord, who was a Mattson supporter, was upset. However, that is where the matter was left. It was not long thereafter that Rolvaag announced his appointment of Mattson as attorney general. After undistinguished service for the remainder of Mondale's term, Mattson did not seek election as attorney general. This opened up the attorney general's spot for endorsement by the Minnesota DFL convention in 1966. I was bothered by the Rolvaag disclosure, but there was nothing I could do about it other than to tuck it away in my memory as to how untrustworthy Governor Rolvaag was.

In the November 1964 election, I was reelected to my fourth two year term in the house. The conservatives/Republicans continued to control both the house and senate. A DFL Governor Karl Rolvaag, and a conservative controlled legislature, set up a clash between the governor and the legislative majorities. There were a dozen or more vetoes by Rolvaag of bills passed by the conservative/Republican majority. Increasingly Rolvaag had surrounded himself with persons who had participated in the successful recount effort. Many, including Jim Rice, were those who had fought the DFL Party leadership in Minneapolis and in other areas. DFL legislative leaders, including myself, had not personally participated in the recount activities. We were busily engaged in fighting a defensive battle in the 1963 session against the conservative/Republican dominated legislature and interim Governor Andersen.

In the 1965 session, Governor Rolvaag's relationship with the leadership of the DFL Party in and outside of the legislature substantially deteriorated. There was little if any communication between those leaders and the governor. The DFL leadership in the legislature created a DFL Legislative Steering Committee. This group of five members from each body was selected to chart a political course for the two caucuses. It was to try to coordinate political and legislative efforts between the DFLers in the legislature and the DFL governor. I was selected as one of the five house members on the steering committee. The efforts of this group of legislative leaders to meet with Governor Rolvaag personally were repeatedly rebuffed by his executive secretary Jim Rice. It was later learned that during many of the times when these appointments were sought that Rolvaag was inebriated or unable to meet because of the effects of alcohol consumption. The DFL Party leaders had the same communication problems with the governor. Thus both the party leadership and the legislative leadership were unable to coordinate legislative and public efforts to chart a course for the forthcoming 1966 elections. This rift was compounded by Rolvaag's standing in the public opinion polls. These polls showed him suffering declines in voter approval.

Chapter Eleven

The Sugar Hills Conference

The DFL Party leadership, led by state party chairman George Farr, Senate minority leader Karl Grittner, and House minority leader Fred Cina, decided to convene a conference of DFL leaders to discuss the party's problems. It was also to prepare for the 1966 campaigns for governor, other statewide offices, and the election of both bodies of the legislature. Among the fears were that the loss of the governor's office, together with continued conservative/Republican control of the legislature, could have a devastating effect on the future of the DFL Party and its policies. This was particularly true since legislative redistricting following a 1964 federal court order was only likely to be accomplished by either a special legislative session or by the legislature seated after the 1966 general election. In fact, redistricting was accomplished in a 1966 special session.

In July 1965, top DFL Party and legislative leaders convened a conference at the Sugar Hills Resort near Grand Rapids. While Governor Rolvaag was invited, he did not personally attend. Several of his staff members did attend. They included Bob Goff and Sally Luther. I attended the conference. I roomed with Senate minority leader Karl Grittner. Grittner, a public school teacher and administrator from St. Paul, had been an effective leader of his caucus in the legislature and in its battles with the conservative/Republican majority. Also attending the conference was Geri Joseph, a Democratic National Committeewoman from Minnesota and one of the party's leaders.

The DFL Party chairman George Farr did an effective job in leading the meeting. It became clear shortly after convening that there was mounting criticism of Governor Rolvaag's relationship with both the party and the DFL legislative leadership. Party leaders from around the state, many of whom had risen through the ranks of the party along with Rolvaag, Freeman and other party leaders of the past, feared that Rolvaag's lackluster record as governor, and his rapidly deteriorating relationship with both the party and the legislative leadership, would lead to a disaster in the 1966 elections.

The sentiment that the party needed new and dynamic leadership to carry it forward to victory in the 1966 election was a carryover from the 1962 DFL convention when many had sought to deny Rolvaag the endorsement for governor and wished to turn to Fritz Mondale as the party's candidate. Lieutenant Governor Sandy Keith, Rolvaag's running mate in the 1962 election, was present at the conference. The decisive moment came when Larry Cohen, 4th District DFL Chair, and later Mayor of St. Paul (1974-1976), moved that contact be made with Governor Rolvaag in an effort to persuade him not to run for reelection. While there were several Rolvaag supporters at the conference neither Goff nor Luther spoke out in his behalf. They listened to the developing consensus that Rolvaag, while he had been a truly faithful member of the DFL, just was not electable again. Many present predicted electoral disaster if he again was the party's leader in the campaign.

For a time following the conference there was some hope that Rolvaag would graciously withdraw and allow another candidate to come forward and be endorsed. That hope proved to be forlorn. Before Rolvaag took any public action in response to the request of the conference attendees, the results of the discussion and deliberations were leaked to the media. In retrospect it was naïve to believe that the results of a gathering of such a large number of DFL leaders could remain private. Rolvaag's public response to the media reports of an effort to dump him were understandable. He became very angry. His anger was stimulated by those surrounding him who stood to lose the most by his withdrawal from reelection efforts. They included Jim Rice and wealthy Minneapolis businessman Robert Short. Short himself was politically ambitious. He was believed to be seeking support of Rolvaag's friends and supporters for a run for lieutenant governor. This prediction proved accurate. Short was a candidate for lieutenant governor on the Rolvaag ticket. In 1982 Short ran against the DFL endorsed candidate for U.S. Senate congressman Donald Fraser. In the 1982 DFL primary, Short was the victor. He lost to Republican Rudy Boschwitz in the General Election.

The Sugar Hills conference was not intended by its sponsors to be a vehicle for any specific alternate candidate for the DFL endorsement for governor. However in the background was an alternative: Lieutenant Governor Sandy Keith. At age 35, Keith had already served seven years in the senate from a basically Republican district in Rochester. Keith's father was a doctor at the Mayo Clinic. Keith, a Yale Law School graduate and Marine Corps veteran, was elected lieutenant governor in 1962. At the time I was serving my third two year term in the legislature. I readily identified both age-wise and philosophically with the intelligent and progressive Keith. Keith had all of the seeming attributes of one who could successfully replace Rolvaag and keep the governor's office in DFL hands. Since Robert Mattson had announced that he would not be a candidate for election as attorney general, the attorney general's spot was open for endorsement and election.

Following the Sugar Hills conference and Rolvaag's decision to contest Keith for the DFL endorsement, I spent much time and effort traveling throughout the state contacting DFL Party leaders and workers looking for their support for my endorsement for attorney general on the Keith ticket. Carolyn and I had developed a close relationship with Sandy Keith and his spouse Marion in the time leading up to and following the Sugar Hills conference. In my opinion the attorney general's post was a perfect one for a lawyer. It was an opportunity to exercise both professional experience and political skills in public service. There was also the opportunity for advancement as evidenced by the career of Fritz Mondale. Mondale went from attorney general to the U. S. Senate to the vice presidency and to candidacy for president. DFL Party tradition had it that the person at the top of the ticket, the endorsed candidate for governor, would have a strong voice in the selection of the party nominee for attorney general and the other constitutional offices.

I knew it was also critical for me to establish a base of acceptability among the party leadership and rank and file throughout the state. I knew that it was important for me to build my own political base. I also was aware that Keith, if chosen as the party's endorsed candidate, would confer with the party leadership, including Vice President Humphrey and Senator Mondale, before making his choice. I also was conscious there had never been a Jew endorsed, let alone elected, to a statewide constitutional office in Minnesota. There were few Jews residing outside the twin cities metropolitan area and Duluth. There were some Jews still living in the Iron Range communities, and few in northwestern Minnesota outside of Moorhead. My legislative record and DFL Party participation over the years had earned me contacts and friendship with DFL leaders throughout Minnesota. As far as back as 1956, I had traveled with state DFL chairman Ray Hemenway during the 1956 presidential primary contest. I was particularly gratified by my reception and strong support from DFL leaders in the 7th Congressional District comprising northwestern Minnesota.

Among my strongest supporters in my quest for endorsement and approval by Keith, were the party leaders in the 7th District such as A.J. "Spot" Reierson, the district DFL chairman, Kay Peterson, the district chairwoman, Greg Powers, a county chair and State Representative L. J. Lee of Bagley. I had also toured the Iron Range with Sandy Keith before the DFL convention. With the aid of then Senator Rudy Perpich I renewed some of the earlier Latz family ties in the range communities of Grand Rapids, Virginia and Hibbing. The multitude of ethnic voters on the Iron Range could readily identify with me as the son of immigrant parents, whose father and uncles had run a dry cleaning business on the range, and whose uncle Hyman had run a dry goods business in Grand Rapids. My religion, to my knowledge, never became a factor either in my quest for endorsement for attorney general or in the subsequent primary election campaign.

Chapter Twelve

The 1966 DFL State Convention

There was a bitter struggle at the 1966 DFL state convention. The months prior to the convention had seen acrimonious battles between the Keith and Rolvaag forces from the party precinct caucuses all the way through county and district conventions and to the state party convention itself. The contest at the convention was a knockdown and dragged out battle. It went on for 20 ballots before Keith secured the necessary sixty percent of the votes for endorsement. There was then neither time nor energy left to deal with endorsements for the rest of the ticket at that convention. A reconvened convention was necessary to fill out the DFL slate for the forthcoming primary election.

However, there were other persons who sought Keith's approval and the party endorsement for attorney general. They included Hennepin County Attorney George M. Scott and State Representative Earl Gustafson of Duluth. Each had strong support in the labor movement. Before the reconvened convention took place, and while I and my supporters continued to try to influence Keith on my desirability and electability as the attorney general candidate, a meeting took place between Keith, Vice President Humphrey and other party leaders. I learned of the meeting in a call from Humphrey. He congratulated me on Keith's decision to support my candidacy for endorsement. I thanked Humphrey for his support. Humphrey, in all candor, told me that he had not originally supported my candidacy. Instead, he said, he had supported Minneapolis Mayor Arthur Naftalin for selection as Keith's running mate for lieutenant governor. Keith, however, had told Humphrey that he favored me for attorney general. It had become clear that both I and Naftalin could not be expected to run on the same DFL ticket for these two offices. Both were from Minneapolis and both were Jewish. Humphrey made known to me his affection and respect for me and our longtime family ties going back to the Rubin Latz's early support for Humphrey's candidacy as Minneapolis mayor. Humphrey said that he understood and respected Keith's choice. He said that he would do what he could to see to it that I was successful in my quest. I thanked Humphrey for his comments.

At the reconvened convention Keith stated I was his choice for endorsement as attorney general. The convention confirmed that recommendation. The endorsement was a very emotional moment for me and my immediate family, my spouse Carolyn and my mother. Rose Latz, herself a veteran of her husband Rubin's career in labor and politics, made an extemporaneous speech from the rear of the convention hall after my nomination. My 4' 11" mother could hardly be seen and heard over the din of the hundreds present at the convention as she sought to be recognized. She did gain recognition and made an emotional and heartwarming speech. She thanked the convention for endorsing her son as the culmination of a lifelong effort by herself and her late husband for the youngest of her then seven children, her son Bob. One can only imagine my emotions at that moment.

But the battle had just begun. After the euphoria of the endorsement process had worn off, Keith and the party leadership recognized that they were in a battle for political survival. Those around Rolvaag were not prepared to concede defeat. Egged on by Rice and Bob Short, who was reputed to have pledged to finance the Rolvaag campaign if he sought to override the endorsement and win in the primary election, the Rolvaag forces refused to concede defeat. They seized upon a great political slogan, "Let the people decide." This theme resonated emotionally with many Minnesota voters. The labor movement was split as was much of the party rank and file. The Rolvaag forces initially filed candidates to oppose each of the party endorsed candidates for statewide office except attorney general. Thus, it appeared that I might

PAID ADV. Ppd., Instd. and pd. for at reg. rates by the Latz for Attorney General Vol. Comm., Stan Efron, Treas., Mpl.

MONDALE ENDORSES LATZ for ATTORNEY GENERAL

U. S. Senator Walter F. Mondale has announced his support for DFL-endorsed candidate for Attorney General Robert "Bob" Latz.

Senator Mondale says: "I am pleased to support our DFL-endorsed candidate for Attorney General Robert Latz. He would make an excellent Attorney General. He has a rich background in public service having served first as an Assistant Attorney General for the State of Minnesota which has given him a deep understanding of the operations of the Attorney General's office, and he has also served with distinction in the Minnesota Legislature. His election as Attorney General would assure that this office is being conducted in the public's interest. I am pleased to recommend him."

No other person is better qualified to recommend a candidate for your support for this important state office.

DFL ENDORSED ● LABOR ENDORSED (MPLS. CENTRAL LABOR UNION — COPE)

Join Senator Mondale and vote for Robert "Bob" Latz for Attorney General on September 13th

Minneapolis Star Tribune, St. Paul Pioneer Press Ad, 1966

be, along with Joe Donovan, the incumbent secretary of state, the only Keith and party-endorsed candidate to be unopposed in the DFL Primary.

This was the situation until 4:15 p.m. on the last day of filing for the primary. Fifteen minutes before filings were to close Wayne Olson, the state Conservation Commissioner under Rolvaag, filed to oppose me. Rumors had it that the Rolvaag forces had been unsuccessful in persuading Hennepin County Attorney George Scott to enter the race for attorney general on the Rolvaag ticket. Scott had served with me in the attorney general's office before becoming Hennepin County Attorney. We had worked closely in the successful prosecution of Gerald Connolly. Scott later was elected to the Minnesota Supreme Court. He served there successfully as an Associate Justice.

The Keith candidacy was tainted by allegations surrounding his involvement with a subsidiary of the American Allied Insurance Company. While Keith had severed his relationship with American Allied before it became controversial, both the Rolvaag forces in the primary, and the Republicans in the general election campaign against Rolvaag, used this alleged "American Allied Scandal" to diminish the candidacies of Keith, Rolvaag and the rest of the DFL ticket. My and Keith's campaign was not helped by my political gaffe at a DFL party rally. In an attempt to rally the troops, I made an unfortunate and unscripted quotation from Senator Eugene McCarthy. McCarthy had, in a previous political campaign against the Republicans, said that "after the Democrats get done with the Republicans, there would be nothing left but to shoot the wounded." The quoted statement was roundly criticized within and without the party. The lesson learned was that one cannot afford to use unscripted references in important political remarks or speeches. Unfortunately, just such unscripted remarks by a close friend of the late Paul Wellstone were to have a devastating effect on the DFL chances to elect Walter Mondale to the vacant U.S. Senate seat following Wellstone's death in a plane crash.

Political observers felt there was an upsurge of a "sympathy vote" for Rolvaag and against Keith and the endorsed ticket. No

matter how dynamic and qualified a candidate Keith was, a candidate taking on a middle-aged incumbent governor did not seem
to sit well with the majority of the voters. In the primary election Rolvaag soundly trounced Keith. Rolvaag received 336,656
votes to Keith's 157,661, a margin of better than 2 to 1. Robert
Short, the Rolvaag ticket candidate for lieutenant governor, polled
310,441 votes to the 144, 582 votes of Gerald Christenson, the
endorsed candidate. A maverick Jewish candidate Joel Saliterman
garnered 12,438 votes as an unendorsed candidate for lieutenant
governor. In the statewide totals I lost to Wayne Olson by 110,000
votes. Olson garnered 262,537 votes to my 152,046 votes. Jack
Omvedt, who had previously run for attorney general in a DFL
primary, received 39,274 votes.[1]

It is interesting that I trailed Keith by only 5515 votes in the
statewide totals. Even more interesting is the fact that in the metropolitan area of the 3rd, 4th and 5th congressional districts, consisting of Anoka County, Minneapolis, suburban Hennepin County,
St. Paul, Ramsey, Washington and Dakota Counties, I outpolled
Keith by a total of 16,740 votes.[2] It is difficult to explain why
I ran ahead of Keith and the rest of the Keith-endorsed ticket.
Perhaps the reason was my ties to the labor unions whose support otherwise went for the underdog incumbent governor. Or
that I was reasonably well known for my activities in the attorney
general's office and during my four terms in the legislature. But
those activities in and of themselves would not seem to be enough
to account for the difference. Perhaps the decisive factor was the
very vigorous campaign that I ran in the heavily populated metropolitan areas. I made effective use of placards on the front and
sides of Metro Transit buses urging voters to vote for Latz for
attorney general. The other factor may have been the radio spot on
the weekend before the election in which former attorney general
and then U.S. Senator Fritz Mondale endorsed my candidacy. An
additional unknown in the election generally was how much of a
crossover there was by Republicans who voted for Rolvaag and
his ticket in the primary. They had the hope and expectation that
by voting for Rolvaag they would be able to get the least electable

DFL candidate to run against the Republican endorsed candidate Harold Levander in the November general election.

In an open primary election system the voter may crossover from voting for a party candidate for one statewide office and then vote for the other party's candidates for the other offices. They can pick and chose whichever candidate of any political party that may suit them. This open primary system is still in effect. Legislators and governors have been reluctant to tamper with the voters' independent choice of candidates, at least in the primary. This system however is inconsistent with an effort to build a two party political system in which voters cannot tinker with the party endorsement process by voting to select the weakest candidate on the other party's ticket. In a general election the voters are confined to voting for candidates of a single political party. They cannot split their votes among several parties' candidates.

In the November 1966 general election, the G.O.P. ticket, led by Harold Levander for governor and State Representative Doug Head as attorney general, swept the state constitutional offices. The sole DFL survivor was Joe Donovan the incumbent secretary of state. The legislature continued to be controlled by the conservatives/Republicans. However, popular Fritz Mondale was elected to a six year term as U.S. Senator over Republican Party State Chairman Robert Forsythe.

I had to give up my quest for reelection to a fifth term in the Legislature to make the run for attorney general. Sandy Keith retired to the practice of law in Rochester. I returned to my law practice and time with my spouse and growing family. I was absent from elective office until my election by the legislature as a University of Minnesota Regent some nine years later. In that same 1966 general election the voters approved a constitutional amendment that would allow members of the legislature to run for other offices during their term of office. For example, a state senator elected for a four year term could run for governor during his/her four year term. If he/she failed in the quest for higher office the candidate was still able to maintain his/her existing seat.

There were several lessons to be learned from the crushing

defeat of the DFL endorsed ticket in the 1966 primary election. It was naïve for otherwise experienced and sophisticated DFL party leaders and legislators to believe that they could oust an incumbent governor of their own party without paying a heavy price at the polls. Minnesota voters like the underdog. The Rolvaag forces sought the sympathy vote with telling effect. Their theme of "Let the voters decide" played to the voters' instinct to reject the choice of so-called "party bosses" as they had in the 1956 presidential primary.

The solid rejection of the DFL Party endorsed slate has led to the diminished effect of the DFL's endorsement of candidates for statewide office. The endorsement process had theretofore been a vehicle by which a qualified candidate for statewide office without access to serious amounts of campaign funding could be elected. The elections of Orville Freeman and Hubert Humphrey were examples of this process. The party endorsement was the vehicle by which Karl Rolvaag was elected lieutenant governor and Miles Lord as attorney general. Rolvaag was the DFL endorsed candidate in his election over incumbent Elmer Andersen in the preceding general election.

I did not participate actively in the DFL Party processes leading up to the 1968 statewide or presidential elections. The DFL Party was torn apart in 1968 over the competing candidacies for president of Humphrey and Eugene McCarthy. It was a battle I had no heart to engage in following the bruising intraparty and primary election battles of 1966.

In 1968, McCarthy refused to announce support of Humphrey until 1½ weeks before the election. Humphrey refused to repudiate President Johnson's actions in the Viet Nam war. In any event, while Humphrey came from behind in the polls, in the final weeks of the campaign he lost the presidency by about 500,000 votes out of a total of over 70 million votes cast.[3] While Humphrey was later returned by Minnesota voters to the U.S. Senate, his life-long presidential ambitions effectively ended with his defeat in the 1968 presidential election by a resurrected Richard Nixon.

Chapter Thirteen

The 1970's

In 1970, I returned to active political work in the DFL. I was elected a delegate to the DFL state convention. At that time there was only a single Jewish legislator. Jack Kleinbaum, a St. Cloud merchant, had been elected to the Minnesota house in 1967. Kleinbaum served in the house from 1967 to 1972, when he was elected to the senate. He served in the senate from 1973 to 1980. The 1970 DFL convention endorsed St. Paul State Senator Wendell R. Anderson for governor and Senator Rudy Perpich of Hibbing for lieutenant governor. DFL Party chair Warren Spannaus gained the nod for attorney general. All three DFL candidates for these offices were elected. However, the conservative/Republicans remained in control of both the house and the senate.

1972 was a landmark election year for the DFL. The party captured control of both houses of the legislature. This was the first time in the state's history that the liberal/DFL held a majority in both houses. That election also saw the election to the Minnesota senate of Allan Spear. Spear was a history professor at the university. He was the first openly acknowledged gay member of the legislature. Spear was elected by his DFL colleagues as president of the senate. As such, he was the senate's presiding officer. He served in that post from 1993 through 1999. Spear also served as a longtime chair of the Senate Judiciary Committee. He retired and did not seek reelection in 2000.

The 1972 election saw Phyllis Kahn's election as a state representative. Kahn is now the longest serving member of the Minnesota legislature. She has been elected for 18 consecutive two-year terms. Kahn has degrees in physics and from the J.F.K. School of Government at Harvard. She has had diverse legislative interests. They include science and technology issues, and the environment and women's rights. Kahn was elected a Fellow of the American Association for the Advancement of Science. She was the sole Jewish woman in the Minnesota house during her first 16 two-year terms in the Legislature. In 2004, she was joined by Representative Tina Liebling of Rochester.

With the 1972 capture of control of both houses of the legislature by the DFL, a historic event occurred. It was the first time in the state's history that the liberal/DFL held a majority of both houses of the legislature and had a DFL governor, Wendell Anderson.

In the 1973 session, DFL legislators pushed through a bill requiring all legislative candidates to run with party designation. Governor Anderson signed the bill into law. This ended Minnesota's so-called non-partisan legislature. Party designation enhanced the power of both major political parties. Party endorsement for legislative office became almost a prerequisite for electoral success. It also created a clear distinction between the candidates running. In that same 1972 session the legislature passed, and the voters subsequently approved, a constitutional amendment permitting the legislature to meet in a regular session every year. Biennial sessions were eliminated as was the likelihood of recurrent special legislative sessions when the legislature could not complete the public's business during the regular session.

1974 was a landmark election year for Minnesota and the nation. The Watergate Scandal caused the resignation of President Richard Nixon and the succession to the presidency of Vice President Gerald Ford. In that election DFL candidates swept all of the state constitutional offices. Swept into office were 26 newly elected DFLers in the house. This gave the DFL continued control of both the house and the senate.

The 1975 session of the legislature was noteworthy for several reasons. I was elected by the legislature to serve on the University of Minnesota Board of Regents. That session also saw the passage of the Minnesota Clean Indoor Air Act. Its principal author was Representative Phyllis Kahn. That law was designed to protect the public health by restricting smoking in virtually all public places. However, there was a noticeable gap in the law relating to bars, restaurants and clubs. This omission became the subject of much controversy in the 2002, 2004, 2006 and 2007 sessions of the legislature. The principal author of the statewide anti-smoking bill was Representative Ron Latz. Latz continued his efforts as a state senator in the 2007 session. The 2007 session saw the passage of the bill prohibiting smoking in bars and restaurants statewide. It was signed into law by Governor Tim Pawlenty.

The 1976 election saw Jimmy Carter elected president and Walter Mondale as vice president. Mondale's election created a vacancy in the U.S. senate seat. Governor Wendy Anderson was at the height of his popularity. He had been a very successful governor. He was identified with a popular proposal to rewrite the Minnesota school aid formula. That legislation became known as the "Minnesota Miracle." Anderson was featured on the cover of *Time Magazine*.

During his term as governor, Anderson had two close political advisors. One was his chief of staff Tom Kelm. The other was David Lebedoff, a Jewish Minneapolis attorney and author. Anderson was faced with a difficult choice. Should he run in a special election to succeed to the Mondale senate seat? Or should he resign as governor and have his successor, Lieutenant Governor Rudy Perpich, appoint him to the senate seat for the balance of Mondale's term?

Political folklore has it that Kelm and Lebedoff disagreed on which route to take. Kelm favored the special election route. Political history in the U.S. was that voters resented a so-called "self appointment" route. Anderson was an extremely successful and popular governor. He would be the overwhelming favorite in a special election. Lebedoff is reputed to have advised Anderson to follow the "self-appointment" route. Anderson chose to resign; have Perpich assume the governorship; and appoint him to the senate seat. This turned out to be a disastrous choice. When Anderson sought to be elected for the regular senate term, he was defeated. This ended prematurely Anderson's very promising career in public office. It was a career that some felt could ultimately lead to his candidacy for president.

Chapter Fourteen

Governor Rudy Perpich

Rudy Perpich was Minnesota's first Catholic governor. Among his closest advisors during his first term was University of Minnesota historian and author Hyman Berman. Among Rudy Perpich's accomplishments in his first term as governor was the appointment of the first woman to the Minnesota Supreme Court. According to Hy Berman who participated in the process, Rosalie Wahl, and Roberta Levy, a University of Minnesota law school teacher were the two finalists for that historic appointment. Perpich chose to appoint Wahl. Levy went on to a distinguished career as a Hennepin County District Court Judge.

Both Governor Anderson and Governor Perpich appointed a number of Jewish attorneys to the District Court. Among those that Anderson appointed were Jonathan Lebedoff and Allen Oleisky. Lebedoff went on to appointment by the U.S. District Court as a Magistrate Judge. He was later elevated to Chief Magistrate Judge. Anderson also appointed Noah Rosenbloom to the district court in rural Lyon, a county in southwestern Minnesota. Lawrence Cohen became Chief Judge of the Ramsey County District Court. In that capacity he played a key role in the historic tobacco trial which resulted in a $6.1 billion settlement with the tobacco industry; the end of cigarette billboard advertising in Minnesota; and the tobacco industry's agreement to cease commenting positively about the health effects of smoking. Among Jewish judges appointed by Governor Perpich to the Hennepin County District Court bench were Myron "Micky" Greenberg, Steven Z. Lange, and Harvey Ginsberg. Interestingly, no Jew has ever been appointed or elected to the Minnesota Court of Appeals.

The 1978 election was a disaster for the DFL. Wendy Anderson was defeated in the U.S. senate race. Both U.S. senate seats were captured by the Republicans. One, Rudy Boschwitz, was the first Jew elected to serve in the United States Congress from Minnesota. The other U.S. Senator elected that year was David Durenberger. Durenberger defeated Robert Short. Short had defeated congressman Donald Fraser in a bitter primary campaign. Fraser held the DFL Party endorsement for that senate seat. The Short-Fraser primary contest was something of a replay of the 1966 Keith-Rolvaag contest. Fraser had supported Keith as a party endorsed candidate. Short was the unsuccessful lieutenant governor on the Rolvaag ticket.

Arvonne Fraser, Don's spouse, was a respected advocate for women's rights. She had been appointed to a prominent position in the Carter-Mondale administration. This post required her to frequently travel overseas. Unfortunately, she was not present during much of the primary election campaign to supply her sophisticated political analysis and organizational ability to Don's campaign. She had done so in his successful campaigns for the Minnesota Senate and for the 5th district congressional seat.

I, along with other friends and supporters of Fraser, urged him to respond to the sharp political attacks on him waged by Short. These attacks had negatively defined Fraser's successful service in public office. As Democrats nationwide were to learn from the 1978, 2000 and 2004 elections, a candidate cannot allow his opponent to define him. A candidate cannot allow attacks on his/her record without making a prompt and pointed response. It is unfortunately naïve to believe that the public does not absorb these negative characterizations of a candidate.

While Short defeated Fraser in the DFL primary, both he and Perpich were defeated in the 1978 general election. At the same time Warren Spannaus was reelected as attorney general and Joan Anderson Growe was returned as secretary of state. Ron Latz interned in Senate Durenberger's Washington office. He worked on healthcare issues.

The inability of the legislature in its 1971 session to come to agreement on the reapportionment of the legislature after the 1970 decennial census resulted in a very unusual situation in the 1979 session of the legislature. The final plan approved by the courts retained the number of Minnesota state senators at 67. However, it reduced the number of house members by one from 135 to 134. In the 1979 legislative session the result was a deadlock. The voters had placed 67 DFLers and 67 Republicans in the house. That deadlock is described in an interesting book by former Minnesota House Speaker Rodney Searle.[1] Searle's story reflects the interplay of the personalities and legislative rules and procedures that resulted from the 67-67 deadlock, and the subsequent narrow DFL control of the Minnesota house following a bitter election contest. There has been no other portrayal in my memory of how personal ambitions and power plays interacted to stalemate legislative progress. It also describes the unusual efforts that allowed the house to function despite the partisan deadlock.

The decline in the value of the DFL Party endorsement for statewide office was evident in the results of the 1982 election. The DFL Party had endorsed Attorney General Warren Spannaus as its candidate for governor. Rudy Perpich returned to Minnesota.

He mounted a vigorous campaign against Spannaus in the DFL primary. This was despite the fact that Perpich himself had been the beneficiary of DFL Party endorsement for office. Perpich defeated Spannaus in the primary election. This was despite my efforts and those of many other DFLers who felt that Spannaus, who had served as a DFL Party state chairman before being elected attorney general, had earned the right for party support as a gubernatorial candidate. Nonetheless, Perpich defeated Spannaus in the primary. He then went on to be victorious against the incumbent Republican Governor Al Quie in the general election.

Chapter Fifteen

The Importance of
Committee Assignments

Observers of the legislature and of the legislative process understand the importance of the member's assignment to particular committees. They also understand how important seniority is. Skill, experience and seniority usually combined to result in a powerful position as the chair of a legislative committee or division. There may be much jousting and negotiation involved in the appointments to various committees as well as who is to chair a committee or a division. Of course, the committees will vary in their importance and their ability to influence public policy. In recent experience there have been three Jewish legislators who have served in powerful positions in the Minnesota legislature.

Senator Richard Cohen from St. Paul has served in the senate since 1986. For the last several sessions Cohen, an attorney, has served as chair of the Senate Finance Committee. He also is a member of the key Committee on Rules and Administration.

Senator Sandra "Sandy" Pappas of St. Paul serves as the chair of the Higher Education Budget Division. She serves as well on the Rules and Administration Committee. Pappas was first elected to the legislature in 1990. Both Cohen and Pappas are DFLers.

Representative Ron Abrams of Minnetonka served in the Minnesota House from 1988, through his appointment by Governor Pawlenty in 2006, as a Hennepin County District Court Judge. Abrams, a Harvard Law School graduate, was a moderate Republican. He chaired the House Tax Committee. In that position he was a major influence on tax bills brought before the house. Abrams also served as Speaker Pro Tem. In that role he served as the presiding officer of the house when the Speaker was taking a break or was absent. Abrams also served on the Rules and Legislative Administration Committee.

During my service in the legislature I was named to important committees while the DFL was in control. I thus was named a member of those committees that dealt with labor relations, state government and on the tax committee. When the Republicans took control in 1963, I was relegated to service on relatively minor committees.

The Rules Committee in both bodies serves a very important function. At the beginning of the session the committee proposes the rules that govern the conduct of the body during the session. The committee also functions as a "traffic cop" at the end of the legislative sessions. This 'traffic cop" function is a particularly important one. During the closing days of the session no bill can be processed for action on the floor of the body without the approval of the Rules Committee.

Politics as the Art of the Possible

Reaching compromises on legislative and political matters in the legislature is maligned by some purists as "selling the cause down the river." However, as one learns early in the political process, in and out of the legislature, politics is really the art of the possible. I learned this early in the 1961 session when we were forced to compromise on the provisions of the fair housing bill by excluding owner occupied duplexes from coverage. The battle may be lost in the short run but won later on, as was the case with the duplex provision.

Even when one changes roles from the majority to the minority in the legislature, that in and of itself does not mean a loss of the ability to influence the process. While in the 1963 Session, when the Republicans regained control of the house, I still maintained a leadership role in the Hennepin County legislative delegation. Substantial unanimity in the delegation was a critical objective as to proposals that affected Minneapolis and/or Hennepin County.

Thus, I was put in a position of being part of a negotiation between Republican Governor Elmer Andersen and the Hennepin County Bar Association leadership as to whether and how many new district court judges would be appointed by the governor for service in Hennepin County. Since I continued to serve on the House Judiciary Committee with conservative/Republican leader George French, that was the initial venue on the new judgeship question. After French and I had negotiated on the subject of how many additional judgeships would be created and appointed the negotiation moved to the governor's office. A meeting took place between myself, Governor Andersen, and attorney Sidney Feinberg. Feinberg, a Republican, was chair of the Minnesota State Bar Association. The result of this three-party negotiation was an agreement, concurred with by French, as to the creation and number of the additional judgeships. Of course, all of these new judges would be appointed by the Republican governor. However, I and other DFLers at the time had confidence that Governor Andersen would be careful and bipartisan in his selection of the new judges. Of course, I had had a previously successful relationship with Governor Andersen in the 1961 session when I had worked together with him and others of a bipartisan coalition of community leaders to secure passage of the Fair Housing Act.

Chapter Sixteen

Hyman Berman
"Minnesota's Historian"[1]

Professor Hyman "Hy" Berman, emeritus professor of history at the University of Minnesota, is the latest among Jewish politicians in Minnesota to serve as a close adviser to a Minnesota governor. Following Abe Harris in the Floyd B. Olson administration; Arthur Naftalin in that of Governor Orville Freeman; and David Lebedoff while Wendy Anderson was governor; Professor Berman was a true "insider" in the first term of Governor Rudy Perpich.

Not surprisingly, all of them served as advisers to Farmer Labor or DFL governors. In the long history of Minnesota politics I am unaware of any Jew who has served as such a close adviser to a Republican governor. None of these advisers still living has been as open and forthcoming about his role as has Hy Berman. His intellect and insight, combined with his engaging personality, has led to his being widely referred to as "Minnesota's Historian."

Given his background and experience it is not at all surprising that Governor Perpich, the news media, and others interested in the history of the Jewish community and of the labor movement, should turn to Professor Berman for his advice, recollections and insights. He has been known as an observer who states forthrightly and with candor his recollections and opinions. His stature and status as a tenured professor at the university made it possible for him to render his advice and opinions candidly. He has been without ambition for elective or appointive office. This has allowed him the freedom to speak up and advise without fear or favor.

Hyman Berman was born in New York City of immigrant,

working class parents. Both of his parents worked in the garment trades. He was the first of his family to go to college. He was fortunate enough to pass an entrance exam to one of the most prestigious public high schools in the country. He then went on to City College of New York which provided Berman and others with free tuition, after having served with the U.S. Army during World War II. In 1948, he received a Bachelor of Science in History degree from City College. He was elected into Phi Beta Kappa. Phi Beta Kappa is the oldest honorary scholarly fraternity in the country. After receiving a Ph.D. degree in history from Columbia University, Berman taught at Brooklyn College and Michigan State University.

He came to the University of Minnesota in 1961. Berman was a teacher in the History Department at the University for 38 years before his retirement in 2004 when he became a Professor Emeritus. At the university he taught American history, Minnesota history, world history and a course in American Jewish history. Berman taught and lectured widely. In 1979, he visited China to give a course on American history to Chinese scholars. He participated actively in faculty affairs. He was a member of the University Senate. In 1996, when some members of the Board of Regents sought to modify the tenure code at the university, Berman said, "The perceived attack on tenure has proved damaging to the university's ability to retain and recruit quality academics."[2]

Berman was one of those faculty members who was active in establishing a Department of American Indian Studies at the University.[3] Among the books and many articles authored by Berman on labor history and anti-Semitism are *Jews of Minnesota,* with Linda Mack Schloff[4] and *Political Anti-Semitism in Minnesota during the Great Depression.*[5]

Berman has become most well known through his frequent appearances on public television's *Almanac* program. His expressed insights into Minnesota history and politics caused him to be named by the program's hosts as "Minnesota's Historian." The title is well deserved. Berman describes himself as a "public historian."

He defines what a historian does as attempts to "translate insofar as possible the latest scholarship for the public at large - to make the past livable for the present." Berman uses history in an effort to gain insight into what is happening today. He quotes the great Spanish philosopher/historian Santayana who said, "Those who forget history are doomed to repeat the errors of the past."

Berman's special interest as a historian has been the history of the American Jewish labor movement. He has written widely on the subject including publications of the American Jewish Historical Society. In 1962, Berman wrote "*A Cursory View of the Jewish Labor Movement; An Historical Survey.*"[6]

The history of the American Jewish labor movement experience ties in with the immigrant experience of Jews in America and in Minnesota. Such organizations as the Workman's Circle and the Jewish Labor Committee had branches in Minneapolis. The Workmen's Circle, locally and nationally, was a "movement for social change. It was a combination of politics, culture, theater, trade unionism, and a hope for a better world." The Workmen's Circle "was an institution that in fact introduced the Jewish worker not only to the broader culture of the United States but to its own culture, the Yiddish culture. It was an instrument of political and social activity as well."[7]

Among the leaders of those organizations were Rubin Latz, Sander Genis and Mike Finkelstein. Genis and Finkelstein were union leaders in the once flourishing garment industry principally centered in downtown Minneapolis. This industry gave employment to many Minneapolis Jews. I had a summer job in the stormcoat manufacturing company headed by Louis Gross. It helped me through college. Louis Gross was one of the early presidents of Minnesota Jewish Council. He is the father of Luella Gross Goldberg. Luella Goldberg has an outstanding record of community service which includes membership on the boards of prestigious business corporations and academic institutions such as Wellesley College. She served as interim President of Wellesley and as chair of the University of Minnesota Foundation Board. The 2000 Session of the legislature elected Gross's other daughter, Linda Cohen, a psychologist, as a Regent of the University of Minnesota.

Among the prominent Jews active in the Minnesota labor movement were John Goldie and Sam Romer. Goldie was long-time attorney for the Minnesota AFL-CIO. Together with his law partner Sam Sigal they also represented many Minnesota labor unions. Romer was a reporter for the *Minneapolis Star Tribune*. His concentration was on labor unions and the labor movement. The Minnesota locals of the Amalgamated Clothing Workers Union, a CIO union, and the International Ladies Garment Workers Union, affiliated with the AF of L, were what Berman calls "Jewish labor unions." He describes them as being "an integral part of the political support base in the Farmer Labor administrations of Floyd B. Olson and his successor Governor Elmer Benson.[8] "At the core of the labor leadership within the Farmer Labor movement in Minnesota were Rubin Latz, Sander Genis and Michael Finkelstein."[9]

With the demise of the Twin Cities garment industry, the political strength and activity of its Jewish union leadership also declined. In more recent years the sole Minnesota Jewish labor leader of note was Jack Mogelson. Mogelson was an activist leader of a Teamsters local and in the DFL Party. Mogelson was also a leader, along with Matthew Stark, of the Minnesota Civil Liberties Union. Consistent with the rough and tumble nature of some Teamsters unions, Mogelson was an outspoken and aggressive union and political figure. His efforts at physical and verbal intimidation offended many in the Minnesota DFL. But because of his union position he had some influence within the party.

The disappearance of the garment trades in the Twin Cities and nationally also resulted in the disappearance of Jews from the industry and the garment unions. According to Berman, "What we saw was that the Jews, not only in Minnesota, but in the United States generally, were a one generation proletariat. The immigrant generation worked in the factories. But their children, because of the fact that their parents worked in the factories and the sweatshops and so on, went on to business and professional careers. They went to college and university graduate schools. They became doctors, lawyers, businessmen and teachers. The social mobility of the second generation, coupled with the disappearance of the garment trades, meant the end of the Jewish labor movement not only in Minnesota but in the United States generally."[10]

Berman has not only been a labor historian. He has studied and lectured widely on political anti-Semitism and anti-Semitism in general. "The stings of age-old prejudices, often masquerading in new guises, in America and abroad," was the subject of a joint presentation of Professor Berman and Mark Massa, a professor of theology and the co director of the Center for American Catholic Studies at Fordham University. The symposium took place at the Jay Phillips Center for Jewish-Christian Learning, a partnership of St. John's University and the University of St. Thomas. On April 12, and April 13, 2005, Berman and Massa participated in a program sponsored by the Jay Phillips Center entitled "What's new about old hatreds?"

Professor Berman's observations about the University of Minnesota, its faculties and administrators, represents a true insider's view of the university. His observations represented a major part of the extensive interview I conducted with him on October 16, 2003. Among his observations as to anti-Semitism among the power structure at the University of Minnesota, Berman states that he "...found no overt anti-Semitism among academic colleagues or administrators during the thirty-some odd years that I have been in Minnesota. I have however found significant evidence of deep seated and deep rooted anti-Semitism in previous University administrations and previous University actions." Berman observed that Dean Nicholson, after whom Nicholson Hall is named on the University campus, "was in direct association and political fellowship with the infamous Colonel McCormick, the publisher of the *Chicago Tribune*, and with William Dudley Pelley, of the American Vigilance Committee." Berman states that Nicholson set up a system of spying among the faculty and students at the university in which Nicholson was looking for, in Nicholson's words, "Kike-Commies." In fact, Berman states that many prominent faculty members and student leaders, none of whom were Jewish, were labeled by Nicholson as "Kike-Commies" simply because "their crime was that they were New Deal Democrats." To Nicholson any New Deal Democrats were "Kike-Commies."

Berman states that "overt anti-Semitism was endemic in the university in the years that Nicholson was Dean of Students. University President Lotus Coffman, after whom the university student center Coffman Union is named, "was in fact instrumental in establishing numerous clauses at the university restricting admission of Jewish students into various professional schools and even undergraduate colleges." In the University of Minnesota Medical School at the time there was a numerical percentage quota as to the number of the entering class who could be Jewish. The way in which admission was administered was that if your name sounded Jewish you were subject to the quota.

Of course during those years the University of Minnesota was not the only college or university that imposed quotas on the admission of Jewish students. In academia there were other graduate schools in the East and throughout the country where admissions counselors suggested to students such as Berman, that "there are certain schools I wouldn't apply to." When Berman was getting his doctorate at Columbia and was looking for a university to teach at he was told by a distinguished professor, "If I were you, I would just go to the City Colleges in New York." When Berman was at Michigan State University and received an appointment at the University of Minnesota, his mentor at Columbia University told him "Hy, that is impossible. You didn't get an appointment at Minnesota. That department (the History Department) is "Udenheim – free of Jews." Dean Harry Carman then corrected himself by stating, "Oh, no, no, there is one Unitarian there who used to be Jewish." While Professor Carman was mistaken, and there were several other Jews already in the Minnesota History Department, Berman believes that his response reflected the reputation of the University of Minnesota in the broader academic community in 1961.

Onward from the 1960's there was a change in the attitude of the University of Minnesota and other comparable institutions as to the admission of Jewish students and the hiring of Jewish faculty members. At the university that change was most notable in the 1960 selection of O. Meredith Wilson as university president. Wilson was a Mormon. Berman believes that rarely would a Mormon be appointed president of a state university. Wilson was a liberal and a New Dealer who believed in equal opportunity. This was most notably evidenced by Wilson's defense of Professor Mulford Q. Sibley. Sibley was a professor of political science who was attacked because he took unpopular political stances. Some right wing politicians, including St. Paul City Council member Milton Rosen, demanded that Sibley be fired. When some regents advocating Sibley's termination asked of Wilson what needed to be done to fire Sibley, Wilson responded "You have to fire me first."

In the mid-1970's, Berman found himself involved in the incidents surrounding the failed candidacy of David Saxon for the University of Minnesota presidency. Berman describes an incident at the time when there was a knock on the door of his office. In walked Regent George Rauenhorst. Berman describes Rauenhorst as a conservative Republican, but a wonderful man, a wonderful human being. Berman quotes Rauenhorst as stating, "Hy, you won't believe what just happened." Rauenhorst then proceeded to tell Berman the story of regents Loanne Thrane and L.J. Lee asking the religious affiliation of Saxon and asking the chair of the University Presidential Search Committee, who was on the Regents Selection Committee with them, to look into it and see whether Saxon was, in fact, a God-fearing American.

Berman agreed to look into the matter. He called and spoke to Regent Neil Sherburne, a good friend of his from the labor movement. In response to the inquiry Sherburne said, "George has it right. That is exactly what happened." Sherburne said, "I was fuming, I was boiling. But you know, we on the Board of Regents have a kind of agreement not to leak things, so I couldn't really tell you, but since George told you, I will confirm it." Berman describes that the next thing he did was to pick up the telephone and call a good friend of his, Bob Lundegard, who was on the *Star Tribune* staff. Berman told Lundegard, "Bob, you won't believe this. Look into it. If there is something there, do something about it." Within the next several days there were big headlines in the *Star Tribune* exposing the whole incident.

As to the troubled presidency of the first Jewish president of the university, Berman is among those who believe that anti-Semitism played a part in the failure of President Ken Keller's term as president. Berman relates an incident in which a good friend from another university related that at a meeting held at a conference of presidents, chairs of boards of trustees and regents, that the chair of the university Board of Regents was "going all over the place, bad-mouthing Ken Keller."

Berman states that, "Mark Yudof's selection (as University of Minnesota President) was of course one that showed that the Board of Regents and the Selection Committee had completely gotten over what had been a history of anti-Semitism at the university." Mark Yudof was overtly and unapologetically Jewish. His wife was an active lay leader in the Conservative Jewish movement." Yudof realized that Hy Berman was, as Berman himself describes it, "kind of a face at the university and with the public." President Yudof was smart enough to realize that the university, and Yudof as president, did not want to lose Berman's presence as it reflected, in part, the knowledge and humanity of the university. Thus, when Berman decided at age 73 that he wanted to retire he got a phone call from Yudof. Yudof said, "What makes you think I or anyone in my office is going to sign your retirement papers?" Berman replied, "Mark, you are a lawyer, but let me tell you I will have you in court so fast." Yudof laughed and said he would come up with a way to keep Berman on as a faculty member for five more years. Yudof made the necessary arrangements, and Berman stayed on the faculty for five more years until he was age 78. After Yudof resigned to become the head of the University of Texas system Berman retired and became a Professor Emeritus of History.

Perhaps most revealing from a political and historical perspective were the insights and stories Berman reveals as a true "insider" in the first term of Governor Rudy Perpich. Berman was part of a group of three who were unofficial advisers to Perpich. The other two were Joe Summers, who became a Ramsey County District Court Judge, and Bill Kennedy who was the Chief Public Defender in Hennepin County. Each of the three had independent economic bases. Therefore, they could afford to give unvarnished advice to the governor free from the fear that the mercurial Perpich would fire them as he could with any of the appointees in his administration.

The evolution of Berman's relationship with Rudy Perpich and his family is described by Berman as "....my associate, my friend, my collaborator, my informant, took me into his family and we became good friends." The relationship began with a University of Minnesota project to study the impact of education on an immigrant community. This was shortly after Berman first arrived at the university. University President O. Meredith Wilson was a historian. He had received a grant for the university from the Ford Foundation. The grant was to study the impact that education had on an immigrant community. The immigrant community chosen for this study was on the Minnesota iron range. President Wilson asked Berman and two of his colleagues in the history department to do that study. They were Professors Clark Chambers and Timothy Smith. Chambers did the segment on the impact of the host community on the immigrants. Smith, a historian of religion, was asked to look at the role of public education. Berman was assigned to look at the role of the ethnic labor communities in the educational process. Thus from 1962-1964, Berman spent most summers and many other parts of the year up on the iron range working on the project. Berman already knew many of the labor and political people on the range. He also got to know the members of the many ethnic communities there: the Finns, Croatians, Slavs, and so on.

Berman states that he really did not have any inside track or view to help him until he met a young dentist who was active politically and who was then on the Hibbing School Board. The following year Rudy Perpich was elected state senator. Rudy Perpich and Professor Berman continued their friendship on and off through the legislative sessions. Berman would visit the Perpich family in Hibbing. When the youngest Perpich son went off to the

University of Minnesota, his father said to Berman, "I want you to look after my son. He is young. He will get lost in the big city." Berman responded, "Well, Rudy is also there." The eldest Perpich responded, "He is a politician, he can't look after him. You look after him." Berman did so.

In 1976, Berman was a Senior Fellow at the Minnesota Historical Society. Thus he spent much time at the state capitol. Rudy Perpich at that time was the lieutenant governor and Wendy Anderson was the governor. When Jimmy Carter and Fritz Mondale were elected president, and Vice President-elect Mondale had to resign from the U.S. senate, a vacancy was created. Tom Kelm, Wendy Anderson's closest political adviser, met with Berman, John Haynes, who was Berman's graduate student, and other staff members at the state capitol cafeteria. The subject was Anderson's plan to resign as governor; to have Rudy Perpich then become the governor; then appoint Anderson to the vacant Mondale seat. Berman cautioned against that plan. He said that if history is any guide that type of plan has failed whenever it was attempted. He would avoid it. Berman felt that the popularity of Wendy Anderson was such that they ought to call for a special election to fill the Mondale seat. Anderson would then resign as governor and run for the seat in the special election. Anderson's popularity was such that he was certainly a heavy favorite to be elected.

When the meeting broke up Berman did not know whether or not his argument had been successful. Several weeks later he discovered that it was not. He learned of the decision by a phone call from Rudy Perpich. Perpich said, "Hy, I am going to become governor. Can Lola and I come over to your house for lunch. Maybe we will get some good Jewish delicatessen; we will have a good lunch; and I want to talk to you." Rudy and Lola Perpich came over to the Berman house. During lunch Rudy said to Berman, "I need your help. I want your help. I am going to be governor." Berman responded that he would be happy to help. Perpich said, "Would you take a leave of absence from the university and join my staff?" Berman thought for a moment and responded, "No, Rudy, I would not want to do that." Perpich said, "Why not?" Berman said, "Well, look, one of the strengths I would have would be as kind of an informal adviser. Doing for you what David Lebedoff did for Wendy. And I don't want to take a leave from the university and become a member of your staff for the simple reason that in a formal way I can't tell you, 'Hey Rudy, you are full of shit.' If I were a member of your staff, and I said that, you would say, 'you are fired.' As an informal person, you can't fire me. I can just go away and not come back again, but you can't fire me." Perpich looked at Berman and said, "You know, Hy, you are right." Berman knew how volatile Rudy could be.

So it was decided that Berman would play an informal role in the Perpich administration. It was a role that he played more or less together with Joe Summers and Bill Kennedy. The role of the three advisers was unique. Berman's teaching position at the University meant that he had more time to spend at the capitol than did Summers who was a fulltime judge, or Kennedy who was a fulltime public defender. Therefore, Berman states that he was "… was practically there fulltime. I had two fulltime jobs, one with Rudy and one with the university." Berman states that he was, "probably the liaison" between he and Summers and Kennedy. They always were talking with him and Rudy was always talking to them. Occasionally the three of them got together with Perpich. That is how it really worked."

Berman said that the first major issue before the Perpich administration was the need to fill a vacancy on the Minnesota Supreme Court. Perpich was determined to appoint a woman. The three of them thought that was a very good idea. Since Summers and Kennedy were much more knowledgeable in this area than Berman, the two of them searched out what they believed to be the most capable women in the legal profession that would be available. Among the number of women considered were Roberta "Bobby" Levy and Rosalie Wahl. Levy at the time was teaching at the University of Minnesota Law School. Later, in 1981, she was appointed a Hennepin County District Court Judge. Had she been appointed to the Supreme Court, Levy would have been the first Jewish woman appointed to the court. (Levy later became the first woman to serve as Chief Judge of the Hennepin County District Court.) The informal screening committee for that vacancy consisted of the governor, Joe Summers, Bill Kennedy and Berman. The governor would not consult with the Minnesota Bar Association leadership. Perpich stated "They are a bunch of right wing Republicans. They have only one agenda. I don't trust them. Here we have two lawyers and two non lawyers. Joe and Bill are the lawyers, and you and I are the non lawyers. We can do it ourselves." It was the unanimous decision to appoint Rosalie Wahl as the first woman Justice on the Minnesota Supreme Court. For an excellent history of the selection of Wahl and other women judges see Center on Women and Public Policy Case Study.[11]

Berman was a speech writer for Perpich. Perpich asked Berman to write a speech he was to deliver at his inauguration as governor. This was a speech that was to define who Rudy Perpich was. This concept was right down Berman's alley. Berman's immigrant working class roots were almost identical to those of Perpich. Both Berman and Perpich were the first of their respective families to go to college. There was a conflict within the Perpich staff as to the theme of the inaugural speech. Ronnie Brooks was a Perpich staff member with close ties to Senate Majority Leader Nicholas Coleman. Coleman and Perpich had a close relationship dating back to their both serving in the senate. Brooks wanted the inaugural speech to be basically an outline of the policy stances Perpich would recommend as governor. Berman prevailed in the debate.

Berman's relationship with Rudy Perpich was radically changed by the events of the "Minnesota Massacre" of 1978. Despite leading in the polls going down to election day, Perpich was defeated in his quest for election as governor. A self appointed Wendy Anderson was defeated by Rudy Boschwitz. After that disastrous election, Perpich became an international representative for Control Data Corporation with headquarters in Vienna, Austria. While Perpich was in New York City preparing for that international post, he called Berman and requested that Berman meet with him in New York City. The two met along with Perpich's spouse and closest political adviser Lola Perpich. At the breakfast meeting Rudy Perpich,

Minnesota's first Catholic governor, stated, "I finally found out why I lost the election. The last weekend, the last Sunday, the Catholic churches made a concerted drive to paint me as a baby killer. They leafleted cars in the church parking lots asserting that Rudy Perpich believed in abortion and is a baby killer." They labeled Rudy Perpich as an abortion supporter. They stated that Perpich's sister in law, Connie Perpich, the wife of his brother Senator George Perpich, was a leading advocate of abortion. Senator George Perpich chaired the Senate Welfare Committee.

Berman states that Rudy turned to him and said, "Hy, I am never going to lose another election. I am not going to be caught in that bind. I am going to revert to my historical roots." Berman replied, "But Rudy, your father is anticlerical. Your father hasn't gone into a church since he was a young man. You weren't brought up in the church." Perpich responded, "For political reasons, I am now a Catholic anti abortion person." Berman responded, "You can't get away with it." Berman stated, "Rudy we are good friends, but I can't go along with you on this one. Political victory is not really, it should not depend on, expediency and opportunism. If you want to go in that direction, good luck."

While Berman states that he and Rudy Perpich "remained good friends," they were "not as close afterwards as they were before." In the next election cycle in 1982, Attorney General Warren Spannaus was the DFL endorsed candidate for governor. Spannaus called Berman and asked if Berman would support him. Berman responded in the affirmative. However, Perpich defeated Spannaus in the primary election. He went on to election for a four year term as governor. Berman states, "I was never the kind of adviser that I was for him as I was in the first two years."

Abortion politics, and the events in 1990 that caused Arne Carlson to replace Jon Grunseth as the Republican candidate opposing Perpich's reelection efforts, caused a rupture in the very close relationship between Perpich and Sandy Keith. Berman describes the two as "probably the closest political and personal friends alive. Both were close, very friendly, and Rudy was one of his (Keith's) early supporters in 1966, when Sandy was running for governor against Karl Rolvaag for the DFL nomination." When there was an opening on the Minnesota Supreme Court for Chief Justice, Berman believes it was natural that Sandy would get it. "Sandy was a good lawyer and a good friend."

The events leading up to that 1990 gubernatorial election, and the 5-2 decision of the Minnesota Supreme Court allowing Arne Carlson to be the Republican candidate for Governor, are well described in Betty Wilson's book on Perpich.[12] Ironically, the majority opinion in that 5-2 decision by the court was written by Justice Rosalie Wahl. However, two other DFLers appointed by Perpich, Supreme Court Associate Justice Peter Popovich and Minnesota Court of Appeals Chief Judge Don Wozniak, were harsh in their blame of Keith for that decision. Popovich had joined Associate Justice Lawrence Yetka in dissenting from that decision.[13] Keith was attending a meeting outside Minnesota at the time. But he participated by telephone in the deliberations of the court on the matter. He voted with the majority. Keith was blamed by Perpich for the decision. However, even if Keith had voted with Popovich and Yetka the vote would still have been 4-3 to allow Arne Carlson on the ballot. According to Berman, Perpich held Keith responsible for the decision. As far as Berman knows, Perpich and Keith never spoke thereafter.

As Wilson aptly points out, the abortion issue played an important factor in Perpich's defeat. Perpich, as he had previously told Berman, was anti abortion. Women voted overwhelmingly to support the pro choice Carlson. Berman describes a unique relationship between Perpich, Popovich and Wozniak. Their relationship went beyond their common ethnic origins. To Berman, "Rudy Perpich was never an establishment DFLer. He was an outsider, even when he became lieutenant governor and governor with the DFL Party endorsement." Perpich had come back from Austria and into the primary election. He defeated the DFL endorsed candidate for governor Attorney General Warren Spannaus. Rudy Perpich apparently never felt comfortable with what he considered to be the establishment DFLers, such as those in Minneapolis and Hennepin County.

One of the important insights reflected in the interview with this distinguished Minnesota historian are his views and analyses of the Minnesota DFL Party. Berman believes that the current ineffectiveness of the DFL Party in electing its candidates can be traced back to the 1970s and the so-called "Fraser McGovern reforms." They were spearheaded by then DFL Congressman Donald Fraser. Those reforms were intended to open up the party processes and to democratize the party by changing the structure of the DFL Party caucuses. The caucuses are where delegates are selected to the next levels of the party activity. There the candidates are endorsed and the party platform is fashioned and adopted. Prior to the Fraser reforms the DFL Party caucuses were a more unified phenomenon. All of the attendees would meet together; select delegates and alternates to the next level caucus or convention; and debate issues and the support or endorsement of candidates. Balloting would take place in a single unified meeting. Under the reforms the structure of the caucuses were changed into so-called "walking caucuses." Attendees would chose caucuses reflecting support of individual candidates and/or support of particular issues or organizations. Thus, there might be a pro choice or pro life subcaucus; a Wendy Anderson for governor sub caucus; a labor subcaucus; an education subcaucus; or a combination of one or more of them. If a single sub caucus did not attract enough adherents to be "viable"; i.e., to have enough members to select one or more delegates to the next level, such as the county or state convention, then the attendees were permitted to walk from a non-viable caucus to another caucus. There their efforts, combined with those of the other caucus members, would be sufficient to elect one or more delegates.

Berman's analysis is that "one of the unanticipated consequences of this process was the development of fragmented politics." And the fragmented politics meant in effect no longer the existence of senior statesmen who were able to ever see the final results." As Berman accurately reflects, "the walking caucuses led in fact to the development of individual issues or groupings, but were so fragmented that they could not talk to one another.

The end result was a weakening of the DFL as a political party." Involved in, and adding to this problem, was the weakening of the Minnesota labor movement and of the Minnesota Farmers Union as important elements of the DFL Party. The end result, Berman observes, "...is that there is no party. There are different interest groups vying with each other for primacy in the party and the platform."

In the years since his retirement from the university Berman has continued to offer his observations on public television's *Almanac* program; as a television analyst on election nights; and as a speaker before organizations on political and historical issues. Retirement has allowed Berman to spend more time with his wife of 56 years, Betty Berman, and with his daughter Ruth and son Stephen and their granddaughter Stephanie. Berman has also undertaken a monumental task. That is the primary authorship of a history of the state of Minnesota. He has left a lasting impression on Minnesota politics and its citizens.

Chapter Seventeen

Burton Joseph

When one identifies husband-wife couples that have had significant impact in politics and Jewish communal life, Geri and Burton Joseph[1] are at the forefront. Burton Joseph and his family have had a leadership role locally and nationally in the Reform movement, in the fight against anti-Semitism, and in one of Minnesota's important business areas, the grain business.

Joseph's parents came to the United States from Rumania in 1892. Burton's father, I.S. Joseph, was a very bright and aggressive young man. The family was desperately poor and needed I.S. Joseph's skill and ambition to survive. Thus, in the 7th Grade, I.S. Joseph left school to go to work and earn money to help the family. He first became a public stenographer. One of his assignments was as a public stenographer at a grain company in the Minneapolis Grain Exchange. By 1913, he had learned enough about the grain business to go into business for himself. He formed the I.S. Joseph Company. Throughout the ups and downs of the U.S. economy in the 1920's, I.S. Joseph became a millionaire, lost his funds in the crash of 1929; and went on to become a very successful man in the marketing of grain and grain byproducts.

The history of Minneapolis' leading Reform synagogue Temple Israel is closely entwined with its first Rabbi, Rabbi Albert J. Minda, and I.S. and Burton Joseph. Burton describes Rabbi Minda as "...a very public figure. He served on many of the public committees around the town. He was instrumental in introducing the Jewish community to the general community. ... He was a man who commanded respect." Burton Joseph believes that Rabbi Minda "...made many openings to the general community for and on behalf of the Jewish people." Both I.S. Joseph and Burton Joseph were congregational presidents of Temple Israel.

Jews Excluded from the Minneapolis Power Structure

The Minneapolis Grain Exchange in the years preceding the accomplishments and breakthroughs of the 1950's and 1960's was a highly restricted organization. Those organizations that excluded Jews from membership included the Automobile Club, the Minneapolis Club and the Minneapolis Athletic Club. The I.S. Joseph Company became the first Jewish member of the Grain Exchange. Burton Joseph describes the Minneapolis Club as "...the highest placed community club in the city." He states that the Minneapolis Athletic Club, which was somewhat less prestigious, also had no Jewish members. The Minneapolis Club reversed itself when Jay Philips was elected to chair the Minneapolis Chamber of Commerce. As Burton describes it, "Jay explained to the leadership of the Minneapolis Club it would be very difficult for him to take that assignment unless he was a member of the Minneapolis Club so he could organize meetings and get together with friends, with people of prominence in the community." Thus, in the early 1950's, Jay Philips and his attorney, Samuel Maslon, became the first Jewish members of the Minneapolis Club.

The U of M and a Career in the Armed Forces

In 1939, Burton Joseph was a freshman at the University of Minnesota. He was 5' 8½" tall and weighed 121 lbs., so as he describes it, "...football was out of the question, as was basketball." Therefore, Burton tried out for the university hockey team and became a goalie. He could not skate but as he described it, "a goalie did not have to skate a great deal." He earned a letter in hockey prior to his graduation in June 1942 when he went into the Air Force. Joseph became a fighter pilot in what was then the Army Air Corp. He flew a fighter plane, the Mustang P-51. He was so proficient with gunnery and fighter aircraft that he became an instructor.

After the end of the WW II in 1945, he was single and decided to stay in the Reserves. In 1950, he was activated from the Reserves to serve in the Air Force during the Korean war. For the next 18 months he was an instructor in fighter aircraft.

In 1953, after having returned from military service, Burton states that he "…was able to get reacquainted with Geraldine Mack who was a reporter at that time for the Minneapolis Tribune. Our relationship developed into great affection, love, and we were married in April of 1953." In 2003, Burton and Geri Joseph celebrated their 50th wedding anniversary.

A Leader in Fighting Discrimination

Burton Joseph has a long and successful history in organizational activity fighting prejudice against Jews and other minorities. His work in Minnesota began in the 1950's, with the Minnesota Jewish Council. This was the organization that was staffed by Sam Scheiner. In the 1950's, the Anti Defamation League of B'nai B'rith opened an office in Minneapolis serving Minnesota, and North and South Dakota. The focus of the Minnesota Jewish Council was in combating anti-Semitism in all phases in life in Minnesota. The Minnesota/Dakotas ADL office, while involved in similar activities, focused itself more on educational policies and practices that could result in more long term change in the relationships between Jews and non-Jews.

In the middle 1950's, Burton Joseph was elected to the National Board of the Anti Defamation League (ADL). Joseph became national chair of the ADL finance committee. As part of that work he led the establishment of the ADL Foundation. The Josephs made the first gift to the foundation of $500,000 in the name of his parents I.S. and Annie Joseph. In 1969, Burton Joseph became chairman of the ADL. He was the first person from outside of New York City to become the chair.

Burton describes the ADL as "… an organization of great skill, success, stimulated in large measure because of the work of Ben Epstein and Arnold Forster." Epstein was the national ADL director and Forster was its general counsel.

Burton Joseph had a business relationship with Duane Andreas, the head of Archer Daniels Midland Company. ADM was a giant international grain company. Andreas was a dear and great friend of Hubert Humphrey. Joseph and Ben Epstein met with Andreas to see if he would be interested in providing the funding for a Hubert Humphrey First Amendment Prize to be awarded by the ADL. That prize would go to an individual or organization which encouraged and supported the work of civil liberties in the U.S. and around the world. Andreas agreed to the request and funded the first award. The first person as awardee was Hubert Humphrey.

Merger of the ADL, Minnesota Jewish Council and Minneapolis Federation Community Relations Committee

As Burton describes it during the early 1970's, it became apparent that the work of three separate Minnesota community organizations involved in community relations, education and the fight against anti-Semitism was not the best use of Jewish community resources. Thus Burton suggested that the organizations be combined into a single organization with an increased budget.

I was selected to lead the merger negotiations. Sam Kaplan represented the federation. After arduous negotiation a merger agreement and new by-laws were agreed upon. Burton requested that I pilot the merger agreement through the ADL National Commission. Burton made the necessary personal contacts with ADL national leadership. The ADL National Commission and the Minneapolis Federation for Jewish Service both approved the merger. The result was establishment of a new organization – the Minnesota Jewish Community Relations Council. The separate ADL office was closed. The first president of the merged JCRC was Marsha Yugend. As a result of my merger activities at the ADL, and on Burton Joseph's recommendation, I was elected to serve on the ADL National Commission. I had served as Chair of the ADL Regional Advisory Board prior to the merger. In 1981,

I was elected to chair the board of the JCRC. I served in that post in 1981 and 1982.

By all accounts the merger was a success. Morton Ryweck was its first Executive Director. However, despite years of success, budget difficulties at the national ADL caused it, in the 1990's, to withdraw from the joint funding arrangement for the JCRC with the Minneapolis Federation for Jewish Service. For several years Stephen Silverfarb served successfully as the executive director of the JCRC. He was succeeded in 2006 by Steven Hunegs, a former president of the JCRC board. Hunegs gave up a successful law practice with his father Richard Hunegs to take on this most important community post.

Relationship with Orville Freeman

Burton Joseph, along with his spouse Geri, had a close relationship with Orville Freeman. This was while Freeman was Minnesota governor and later as the Secretary of Agriculture under presidents Kennedy and Johnson. Despite Freeman's service as Minnesota governor, Freeman had little background in national and international agricultural matters when he was appointed by President Kennedy as Secretary of Agriculture. Burton Joseph's relationship with Freeman allowed Freeman access to Burton's knowledge of the grain business. Freeman was Secretary of Agriculture for eight years.

Early in 1962, Joseph read a story in the *New York Times* about a Russian grain delegation in Ottawa, Canada. The Russians were in Canada to buy grain. Russia had a failure in its grain crop that year due to a drought. Burton describes the New York Times story as mentioning that the Canadians did not have enough grain to export to Russia to take care of the Russians' requirements. The story named the leader of the Russian delegation who was in Canada to buy grain.

This was at a time when the United States had an embargo on grain shipments to the Soviet Union because of the cold war disputes between the United States and the Soviet Union. Despite the embargo, Joseph decided to call the Russian leader and to let him know that he had a relationship with the Secretary of Agriculture. Joseph stated that perhaps they could put together a program where the Russians would consider buying U.S. grain. Joseph states that "I will never forget his first words to me after I explained who I was. He said, "By all means come to Ottawa and bring offerings.""" Joseph then knew that a successful result of shipping American grain to the Soviet Union was possible. This was in early 1963. Joseph called Freeman who at the time was in Duluth visiting on behalf of an export operation of U.S. grain. Joseph told Freeman about the telephone visit he had and the Russian's statement to "bring offerings." Freeman responded, "Let me go talk to President Kennedy, and we will see if we can put together a program for you and a delegation of American grain leadership to go to Ottawa."

Freeman did talk to President Kennedy. Freeman called Joseph back and said, "It is okay to open discussions, but do not sell anything until we discuss in Washington the political consequences of opening trade with the Soviet Union." Joseph agreed. He then called various friends who were leaders of the major companies that would be involved. They included General Mills, Pillsbury, Archer Daniels Midland, Conagra, Cargill and half a dozen other major companies. Joseph organized a group to go and assemble in Ottawa and to meet with the Soviet delegation. They did so and received a very positive response.

Joseph then came back to Minneapolis and called Freeman. He reported, "I think we have a wonderful opportunity to sell grain. They are looking for a huge amount. 28 ½ million tons." Burton describes this as, "This would have been the largest grain export sale in the history of the country." Freeman responded, "We like this. Let me talk to the President. I can't reach him now, but I will as soon as he returns from a political trip to Dallas, Texas." The tragedy of Dallas and President Kennedy's assassination occurred that weekend on that trip to Dallas. They were not able to go forward with the program until Lyndon Johnson had an opportunity, among other immediate requirements of his new presidency, to give Joseph and the others the okay.

Chapter Eighteen

Geri Joseph

No other Jewish woman in Minnesota has had a more varied and successful career than Geraldine (Geri) Joseph.[1] From her first days with the *Minnesota Daily*, the student newspaper at the University of Minnesota; as a reporter for the *Minneapolis Star Tribune*; as a national mental health advocate and as a pathfinding woman in DFL and national politics would be enough to ensure being at the pinnacle of those Minnesota Jewish women who have done it all. When we add being a successful wife and mother, as Ambassador to the Netherlands, and as a board member of leading Minnesota corporations, there isn't much more to write about.

Career in Journalism

Geri Joseph's career as a journalist began with the *Minnesota Daily*. She became manager editor while a student. It was at the *Minnesota Daily* that she had her first exposure to Hubert Humphrey. When she went to work as a reporter for the *Minneapolis Tribune* she wrote stories in the areas of health, welfare and education. Her interest in the mentally ill and mental health programs began with a series she was asked to do for the *Tribune*. The Unitarians had done a study of the mental health hospitals in Minnesota. A local head of the Unitarian church, Reverend Arthur Foot, brought their report to the newspaper. Joseph describes that report as having "…had a lot of very harrowing details in it." Joseph took the report to the *Tribune* city editor Bower Hawthorne. She recommended that the paper do a story on the subject. Hawthorne agreed. He did suggest that Joseph see Governor

176

Luther Youngdahl and describe to him what they wanted to do. They did not want it to be one of those things where you spring "a kind of trap" on the governor and his administration. They wanted the governor's cooperation. At first Governor Youngdahl "…was very apprehensive. He didn't want us to do it. He told me if I pursued this he would have my job. It was a strange Luther Youngdahl, because that was not in character for him." Geri went back to the newspaper and related the conversation to Hawthorne. Hawthorne suggested that they both go over and talk to the governor. They did and told Youngdahl exactly what they wanted to do. They told Youngdahl that they would let him see the articles. He could not prevent them from being run or edit them, but he could see them. They also said that they were going to go in with a photographer into all the mental hospitals. At that point Youngdahl agreed, even though they did not need his approval. Those were public institutions. While action and mental health reforms would require action by the legislature, they did need the support of the governor.

Joseph and photographer Arthur Hager went into all of the state hospitals. She said, "We lived in them. We ate in them. They were true horrors. They were just awful. They had been stripped of everything, because after the war the economy was not that great. I mean people slept on bare mattresses that were just filthy. The people who were in there working as aides were by and large untrained people who just came in off the streets. They probably couldn't have held any other job. It was…for weeks afterwards the clothes that I had worn in these hospitals, I couldn't get the smell out of them. I turned my head, I could smell it in my hair. It was quite an experience. And I was a lot younger. I had never been through anything like that. Some of the hospitals even from the outside looked like dungeons. And many people had been there for so long that they had lost all contact with friends and family. They had just been there for their whole lives."

So much momentum was created as a result of the mental health series that the legislature the following year appropriated a significant amount of money to deal with the problems that

Joseph and the newspaper found. That activity spurred Joseph to join the Mental Health Association of Minnesota. She rose in that organization at the national level to be elected the Mental Health Association's national president. Her job as national president took her to a number of states. She spoke to state legislators. She did organizational fundraising.

Joseph's activity with the Mental Health Association greatly influenced her attitude toward politics. She states, "…that there is no way you can really get very much done without some political access. Whether it is going to the legislature. Whether it is persuading people to vote for this one or that one."

An unusual result of her activities in mental health was an award which she received from Sigma Delta Chi, the men's journalism fraternity. They had apparently never given an award to a woman. At the award ceremony she experienced what must have been a feeling that would have been shared by other women who had succeeded in what was then a men's world. At an award ceremony at the Waldorf Hotel in New York City, Joseph describes how she felt as being the only woman. She states that she, "…had to walk all around this enormous room to get to the podium where they were giving this award. You almost feel that it is not really you, Geri Joseph, a person. It is really some Geri Joseph who is playing a role. That really is the feeling you have." Of course, it was a very good role.

Career in Politics

Joseph's first exposure to the political dynamo that became a great Minnesota and national political leader came while she was managing editor at the *Minnesota Daily*. Hubert Humphrey came to the Daily office when he was running for mayor of Minneapolis. He seated himself and proceeded to talk about a whole range of subjects. This included the fact that there was no housing on campus for the returning veterans who were going to the university. Humphrey laid out for Joseph and others an editorial campaign urging the university to build housing on campus. It resulted in quonset hut housing.

Joseph underscores the importance of stating the tremendous appeal Humphrey had to those in that campus small office. She said that within minutes of his being there the news got around the entire building, Murphy Hall, the journalism building. It resulted in an absolutely packed office to hear Humphrey. She states that Humphrey, "… was very compelling. He was talking without notes, as he often did, and there was something really magnetic about him, something very exciting."

In 1953, after Geri and Burton Joseph were married, Geri left the Minneapolis Tribune. She did some freelance writing for them. In 1956, Eugenie Anderson of Red Wing, who was one of the most outstanding women in Minnesota DFL politics at the time, urged Geri to become the chairwoman of the Volunteers for Adlai Stevenson. She agreed to do so. That role was her first introduction to a political campaign. The DFL was split in 1956 between the forces supporting Illinois Governor Adlai Stevenson for the Democratic nomination for president and those supporting Tennessee Senator Estes Kefauver. As she and others campaigned through the state on behalf of Stevenson, she became aware about how tough it would be to sell Stevenson to Minnesota voters. Stevenson was an intellectual and a wonderful speaker, but he did not have the kind of personal appeal that Humphrey had. Stevenson really appealed, as Joseph put it, "to your head, and not particularly to your emotions. He couldn't grab you the way Humphrey grabbed you. But he was very thoughtful." Kefauver defeated Stevenson in that 1956 DFL presidential primary. Stevenson went on to capture the Democratic nomination for president. He lost to Eisenhower in the November election.

The 1960 Presidential Primary Campaign

By 1960, Geri Joseph had gone from chairwoman of the state DFL party in 1958 to the committeewoman representing the Minnesota DFL on the Democratic National Committee. Her male counterpart was 8th District Congressman John Blatnik. In 1959, Joseph's political relationship with Humphrey had expanded. That year Humphrey asked Joseph and several others to go with him out to the west coast to test the waters for his 1960 run for the presidency. Joseph traveled to Seattle, Oregon and California with Humphrey. In 1960, Joseph was very much involved on behalf of Humphrey's candidacy for the Democratic nomination. She traveled with Humphrey in the presidential primary campaign in Wisconsin. While Humphrey lost that primary election to John F. Kennedy, Humphrey told these insiders that because he had picked up the western part of Wisconsin that it was something of a victory considering the forces he had been up against with the money and the Kennedy family.

Joseph, Humphrey's administrative assistant Bill Connell, his press secretary Norman Sherman, Pat O'Connor, Gerald Heaney, Eugene Foley and Muriel Humphrey were gathered in the Schroeder Hotel in Milwaukee on primary night. They went around the room to see how each felt about whether Humphrey should go into the primary election campaign in West Virginia. No one said yes. They were already in debt. They didn't have the money to go into that primary. They knew that the Kennedys had the resources to spend much money there. Joseph recalls that there was even talk of how the Kennedys were giving out dollar bills folded in matchbooks to the people who were of some influence at the very local level in West Virginia. However, Humphrey was "feeling very triumphant, even though he had lost."

While they were commiserating over Humphrey's loss in the Wisconsin primary, there was a knock on the door. There was a phone call from the hotel desk telling them that Bobby Kennedy was coming up. He came in. Joseph describes Bobby Kennedy as "full of happy, he was happy, and Hubert was right by the door." Bobby Kennedy came in. He shook Humphrey's hand and urged him to come over to their headquarters. Joseph describes a "dead silence in the room." Muriel Humphrey was standing next to her, and she was absolutely shaking. After some exchange between Bobby Kennedy and Hubert, Hubert agreed to come over. After Kennedy left, Muriel Humphrey "just about hit the ceiling." Muriel said, "I am not going. I am not going in there." Humphrey then said, "Geri, you come along, and Muriel just drive in the car with me. Geri you come along, and then you can bring Muriel back. And I will go in." That is what they did. Joseph describes it as a "very, very depressing time."

The 1960 Democratic National Convention was in Los Angeles. I was elected a delegate to that convention. As national committee members, Geri Joseph and John Blatnik were delegates to the convention. Blatnik and Joseph were asked by Walter Ruether, the head of the United Automobile Workers Union, and Arthur Goldberg, who was the union's legal counsel, if they could meet with them. This was during a confusing and contentious time at the convention. Governor Freeman was going to be one of the nominators of Jack Kennedy for president. Gene McCarthy was going to be nominating Adlai Stevenson. For the most part, the Minnesota delegation was going to stick with Humphrey who was still a candidate for the nomination despite the probability that Kennedy had the votes for the nomination. Ruether and Goldberg met with Joseph and Blatnik. Joseph states that Ruether and Goldberg told them that the UAW, a large and powerful union, was not going to stick with Humphrey. Instead they were going to support Kennedy, because they thought Kennedy could win, and that Humphrey could not. While both Blatnik and Joseph were very upset, Blatnik was calmer than Joseph. Joseph was furious. She said to Ruether and Goldberg, "So that is what Humphrey gets for carrying water for you guys. You are simply going to abandon him?" As they were all leaving the room, Joseph stayed kind of behind. She describes herself as being "so furious I could have gone right through the ceiling." Arthur Goldberg came back and said, "Geri, you know if you are going to be in politics you have to understand that these are the kinds of things that happen. They are cruel things, but they are what happens." Joseph replied, "Well, thanks for telling me that. I will never forget it."

The Minnesota delegation never got to vote for the presidential nomination. Kennedy had already been nominated by acclamation before Minnesota ever got to cast its vote. The Minnesota delegation stuck with Humphrey to the end.

After the convention had nominated Kennedy for president, Geri and others were with Humphrey in his suite. There was a

knock on the door. It was Bobby Kennedy. He came in and confronted Humphrey. Joseph states, "He (Bobby Kennedy) berated
Humphrey up one side and down the other. Told him that there
would be repercussions from this. He would never have any more
authority." Joseph describes the scene as being "just horrible."

The confrontation between Kennedy and Humphrey had
occurred in Humphrey's bedroom. Humphrey said, "Did you hear
that?"

Joseph had heard it. Humphrey walked her over to the window. He was quite depressed, which was unusual for Humphrey.
Humphrey said to Geri, "I don't know, does that really mean the
end of my influence in the Senate?" Humphrey went on just kind
of talking to himself. He said, "I can still work in the Senate. John
Kennedy will need me. And I will be there. I will be there for
him." Joseph describes her thoughts at the time as being "what
an incredible guy" Humphrey was. People used to criticize Humphrey because he never held a grudge. He just didn't have that
ability to really drive the knife in when he could have. Joseph said
she told Humphrey at a later time, while they were having lunch
at his Senate office, "How can you be like this. How can you never
have it in for anybody who has really harmed you?" Humphrey's
response was something that really struck Joseph. He said, "Geri,
there are a lot of things that I want to do in my life. If I were to
stay angry, if I were hold to grudges, where I would get the energy
to do all these other things?"

The 1968 Presidential Election

Joseph was closely involved in the Humphrey campaign for
the presidency in 1968. One of the key decisions facing Humphrey in that campaign was whether he should reject the Viet
Nam policies of President Lyndon Johnson. Joseph says that
there were many who advised Humphrey to disassociate himself
from Johnson and Johnson's Viet Nam policies. These included
Larry O'Brien the chair of the Democratic National Committee.
O'Brien is described as being quite upset with Humphrey because

of Humphrey's refusal to disassociate himself from Johnson. Joseph's observation provided a key to Humphrey and his philosophy. Humphrey was loyal. It was not loyalty to Johnson the man, but for the office of the President. Humphrey felt very keenly that as the Vice President, he could not turn on the person who was in that office unless that person had committed some kind of crime.

Reflections on Humphrey as President

Joseph reflected on what kind of president she believed Hubert Humphrey would have been had he been elected in 1968. Several questions were present. Would he have had really strong people around him? Could he have bypassed them? Could he have somehow just seen his own way clear to either not have those people as close advisors, or really not have them around at all?

Joseph believes that "Humphrey was a very adaptable guy." He was able to take an idea from someone else and make it his own. He was "very creative." Joseph believes that Humphrey "could have done much better in the international field." Humphrey had a real feeling for international affairs and economics. She believes that he "…would have been a good president." He would have been "a president who made people feel this was really their government." When Joseph was asked as to whether she would have been in Humphrey's cabinet had he been elected president, she said that she just didn't know. Her kids were still young. She didn't know whether the timing was right for that post had she been offered it. She believes that timing for women is perhaps more important than it is for men, particularly because of the age of their children and family responsibilities.

Appointment as Ambassador to the Netherlands

At the time that Fritz Mondale became Vice President in 1975, things were different in the Joseph family. Her children were all grown and had families of their own. Nevertheless, when Mondale called her and asked her if she would be interested in being an ambassador, she says that she "was totally taken aback." She didn't believe in growing up that she was going to be an ambassador. She always figured that ambassadors came from service in the State Department or in the Foreign Services. Notwithstanding her indecision, she acknowledged that she might be interested. She never thought that it would happen. About a month and a half later Mondale called her back. She states, "Fritz called, I was down in the basement ironing and it is Fritz on the phone, and he says, "Geri, congratulations, Madame Ambassador.""

At first Joseph reflects that she was terrified at the prospect. She would be alone in the Netherlands. Burton had his company to run and was still involved in the Anti-Defamation League. He would be able to come over perhaps every several months. She would miss her kids and their families. Most importantly, she really did not know what an ambassador's duties were. On a personal level Burton was pretty upset with her, because he had never made a meal in his life up to that time. Geri was concerned as to who was going to take care of him. His response was that he would buy a microwave. He would stay here with the family and run his business.

One of the things that influenced Joseph to accept the ambassadorship was that she had been doing a lot of writing about the importance of women accepting some of these political responsibilities. To reach out "…reach out for the higher rungs." She thought, "My God, how can I not do it now." Joseph describes her service as ambassador to the Netherlands as "the highlight for me of all the different things I have done."

Joseph did not speak the Dutch language at the time she was appointed. She learned the language while she was ambassador. She was assisted in her ambassadorial duties by about 250 people in the embassy. They included Foreign Service career people, military officers, and people from the drug enforcement administration. From the outset she told the assembled staff that she needed them more than they needed her. It was a successful relationship with the staff. They did everything to make her tenure successful.

She finally realized that she could deal with all of the challenges presented by being an ambassador. It was really the culmination of all of her previous experiences in journalism, service on corporate boards, and her efforts in politics.

Geri Joseph was the first woman ambassador to the Netherlands. That meant that she was in the spotlight with the Dutch people and the Dutch government. She was acutely aware that she was in a job where there were very few women.

Joseph's service as ambassador was not without its threats and harrowing experiences. She had become close with the Israeli Ambassador to the Netherlands. He was assassinated in London. There were threats to kidnap her as the American Ambassador. She had Dutch security people with machine guns and all of the rest of security devices for several months. The stress of the position affected her health. It took her a year to recover after she came back to Minnesota. She left her post with a tremendous respect for the career Foreign Service people.

On Being Jewish in Politics

In all her varied careers in politics Joseph never encountered any problem in being Jewish. She was never confronted in any nasty way about that. Whatever private thoughts individuals may have had on the subject of her religion, people always kept it to themselves. She never ran into overt signs of discrimination in politics. She believes that this was a wonderful thing. She believes that it may have well been there, but if it was she personally never encountered it.

Reflections on Eugenie Anderson and Women in Politics

Eugenie Anderson of Red Wing was the other woman ambassador from Minnesota. She was appointed by President Truman as the Ambassador to Denmark. Anderson was the first woman ambassador. She was a mentor to Geri Joseph as well as to myself. I was the assistant attorney general assigned to the Fair Employment

Practices Commission which Anderson chaired. Joseph says that Eugenie Anderson, "had a special way about her. She had a rather queenly manner about her. She was very sensitive. She knew a lot about issues and could explain them. Women were very devoted to her." As with many others, Anderson who was a wonderful pianist having studied at the Julliard, had come under Hubert Humphrey's spell. Anderson was very devoted to Humphrey. She was a key advisor to him at a time when, as Joseph puts it, "women were pretty much all behind the scenes in politics in Minnesota and elsewhere." At that time women did what she called the "grunt work of politics. They helped organizing meetings, and put together agendas. They ran the offices and sent out the mailings. They were rarely out front, no matter how smart they were."

The 1958 Campaign Anderson versus McCarthy

In 1958, Eugenie Anderson and Congressman Eugene McCarthy contested for the DFL nomination for U.S. Senator. Joseph observes that there were many women, as well as some men, who were involved and worked hard in the Anderson campaign. They all worked very hard on behalf of Anderson who campaigned all over the state. Joseph believes that Anderson felt that she had a real chance at winning. She observes that perhaps this was kind of a "trap" for women candidates, because nobody wants to hurt their feelings or offend them. Therefore, everyone may say that they are for you and encourage you to win despite their having other reservations on the subject. Unfortunately Hubert Humphrey, with whom Eugenie Anderson had been very close, did not take a position on the Anderson-McCarthy contest. Orville and Jane Freeman supported Anderson. Joseph observes that Jane Freeman was a person in politics in her own right and could have been elected governor or U.S. senator had she run. When McCarthy was successful and was ultimately elected to the senate seat, Eugenie Anderson was "very hurt by this. It took her a long time to recover." Joseph says that Anderson felt a sense of betrayal.

Joseph reflects on the evolution of the role of women in politics and in elective office in Minnesota. When Eugenie Anderson ran in the late 1950's, Minnesota and the DFL Party were not quite ready to view the role of a woman as being ready for elective office. Even when women such as Joan Growe ran, who had a very good record as Secretary of State and a well-financed campaign for the U.S. Senate, she was still not successful. Joseph reflects that times are changing, and that one can now feel encouraged by the emergence of women as members of the Minnesota legislature and as mayors, council members, and county commissioners. People are now beginning to realize how much influence and power these women elected officials have in the roles in which they now serve. There are now more women in the business world, some of them in "very high positions." On the role of financing women candidates for public office, Joseph states that in the early 1980's, a group of women got together and organized a Minnesota Woman's Campaign Fund. She co-chaired the fund for the first couple of years. Each of the founding members put in $1,000. They then were asked to call ten other people to ask them to contribute. It was very successful. Joseph believes that progress has been made although not as much as she and other women would like.

Joseph on the Current DFL Party and Its Agenda

Joseph describes the feelings of herself as a DFL "oldtimer." She reflects that the DFL Party does not have the same vitality as in prior years. In part it may be because the times with people like Hubert Humphrey were unusual. They were exciting leaders with ideas who wanted to have a role in what was happening in the country. She doesn't see that as happening today with the Minnesota DFL. Perhaps the issues that she and other DFL leaders cared about have been resolved, and the party hasn't found a new agenda for itself.

Part of it may be that we are now living in a different world where international issues have eclipsed the domestic ones. She believes that "you are not going to persuade Iran or North Korea to do what you want them to do just because you want them to do it. There has to be a quid pro quo." Joseph believes that the current administration in Washington has "failed in that terribly." She believes it to be the most "arrogant administration that [she] can recall since [she] has been involved in politics."

Service on Corporate Boards

Geri Joseph was a pathfinder for women in general and Jewish women in particular in her long term service on major corporate boards. Beginning in the early 1970s with her selection to the Board of Northwestern National Bank, she also served on the boards of Northwestern Bell Telephone, Honeywell, Hormel and Twin City Barge Co. Service on each board presented Joseph with an opportunity for service, innovation and promotion of other women to board service.

Joseph describes her service on her first board, that of the Northwestern National Bank, "...as an absolutely fascinating learning experience." There were 24 CEOs on the board and her. She was the only woman. Since everyone knew that she was something of a neophyte that gave her the opportunity to ask some pointed questions that others may have been reluctant to ask. Thus she succeeded in the board adopting for the first time board agendas. The other was orientation sessions for board members. This was particularly important since the issues in the banking industry are unique even to CEOs of other major corporations. When Joseph was selected ambassador to the Netherlands, she was asked for the names of other women who might be appointed to the board. She suggested the late Barbara Stuhler at the University of Minnesota and a Black woman, Reatha Clark King. Both of them were appointed to the board. When Joseph returned from the Netherlands she was asked to come back on the bank board.

Elmer Andersen suggested Joseph for service on the board of the Hormel Company in Austin. The selection for service on the Hormel had a Jewish side to it. Since Hormel was a major producer of pork products, the CEO of the company was concerned as to whether Joseph's being Jewish would interfere with her service on the board. At the meeting with the company CEO, Joseph told a story about how on a family wilderness trip a bear had come into camp and swiped a big package of bacon off a table. She assumed that once the CEO figured that she ate bacon that she would not be anti-Hormel. So they appointed her to that board which she described as a "a great, great experience." She served on that board for approximately 25 years, well past retirement age. The CEOs of Hormel have been very supportive of the Anti-Defamation League. Both Richard Nolton and Joel Johnson were willing to serve as honorees for major fundraising dinners for the ADL.

Joseph admits to some trepidation when asked to serve on corporate boards such as Honeywell which had diverse interests, particularly at the time in computers. She would ask herself a question, "Would I know enough to be a good board member?" She obviously did. With Honeywell her experience was especially significant because it was at the time of the beginning of computers. Also Honeywell had a major international business. Thus the service on the board provided a great learning experience. She also believes that her corporate board experience provided a great learning experience for her about the people who served on these boards. They were your leaders in Minnesota business and industry. Her service also helped break down stereotypes about Jews.

Geri Joseph observes that "the main thing about being on these boards is what you learn, and what you can bring to that board." Also, you can't have people on a board who only say "yes."

You must have people on that board who will ask good questions and will kind of keep the company's toes to the fire. We certainly have seen the consequences of a lot of places where they didn't do that."

As Geri Joseph retired from her service on these major corporate boards, she has been succeeded by another very capable Minnesota Jewish woman Luella Goldberg. Several years ago Dick Nolton of Hormel asked Joseph if she knew Luella Goldberg, and

what did she think about the possibility of bringing another woman onto the board. Joseph had been really going after them about
it being time that they should have another woman on the board.
Nolton and Joseph met with Luella Goldberg to see if Goldberg
was interested. They selected her to the board. She and Joseph
served on the Hormel board at the same time. Goldberg has gone
on to service on other major corporate boards including that of
ING. ING is a major international insurance company.

Geri Joseph and the University of Minnesota

G eri Joseph has had a longtime positive relationship with
the University of Minnesota. When she returned from the
Netherlands, Joseph went to work at the Humphrey Institute. She
first worked with Harlan Cleveland. Muriel Humphrey had called
Joseph in The Hague in the Netherlands asking her if she could
be in London for a fundraising event for the Humphrey Institute.
Geri joined Muriel Humphrey at that event. At that point Harlan
Cleveland, who was going to be the first director of the Humphrey Institute, asked her to come and see him when she returned
from Holland. He would like to have her affiliate and work at the
Institute.

Later, in about 1984, Joseph was named a Senior Fellow at the
Humphrey Institute. She taught classes together with Cleveland
on successful international institutions. She also taught a class on
"What Works" in international institutions. Joseph also worked
with Fritz Mondale in setting up the very successful Mondale
Forum. She is extremely proud of her work at the Humphrey
Institute, because it involved young people that they assumed
would be moving out into society and becoming leaders in their
various fields.

Joseph's desire is that the Humphrey Institute "can really
become one of the very top public affairs schools in the country."
She believes that Hubert Humphrey and the state of Minnesota
deserve that. Geri Joseph currently serves on the Humphrey Institute Advisory Board.

Chapter Nineteen

Arthur Naftalin

A rthur Naftalin, former Mayor of Minneapolis, passed away at age 88, on May 16, 2005. At the celebration of his life appropriately held at the Humphrey Institute Atrium, former Vice President Fritz Mondale described Naftalin as a "scholar/politician." Indeed Naftalin combined the positive attributes of a college professor of political science and public administration with vast political experience dating back through his days as a student at the University of Minnesota. It extended through service in a key role in the administration of Governor Orville L. Freeman.

Naftalin became Minneapolis Mayor in 1961. He served through 1969. Before embarking on his academic and political careers Naftalin was a journalist. After serving as Managing Editor of the *Minnesota Daily* in 1938-1939, he was a reporter for the *Minneapolis Tribune*. Naftalin, a native of Fargo, North Dakota, began a career of political activism on the university campus in the 1930's. He was a contemporary of campus political activists such as Eric Severeid; Richard Scammon, "who later headed the U.S. Census Bureau;" Earl Larson, who became a U.S. District Court Judge; and Lee Loevinger, "who became a Minnesota (state) Supreme Court Justice and Federal Communications Commissioner;". They all belonged to a campus non-Greek fraternity called the Jacobins, a name derived from the political group in the French Revolution known for extreme egalitarianism."[1]

Naftalin was an early supporter of Hubert H. Humphrey. This led him to be one of the founders of the merged DFL Party. Naftalin's Ph.D. thesis was "A History of the Farmer-Labor Party in Minnesota."[2] When Humphrey was elected Mayor of Minneapolis he appointed Naftalin as his secretary. I first met Arthur Naftalin in 1954, in a course Naftalin taught at the university on politics and public affairs. Naftalin's teaching assistant in that course was North Minneapolis native Earl Cheit. Cheit went on to become a distinguished professor and Vice Chancellor at the University of California, Berkeley.

When Orville Freeman was elected governor in 1954, he was quick to appoint Naftalin as his Commissioner of Administration. Commissioner of Administration was a key position in state government. In memorializing Naftalin at the celebration of his life, Freeman's widow, Jane Freeman, described the Commissioner of Administration as "like deputy governor." As Commissioner of Administration Naftalin was a close advisor to Freeman. Most importantly, he kept the wheels of state government running smoothly while the governor attended to the many other issues facing him in that office. With John F. Kennedy's election as President Orville Freeman went to Washington as Secretary of Agriculture. Naftalin had an opportunity to go to Washington and serve in the Kennedy administration. He turned down that opportunity to remain in Minnesota.

As Mayor of Minneapolis Naftalin was a civil rights supporter and activist. He participated in the 1963 march on Washington where the Reverend Martin Luther King, Jr. delivered his famous speech. Among the participants in that March was Max Fallek. Fallek represented Temple Israel. Naftalin was Mayor during the infamous riots on Plymouth Avenue. His leadership and style helped defuse the confrontations between the communities. Naftalin, working together with prominent Minneapolis business and civic leaders, was instrumental in forming the Minneapolis Urban Coalition. There were a number of other prominent members of the Jewish community who were involved with the Urban Coalition. They included Rabbi Max Shapiro of Temple Israel and Beth El Synagogue's Rabbi Kassel Abelson. Real estate developer Ray Harris and I served on the Urban Coalition Housing Taskforce.

As mayor Naftalin spearheaded the organization and development of the Minneapolis Civil Rights Commission. The formation of the Metropolitan Council with Naftalin's participation helped bridge the gap between Minneapolis and the suburbs. A participant at the celebration of his life was Marilyn Gorlin, one-time Vice Chair of the Minnesota DFL. She described Naftalin's efforts through the Met Council to eradicate mosquitoes. Gorlin, a Golden Valley resident, recalled how Naftalin said that mosquitoes cannot tell the difference between Minneapolis and Golden Valley. There must be joint efforts to stop their breeding and proliferation.

Naftalin's ambition to achieve higher public office met with what Jane Freeman described as "unfulfilled promise." In 1966, he made an unsuccessful bid for DFL endorsement as lieutenant governor on the Sandy Keith ticket. Naftalin's political ambitions were cut short by unsuccessful vocal chord surgery which left him with an impaired speaking voice. He did continue as a Professor of Public Affairs at the University. He produced and hosted a weekly public affairs program on public television entitled "Minnesota Issues." For public television he also produced a series of documentaries on Minnesota governors. Naftalin was a founder of the Minneapolis Citizens League and of the Minnesota chapter of the Americans for Democratic Action. These organizations encourage citizen participation in public affairs.

After serving as mayor Naftalin was active as a spokesman for the Minneapolis Friends of Public Education. This organization, among other things, was known for its opposition to the school voucher movement. In 1969, Naftalin was awarded an honorary Doctor of Laws degree from the University of North Dakota. In 1986, he retired as a Professor of Public Affairs from the university. Naftalin was married for 63 years to Frances, who is not Jewish. Art was always conscious of his Jewish heritage. He was a member of Temple Israel. Art and Frances raised two sons and one daughter. The eulogy delivered by their son Mark made it clear that Jewish tradition had a significant presence in the Naftalin household.

Chapter Twenty

Hubert Humphrey's Third Quest for President

In 1976, Hubert Humphrey had returned to his seat in the U.S. Senate. He was determined to make his third (and last) effort to win the presidency. His forces needed to secure the selection of Humphrey pledged delegates to the national convention to be held in Miami, Florida. While delegates had been selected in the individual congressional districts, a bloc of delegates was to be chosen by the DFL State Convention convening in Rochester. I was selected to be the co-floor leader of the Humphrey forces. I served with Terry Montgomery, chief of staff to Governor Rudy Perpich.

It was a cantankerous convention. Spirits were high, caused in part by the emergence of a new group of gay DFL delegates who were identified by their purple tee shirts. There was also a vigorous group of feminists. It was among the most difficult political tasks I had ever undertaken. I had previously chaired a series of DFL congressional district and state conventions. The floor leader's role at that convention involved constant contact with delegates, involvement in vocal floor fights, and parliamentary skirmishes. At the end of the convention I was physically exhausted. I also lost my voice from a traumatic nodule on my vocal chords. It required surgery which was successful.

The Humphrey forces were only partially successful at the state convention. But Humphrey went on to keep himself in the race at the Miami convention, although with little apparent hope of success. Following the state convention Humphrey offered me an opportunity to serve on the National Democratic Party Platform Committee at the Miami convention. A combination of my voice problems, and the demands of my law practice, caused me to turn down the offer. This was a rejection I was later to regret.

As events turned out, I ended up at the Miami convention, although in an unexpected role. As a Minnesota legislative lobbyist I represented a coalition of individuals and groups interested in securing appropriations at the federal and state levels for childcare facilities and programs. These included funding for food programs for children in daycare facilities. There was a proposal in the Congress for a significant appropriation. It involved federal money for the states, including Minnesota. Our state was in the forefront of the childcare movement.

My clients requested I go to Miami and to attempt to meet with the key congressional leaders who were considering the appropriation. Apparently the childcare lobbyists on Capitol Hill had been unsuccessful in dislodging the funding measure from the House Appropriations Committee. That committee was chaired by Congressman Wilbur Mills of Arkansas. I knew that making contact with Mills would be very difficult. I realized that the best bet would be to try to get on to the floor of the convention. There is a good deal of free time at a national convention during lengthy speeches and debates. However, I did not have a floor pass which was necessary for access to the convention delegates.

Even without guaranteed access, I flew to Miami in hopes of finding a way to make the necessary contacts. On arrival I reached Minnesota DFL Chairman Richard "Dick" Moe. Moe was a longtime friend dating back to the early 1960's. Moe later became the top aide to Vice President Fritz Mondale and also to President Jimmy Carter. He secured me a floor pass. Congressman Don Fraser, himself deeply interested in daycare legislation, suggested that the key to access to Mills was through the chair of the Arkansas convention delegation. That was Arkansas Governor and later U.S. Senator Dale Bumpers. Fraser also suggested a contact with Georgia Governor Jimmy Carter.

The first approach was to Jimmy Carter. This was eminently unsuccessful despite my dropping Fraser's and other names. Carter fixed me with those cold blue eyes. He shrugged me off without listening to my story. The result was different with Governor Bumpers. He was most gracious. Since chairman Mills was not on the floor of the convention at the time, Governor Bumpers suggested that the best time to meet with him would be following a caucus of the Arkansas delegation. It was to be held at their hotel the next morning. He suggested the time I should show up and simply wait until the caucus adjourned and Mills exited. Bumpers said that he would make a contact with Chairman Mills to set the stage.

The next morning I promptly arrived at the hotel and waited patiently until the caucus adjourned. Mills was well known through the extensive publicity he had received in his long and successful position in Congress. I approached him when the caucus adjourned and introduced myself. Mills was very gracious. Obviously, Bumpers had paved the way. Mills explained the difficulties in getting significant appropriations through his committee even for what most might consider valuable projects. While he made no firm commitment, he indicated that he would do what he could to see that an appropriate level of money was approved for daycare programs. On my return to Minnesota I made a report to my clients. We hoped for the best. Our hopes were partially realized when the committee and the Congress did approve a proposal, although it was more modest than we would have liked.

Chapter Twenty-one

Hubert Humphrey's Last Hurrah

The final episode in my long family and personal relationship with Hubert Humphrey came in a very sad but meaningful way. As a University of Minnesota Regent I was invited to attend a testimonial dinner in Washington, D.C. for Senator Humphrey. Humphrey was stricken with terminal cancer. It was to be his last major public appearance. Carolyn and I were joined in the trip by Regent David Utz, a renowned Mayo Clinic urologist, and his wife Ginny.

The dinner was preceded by a reception at the residence of Vice President Fritz and Joan Mondale. The residence was a stately building in an exclusive Washington neighborhood surrounded by foreign embassies. Joan Mondale was known affectionately as "Joan of Art." She had secured notable works of art which were featured prominently throughout the residence. Attending the reception and dinner were a long list of political notables. They were of both political parties. They included a number of national television and newspaper correspondents and columnists.

For the Minnesotans the "people watching" was outstanding. One situation occurred which is still vivid in my memory some 30 years later. While we were standing with the Utz's and enjoying the scene, in walked Republican Senator John Warner of Virginia and his then wife Elizabeth Taylor. Taylor was stunning. She wore the Hope Diamond given to her by Richard Burton. Her violet eyes were absolutely luminous. All four of us just stood there in awe. What was interesting was that Senator

Warner left Elizabeth Taylor standing by herself while he went off apparently to do some politicking.

The scene reminded me of what Governor Karl Rolvaag had done to his spouse at the Polish National Alliance Hall in Minneapolis many years earlier. The Utzs and the Latzs quietly debated among themselves whether we should approach Elizabeth Taylor and introduce ourselves. The men were too shy to do so. Therefore, Carolyn and Ginny took it upon themselves to make the approach. They walked across the room and introduced themselves to Taylor. After a few moments they motioned Dr. Utz and I to come over. We introduced ourselves. Taylor was most gracious. It was clear that she was very uncomfortable in her role as the spouse of a politician. She was just not used to being left to fend for herself in this kind of social scene. It was not long afterwards that she sought and obtained a divorce from Senator Warner.

The dinner itself was a very emotional experience. We were seated with Republican U.S. Senator from Pennsylvania Richard Schweiker. He was also very gracious and interesting. He told us how Hubert Humphrey's personality had bridged across the otherwise vast gulf between the Republicans and Democrats in the U.S. Senate. Everyone present knew that Humphrey was dying. His gaunt appearance told everything. He gave a very emotional farewell speech. The evening concluded with Australian singer Helen Reddy singing "You and Me Against the World." There was not a dry eye in the entire house.

Chapter Twenty-two

Anti-Semitism Intrudes in Selection of University President

My election as a University Regent came about through unusual circumstances. There had not been a Jewish member of the board since 1934, when George B. Leonard was appointed by Governor Floyd B. Olson. In 1974, the Regents were required to select a new university president to succeed the retiring Malcolm Moos. One of the candidates to succeed Moos as president was Jewish. He was David Saxon, Chancellor at the University of California Los Angeles. In response to questions by Regent L.J. Lee of Bagley, Saxon said he was a non-observant Jew. Lee was a former DFL State Representative. I served with him in the Minnesota House during the 1960's.

According to news reports, Lee raised the question about Saxon's lack of observance or commitment as a Jew. Lee questioned whether the university was ready for a person who did not have sufficient religious identification or commitment to observe his faith's religious practices. Disputes arose as to the full thrust and meaning of Lee's remarks. This led to a Minnesota Senate investigation of the presidential selection process. In September, 1974, the chairman of the Senate Education Committee, Senator Jerome Hughes appointed a special subcommittee "to investigate the process by which a new president had been selected for the University of Minnesota."[1] The subcommittee consisted of three DFLers - senators Hughes; Hubert H. "Skip" Humphrey of New Hope, Plymouth and Crystal; B. Robert "Bob" Lewis of St. Louis Park, and Republicans Joseph O'Neill of St. Paul and Robert Dunn of Princeton.

Each of the subcommittee members had achieved a solid reputation in and out of the senate for their experience, integrity and insight. At the time the DFL had majority control of the senate. Senator Nicholas Coleman was the Senate Majority Leader. The charge to the subcommittee was expressed by Senator Hughes in a letter to each subcommittee member. Senator Hughes wrote, "that the interest was legitimate because of the senate's customary participation in the selection of the regents, "…it is imperative that the legislature monitor the actions of those it appoints during their term in office." Hughes went on that, "the subcommittee was to serve as a vehicle for the senate's expression of concern over the highly publicized allegations of impropriety in the Presidential selection process."[2]

This subcommittee "Charge" was significant beyond the issue of the alleged improprieties in the presidential selection process. It was the first time in memory that any body of the legislature had conducted an investigation of the internal workings and processes of the Board of Regents and its members.

The subcommittee held six meetings. Unfortunately, it was "not deemed necessary that testimony be taken under oath."[3] The subcommittee met from September 1974 through January 1975. It took testimony from Regents Elmer Andersen (Regents' Chair), Neil Sherburne, Lauris Krenik, Wenda Moore, Lester Malkerson, Loanne Thrane, L. J. Lee, and Katherine Vander Kooi. The subcommittee also took testimony from Senator Coleman and professor Warren Ibele. There was a meeting reserved for public testimony. The only witness to appear was professor Irwin Marquit.

The subcommittee report set forth facts that clearly indicated the significant involvement of the question of religion, and Saxon's religious affiliation or connections, in the interview and selection processes. Both the University Charter and Minnesota laws against discrimination prohibit inquiries into the religion or religious affiliation of any prospective employee, whether it be in a public institution or in the private sector. Yet the senate inquiries disclosed that "the religions of some of the candidates were listed in their dossiers and some were not."[4] Apparently Dr.

Saxon's dossier did not disclose his religion. Regent L. J. Lee thus inquired as to Saxon's religious affiliation. Professor Warren Ibele, in a telephone conversation with Regent Sherburne, "expressed his dismay, displeasure and disappointment that this [religious] issue had been raised and stated that the issue was not relevant or significant from the viewpoint of the faculty and the student body."[5] Regent Lee testified before the subcommittee that Regent Sherburne never brought these faculty objections to his attention.[6] Whether any such communication would have caused Lee or other Regents to end their injection of religion into the selection process is unknown. In any event, at a meeting of the Board of Regents on February 7, 1974, attended by all but one regent, Regent Lee "…again mentioned that the religious affiliations of the nominees were included in some of the dossiers but not in others."[7] None of the regents present apparently objected to this comment.

The references to religion or religious affiliations did not end with that February 7 meeting. It continued when a five person recruiting team visited Dr. Saxon in Los Angeles. Regents Andersen, Sherburne and Krenik and professors Krislov and Heller were present at this meeting, the primary mission of which was "…to investigate and recruit Dr. Saxon and to interest him in the presidency of the University."[8]

During this visit with Dr. Saxon, Regent Krenik "questioned Dr. Saxon about his political activities, community activities, hobbies and *religious* activities."[9] In defense of his questions, Regent Krenik stated to the subcommittee that he felt "that it was relevant in a state like Minnesota also to ask about participation in *formal* religious activities."[10] While Dr. Saxon told the subcommittee in a letter "that his religious views" were never solicited during the screening process, in my opinion the inquiry about "formal religious activities" is simply a backdoor means by which the person's religion is to be discovered by the prospective employer. When one discloses "religious activities," one cannot but disclose the person's "religious affiliation." What continues to be distressing is that the two other regents present at the meeting with Dr. Saxon did not raise any objection to Krenik's questions. While the reason may be that they did not want to show disagreement among regents during a recruiting visit, there is no evidence that either regent spoke to Regent Krenik at a later time about the impropriety of his question.

It was up to a Jewish faculty member, Professor Samuel Krislov, to raise objections to the Krenik questioning. Upon his return from California, professor Krislov "… communicated to the University Consultative Committee that he was unhappy and displeased that Regent Krenik had raised the question of Dr. Saxon's religious affiliation or preference."[11] Krislov communicated to the committee that he felt it was inappropriate and contributed nothing to the search process. "The consultative committee unanimously agreed that any questioning regarding religion was not only improper, unethical, and out of line, but was also illegal."[12]

At the committee's request, the chairman of the Consultative Committee, Professor Warren Ibele, telephoned Regent Sherburne and "…told him in unequivocal terms that these questions were inappropriate and irrelevant."[13] Regent Sherburne was reported by Professor Ibele to have added that the questions were also possibly illegal. However, in his testimony to the sub-committee Sherburne denied that the question of religion was raised on an outstate trip.[14] These inconsistencies in the testimony were never reconciled. Regent Krenik testified to the subcommittee "…that Regent Sherburne never contacted him to state that a complaint had been made."[15] Thus, yet another opportunity to call a halt to these improper religious inquiries was missed.

The inquiry into information about a candidate's religious views did not end with Saxon. Regent Lee used Regent Loanne Thrane to find out the religion of Dr. Peter Magrath. Regent Thrane determined that Dr. Magrath was an Episcopalian. She then responded to Professor Murphy who had found the information for her, "Oh, thank God!" Dr. Magrath was not questioned about his religion during a trip to Syracuse, New York to interview him.[16] Once the regents knew that Dr. Magrath was an Episcopalian, they did not inquire of him about his "religious activities" as Regent Krenik had of Dr. Saxon.

Regent Lee would not let go of this subject of religion. At a March 7, 1974 meeting of the board, "Regent Lee inquired of the California team if they had information about Dr. Saxon's religion." When the members of the California visiting team indicated they did not have the information, "Regent Lee then said that he understood Dr. Saxon was Jewish." When, finally, Regent Wenda Moore objected and asked "What difference does that make?" Lee replied, "None at all." Regent Lester Malkerson also raised the issue of the legality of such inquiries and stated to the board that "no single ethic should be considered preferable by the board."[17] Regent Vander Kooi then stated that she believed that "...a person have some moral code which he can refer to in making decisions." However, Regent Vander Kooi later testified that "...she did not attempt to find out about the moral code of any candidate other than Dr. Saxon, about whom she had made inquiries "to a mutual acquaintance."[18]

Regent Lee, in his testimony before the subcommittee, attempted to justify his questioning about Saxon's religion by stating that he believed that "religion and nationality are not connected; that he believed that a statement that a person is Jewish was "a statement of nationality and not a statement of religious preference."[19] There is no indication in the subcommittee report that Lee was questioned about how "nationality" and "religious preference" differ. This is borne out in a March 17, 1974 dinner held at the governor's mansion for Dr. and Mrs. Saxon and members of the Board of Regents. During the conversation with the regents and the Saxons, "...Regent Lee said that his constituents would be curious about the religious affiliation of the new president. He asked Dr. Saxon what his religious affiliation was." There was no question as to what Dr. Saxon's "nationality" was as compared to his "religious affiliation." It was then reported there was a "general discussion among those present with Dr. Saxon about the importance of a religious affiliation for any individual selected as president." Whether the question to Dr. Saxon was as to what was his religious affiliation, or as another Regent indicates, the question was "Do you belong to a church?", Dr. Saxon is reported to have replied, "that he was not a joiner, that he was a Jew, but that he did not belong to any church or congregation."[20] Once again Regent Lee sought to explain to the Senate Subcommittee that his question was an attempt to learn about Dr. Saxon's "philosophy." We leave to the reader a determination as to the motivation behind the twists and turns of Regent Lee's explanation for his repeated and reported inquiries about Dr. Saxon's religion.

At one time Dr. Saxon had, in a straw poll of the regents, a majority of seven regents voting to make him the university president. Dr. Magrath had five votes. Four of the five initial votes for Dr. Magrath were from individuals who had raised questions along religious lines, Regents Krenik, Vander Kooi, Thrane and Lee. (There is no indication that the third candidate for University President, Dr. Richard Cyert of Carnegie Mellon University, was ever subject to any inquiry during the interviewing process relating to his religion, philosophy, moral code, or religious activities. Dr. Cyert withdrew his candidacy when the names of the final three candidates were published in the St. Paul Pioneer Press of April 5, 1974.)

Ultimately, Dr. Saxon was not chosen as the university president. The rationale "by nearly all Regents testifying before the subcommittee was that the critical issue in the vote was Dr. Saxon's remarks about the coordinate campuses of the university."[21] Those remarks in addressing a luncheon meeting of the news media, agricultural and business leaders and alumni representatives was that "he believed Minnesota should have only one great university in the major population center of the state, and that the coordinate campuses should be "satellite and subsidiary" to the main university."[22] There is no evidence cited in the subcommittee report of any outcry or criticism of that statement by any of those present at the luncheon meeting or by other constituencies of the university outside of the twin city metropolitan area. Apparently no regent testifying before the subcommittee was asked to provide evidence specifying any such criticism of the Saxon statement.

In fact the Saxon statement expressed what I believe to be

a commonly held view: that while the coordinate campuses are important to the mission of the university, they certainly are not equal in importance to the university's overall mission as compared to the Twin Cities campuses where the largest number of students from all over Minnesota receive their undergraduate and graduate education. Nor is there any evidence that any regent sought any follow up inquiry of Dr. Saxon after his March 18 statement to have him amplify or explain those remarks.

It was not until three weeks later, over the weekend of April 5-8, that Dr. Saxon's seven-to-five majority among the regents was changed to an eight-to-four, two-thirds majority vote of the board for Dr. Magrath. This followed a procedural change suggested by Regent Chairman Andersen that no candidate should be offered the position of president without having a minimum two-third's vote of the board. The change from a majority in favor of Saxon to a two-thirds majority in favor of Magrath was initiated by a change in vote by Regent John Yngve from Saxon to Magrath.[23]

Yngve was my predecessor on the board. Yngve sought reelection to the board but was defeated by me in the 3rd Congressional District Caucus. At no time during my six-year tenure on the board, including my two years as Vice Chairman of the Board, was there ever a debate or discussion over the Saxon remarks about the relationship between the Twin Cities campuses and the coordinate campuses. Both the senate committee's conclusion, and my belief is, that none of the controversy over the candidacy of Dr. Saxon should reflect negatively on either the candidacy or the presidency of Dr. C. Peter Magrath. I worked closely with Dr. Magrath throughout my tenure as a regent, and particularly during my two years as Vice Chairman. I have only the highest respect for Dr. Magrath and his leadership of the university during his time as president.

The final facts found by the senate subcommittee leading up to its conclusions were two-fold: Professor Hyman Berman, then President of the University of Minnesota Federation of Teachers, concluded, based on a conversation that he had with Regent Rauenhorst, "...that anti-Semitism on the part of Regents Lee and Thrane had been a factor in the presidential selection process." Regent Rauenhorst agreed that the conversation took place but told the subcommittee that he remembers nothing about anti-Semitism. He stated that it was not a factor in the deliberations.[24] Senators Nicholas Coleman and George Conzemius testified that at a breakfast meeting Regent Sherburne "...told five state senators that anti-Semitic attitudes on the parts of Regents Lee and Vander Kooi played a part in the presidential selection." Regent Sherburne testified that he did not make such a statement, but that it was possible he had been misunderstood.

In its Conclusions the Subcommittee found that while improper and repeated raising of the religion question during the selection process took place, that, after hearing all the evidence, that anti-Semitism was *not* involved in the final selection.[25] The Committee did find that, "the inappropriate topic of religion was raised repeatedly during the selection process." "There is evidence that information about the religious affiliations, connections, and activities of the candidates was actively sought by at least three of the regents. These questions about a candidate's religion did not accurately address the concerns the regents professed to have, namely, that the individual have a life ethic. Answers to questions about religious affiliation may not accurately reflect an individual's philosophy. By failing to distinguish between philosophy and religious affiliation, the regents failed to obtain the information they sought and inserted the inappropriate and irrelevant criteria of religion into the selection process."[26]

The Subcommittee condemned these inquiries and found that they were in violation not only of the University Charter, but also of other applicable state and federal laws. The Subcommittee strongly condemned the "appearance" of religious discrimination in the selection of a university officer. They found that it is not only actual discrimination based on religious beliefs or the lack thereof that should be condemned as illegal and improper, but on this rightfully sensitive issue the *appearance* of such discrimination in the selection of the university officer should be closely guarded against and strongly condemned.[27] In an important conclusion as it relates to the functioning of the Board of Regents, the report concluded:

"The vote change that took place over the weekend of April 5-8 was conducted in a closed manner over the telephone on a one-to-one basis. There was no opportunity for the free exchange of ideas among the regents, or for the proponents of one candidate to rebut any arguments offered on behalf of another. The final decision thus came in a situation at odds with the board's professed spirit of openness. The meeting on April 8, in which the regents voted to offer Dr. Magrath the presidency, had little relation to the events that transpired in private."[28]

Those who have served on boards, particularly those with relatively small numbers of members, are keenly aware of the importance of the interaction that takes place at a board meeting. The debate and discussion of the merits of an individual's candidacy, or on other important issues, can have a significant effect on the thinking and vote of board members. While the tactic of one-on-one discussions of board members, or private meetings of board members that represent less than a quorum of a committee or board, may be a fairly common tactic to avoid the letter of the open meeting law, or to achieve a consensus in a controversial matter without provoking public discussion and conflict, it does not advance the interests of those to whom the board members, individually and collectively, are to serve. This is true whether it be the legislature, the general public, the faculty, or the students. While the end result in the university presidential search process was a satisfactory one, the way in which it was achieved diminished the credibility of the board members individually and collectively. That process only reinforced the recommendation of the Senate Subcommittee "that the board of regents shall conduct all of its business in *total compliance* with the Minnesota Open Meeting Law."[29]

The subcommittee made another recommendation that pointed out the built in conflict that occurs when regents' membership is along geographic lines. Membership on the board consists of eight persons, each of which represents one of the state's eight congressional districts. The other four members are elected at large. If the ultimate decision to deny the presidency to Dr. Saxon was not based on some regent's views as to his religion, then it must have been Saxon's statement about the relative lesser importance of the coordinate campuses compared to the Twin Cities campuses. The Subcommittee's criticism was that some regents may have viewed their service on the board as "being solely representative of regional or provincial interests." Since "…decisions of the board have broad implications for the welfare of the entire state," the committee felt that a reexamination of this apparent position, by both the legislature and the regents themselves, would seem advisable.[30]

While some of the members of the board in 1974 may have viewed their service as "solely" representative of the regions or geographic areas they were elected to represent, my experience is that few regents are that parochial in their positions. It is accepted within the board that those regents from districts with coordinate campuses will guard with diligence those campuses, whether they be in Duluth, Morris, Crookston, or Waseca. By the same token, regents resident in the 3rd, 4th and 5th Congressional Districts encompassing the Twin Cities and their suburbs will have an inclination to focus on the Twin Cities campuses. A physician, lawyer or dentist board member will be inclined toward the interests of their particular profession in the same way that a farmer, teacher, union business agent, Jew or African American regent would be sensitive toward issues that directly affect them. It is this diversity that makes the board under its current structure representative of the entire State of Minnesota despite occasional lapses as evident in the subcommittee report on the Saxon candidacy. Gubernatorial appointments subject to confirmation by the legislature, or direct election by the voters, are unlikely to resolve issues raised by the diverse interests that are served by the University of Minnesota. They may only compound them.

In a Minority Report, Chairman Lewis made a singular recommendation: "that Regents L. J. Lee and Lauris Krenik not be elected to the board by the 1975 Legislature."[31] Regent Lee did not seek reelection to the board. Regent Krenik continued to

serve. In 1983, Krenik was elected chair of the board. Neil Sherburne had succeeded Elmer Andersen as board chair and served
as chair from 1975 to 1977. The two Republican members of the
Subcommittee issued a separate Minority Report. They strongly
endorsed the committee's report. They stated that the report "...
shows the excellent tool a legislative hearing can provide in determining just what are the facts concerning a *highly notorious* and
potentially damaging series of events to which the public deserves
to know the truth."[32] However, Senators O'Neill and Dunn went
on to criticize Senator Coleman and the DFL Senate majority
leadership in refusing to allow the senate to meet with the House
in Joint Convention in 1973 to elect regents, although the house
was ready and willing to do so. The stated reason by Dunn and
O'Neill "was that two of the four regents (up for election in the
1973 Session) were not members of the DFL Party." This they
described as a "very poor reason" for thwarting "what would have
been the will of the majority of the representatives and senators in
the State of Minnesota."[33] The impasse was solved when Governor
Wendell Anderson appointed four members to the board. Two of
them were Republicans, former Governor Elmer L. Andersen and
Lauris Krenik. At the time it was thought by some that former
Governor Andersen was Coleman's real target.

Another significant conclusion of the Subcommittee related to
discussions that Regent Sherburne, the Chair of the Search Committee, had with members of the "majority caucuses of both houses
of the legislature". The Report stated:

"Regent Sherburne indicated that during the selection process he had discussed selection procedures with members of the
majority caucuses of both houses of the legislature. The political
implications of such an action do not seem appropriate in a process in which the legislature has no direct responsibility."[34]

The "majority caucuses of both houses of the legislature" were
composed of DFL legislators. While the report does not indicate
the purpose for which Sherburne had these discussions, I would
agree with the subcommittee that such discussions, particularly
with members of only one political party, whether they be in

the majority or the minority, would represent an inappropriate involvement of the legislature in the presidential selection process. While obviously there will always be contact between legislators and regents on important issues before the board, a discussion of presidential "selection procedures" should be an internal matter within the board, and perhaps with involvement of the faculty, students and alumni association representatives. There should be no involvement with legislators of either political party. Discussing it with only members of the majority caucuses can only serve to give the impression of political partisanship in the presidential selection process which would not well serve the university or the board.

It should be noted that in an interview with the *Minnesota Daily*, Regent Lee stated that when he appeared before the senate subcommittee he stated that religious considerations had nothing to do with the final presidential choice. He said that he was within his rights to ask such questions, because he was trying to find out as much as he could about the man. Lee defended his record of over 30 years of public service, stating that it was "clear" that he had always been against discrimination of any kind, and that he was "ready to bring suit for libel if there are any further accusations."[35]

In an interview with the *Daily*, Dr. Saxon stated that the regents never asked whether he believed in God or if he ever prayed. "All they asked is whether I belong to any church." Saxon said he told the regents he was not a member of any church.[36]

University Associate Professor of Physics and Astronomy Irwin Marquit was quoted in the *Daily* as telling the Senate Subcommittee that the university's presidential search was influenced by "anti-Semitism." Marquit stated that he learned from another faculty member that Regent George Rauenhorst had said that Regent Lee once commented, "The University of Minnesota was not ready for a Jew as president."

According to the *Daily*, Regent Neil Sherburne also testified that Lee had said the university was not ready for a Jew as president. The *Daily* article went on to state that in the *Minneapolis*

Tribune in September 1974, Regent Chairman Elmer L. Andersen
was quoted as stating that Lee had made a remark that the University of Minnesota was not ready for a Jew as President. When
the *Daily* asked Andersen about the statement in the *Minneapolis
Tribune*, Andersen retracted the statement.[37]

While regents denied that the allegations about the injection of religion into the search process had led to the selection
of Magrath as university president, Majority Leader Nicholas
Coleman was not as sanguine as the regents. He observed, "If not
the only factor, religion was one of the factors that went into the
decision."[38]

In 1975, David Saxon went on to be elevated from Chancellor
of the University of California to its president. In a Resolution to
President David S. Saxon passed by the Assembly of the Academic
Senate on May 25, 1983, the following statement was made:

"For the past eight years the university has had the great fortune
to have been led by a gifted teacher. For the past eight years David
Saxon has made California his classroom, educating governors, legislators, anyone who would listen, and even those who would not,
about the value and meaning of education. He has piloted the university through the worst financial straits it has ever experienced,
fighting the political battles, making the tough decisions, all to protect and nurture the cause of excellence. He has recognized the need
to foster academic excellence at all levels of education in California
and has taken the first steps to coordinate efforts toward the same."

Chapter Twenty-three

Aftermath of the Saxon Controversy

The reports of the statements and questions by Lee and other regents, and the subsequent selection of a president other than Saxon, reverberated strongly in both the Jewish and non-Jewish communities. They raised questions of anti-Semitism. Many wanted to know why no one on the board had strongly criticized Lee and the others for their questions and remarks with their anti-Semitic overtones. There was at that time no Jewish member of the board. There had not been one since the mid-1930's. Members of the Jewish community, and especially the Jewish human relations agencies, began to question why there was no member of the Jewish faith on the governing board of the university.

At the time I was the Chairman of the Regional Advisory Board of the Anti-Defamation League of B'nai B'rith for Minnesota and the Dakotas. As such, I met with Governor Wendy Anderson. Anderson was a former legislative colleague of both myself and Lee in the Minnesota House. This was before Anderson's election to the state senate and then to the governorship in 1970. The purpose of the meeting was to sound out the governor on the way in which the L. J. Lee incident could be dealt with and, as subtext, what could be done to find a Jewish candidate for membership on the Board of Regents. Governor Anderson questioned whether Regent Lee was an anti-Semite. He brought out the Legislative Manual for the 1961 Session of the legislature. He pointed out that then State Representative Lee had been a co-sponsor with me of the bill for the passage of the Minnesota Fair Housing Act. Anderson also pointed out that Lee had been my strong supporter in my efforts to secure the DFL nomination for attorney general.

While these comments were persuasive, on a level of the absence of "personal" anti-Semitism, they did not meet the perception that the comments by Lee and other regents had infected the presidential selection process and resulted in the defeat of the Saxon candidacy. Nor did it diminish the belief that such challenges to a Jew's faith, religious observance or convictions would likely not have occurred or gone without a serious public and private challenge if there had been at least one Jewish member of the Board of Regents at the time.

Since there were no vacancies on the board at that time, Governor Anderson was without power to appoint anyone to the board. However, there were several seats on the board subject to legislative election in the 1975 session. This created the opportunity for at least one Jew to enter the race for election to the board. There were three congressional district seats up for election. Two were in the heavily DFL 5th and 8th Congressional Districts. The 5th encompassed the city of Minneapolis. The 8th was Duluth and the Iron Range. For the first time in political history there were a majority of DFL House and Senate members in the 3rd Congressional District. The 3rd District was made up of a small sliver in north Minneapolis with the balance in Hennepin County, including Golden Valley and St. Louis Park. I was then a resident of Golden Valley. My family and I had moved to the suburbs following my defeat in the 1966 primary election for attorney general. I had not considered running for a seat on the Board of Regents. I was busy raising a family, practicing law and lobbying at the legislature. My clients included the Minnesota Beer Wholesalers Association, a trade association of businesses engaged in selling beer to retailers. I had successfully represented that association for several years. I intended to continue the representation into the future.

The situation changed dramatically with a phone call from Representative John Arlandson who represented Golden Valley and St. Louis Park. Arlandson indicated that he and Representative Pete Petrafeso, who represented the balance of St. Louis Park, were searching for a Jewish candidate to run for regent in the 3rd District. Since the DFL had a majority of legislators in the 3rd District caucus, a DFL majority would be able to recommend a candidate for 3rd Congressional District Regent. That candidate would have a strong potential for success given the legislature's traditional selection process which was to ratify the candidate selected in a congressional district caucus. With the legislative deadlines for nominations to the board fast approaching, I was given only 24 hours to decide whether to throw my hat in the ring. After serious discussion with my spouse Carolyn about reentering the political process, I decided to go for it. I was a graduate of the university and its law school. The Jewish community had strong feelings of support for the university. It was not however a clear shot. There were other DFL candidates. Dr. Fred Lyon, a prominent physician and human rights activist, was supported by Senator Bob Lewis. Attorney Kingsley Holman, a longtime DFL leader from Bloomington, also was a candidate. The Republican incumbent regent, former Representative John Yngve of Plymouth, sought reelection to the board.

The 3rd District DFL House and Senate members met. I succeeded in gaining their support by a margin of one-half vote. The only half vote was supplied by North Minneapolis Senator Carl Kroening. (There were half votes cast because one legislative district covered that part of Minneapolis in the 3rd District and a portion of suburban Hennepin County.) I went on to prevail in the caucus of all 3rd District legislators by a one-vote margin on a straight party-line vote. The recommendation by the 3rd District legislative caucus was then forwarded to the House and Senate Education Committees slated to meet jointly and to make recommendations to the entire legislature.

However, the path to election as a regent was not yet clear. There not only needed to be the Education Committees' recommendation, but the ultimate majority vote at the Joint Convention. A problem with my nomination then surfaced. Senator Nick Coleman, a DFLer and Senate Majority Leader, publicly stated that he could not support the election as a University Regent of a "beer industry lobbyist." This represented a major obstacle to my election. Coleman was a popular and effective leader. He possessed significant influence with his colleagues. Given his public statements over the L. J. Lee incident, one could have expected his support for a Jewish candidate. I had a good relationship with Coleman during my service in the legislature. We had served together on the Steering Committee of DFL legislators during the term of Governor Rolvaag.

I and my supporters were thus mystified by Coleman's opposition. The real reason for Coleman's opposition has never before been publicly stated. It went back to a previous session of the legislature in the early 1970's when, as lobbyist for the Minnesota Beer Wholesalers Association, I was successful in the late hours of the legislative session in amending a Coleman sponsored bill. In the bill Coleman sought to restrict the rights of Minnesota liquor, wine and beer wholesalers to have exclusive franchises for their products to be sold in Minnesota. Almost all of the Minnesota liquor and wine wholesalers were Jewish owned. Coleman had good cause to challenge the monopoly of the liquor wholesalers and their sales practices. There was no such evidence as to the beer wholesalers. Extensive competition took place between brands and wholesalers. Only one small Minnesota beer wholesaler was Jewish.

The amendment that I was able to get adopted on the floor was a technical one. It took both beer and wine products out of the Coleman legislation. It left in the restrictions against the liquor wholesalers. I am convinced that Coleman's opposition to my candidacy as a regent was a thinly veiled payback for my successful lobbying effort. In memory, no other regent's candidacy for the board had been challenged on the same or similar grounds. Nor had my lobbying effort on behalf of other clients been challenged for acceptability in the legislative process. I had done nothing unethical in my lobbying efforts on the Coleman bill. I had simply prevailed with the argument to legislators that Coleman had not established a need to restrict the franchise rights of beer wholesalers. Wine was omitted from the Coleman bill because of a technicality involved in amending the bill on the floor. In any event, I had a difficult choice to make. Give up my main lobbying client, which provided a substantial source of my income and that of our small law firm, or withdraw my candidacy for regent. Coleman's opposition made my candidacy problematic. The choice was a family and professional one. The final choice was that I unilaterally agreed publicly I would not lobby for that client during my six year tenure as a university regent. Senator Coleman then did not publicly continue his opposition to my election.

With that final obstacle out of the way, I went on to election by the legislature. At the same 1975 session Irwin Goldfine of Duluth was elected as the 8th Congressional District Regent. During my six years as a regent I was often asked how much time was devoted to attending to regent's duties. Separate and apart from the committee meetings and regent's board meetings, there is a tremendous amount of reading and preparation. This is in addition to any leadership position as a committee chair or Chair or Vice Chair of the Board. This is all time taken away from family and one's occupation or profession. Regents receive no compensation. It is an effort that takes an average of 40 hours each month. The equivalent of a full work week. Why then would one work so hard to be elected a university regent? For me there were several reasons. I was a university law school graduate. There had not been a Jew selected as regent for 40 years. The University of Minnesota, and especially its Twin Cities Campus, is a place close to the hearts and minds of the Minnesota Jewish community. Spreading financial success in the Jewish community made it possible for immigrants to consider other choices in higher education. The university was the singular pathway for post secondary educational opportunity to our sons and daughters.

The flagship Twin Cities Campus was not only a place to earn a degree in law, medicine, dentistry, education and the arts. It also presented an opportunity for young Jewish men and women to meet each other and to engage in a variety of social, cultural and educational activities. Jewish fraternities and sororities presented social opportunities to those young Jews whose parents could afford them. The most prominent of these organizations were the

Sigma Alpha Mu and Phi Epsilon Pi fraternities and Sigma Delta Tau and Alpha Epsilon Phi sororities.

Until the 1970's, these fraternities and sororities were almost exclusively Jewish. Almost all other fraternities and sororities did not solicit or admit Jewish students. This was the case both at the University and nationally. There were also Jewish professional fraternities in engineering and medicine, but no separate fraternity for Jewish law students. There was the Hillel Foundation on campus. Hillel was mainly supported by B'nai B'rith, a Jewish fraternal organization. It provided students with religious, cultural and social activities. Some members of Jewish fraternities and sororities achieved prominence in the community after graduation. They included "Sammies" Burt Cohen. Cohen became the publisher and editor of Minneapolis-St. Paul Magazine and MSP Publications. Lawrence Cohen was prominent in the DFL party. He was elected Mayor of St. Paul. He later served as Chief Judge of the Ramsey County District Court and as chair of the Ramsey County Board of Commissioners. Steven Lange retired in 2006 as a Hennepin County District Court Judge.

Prominent "Phi Ep's" included businessman and author Harvey Mackay and grain merchant Burton Joseph. Other prominent "Phi Eps" included twin cities attorneys Allen Saeks, Ron Simon and Sherman Winthrop. Simon and Mackay were student athletes who became prominent in the M Club. Simon also served as President of the University of Minnesota Alumni Association.

The two Jewish sororities on campus housed women from non-metro Minnesota and elsewhere. Members included SDT Marsha Yugend of Little Falls. Yugend later became the first president of the merged ADL-JCRC Board. While there was a University coordinate campus in Duluth, known as UMD, most Jewish students from Duluth and the Iron Range came to the twin cities campus. The twin cities campus provided many more social opportunities for these young Jews to meet, marry and establish lifelong ties with other Jewish young people from the twin cities and from other parts of Minnesota and elsewhere. The University of Minnesota Duluth had excellent programs. However many young people from Duluth and the Iron Range came here not only for the social opportunities, but also because the twin cities campus provided a broader range of educational opportunities. These choices included the law, business, medical and dental schools and such specialized areas as engineering, nursing and architecture.

Chapter Twenty-four

The Legislature and the University

There is an inevitable tug of war between the Minnesota Legislature and the governing bodies at the university. Despite the fact that the *Chase* decision and its progeny limited the legislature's specific control over the university, there has been, over the years, efforts by legislators to exercise various measures of influence or control over the university's leaders, faculty members and policies.

In the 1960's, there was controversy and legislative pressure to require the removal of an avowed Socialist professor at the University, Mulford Q. Sibley. Unfortunately, a Jewish St. Paul City Council member Milton Rosen, engaged in demagogic attacks on Sibley reminiscent of Senator Joseph McCarthy of Wisconsin. University President O. Meredith Wilson is reported to have told the regents that he would resign if the regents acted to remove Sibley. Instead, Wilson convinced the regents to draft a strong statement in support of academic freedom.[1]

Wilson's strong leadership contrasted with the indecisiveness exhibited by university president Malcolm Moos in 1974. Former Governor Elmer L. Andersen was chair of the Board of Regents. There was considerable conflict with Senator Nicholas Coleman. Coleman requested the university provide information from class enrollment lists of professors who he suspected might be neglecting their classes because of outside commitments. A series of four articles in the *Minnesota Daily* concluded that the power of President Moos was eroding. There was a feeling among the regents that Moos was indecisive. Some felt he delegated too much authority to his vice presidents rather than making the decisions on what matters should or should not be decided by the Board of Regents. The *Daily* writer observed that: "the board's powerbase is shifting from a collection of men who considered a position as regent as great public service, to a more representative, diverse group of individuals who formed shifting coalitions around issues that concerned them." The writer went on: "As members of a lay board, they [Regents] are often unaccustomed to academic politics. The label "activists" applies largely to topics which they understand or for which they have some definite feelings. On less familiar topics they defer to more experienced colleagues or to those regents with broad political knowledge."[2]

A university president may well be caught between two conflicting and powerful forces: the legislature with its control of the purse strings on the one hand, and an activist Board of Regents on the other.

Since regents are usually elected by a vote of the legislature, it is not surprising that legislators, and in particular legislative leaders, would demand accountability from the regents as to actions taken by the university. These demands can clash with the principle that the regents should usually defer to the recommendations of the university president and not meddle in what some would call the day-to-day governance of the university. Of course "meddling" is in the eye of the beholder. It is indeed a narrow line to which regents are expected to adhere. In the instance of President Moos, a president's real or apparent indecision can lead the regents individually and collectively to assume a greater role in university governance. With a more decisive and stronger willed president, such as O. Meredith Wilson, there is more likelihood that the regents would defer to presidential initiatives and governance.

The university president's role in relationship to the Board of Regents is also shaped to the degree to which the president attends to what some observers may call "the care and feeding of regents." Compare the excellent relationship with the Board of Regents of President C. Peter Magrath with criticism of his successor President Ken Keller. Keller's inability or failure to establish strong relationships and avenues of communication with the board, led, in part, to diminished board support. When his policies came under harsh criticism from within the board and from the legislature, Keller, the university's first Jewish president resigned.

The line between making policy and interfering with administrative activity is a narrow one. However, a regent has an accountability to the legislature which elected him/her. This requires, at a minimum, the asking of the pertinent questions as to the reasons for and results to occur when both types of decisions are being considered. Those regents with prior legislative experience are uniquely suited to ask the hard questions on issues that are likely to need approval by the legislature. This is particularly true as to the formulation of the university budget and building proposals. To be approved they need strong legislative approval on a bipartisan basis. Likewise, regents with legislative experience can be helpful in securing legislative approval for university proposals. An example is my 1976 effort to help secure bonding approval for the construction of a new law school building. It was successful.

Chapter Twenty-five

The University of Minnesota Faculty

Teachers at the University of Minnesota do not confine their expertise and teaching skills to their students. Through their participation in community organizations, and lectures to various groups, they can transmit their knowledge and experience in many ways that can influence policy. Through the years university faculty have personally participated in Minnesota political parties. They have served as consultants to municipal and community organizations that helped to shape public policy such as the Citizens League. They have also testified in court and before legislative committees on their areas of expertise. When they have done so, it is always with a disclaimer that they are only speaking personally, and that they do not express any opinions on behalf of the university. Professors Hy Berman and Arthur Naftalin are two of the most prominent Jewish faculty members who were very influential in shaping public policies through their service to governors Rudy Perpich and Orville Freeman respectively. Sociology professor Arnold Rose served in the legislature. Jewish university scholars have influenced students, other faculty in and out of the university, and public policy makers through their books, articles and university lectures.

Professors who have received national or international acclaim for their research and writings in the areas of their expertise helped build the reputation of the institution. That reputation not only serves to attract others to the faculty to work with the so-called "stars" in their fields. They also serve to build up the reputation of the university at the legislature. This may create a better opportunity for the university to meet a favorable reception at the legislature when its budget proposals are presented. This is particularly true since the university is in competition with the state universities and colleges for the funds available to fund institutions of higher education.

External influences, public and social policies, are not the only area where the university faculty can be influential. The internal governance structure of the university really has three power bases: the university president and his administration; the Board of Regents; and the university faculty organizations. The twin cities campus is not unionized. Thus, faculty governance structure speaks for all the faculty members in university policy matters. Preeminent of these faculty organizations is the influential University Senate Consultative Committee. Political science professor Samuel Krislov has served as chair of this committee.

Author Saul Bellow was on the university English department faculty for the "better part of five years in the mid-1940's and 1950's. It was after Bellow left the university in 1976, that he won the Nobel Prize for Literature and the Pulitzer Prize."[1]

It was not until well into the 1950's, that there were significant numbers of Jewish faculty at the university. They were initially concentrated in the social sciences and in the medical school. Notable political science professors other than professor Krislov included professor Werner Levi. In the sociology department, beside Arnold Rose, there was David "Dan" Cooperman. It was not until fall 1955, that the law school hired its first Jewish professor. He was Michael Sovern. After Sovern left the university he became Dean of the Columbia University Law School. In 1980, he became president of Columbia.

Yale Kamisar taught at the university and later at the University of Michigan Law School. He taught and wrote in the areas of criminal and constitutional law. He is known as the "father of *Miranda*." The *Miranda* decision by the U.S. Supreme Court established the principle that persons taken into criminal custody are entitled to be advised of their right to consult with an attorney before being questioned about the possible commission of a crime.[2] Fritz Mondale, while Minnesota Attorney

General, was instrumental in organizing the attorneys general throughout the nation in support of the establishment of the "Miranda Rights."

Other university law school faculty have written and lectured on a variety of important public policy and legal issues. Professor Jesse Choper has written and lectured on constitutional law and issues relating to religious liberty. Professor Robert J. Levy is an internationally known scholar in the areas of family law and of children and the law.

Professor Carl Auerbach, who also served as Dean of the law school, is a scholar in the areas of administrative and constitutional law. One of his areas of expertise was on legislative and congressional redistricting. On this very politically sensitive subject he testified before the Minnesota Senate Elections Committee. His spouse Laura Auerbach was an aide and speech writer for Governor Wendell Anderson.

Regents' Professors

Deserving of special mention are those whom the Board of Regents, upon recommendation of the faculty, have named as Regents' Professors. This is the highest honor that can be afforded by the university to one of its faculty members. It is afforded only to those who have achieved preeminence in their chosen field.

One such person is Regents' Professor Leonid "Leo" Hurwicz. Hurwicz came to the university in 1951 at the urging of economics professor Walter Heller. Heller later became chief economic advisor to President John F. Kennedy. Hurwicz has been called "one of the nation's most distinguished economic theorists."[3] Hurwicz combined his academic pursuits with active participation in the DFL Party. Two Jewish theorists in the mathematics department achieved Regents' professorships. They are professors Avner Friedman and Laurence Markus. Friedman and Marcus were both selected as members of the prestigious National Academy of Sciences.[4]

The University of Minnesota Medical School

The university medical school had a quota for the admission of Jewish students at least until after the decade of the 1950's. However, there was no lack of prominent Jewish faculty in the medical school. Each of those mentioned have contributed significantly to life saving research, medical education, and the training of medical students. All of these virtues have contributed to improved patient care. Their contributions through their research, writings and lectures all over the world have not only a created a great reputation for the school. They have also contributed to making the school nationally and internationally known for advancement in medical science, and life saving medical and surgical processes and techniques.

Dr. A. B. Baker, was a world renowned neurologist. He was described as "...the man who became the leading force in American and world neurology in the mid-twentieth century. He was the main founder of the American Academy of neurology.[5]

Dr. Leo J. Rigler was the chairman of the Department of Radiology from 1933 to 1957. "He was a leader in the development of academic radiology and did as much as anyone to develop American diagnostic radiology into a clinically-oriented consultative specialty and unique academic discipline."[6] Rigler was the author of over 250 medical articles and books.

Regents' Professor Dr. Robert J. Gorlin was a distinguished oral pathologist and geneticist. He was an emeritus member of the dental school faculty. Gorlin was the 2003 recipient of the American Dental Association Gold Medal Award for excellence in dental research. Gorlin discovered more than 100 syndromes and diseases, several of which bear his name. His text, "Syndromes of the Head and Neck", is the foremost reference in the field.[7]

One would be remiss in not mentioning several other physicians whose research, teaching and treatment of patients has added to the world's medical knowledge and prepared students for contributing their own gifts to the state, nation and world. They include Dr. Marvin Bacaner, a physiologist; Dr. Henry Buchwald, professor of surgery and biomedical engineering; Dr. Jay Cohen, a cardiologist; Dr. Arnold F. Leonard, surgeon and cancer researcher; Dr. Malcolm Blumenthal, a specialist in asthma and allergies; and the late Dr. Milton Orkin, a specialist in dermatology. Dr. Kenneth Swaiman a specialist in pediatric neurology. Dr. Harold Wexler, a specialist in internal medicine, was honored by the university in 2003 with the creation of an endowed chair for his contributions to teaching with emphasis on patient care. Dr. Aaron Lerner, a dermatologist. His work "...led to cancer treatments and the discovery of vital hormones."[8] He is the brother of Harry Lerner, children's book publisher.

In academic medicine, Cherie Perlmutter has served as Acting Vice President for Health Sciences. Dr. David Brown served as Dean of the medical school in the late 1980's and early 1990's.[9]

These university physicians not only pioneered techniques that have saved and prolonged lives. They have also had worldwide influence as teachers. Their students from all over the nation and the world have gone on with their careers that have had a significant influence on medical care and teaching. The research and writings have added significant sums of money to the university from research grants by such prestigious institutions as the National Institutes of Health (NIH).

Chapter Twenty-six

Jay Phillips

O ne would not usually consider inclusion of a successful busi- nessman and philanthropist as a person involved in "politics" as such. Success and the accumulation of wealth in and of them- selves may add little or nothing to the quality of life of their core- ligionists or other citizens of state. Any such exclusion, however, overlooks the influence of the accumulation of the wealth and the uses to which these funds are put may have on public policies and their fellow citizens.

I am not here describing the influence of political contribu- tions to candidates and causes as they affect candidates for public office. That subject is described in the chapter on "Shaking the Money Tree." Use of accumulated wealth, personal contributions, or through foundations in the Minnesota Jewish community, has centered on Jay Phillips. The late Phillips founded and built a very successful company that distilled and distributed alcoholic bever- ages. He created the Phillips Family Foundation which continues today. Its philanthropic endeavors continue through Jay's grand- son Edward "Eddie" Phillips.

The record of Jay Phillips and his charitable contributions to community institutions is so long that it must be focused on some of those contributions that directly affect the Minnesota Jewish community, and which have affected directly the spirit of the con- cept of "let justice prevail." Into the early 1960's, the restrictions on admission of students into the university medical and dental schools were mirrored by the exclusion of Jewish doctors from staff membership and treatment privileges at twin cities hospitals. The one notable exception was the Minneapolis Swedish Hospi- tal. There surgeon Dr. Samuel Balkin had medical staff privileges.

These discriminatory practices impacted on the availability of medical care to the Jewish community and other minorities. They led to the construction of Mount Sinai Hospital. Mount Sinai opened its doors in 1951. Mount Sinai made available superb medical care on a non-sectarian basis as to both patients and medical staff.

At the University of Minnesota a Phillips' donation provided the major funding for a medical school building named in honor of pioneering university surgeon Dr. Owen Wangensteen. Wangensteen was not Jewish. As a regent I was honored to make a presentation to Jay Phillips at the dedication ceremony for the Phillips-Wangensteen facility.

Jay Phillips has been described as a "pioneer in fostering Jewish-Christian understanding."[1] The founding of a chair in Jewish Studies at St. John's University in Collegeville chair evolved into the Jay Phillips Center for Jewish-Christian Learning at the University of St. Thomas. The rabbis/scholars who served at the Jewish studies program at St. John's University in Collegeville and the Jay Phillips' Center at St. Thomas have "…over the years taught courses in Jewish religious thought to undergraduates and seminarians, hosted scholars as lecturers at the university, and participated in general campus life.[2]

Two of the prominent benefactors besides Phillips to the creation of the Jay Phillips Center was the late Sidney R. Cohen and Thomas P. Coughlan. Rabbi Max A. Shapiro became the founding director of the Center. Rabbi Shapiro, upon his retirement as Senior Rabbi at Temple Israel in 1985, served as the director until 1996. He is now director emeritus. The center is now guided by Rabbi Barry D. Cytron. Rabbi Cytron previously served as the rabbi at the Adath Jeshurun Synagogue in Minneapolis.

In 1944, Jay and his wife Rose created the Jay and Rose Phillips Family Foundation. The foundation website well describes their intentions; "as children of Russian Jewish immigrants, Jay and Rose Phillips both grew up in hardworking families that placed great importance on the Jewish values of charity, lovingkindness, and social justice."

Chapter Twenty-seven

Inside the
Board of Regents

I have over 100 years of cumulative service on boards of organizations in the Jewish and general communities. However, nothing has provided me with more feeling of accomplishment than my six years of service on the University Board of Regents. The twelve-person board sets the policies for the largest and most significant institution of higher education in this state. These policies affect thousands of students, faculty and staff. The regents' decisions have impact on the quality of education offered. They also impact the reputation of the state through the accomplishments of the students, faculty and athletic programs. Tuition policies alone impact who is able to gain entrance and continue to pursue their college degree. The discoveries of its faculty members in every discipline affect the culture, economic wellbeing and health of Minnesotans, citizens of the United States, and of the world.

On a personal level, regents interact with some of the brightest and most accomplished persons in our state and world. These interactions provide opportunities for personal growth that are unmatched in service on other boards and with other organizations. Service on the board is unlikely to be matched in prestige with comparable organizations.

Thus, it is not surprising that there is vigorous competition for election to the board. Despite efforts at reforming the regents' selection process, it remains essentially part of the political process. This is true whether election by the legislature is sought in the usual process, or gubernatorial appointment occurs to fill a vacancy. As may occur in a competitive political process, eminently qualified candidates with significant community and university service may lose out in the process.

Two such persons who unsuccessfully sought election to the board by the legislature were attorney Marvin Borman and Luella Goldberg. Both have served as chair of the University of Minnesota Foundation. The foundation is itself a very prestigious organization. It is an organization of "heavy hitters." It is responsible for raising millions of dollars to support university building projects, programs and endowed professorships.

Borman has served in leadership capacities in diverse organizations. They include the presidency of Temple Israel, and as President of the Minneapolis Club. Goldberg has served as Interim President of Wellesley College. She also serves on the boards of numerous corporations. She is the only woman member of the Board of Directors of ING, an international insurance company.

The interaction with other regents also can serve as an enriching experience. The requirement that there be a regent elected from each of the state's congressional districts assures diversity in membership with accompanying differences in political, cultural and social opinions. The selection of a Student Regent as an at-large representative has brought yet another and welcome dimension. The election of at-large regents assures a point of view that can counterbalance a parochialism of the congressional district regents. The tradition of one at-large regent coming from the leadership ranks of organized labor, together with a Mayo Clinic representative from the First Congressional District, brings yet another dimension to the board.

This diversity can bring conflict in philosophies and approaches as it would with any board that may include racial and religious minorities, farmers, businessmen, women, physicians, dentists, lawyers, teachers and a student. Each of the regents' committees also has a student representative who is in addition to the student regent serving on the board itself. In a sense, students are the constituents of the university and its board.

During my service on the board there was also a continuation of minority representation first achieved by the appointment of Josie Johnson by Governor Wendell Anderson. Wenda Moore, also an African American woman, served with me during my six years of service 1975-1981. Moore was vice chair, and then chaired the board. I served as vice chair for the last two years of my term. Moore was the first woman to chair the board. We met with President C. Peter Magrath to discuss university policies and to fashion the agenda for monthly board meetings. This was an opportunity for me to work inside the decision-making process at the university. Under traditional practices, I would have been elevated to chair the board. Despite a concentrated effort to be reelected to a second six year term, my reelection efforts failed at the legislature. By 1981, the legislative composition of the Third Congressional District had changed. Republicans had regained the majority of that legislative delegation. They nominated a Republican businessman to replace me. Even some Democrats at the legislature were unwilling to change the tradition of legislative ratification of the choice of a congressional district caucus. Of course, it is by that same traditional process that I had been elected. The result disappointed me and my supporters on the board and many members of the legislature.

The 1975 legislative session had seen the election of two Jews to the Board. Duluth businessman Irwin Goldfine and I were the first Jewish regents in over 40 years. A year later Governor Wendell Anderson appointed Minneapolis attorney and author David Lebedoff to fill a vacancy as Fifth District Regent. From no regents to three in a space of two years. All in the aftermath of the rejection of the candidacy of David Saxon amid allegations of anti-Semitism on the part of several regents.

Of course, being of the same religious faith does not necessarily result in a congruence of attitudes or philosophies toward higher educational institution policies and practices. More often than not, Regent Goldfine and I had similar views on policies and people. I recognized that coming from Duluth Goldfine would have strong feelings in support of the University of Minnesota Duluth (UMD). After his retirement, Goldfine's contributions, personal and financial, to UMD and the university, were honored by the award of an honorary degree and the naming of student residences at UMD in his name. Goldfine's views were little different than those of other regents with a university coordinate campus. So long as one knew where the others were coming from, whether it be in support of the law school, the business school, the College of Veterinary Medicine or programs involving Greater Minnesota, compromises and understanding of positions took place. It was rare that personalities intruded on policy, opinions and debate.

There were three lawyers on the board: myself, Lebedoff and former State Senator William Dosland of Moorhead. Dosland, a Republican, was an experienced lawyer and legislative veteran. He provided a connection to Republicans in the legislature in the same way Lebedoff, Goldfine and I provided links to the Democrats.

Democrats on the board ranged from liberals to conservatives. Regent Lloyd Peterson, a successful farmer and agribusinessman from Paynesville, was a conservative Democrat. While our philosophies sometimes failed to mesh, Carolyn and I achieved a personal relationship with the Petersons. Ardy and Lloyd Peterson had a strong respect for their Swedish heritage. We learned much about their roots in our social interaction.

It was more often the origins, occupations and professions of the regents that shaped their views on university policies. It also shaped the degree to which I and individual regents were thought to be intruding excessively in the day-to-day operations of the university as compared to restricting ourselves to policy matters. Regent Lester Malkerson, who was the longest serving regent on the board at that time, and its former chair, often objected to what he believed to be an inappropriate intrusion of individual regents into the operational decisions of the president and his central administration. In this regard Malkerson was continuing a challenge to the increasing activism of regents that began under the administration of President Malcom Moos.

In 1979, I was elected Vice Chair of the Board. I look back with much satisfaction on my relationship with Board Chair Wenda Moore and President Magrath. Moore and I were most often in agreement on university policies and strategies. We presented a united front in reflecting the views of the board in our meetings with Magrath. Magrath often used our meetings as a sounding board for policies that would later be brought to the full board. These meetings also included Duane Wilson, the secretary to the board. Wilson headed the administrative staff for the board. He had served as Commissioner of the Department of Agriculture under Governor Al Quie. Since Moore and I were both from the metropolitan area, Wilson could add insight and opinions of caution on subjects that affected coordinate campuses and Greater Minnesota.

Wenda Moore had a strong but gracious style that served her and the university well. After completing service as a regent, she was elected to the board and then to chair the Kellogg Foundation. The Kellogg Foundation, with its important international programs, serves as an opportunity for Moore to continue to devote her talents to the service of others.

Contrary to his successor Ken Keller, President Magrath spent what I believe to be appropriate amounts of time tending to the "care and feeding of regents." This was a positive dimension of his presidency. Magrath had a pleasant style and an instinct for where his policies would go with the board. He was rarely too far out in front of the board. The president, his assistants Mitchell Pearlstein and Jeanne Lupton, and his vice presidents, knew that most regents had ties to the faculty as well as into the political process with both parties at the legislature. Magrath welcomed input from regents whether or not their opinions ultimately coincided with his views and recommendations. While not all faculty viewed him as a strong president in the mold of an O. Meredith Wilson, Magrath impressed me as being as strong in his views as the circumstances dictated. His political instincts were good. I view his ten years as university president as successful ones.

The Move of Memorial Stadium

That is not to say that both Magrath and the board made all the right decisions and at the right times. One of the wrong decisions is the one that I regret most as a regent. It was the vote to move university football games from Memorial Stadium on campus to the Metrodome in downtown Minneapolis. There was enormous pressure from some university alumni and downtown business interests to relocate football from the aged Memorial Stadium to the weatherproof confines of a domed stadium. Business interests saw university football downtown as a boon to development of the areas surrounding the dome, as well as providing customers for downtown bars and restaurants.

I can remember spending many a sunny fall afternoon viewing Gopher football at Memorial Stadium. It was both as a university student and as a regent. Some of those days were also cold or wet. I and other alumni view with nostalgia the homecoming decorations and parades down University Avenue led by the university marching band. Yes, it would have cost a considerable sum to remodel Memorial Stadium into a modern football facility. But events since that move have established that there is an unmistakable loss of student participation and spirit when university football is moved off campus. While certainly student attendance at football games is tied in part to the quality and success of the football team, the move of university football to a new stadium near the site of the old Memorial Stadium, will prove to be a successful investment of public and university funds. It will provide a renewed campus spirit and interest in Gopher football.

Regents, like other elected officials, frequently are lobbied by individuals or groups having their own agendas. They may be by university benefactors in the business community, unions representing university staff, or supporters of various schools or units within the university community. A regent's analytic powers and fortitude frequently come into play. Some regents, myself included, were criticized for asking too many questions about proposals coming before the board. It is better to have asked the questions, and hopefully received the answers, than not to have questioned and be sorry about it later. It is easy to be caught up in a proposal, and the emotions or forces that support or oppose it. One can assume the best of intentions of those proposing the course of action. It is better to be a skeptic than to later regret a vote because the right questions were not asked.

Proposals brought before the Board of Regents do not have the same checks and balances as with bills proposed at the legislature. One may pass a bill through a legislative committee, but it still must be voted on by the whole body. It then is subject to the same process in the other body. Then the governor must agree to sign it into law. With a small board, such as the regents, the buck stops with the board. It only takes a simple majority of the twelve to pass a proposal. This places a significant burden on each regent in reaching a conclusion as to how to vote on an important or controversial measure. The ability to cast an educated vote is only as good as the information that reaches the members in the decision-making process. There is always significant pressure to concur in the recommendations made by the president and his/her vice presidents and administrators. Prior to the president's recommendations, faculty members, school and department heads and other campus leaders may apply not only input into the decision making process. They may also exert pressure for the president to concur with or oppose actions that may have been taken within a particular school or department.

Chapter Twenty-eight

The Landmark Rajender Litigation

An example of the decision-making process at the Board of Regents, it is the history of the discrimination claims of Shyamala Rajender. Rajender is a native of India. After receiving her Ph.D. in chemistry, she received a research grant for post doctoral work from the university. She was later offered a teaching position in the chemistry department as an assistant professor. She sought a tenure track position leading to a position as a tenured faculty member in the chemistry department.

In 1973, the chemistry department was all male. There was no female member of the tenured faculty. Rajender was denied a tenure track position. When she asked for a reason, she alleged she was told, "We have 46 faculty members and all are men. We cannot give you tenure because being a woman, they won't like you there, and also because of your national origin they will not accept you."[1]

Rajender filed a Charge with the Equal Employment Opportunity Commission (EEOC). She then filed a sex discrimination suit alleging discrimination in violation of federal law by the university and its chemistry department faculty. The suit was assigned to U. S. District Court Judge Miles Lord. Lord was a former Minnesota attorney general and U.S. attorney for Minnesota. Rajender was represented by attorney Paul Sprenger. In one of a series of errors on the part of the university administration, the university attorney allowed the chairman of the chemistry department to designate the outside attorney to represent the university and conduct its defense to the charges. The error, which was later to prove fateful, was in failing to select an attorney who knew Judge Lord well enough, and was strong and aggressive enough, to withstand Lord's well known and sometimes heavy handed actions in presiding over important lawsuits.

I was well acquainted with Judge Lord. I served as an assistant attorney general under Lord for over three years. Lord was well known in the legal community for his liberal views. On occasion he would take the questioning of witnesses out of the hands of the litigant's attorneys and cross examine witnesses himself. This was particularly true when Lord felt that the whole story was not being told. Or when the testimony did not coincide with Lord's views on the matter.

Lord certified the Rajender suit as a class action. This meant that the result would affect not only Rajender's individual discrimin-ation claims. The findings and conclusions could apply to all women in the faculty at the university. The Rajender lawsuit had been commenced before C. Peter Magrath became president. It was also prior to the time when I, David Lebedoff and William Dosland had come on to the board. Information on the Rajender claims, and opinions as to their merit, came from the then university attorney; the outside counsel retained to represent the university; and the strongly expressed views of the leadership and faculty of the chemistry department. The conclusion at the time was that Rajender's claims were without significant merit, and that the university should continue to vigorously defend against the claims. This was not because there were assumptions made that there was not any gender based discrimination among the faculty. Rather the conclusion was that Rajender did not possess the qualifications justifying her appointment to a tenure track position. Thus, the university rejected an opportunity to settle Rajender's initial complaint for the sum of $50,000.

As the trial before Judge Lord proceeded, Lillian Williams was called as a witness. Williams was the head of the university Department of Equal Opportunity. Judge Lord took over the questioning of Williams from the attorneys. The impact of any judge, let alone one as strong-willed and persistent as Judge Lord, would be enough to intimidate almost any witness. Lord's questioning of Williams had precisely that result. The result of William's admissions under this questioning was to, in effect, pull the rug out from under the university's defenses to the suit. Unfortunately, the university's trial attorney failed to make objections for the record during Lord's questioning. Objections would have made a record for an appeal of Lord's action to the Eighth Circuit Court of Appeals.

Attorneys knowledgeable with Judge Lord's approach in similar situations knew that he would occasionally go well beyond what is appropriate for a judge in taking over a case from the litigants. The only alternative was for the attorney to make sufficient objections for the record so that the Eighth Circuit, as it occasionally did, could reverse conclusions based on Lord's excesses. The university's trial attorney remained silent while Lord pushed Williams so hard that by the end of her testimony the university's defense was in tatters.

The matter then came before the regents. We were all presented with a transcript of the Williams' testimony. The three lawyers on the board, myself, Lebedoff and Dosland, perhaps among others, read the trial transcript of the testimony in detail. When the review was completed there was unanimous opinion on the part of the three attorneys that the university was certain to lose the case. The university attorney was instructed to enter into negotiations for the settlement of the Rajender action.

In 1980, Rajender and the university entered into a Consent Decree. Rajender received a settlement in the amount of $100,000. She did not achieve the position in the chemistry department that she sought. During the eight years that the case was pending Rajender had entered and graduated from the Hamline University School of Law. In 1976, she became an attorney and was admitted to practice in the State of California. She practices law in Danville, California.[2]

The settlement embodied the Consent Decree, not only involved Rajender. It covered the entire class of women faculty at the university.[3] The Rajender Consent Decree was only in effect until the 1991-1992 academic year. Under the decree the university was required to conduct a nationwide search to fill any academic non-student position. The university "must also make a good faith effort to hire "approximately equally well qualified" female candidates under an affirmative action plan until the percentage of women employed at all levels within a university department is equal to the percentage of women available for hiring."[4]

To comply with this requirement the university annually compiled faculty gender statistics of the percentage of women employed at each level within each department of the university. As part of its good faith effort the university has written hiring guidelines for each department. The hiring guidelines require each department to keep extensive records of its hiring process. These hiring guide-lines, however, are not part of the Rajender Consent Decree."[5]

Under the Consent Decree the university is committed to conducting what has become known as a "Rajender search." The university department "... must first form a search committee. The committee's job is to make a final selection for the advertised position based on characteristics such as a candidate's training, his or her experience, the quality and quantity of a candidate's published works, and the academic recommendations submitted on behalf of each candidate. If a Rajender search results in the hiring of a male candidate, the search committee must list the three most qualified women who were considered and document the committee's reasons for not hiring one of these women."[6]

In 1983, several female faculty members filed petitions under the Rajender Consent Decree alleging continuing discrimination by the university. The claim this time was discrimination in compensation. The district court certified the female faculty members as a class. In 1989, the claim was settled with the university entering into a second consent decree. This decree became known as *Rajender II*. The consent decree in *Rajender II* provided for the distribution of $3 million to female faculty members as salary increases.

A unique aspect of the original Rajender settlement was the creation of a panel of three special masters to hear and determine the claims of other women at the university who believe they have been subject to discrimination. Judge Lord, with the concurrence of the university, appointed three experienced attorneys as special masters to hear and determine such claims. They were the late Leonard Lindquist, an experienced labor and employment lawyer with vast experience; retired Hennepin County District Court Judge Edward J. Parker, a former assistant attorney general; and the late Viola Kanatz, a lawyer and arbitrator.

The procedure was to have one of the panel members serve as the neutral arbitrator. Each party, the university and the claimant, would appoint a panel member. A decision by the majority of the panel would be binding. However, more claims were mediated by one of the panel members than were decided by the three person panel.[7]

Along with opening the doors to equal opportunity for women in the faculty, there was another positive result of the Rajender litigation. It was the creation of a new position of General Counsel to head the University Attorney's Office. The scope of the legal needs of the university had created need for a more sophisticated and experienced attorney to represent the university. The position had also outgrown the ability of one person to handle the ever growing complexity of the university's need for legal advice and service. I served as the point person on the board in urging the president and the board, in the aftermath of the Rajender experience, to upgrade the position. It was also to regularize the procedure in the appointment of outside counsel to assist in the university's litigation needs.

The university attorney's office is now known as the Office of the General Counsel. It is directed by Mark B. Rotenberg. Rotenberg has a staff of approximately 20 attorneys. They are assigned to cover such diverse topics as healthcare law and issues relating to the Academic Health Center; contracts; employment discrimination and affirmative action; copyrights; trademarks; technology transfer; real estate and lawsuits and legal claims. The geographic scope covers the twin cities as well as the coordinate campuses.

Federal and state laws generally, and as to equal opportunity policies in particular, had grown enormously in their reach and complexity. The consequences of discriminatory policies and practices as to all protected classes under these laws required changes in administrative procedures. They also created a need for people with the capabilities to assess the legal consequences and advise university administrators and faculty accordingly.

Post Rajender decree action continued with other efforts to mobilize University resources to assess and improve the "University's climate for women and plan activities related to climate assessment and improvement."[8] What became known as Minnesota Plan II resulted in the hiring in 1988 of Professor Janet Spector. Spector "helped found the Department of Women's Studies and the Center for Advanced Feminist Studies at the University." In 1988, she was appointed "special assistant to the Vice President for Academic Affairs and Director of Equal Opportunity/Affirmative Action."[9]

The University's Lobbying Efforts

During my time on the board, I, as a former legislator and lobbyist, expressed concern at the lack of backup for the university's lobbying efforts at the legislature. Other organizations with constituencies, such as organized labor and farmers, frequently called upon their members to lobby legislators in their home districts on issues that affected them. From my own professional experience I knew that private business interests, such as statewide trade associations, used the same legitimate methods to plead their case to individual legislators. They did so either at the capitol or back at home during legislative campaigns and during the legislative session. Legislators would more likely be influenced in their acceptance of arguments for or against a proposal from those who would be voting in the next election in their home district. Also, contacts made away from the stress and time constraints of the legislative session were likely to be more successful. This was especially true during a legislative campaign when the candidate would know that his/her response might influence votes at election time.

The university's lobbyists, Stan Wenberg, and later, Stanley Kegler and George Robb, were experienced and skillful. They had many legislative contacts among legislators and key staff persons. But the grassroots resources they had available to call upon were very limited. They could, of course, call on faculty members to testify on areas within their expertise. One example was Dean Auerbach's lobbying on behalf of the new law school building.

But beyond these resources there was no widespread group through-out the state that the university and its lobbyists could call upon to make its case on a one-to-one basis. My concept was to use alumni and university faculty in an organized effort directed by the univer-sity central administration and the university's lobbyists to engage in a year around effort. Both during the interim and in legislative sessions these persons would make the case as to the university's needs. They could, as well, respond to the university's critics.

One idea was to take a leaf from candidates for the legislature by holding coffee parties in the individual districts. A prominent professor or alumnus could invite a group of neighbors, including parents of students, to convene in a home. They would invite legislative candidates to attend. The university's needs could be highlighted, and the candidate's questioned as to their positions and records. Following such meetings the information obtained could be spread through a network of university supporters.

The creation of a widespread network was the key to the success of the proposal. The university had a broad array of faculty, staff and students who, together with alumni, had the potential for vast outreach on behalf of the university. The idea did not gain enough traction during my time on the Board of Regents. However, in January 1983 "...more than three hundred alumni came together as a presidential network to help lobby for the university's needs with the legislature." Harvey Mackay was among the Minnesota Alumni Association volunteers who "continued and strengthened the legislative advocacy."[10]

I am familiar with two recent examples of the success of this legislative network. A coffee party was hosted by Marilyn Gorlin the spouse of the late Regents' Professor Robert Gorlin. Marilyn is a DFL activist in her own right. The other was hosted by former

University Vice President for Academic Affairs professor Marvin Marshak. Reports received from then legislative candidate Ron Latz were that both events were successful. Their success was achieved because they were convened by persons of stature in the community whom Ron knew would spread information about his views among their friends and neighbors.

The Lettuce and Grape Boycott

President Magrath's ability to guide the regents and the university through difficult policy decisions was demonstrated early in the Magrath administration. It revolved around whether the university should support a boycott of lettuce and grapes harvested by nonunion labor. The national effort to boycott such products was initiated by Cesar Chavez and the United Farm Workers Union. Chavez had made a major effort to organize the workers. Many of them were Mexican immigrants whose stoop labor harvested these products in California. Liberal groups throughout the country, including students at colleges and universities, rallied around Chavez's call.

The call was that people should not purchase, and colleges and universities should not serve, lettuce and grapes produced by the nonunion labor. Lettuce and grapes were served at student unions and residence halls at the university and elsewhere. Despite questions as to the legality of the institution supporting a boycott, there was more discussion at the regent's level over the tactics in resolving the confrontations that the boycott created. There was student picketing and fasting. Regents from the rural areas were much more hesitant at supporting the boycott than were regents from a metropolitan area that had liberal and labor affiliations. Encouragingly, the legislature did not intervene in these policy discussions or try to influence the results.

After soliciting student opinion in the residence halls, President Magrath found a satisfactory compromise. With board approval, he instituted a "two bowl" policy. Students were given a choice between ordering union grown lettuce and produce or those from nonunion sources. Some thirty plus years later, the efforts led by the now deceased Chavez to form a viable farmers' union, and to achieve progress in negotiating contracts with California growers, are still largely unsuccessful.

Chapter Twenty-nine

The *Minnesota Daily*
"Humor Issue"

President Magrath and the regents were much less successful in resolving the controversy which erupted from a so-called "humor issue" of the *Minnesota Daily* published during finals week in 1979. The facts surrounding the dispute are set forth in the opinion of the U.S. Court of Appeals for the 8th Circuit in *Stanley v. Magrath*, 719 F. 2d 279 (8th Circuit 1983). The Court stated that the: "Humor Issue" was "... styled in the format of sensational-ist newspapers, contained articles, advertisements, and cartoons satirizing Christ, the Roman Catholic Church, Evangelical reli-gion, public figures, numerous social, political, and ethnic groups, social customs, popular trends, and liberal ideas." In addressing these subjects, the paper frequently used scatological language and explicit and implicit references to sexual acts. There was, for example, a blasphemous "interview" with Jesus on the Cross that would offend anyone of good taste, whether with or without reli-gion. No contention is made, however, but the newspaper met the legal definition of obscenity."[1]

The *Daily* issue not only outraged the regents but many leg-islators as well. Legislative hearings were held in both the House and Senate. As the court noted, members of the Board of Regents and university administrators received numerous letters deploring the content from church leaders, members of churches, interested citizens, students, and legislators.[2] There was significant pressure on President Magrath and the regents to take action against those responsible for the offensive publication. Easy answers were not forthcoming. Despite the acknowledged offensive nature of the publication, there were issues raised involving freedom of the press, and the right of the *Daily* to publish even acknowledgedly offensive material.

All members of the board, without regard to their religious affiliation, acknowledged that they were offended by the contents of the *Daily* issue. There was much internal debate among the regents, and in discussions with President Magrath, as to how the university administration and its governing body should react. "On June 8, 1979, the regents unanimously passed a resolution stating that they were "compelled to deplore the content of the June 4-9, 1979 issue of the *Minnesota Daily*."[3] The regents and Magrath wanted the Board of Student Publications, which governed the *Daily*, to take some corrective action in response to the regent's resolution.

On July 13, 1979, when the issue remained unresolved, the regents unanimously passed another resolution. In that resolution "the regents stated the issue in question was "flagrantly offensive." They established an ad hoc committee "to review with the president the concerns expressed and the recommendations of the president regarding the *Minnesota Daily*. Among other things, the regents directed the special committee to consider the "appropriate mechanism for circulation and financial support for the *Minnesota Daily*."[4]

The issue was how to appropriately respond to the *Daily's* action in such a manner as to clearly indicate not only displeasure with what had taken place but also to insure, to the degree possible, that the action would not be repeated in the future. The only available avenue appeared to be addressing the financial support of the *Daily*. Most of the revenue supporting the *Daily's* operations came from a portion of the mandatory service fee paid each quarter by every university student. The amount of the student service fees, and the allocation of those fees to various student organizations, was determined by the regents on an annual basis upon recommendation from the president. The University Attorney rendered an opinion that "changing the fees immediately following the "humor issue" could be viewed as punitive action in

violation of the First Amendment."[5] The issue of allowing students a means with which to withdraw their individual financial
support from the *Daily* had come from the House Education
Committee, Higher Education Division, in December 1979. "The
House Committee Chairman wrote the chairman of the Board
of Regents stating that the vast majority of the division recommended that the "Regents allow students a means to withdraw
their individual financial support from the *Daily*."[6]

Since the timing of any action involving the *Daily's* financial
support had significant legal effects, the matter dragged on to
spring 1980. Then the student service fee determination process
came into play. That process provided for a Student Services Fees
Committee to make recommendations as to the fees for the forthcoming year. That committee was composed of "elected students,
faculty members, and administrators." In a 6-5 vote that committee rejected the institution of a refund system. Along with that,
it recommended that the fees supporting the *Daily*, the Board of
Publications fees, be increased by 11.6 percent.[7]

However, President Magrath did not concur with this committee action. The following month he recommended to the regents
that the students who objected to paying for the support of the
Daily from their service fees would have the right to have the
Daily portion of those fees refunded. There was precedent for the
refund procedure. Both the Student Health Service and the Minnesota Public Interest Research Group were subject to having the
funding from service fees refunded at the request of students. In
the case of the Health Service this was because some students had
health insurance coverage that made the support of the Health
Service duplicative. The political advocacy of MPIRG was controversial. The campus wide organization of students was the Twin
Cities Campus Assembly. After reviewing President Magrath's
recommendation for a refundable *Daily* fee, the assembly voted
99-7 in opposition.[8]

The ball was then resting firmly before the Board of Regents.
On May 9, 1980, on a 8-3 vote, the regents adopted a resolution
"…that instituted a refundable fee system for a one year trial period,

allowing objecting students to obtain a refund of that part of the service allotted to the Board of Student Publications."⁹ At the same time, the regents voted to increase the fee support for the *Daily* for the 1980-81 school year. They did so again the following year, while voting in favor of retaining the refund system. (Regents Lebedoff, Schertler, and Unger voted no on the May 9, 1980 resolution.)¹⁰ The *Daily* would continue as a student newspaper distributed free to all students, faculty and staff at the twin cities campuses of the university. The *Daily* would also have for its financial support revenues derived from advertising. Those regents who supported the resolution, including myself, hoped that what they considered to be a reasonable compromise would satisfy both the moral, political, and legal issues presented and put the controversy to rest. The *Daily* would have an increase in its overall revenues. Those who objected to getting the *Daily* could apply for and receive a refund of that portion of their student service fees that were allocated to the Board of Student Publications and the *Daily*.

STANLEY v. MAGRATH

The *Daily* and its supporters sued Magrath individually and as president of the university. Each of the regents was also sued individually and as members of the Board of Regents. The plaintiffs were the editors of the *Daily*. They alleged that the action of Magrath and the regents in changing the method of funding the *Daily* violated the First Amendment's guarantees of freedom of the press. The action was commenced in the U.S. District Court for the District of Minnesota. It was assigned for trial before U.S. District Judge Robert G. Renner. Renner was a former member of the Minnesota House of Representatives. He had served as U.S. Attorney before his appointment as a federal judge. Renner, from Park Rapids, was a moderate Republican known for his insight and fair demeanor. I had served for several years in the Minnesota House with Renner.

Renner heard the injunction action without a jury. The university was represented by a team of attorneys led by an experienced and skilled attorney Leonard J. Keyes. Minneapolis attorney Marshall Tanick represented the *Daily*. He took the case on without guarantee of payment of any fee. He would be compensated only if he was successful. Tanick was an honors graduate of both the University of Minnesota, majoring in journalism, and the Stanford University Law School. During pretrial discovery proceedings Tanick took the depositions under oath of the individual regents. Like my own, Tanick's roots were in North Minneapolis. He was the son of Jack Tanick, a former vice president of the Laundry Workers and Dry Cleaners Union that my father Rubin Latz had led some 40 years previously. Tanick thus had a liberal and labor background. He was a firm believer in the First Amendment guarantees involved.

When Tanick cross-examined me during my deposition, I was irritated by the aggressive nature of his questioning. Thus at one point during the questioning, I interrupted Tanick to complain, "Marshall, if you don't stop badgering me I will tell your father on you." The statement took Tanick by surprise. He was momentarily taken aback, but then proceeded with his interrogation albeit on a slightly less confrontational course.

The testimony by six of the regents, Casey, Peterson, McGuiggan, Goldfine, Krenik, and me, according to the appellate court, established that "…that one of the reasons that they voted in the favor of the resolution was that students should not be forced to support a paper which was sacrilegious and vulgar."[11] The District Court's opinion had emphasized that refund systems, coupled with the simultaneous increases in the amount of fees supporting the *Daily*, did not actually reduce the total amount of the fee support to the *Daily*. Thus the court noted when the money lost due to refunds was balanced against the increases for the 1980-81 school year, the net gain to the *Daily* was $15,826.22. This was greater than the amount received in 1979-80.[12]

After trial the District Court dismissed the action. "The District Court's key finding was that "[one] of the motivations for the establishment for the refundable fee system was to respond to the concerns of those students who objected to being coerced into giving financial support to the *Daily*." The District Court had concluded that the regent's action was "rational," and held that the First Amendment had not been violated."[13]

Following the adverse decision in the District Court, the *Daily* plaintiffs appealed to the Eighth Circuit Court of Appeals. On October 11, 1983, that court unanimously reversed the decision of the District Court. After extensively reviewing the history of the ill-fated "humor issue," and the private, public and regential reaction to it, the appellate court concluded that the decision by the regents was in response to the content of the "humor issue"; that the regent's decision was adverse to the plaintiff; and that the decision was substantially motivated by the content of the newspaper. Thus the court concluded that the First Amendment was violated. The Amendment "...prohibits the regents from taking adverse action against the *Daily* because the contents of the paper are occasionally blasphemous or vulgar."[14] The Court held that "if the Board of Regents would have changed the funding mechanism simply because of students' objections, it should prevail, here, even if opposition to the *Daily*'s contents was also in the board's collective minds." The regents did not show that this was the sole motive for its action involving the *Daily* and its funding. From the testimony of the regents, the appellate court concluded that "the regents' two resolutions which deplore the contents of the "Humor Issue" also furnished strong evidence that the regents were reacting to the contents of the paper and to the disapproval that others expressed as to the contents."[15] This testimony was evidence of the regents "improper motivation." The court also found it significant "...that the regents did not move to establish a refund system at the Duluth, Morris or Waseca campuses of the university." The court went on to state that "if the regents had truly been motivated by the principle that a student ought not to be forced to support a newspaper that espouses views the student opposes, then one would expect that they would have taken some action in regard to the newspapers at the other campuses. Yet in 1981, when the refund system was instituted, the regents took no such action. No motion was even made that the board conduct a study of the feasibility of instituting the refund system at the other schools. In 1981, a motion to institute the refund system at these other schools was made and defeated."[16] The Eighth Circuit ruling ordered the U.S. District Court to render "injunctive relief" ending what is considered to be an illegal fee structure.

"Magrath considered the position he took in the *Daily* case as one of the mistakes he made as president. "I think I was wrong…if I had to call that one again, I'd call it the other way. I feel badly about that because I feel so strongly about the First Amendment."" "The humor issue (of the *Minnesota Daily*) was an anomaly. For many years the *Minnesota Daily* had been among the most respected student newspapers in the United States."[17] I agree with that assessment. President Magrath may well have, in retrospect, proved correct. One can only speculate as to what would have occurred had he and the regents stood up to the criticism of that one issue of the *Daily* and allowed it to pass without imposing sanctions. Like other First Amendment issues, there does not seem to be a way to find a bright line principle on which to base a decision. At one end of the spectrum is the unfettered right to say and print what one believes. On the other, courts ruled early on that the constitutional principle of free speech does not protect one who "cries fire in a crowded theater." In *Stanley v. Magrath* the appellate court ruled that the university could not change its funding policy for a student paper based on the "hue and cry" of the public objecting to a particular issue. On the other hand, the court noted that the university could establish a policy which allowed students a refund of the portion of their activity fee that supports a student paper that the students oppose. The difference is that while a refund policy can be established, such a policy cannot be initiated in response to public criticism of the publication, even with the concern that the publication, as a school sponsored activity, can adversely affect the reputation of the school.

Some courts have ruled that if the material in the publication is libelous or obscene or encourages others to engage in dangerous or unlawful activity, then the publication may be confiscated and the students responsible can be punished. However, mere discussions of controversial issues, be they material dealing with war, drugs, abortion, birth control information and like subjects, cannot be barred from student publications even at the high school level.

Because of its wide distribution to those within the university community, as well as to those outside, such as members of the legislature and others in government, it is easy to forget that school sponsored publications, such as the *Minnesota Daily*, are designed to reflect the views and opinions of the students. As is the case with newspapers in the private sector, it is increasingly difficult to discern where what is reported/printed are only facts or instead represent the opinions of the writer. One other message that I learned to my regret in the course of my political career is that the attempted use of humor is very dangerous. One, who in public life or public office, is inclined to attempt to use humor to prove a point proceeds at his/her peril.

Chapter Thirty

The Two Jewish University Presidents

There have been two Jews elected as president of the University of Minnesota who merit special mention because of their unique stature and accomplishments in public policy and the political realm. One is Professor Kenneth Keller. The other is Mark Yudof.

Kenneth Keller

A prominent Jewish faculty member became the first Jewish president of the university. He was Kenneth Keller. Keller, a noted biomedical engineering researcher, served as University president from 1985-1988. Keller's tenure as president was noted by significant accomplishments and major controversy. His tenure as president was highlighted by the Minnesota Campaign. The fundraising venture raised over $300 million in private gifts for programs and endowed professorships at the university.[1] One cannot underestimate the importance of this type of fundraising venture. The creation and sustenance of endowed professorships at a university enables the institution to attract and retain the most sought after scholars from around the world.

A university planning document titled "Commitment to Focus" proved to be both necessary and controversial. It created a division between Keller's supporters and opponents on the Board of Regents. Critics complained of elitism. There were fears of restrictions on open access to the university.[2] There was also controversy over the cost of remodeling the university president's residence.

The controversies surrounding Keller were fueled in part by beliefs by some Jewish faculty members of anti-Semitic attitudes toward Keller which in part were the cause of Keller's 1988 resignation. (See Hyman Berman interview.) In a December 1997 interview, Keller noted that "there were some things that happened that raised the issue of whether there was any anti-Semitism at work...I need to state for the record that I never felt it."[3]

The allegations of anti-Semitism directed toward President Keller centered around Regent Charles McGuiggan. McGuiggan was Regents' Chair during part of Keller's presidency. Keller admitted that "hubris" and failure to establish personal relationships with some board members, including McGuiggan, left him with limited support on the board when he came under fire over the cost of remodeling the president's residence and the commitment to focus.[4]

Keller's admitted failure to establish personal relationships with some board members can be contrasted with the record of President C. Peter Magrath. Magrath made a genuine and successful effort to establish personal and professional relationships with members of the Board of Regents. Thus Magrath established a reservoir of support from the regents during several troubled and controversial issues and decisions that were made by him and the board during his presidency.

Mark Yudof

The July 1997 selection of Mark G. Yudof as president of the University of Minnesota was in sharp contrast to the religious issues surfacing during the Saxon candidacy. In the selection process Yudof was literally Jewish. Yudof, and his wife Judy, made no secret of their religious commitments and involvement. Judy Yudof had an impressive community career in Austin, Texas. She served on boards and commissions in both the Jewish and secular communities. She became the national president of the United Synagogue of Conservative Judaism. This was a high honor in the national Jewish community. Prior to his election as president of the University of Minnesota, Yudof had been the Dean of the University of Texas Law School. He then became Executive Vice President and Provost of that university. That was a position which was next in rank to the university president.

In his inaugural address President Yudof was clear on his views on the continuing debate as to whether the university's land grant status with its emphasis on accessibility to the university could survive with the mission to propel the university into the front ranks of public universities in the nation. In that address Yudof stated:

"Minnesotans expect us to be fair in providing access for their sons and daughters. If we do not provide reasonable access-*including access for those who are underprepared and historically underrepresented in higher education and in the upper levels of our socioeconomic life*-the taxpayers and state government will turn their backs on our graduate, research, and out-reach functions."[5]

When the opportunity came in for Yudof to return to Texas as the president of the University of Texas at Austin, he took the opportunity to return to that state. Observers agree that his tenure as the University of Minnesota president was a successful one.

Robert Bruninks served Yudof and the university as Executive Vice President and Provost. This was the number two spot at the university. Continuing to serve as the Dean of the College of Liberal Arts, the largest college in the university, is Steven J. Rosenstone. Rosenstone's academic expertise is in the area of electoral politics. He taught at the University of Michigan.

Chapter Thirty-one

The Two Professors

There are two university of Minnesota professors who merit special mention because of the unique stature and accomplishments in public policy and the political realm. They are the late Professor Arnold Rose and Professor Allan Spear.

Allan Spear

Allan Spear is a now retired university history professor and former state senator. Spear served 27 years in the Senate, from 1973 to his retirement in 2000. He represented a staunchly liberal district which encompasses the University of Minnesota Minneapolis campus and the surrounding residential area.

Spear was Minnesota's first openly gay legislator. As such he attracted national renown. There was no indication of homophobia following Spear's disclosure. He was elected by his DFL senatorial colleagues as President of the Senate. As such he presided over the body during legislative debates. Spear also served as chair of the Senate Judiciary Committee. Spear's longtime aide was Marcia Greenfield. Greenfield is the spouse of now-retired Representative Lee Greenfield. Greenfield represented part of the senate district that Spear represented.

Arnold Rose

Best known in academic circles nationally and worldwide was the late Arnold Rose. Rose was a professor in the University Sociology Department prior to and during his one term in the Minnesota House in 1963-1964. Rose served in the Sociology

Department from 1949 until his death from cancer at age 50 in in 1986.

Rose was most noted as a coauthor with Gunnar Myrdal of the classic study of race relations in America detailed in *An American Dilemma* (1944.) Rose prepared a condensed version of the text entitled *The Negro in America* (Harper Torchbooks, 1964.) Among his many other articles and publications, Rose authored *"The Power Structure: Political Process in American Society"* (Oxford University Press, 1967.)

Rose's prominence as a sociologist and academician on race relations was not enough in and of itself to raise Rose to become a target of right wing extremists. With his election to the legislature in 1963 his profile was raised significantly. In echoes of the McCarthyite attacks of the 1950's, with their allegations of guilt by association and Communist collaboration, Rose became the subject of an attack by Gerda M. Koch. Koch's organization, Christian Research, attacked those she believed were communist collaborators.

In 1963, Koch's organization published a pamphlet entitled *Facts for Action. Facts for Action* stated: "Arnold Rose, Minnesota University Professor and State Legislator, collaborates with Communists and Communist Fronters." The guilt by association was that Gunnar Myrdal was "a notorious Swedish Communist," and that Rose, as a coauthor with Myrdal, was a person who "collaborates with Communists and Communist Fronters."

Rose did not stand idly by after these attacks. He sought the assistance of prominent Minneapolis attorney Norman Newhall. Newhall represented Rose without a fee in a libel lawsuit against Koch and Christian Research. After a lengthy trial in the Hennepin County District Court, presided over by the experienced and able Judge Donald Barbeau, a jury returned a verdict in favor of Rose. However, on appeal to the Minnesota Supreme Court, the jury verdict was overturned in an opinion authored by Associate Justice C. Donald Peterson. Peterson served in the Minnesota House before his election to the Supreme Court.[1]

The defendants contended before the District Court that the statements about Rose "were not defamatory and were, in any event, the truth." However, the Supreme Court held that "the jury's verdict, under proper instructions from the trial judge, clearly settled that issue. The jury gave Dr. Rose total vindication of his reputation."[2] As the Supreme Court stated, if there was any doubt as to the defamatory references they were removed in the opening statement by defendant's trial counsel to the jury:

"…[Rose] is one of the most resourceful Communists in the whole United States…"

"….[he] actually collaborated with Communists in the publishing of this book and has been collaborating with them and has entered into a course of conduct over a long period of time of collaboration although he does not come out openly;…"[3]

Koch's attacks on Rose brought out of the woodwork other efforts by extremists to discredit him. Thus, as the Supreme Court noted, "Dr. Rose and his family were subjected to nasty telephone calls and other crude harassments."[4] In March, 1963, the Chief Clerk of the Minnesota House of Representatives received an envelope containing a communication from a stranger to this action. Justice Peterson described the communication as one "… which can best be described as a most venomous diatribe against Jews and Negroes in which Rose, linked by that stranger to the members of the United States Supreme Court, was called 'one of the *most dangerous* men in America.' Dr. Rose is a Jew."[5] The Court noted that Rose's counsel "conceded on oral argument, however, that defendants were not responsible for that communication."

To their credit leading Conservative legislators and other public officials testified as to their respect for Rose. One testified that he had not "the slightest [reason] to think of him as a Communist sympathizer."[6] What is most significant historically, and instructive as to candidates for public office, is that they are not insulated from libelous attacks on their integrity or character even if, as in Rose's case, a court finds that the attacks/statements are not true. In *Rose v. Koch* the Minnesota Supreme Court applied retroactively, that is for the first time, a decision by the

U.S. Supreme Court in *New York Times v. Sullivan,*[7] Since Rose was both a "public official" and a "public figure" (author and educator), when the inflammatory pamphlet was published, Rose was required to prove "actual malice" on the part of those making the statements. It was not simply enough to sustain a verdict to prove "ill will." The Minnesota Supreme Court found that the plaintiff, Rose, under the *New York Times v. Sullivan* standard, must prove that "...defendants acted with knowledge that their defamatory publications were false or with reckless disregard of whether or not they were."[8] For an excellent discussion of *Rose v. Koch* and *New York Times v. Sullivan* see *The Hennepin Lawyer,* July-August 1984, an article authored by attorney Marshall Tanick.

There were two effects of the entire *Rose v. Koch* litigation. One, and most importantly, is that there is a broad reach legally to the definitions of a "public figure" or "public official." *New York Times v. Sullivan* continues to apply to those seeking or elected to public office or those who, such as university professors, will fit into the broad category of "public figures." If one fits in either category, and believes that he/she has been libeled or slandered, the person "must show fault by the defendant regarding the truth or falsity of the defamatory communication. He must show that the defendant knew the communication was false or acted with reckless disregard as to whether it was false. The burden of proof is on the plaintiff to prove the statement was false."

While Arnold Rose did not receive any money damages in his lawsuit, his personal and professional reputation were cleared both by the jury verdict and by the Minnesota Supreme Court opinion. Christian Research is described as a "right-wing extremist group" in a publication entitled *Arnold M. Rose, Libel and Academic Freedom; A Lawsuit Against Political Extremists* (University of Minnesota Press, 1968.) The increasingly adversarial and personal nature of the political process requires persons who consider a life in politics and public office to be aware that their personal reputation and history are not only subject to careful examination by their adversaries. Their opponents are shielded by the free speech guarantees of the U.S. Constitution from all but the most egregious circumstances in which actual malice can be proved to the satisfaction of the court and the jury. One with knowledge of the vagaries of the legal system, and decisions by a jury, must proceed with appropriate trepidation before entering into the political arena. The legacy of Arnold Rose lives on in political annals through this landmark decision in *Rose v. Koch* as well as through his distinguished although shortened career as a legislator and world recognized sociologist.

Chapter Thirty-two

The Art Of Lobbying:
Power, Politics and Persuasion

No discussion of Minnesota politics would be complete with-out an exploration of the role of the members of the Jew-ish community in the art of lobbying. Lobbying is the process of influencing elected officials at all levels as to their actions or votes on behalf of, or in opposition to, matters of legislation or public policy. The term "lobbying" is derived from the "lobby," the waiting room or entrance to a legislative chamber. Lobbying is simply the exercise of rights guaranteed under the U.S. and Min-nesota Constitutions. It is petitioning the government for redress of grievances.

In Minnesota lobbying has great historical precedent. On April 5, 1936, during a great debate over a tax bill, two thousand people calling themselves "the People's Lobby" spent the day at the State Capitol lobbying on behalf of the Farmer-Labor/Benson tax bill. The house was then controlled by the Farmer-laborites. The senate remained in conservative control. The People's Lobby represented a broad cross section of the rank and file members of the Farmer-Labor Party. There were contingents from the Worker's Alliance, the Timber Workers and other CIO unions, the Farm Holiday Association, and Farmer-Labor clubs from around the state.[1]

Lobbying has been so pervasive and influential at all levels of government that it has been called the "fourth branch of gov-ernment." Throughout the years there has been much controversy surrounding lobbyists and lobbying tactics. This is particularly true at the national level. 2005 was a year in which scandals erupted in the nation's capitol involving some members of Congress and the well known lobbyist Jack Abramof. Lobbying is an area very well known to me. I spent some 35 years as a lobbyist following my 1966 retirement from the legislature. I acted as a lobbyist for public interest groups and business trade associations. They included the Minnesota Children's Lobby, the Minnesota Speech and Hearing Association and the Minnesota Beer Wholesalers Association. My lobbying efforts were instrumental in the enactment of the Minnesota Childcare Facilities Act which provided funds and administrative support for the hearing impaired. My efforts also included the passage of the Beer Wholesalers Franchise Act. To avoid conflict of interest issues, I retired as a registered legislative lobbyist when Ron Latz was elected to the legislature.

Lobbyists play many different roles in the governmental process. The most visible lobbying activity may be shown in pictures of legions of lobbyists milling around the entrances to the legislative chambers. They are there hoping to achieve a few minutes of time to plead their cause with their targeted legislator. While occasionally a lobbyist may make an appearance before a legislative committee, most lobbying activities are not as visible. The most significant role of the lobbyist is providing a busy legislator with information supporting the client's position. Legislators traditionally have been overwhelmed with the need for facts and precedents supporting or opposing proposals. While staff support at the legislative level is now greater than ever before, even today those support levels are not adequate for the legislator to obtain necessary information. On controversial matters a legislator may be bombarded with facts and arguments on several sides of the issue. It is then up to the legislator to sift through the merits of those arguments in the decision making process.

Lobbying is indeed an art form. It combines elements of political power, an intimate knowledge of the political process, and the ability to persuade. Both the time and attention span of busy legislators requires a lobbyist to have the ability to express arguments for or against a proposal as succinctly as possible to achieve and hold the attention of the targeted official.

A major and controversial part of a lobbyist's role is the raising of campaign funds for public officials who have influence over issues affecting the lobbyist's clients. The money raising side of lobbying has led to abuses that have surfaced in Washington and in state legislatures. The most notable of these include the providing of campaign funds, directly or indirectly, beyond the limits of the law; providing trips to exotic locations in the guise of congressional fact finding; and expensive meals and free plane rides on corporate jets to and from the lawmaker's home state.

Federal campaign laws are so vague and riddled with exceptions that there are many loopholes through which disguised campaign contributions are channeled by interest groups on both sides of the political aisle. Minnesota has severe restrictions limiting the value of meals and so on provided to legislators. This has led to a claimed lack of social exchange between legislators of the two parties, and a subsequent loss of collegiality between partisan legislators. However, most recent efforts in the 2006 Session of the legislature to amend these limits failed. This was most likely a legislative reaction to the Washington scandals involving Abramof, Representative Randy Cunningham of California, and former House Majority Leader Tom DeLay of Texas.

It is without doubt that campaign contributions will buy a lobbyist access to the politician. They will provide or enhance the lobbyist's possibility of communicating face to face with the lawmaker or his/her staff. However, as the amount of the funds raised and contributed to an elected official increases, the question is necessarily raised as to whether what is being sought is more than an opportunity to plead the client's cause to a willing listener. No one yet has been able to draw a bright line as to whether it is appropriate access that is obtained. Or whether an unethical, if not illegal, contribution is being made in an effort to "buy" the lawmaker. The cost of campaigning, with media buys for television and radio commercials and so on, has sharply increased. Thus the candidate's need for funds has multiplied, and with it pressure on lobbyists and their clients to contribute.

There are several different categories of lobbyists. There are individual citizens who are petitioning a lawmaker or lawmaking body at every level for the redress of their particular grievance. It may be a zoning change to accommodate a particular residential or commercial building site. Or it may be an individual who lobbies a legislator by mail, by telephone or through email. Many of these seemingly individual pleas for or against a pending matter may be initiated by a special interest group. They acknowledge, appropriately, that public officials are much more likely to listen to the voters in their district than to the arguments of a professional lobbyist.

Public interest groups may be environmental or social action groups representing segments of the religious community such as the Joint Religious Legislative Coalition. The AFL-CIO and labor unions representing public employees and teachers have their lobbyists. The same is true for groups promoting or opposing other controversial actions, such as limits on abortion rights or same sex marriages.

Business groups represent a large category employing lobbyists. Business trade associations, such as in the licensed beverage industry, the Minnesota Business Partnership, the various chambers of commerce, and the Minnesota Taxpayers Association all employ lobbyists representing their individual points of view. Often individual business owners become quite experienced and adept at lobbying for their particular individual and collective interests before city councils and the legislature. Two of those individuals from the Minnesota Jewish community were Minneapolis businessmen Darrell Ansel and Norman Pink.

Large business entities, such as Target Corporation; individual banks; 3M Corporation; Northwest Airlines typically have an in house director of governmental relations. They also will retain individual lobbyists or lobbying organizations. The in house officials will normally serve as the interface between the lobbyists on site at the capitol. Then they communicate the results to their superiors in the organization. One example is Nathan Garvis. Garvis is Vice President for Governmental Affairs at Target Corporation. The Humphrey Institute at the University of Minnesota named Garvis as one of the recipients of the 2004 Hubert H. Humphrey Public

Leadership Award. In noting that honor, Garvis was referred to as "gifted and nationally regarded."

Lawyers also make up a group of Minnesota legislative lobby-ists. Contract lobbyists are where a law firm or other body enters into a lobbying contract with a business or organization. Sandra "Sandy" Neren, a non-lawyer, is a longtime and effective lobbyist with the Messerli and Kramer law firm. Another member from the Jewish community active in St. Paul is Judy Cook. Cook is a former executive director of the Minnesota Retail Association. She is now a name partner in the Cook, Girard lobbying firm. The Cook Girard firm also has a stable of lobbying clients. Cook is not a lawyer. Marcia Avner is a lobbyist for the Minnesota Council of Non Profits. Now retired is Abe Rosenthal. Rosenthal was a longtime lobbyist for a trucking association. Former State Rep-resentative Lee Greenfield, who chose not to run for re-election to the legislature, has used the expertise in healthcare matters he acquired during his legislative service, and as chair of the House committee on the subject, to consult and lobby.

A lawyer-lobbyist has a number of ethical responsibilities. The lawyer-lobbyist must abide by all of the general state restrictions on lobbying activities, including registration and disclosure of the lobbyist's clients. The lawyer-lobbyist must also adhere to the eth-ics of the legal profession.[2]

The dual nature of the relationship between lobbyists and the Congress was set forth succinctly by Minnesota native and congres-sional expert Norman J. Ornstein in his book, written with Shirley Elder, *"Interest Groups, Lobbying and Policy Making,"* 1978. There Ornstein states "Members of Congress in turn rely on groups to provide valuable constituency, technical, or political information, to give reelection support, and to assist strategically in passing or blocking legislation that the members support or oppose. *Groups need Congress and Congress needs groups."* (Emphasis added.)

What has helped give lobbying a bad name is the increasing use of sophisticated telemarketing calls and television ads to get an industry's or special interest group's message across. The effort of the pharmaceutical industry to influence the Minnesota legislature to defeat prescription drug bills is a case in point. The effort is set forth in an article in the *Star Tribune* of Sunday, November 16, 2003. It points out that, "Since 2000, the (pharmaceutical) industry, led by its trade group, The Pharmaceutical Research and Manufacturers of America (Ph. RMA), has spent at least $2.6 million in Minnesota on public relations, lobbyists, political advertisements and federal and state campaign contributions." Among other efforts the pharmaceutical industry has used "…methods designed to create the appearance of a grassroots surge of concern when the effort is driven by drug interests." Efforts were devoted to defeating price control measures on drug prices and successfully opposing bills that would have required substantial rebates or discounts from pharmaceutical companies.

"One of the questionable techniques used by pharmaceutical manufacturers is a 'sophisticated telemarketing technique' known as 'Astro Turf Lobbying.'" This technique creates an '…..artificial grass-roots political movement(s) designed to flood legislators' offices with faxes, letters and phone calls to create the appearance of a groundswell of constituent concern.' The article states that "…nearly all major public relations firms now provide similar lobbying efforts for their corporate clients." "The industry organizations often use 'consumer-friendly' names to disguise their true purpose." Often, if the Minnesota resident is amenable to the message received from the telemarketer, they are immediately patched through to the state legislator to whom they express their views. Pharmaceutical industry political spending in Minnesota in 2000-2002 totaled $602,968.00. These expenditures included a total number of Minnesota lobbyists at 38 lobbyists and 1,334 television ads.[3] [Sources noted as Minnesota Campaign Finance Board, Campaign Finance Analysis Project, estimates from the Wisconsin Advertising Project.]

Chapter Thirty-three

Shaking The Money Tree

Providing the seed money necessary to build a public facility such as the Wangensteen building or the Mount Sinai Hospital is only one example of the efforts by individuals and their families to create facilities and services that redound to the benefit of the public. Another method of financing involves candidates for public office and funding for passage of laws in the legislature and the adoption of constitutional amendments. These financial efforts were aptly phrased by the late Speaker of the U.S. House of Representatives "Tip" O'Neil of Massachusetts. O'Neil coined the phrase, "Money is the mother's milk of politics." And how right he was. No political campaign from the lowest level up through the President of the United States can hope to succeed without adequate funding by which they hope to influence the voter to their cause. The higher the elective office, and the broader the geographic and population sought to be reached, the greater is the need to raise substantial funds. In today's environment this has become not just millions of dollars but hundreds of millions. Observers have estimated that it will take approximately $100 million each for prospective presidential candidates in the 2008 elections to be viable.

Funds are used for television and radio advertising, newspaper ads, polling, literature extolling the record and virtues of the candidate, and simply paying the cost of staff and travel. Money may be raised and donated to the individual candidate, to the political party, or to a political action committee (PAC). The purpose is not simply to elect or reelect a candidate who shares the views and philosophy of the donor or fundraiser. Money donated will not only shape the message of the candidate. It also influences his/her agenda once office is attained. Money contributed is also used simply to gain access to the candidate once elected. Access provides an opportunity for the expression of opinions.

Contributions also are a means of ego gratification. They allow the donor to share in the reflected glory of the candidate be he/she a governor, U.S. senator, or president.

It often does and should shake the sensibility of the viewer to read or hear of a wealthy person who donates a large sum of money simply to attend a reception and have his/her picture taken with the president. For some, such as former Senator Rudy Boschwitz, raising huge sums of money can lead to an ambassadorship to a body of the United Nations. For others, either Democrat or Republican, it can lead to a prestigious diplomatic post in England, France, Germany and the like. Or it may lead to a position in state or federal government for which the person may or may not be qualified. The appointees' ineptitude is often not discovered until a crisis occurs such as in Hurricane Katrina.

Many books have been written about campaign financing; the laws that regulate money in politics; and the individual fundraisers who provide the fuel to keep the political money machines running. Most state laws, like Minnesota's, are designed to limit or prohibit campaign contributions by business corporations. However, there are so many devices conjured up by clever lawyers and politicians, that these restrictions have become meaningless in the real political world. There are so many ways to hide the origin of such contributions. Corporate officers may implicitly or explicitly "require" highly paid corporate officers to donate to the candidate of the business' choice. Or they "launder" funds through various campaign committees or political action committees (PACS) in a way that the restrictions become almost impossible to enforce.

The fact that criminal penalties are affixed to campaign violations does not appear to have provided much of a deterrent to the use of the loopholes in the laws. Even when one believes that he has a "smoking gun," providing written evidence of a laundered contribution in violation of Minnesota law, the proof of an intentional violation proves to be almost insurmountable. Witness the

2005 prosecution of a former Republican State Chairman for a claimed violation of Minnesota's law against corporate political contributions. The jury, after a relatively short deliberation, reached a verdict of "not guilty."

The political contributions can come in large or small amounts. A president's campaign can charge thousands of dollars to attend a luncheon to hear the president or have a picture taken with the president. But the candidates do not overlook the smaller donors who may give simply because they like the candidate's stand on an issue such as abortion or are "...very impressed by his (President Bush's) faith."[1]

In 2000, Rudy Boschwitz, the co-chair of the president's Minnesota campaign, along with his wife Ellen, each gave $2,000.00 to the president's campaign. "Boschwitz, one of the elite group of fundraisers invited to a barbecue at the President's ranch in Texas earlier this month, raised at least $388,000 for Bush in 2000..." In 2003 the Minnesota presidential campaign of Senator John Kerry raised, through June 30, more money - $114,940 - than President Bush's $107,600.[2]

For many years before Rudy Boschwitz's and Norm Coleman's elections to the U.S. Senate the most visible Jewish fund raisers in Minnesota were Democrats. Avid fund raisers for Republican candidates, such as Alan "Buddy" Ruvelson, kept a low public profile while raising substantial sums quietly from Jewish businessmen. These were Jews with more conservative political interests than the liberal supporters of DFL candidates.

There were, and are, a number of notable leaders in the Minnesota Jewish community who have been publicly and privately identified with raising money for Democratic-DFL candidates. Their efforts may have been limited primarily to individual candidates, such as businessman Ted Deikel for Governor Wendell Anderson. The late Milton Altman, a St. Paul attorney, was also an active DFL fundraiser. He also encouraged his law partner, St. Paul insurance company attorney James Geraghty, to become co-chair of the Lawyers For Latz volunteer committee in my campaign for attorney general. Or they could be more broadly identified with support for liberal causes and candidates. Through the years there have been a handful of Minnesota Jews who have raised very substantial sums for liberal causes and candidates. Several, like Ruth Speigel Usem and Sam and Sylvia Kaplan, have also offered their personal residences for fundraising events. These have been for political aspirants at levels from local municipal offices to candidates for president and vice president.

Others have been both major donors and also fundraisers. Successful Jewish Minnesotans, such as retired retail merchandiser Harold Roitenberg, and real estate developer Gary Tankenof, have not only been major supporters and fundraisers for causes in the Jewish community. They have also raised and contributed substantial amounts to primarily Democratic candidates.

Perhaps the most visible and successful Jewish political fundraisers for Democratic causes and candidates at many levels are Minneapolis attorney and banking entrepreneur Samuel Kaplan and his restaurateur spouse Sylvia. The Kaplans have for years been active in the Minnesota Jewish community. Sam Kaplan is past president of the Minneapolis Jewish Federation. He has a long record of identification with and support for human rights and social justice issues. Sylvia Kaplan in her own right has a long-standing record as a human rights activist. At age 22, and with little children at home, Kaplan was a leader in educating Golden Valley residents "… about prejudice and anti-Semitism." She helped organize the Golden Valley Human Rights Commission "…which became the first official HRC in the state."[3]

Along with 27 other influential Twin Cities couples that included Dr. Stanley Goldberg and Luella Goldberg and Dr. Alvin Zelickson and Sue Zelickson, Sam and Sylvia Kaplan were honored by being selected by *Minneapolis/St. Paul Magazine* as the most significant "Power Couple" on the list.[4] The article describes Sam and Sylvia Chessen Kaplan as "king makers, political heavyweights, power brokers."

While the Kaplans have been identified with many social and political causes and candidates they are best known for their financial support and mentoring of the late Senator Paul

Wellstone. Sam Kaplan was chairman of Wellstone's 1990 and 1996 successful campaigns. However, the Kaplans' relationship with Paul and Sheila Wellstone went far beyond the typical hosting of fundraising events and raising campaign contributions. There was a close personal relationship between them. The Kaplans were political and strategic advisors as well as fundraisers. In 1990, the front end money the Kaplans raised helped propel Paul Wellstone from relative obscurity into the Senate over Rudy Boschwitz.

The Kaplans gave the relatively unknown Wellstone the credibility he needed to compete with the better known and well-funded incumbent Jewish Senator. Boschwitz, a successful businessman as well as a well known conservative Republican, had the political acumen and financial resources to be elected and serve in the U.S. senate. Most observers believe that but for the financial and political advice and efforts of the Kaplans that Paul Wellstone would not have eked out his very narrow victory over Boschwitz in 1990 and repeated that success in 1996. Wellstone was widely expected to triumph over St. Paul Mayor Norm Coleman before the Wellstones' deaths ended that campaign. The death of the Wellstones has not ended Sam and Sylvia Kaplan's involvement with liberal causes and candidates. Their home situated on the banks of the Mississippi continues to be the site for fundraisers for their candidates and causes.

Lobbying and Lobbyists

The activities of those Jews described in the chapter on "Shaking The Money Tree" do so for a variety of reasons. They may raise and contribute funds simply in support of a particular cause or candidate. Or, as the case with former U.S. Senator Rudy Boschwitz, they also seek to maintain influence in the inner circles of government on behalf of their favorite causes such as support of the State of Israel. Or the motivations may also include the degree of involvement with an individual candidate so that they may serve as a mentor to the candidate. This was the case with

Sam and Sylvia Kaplan.

As a rule these activities are governed by state and federal laws on campaign financing. Their activities do not usually constitute "lobbying" in the legal and traditional sense. They do not on any kind of a regular or specific basis seek to influence local, state or federal persons or lawmakers. Those who do so are required to register as lobbyists under federal and state law. As in Minnesota, their activities, including providing favors such as meals and entertainment, are severely restricted. Until recently, with the emergence of the scandals in Washington involving Jack Abramof and several members of Congress, the regulations affecting the federal government and the Congress were riddled with loopholes and exceptions. It remains to be seen how successful the new Democratic Party control of the Congress will result in legislation sufficient to close the loopholes that led to these abuses.

Lawyers who seek to lobby on behalf of clients in Minnesota are subject to dual regulations. They are required to register and comply with the Minnesota law on lobbyists. In addition, they are governed by the Rules of Professional Responsibility governing the conduct of all Minnesota lawyers.[5]

Even after a lawyer in private practice becomes a judge his/her conduct while a practicing lawyer may result in removal from office as a judge. This was the case in a matter brought before the Minnesota Board on Judicial Standards in 1978. I was retained as a Special Counsel to represent the board in removal proceedings involving a sitting district court judge, Jack Gillard. The proceedings involved questions as to the conduct of a sitting district court judge for claimed ethical violations occurring *before* he became a judge and while he was acting as an attorney in his private law practice. It was alleged that while in private law practice Gillard had represented an Iowa insurance company that sought to be licensed to do business in Minnesota. In the course of that representation, Gillard was alleged to have told Iowa insurance executives that he had a relationship with a prominent politician who could exert influence on the state licensing officials to grant the license. In his request for a substantial retainer fee Gillard was alleged to have asked for such a large fee that the insurance executive believed that much of the money was to be used to improperly influence the issuance of the license. The Board on Judicial Standards heard the evidence of the alleged unethical conduct.

The board determined that while the conduct occurred while Gillard was acting as a practicing attorney, and was therefore subject to his disbarment to the practice of law, that such conduct would require removal of Gillard from office as a judge. This followed because the Minnesota Constitution requires judges to be licensed to practice law. If a judge is no longer able to practice law, he/she is no longer able to serve as a judge.

Since the issues involve interpretation of the Minnesota Constitution, the board's action removing Gillard was appealed by Gillard directly to the Minnesota Supreme Court. It came before the court on two separate occasions. The Supreme Court ruled that Gillard was to be removed from office as a judge.[6]

Chapter Thirty-four

The Minnesota Triplets:
Rudy Boschwitz, Paul Wellstone, and Norman Coleman

Minnesota is unique in the nation in having three U.S. Senators who are publicly identified as Jews. There are other states, such as California and Wisconsin, that have had as many as two Jewish senators serving at the same time: California with Barbara Boxer and Dianne Feinstein, and Wisconsin with Russell Feingold and Herbert Kohl. Each state is allotted two U.S. Senators regardless of its population.

The Minnesota Triplets did not all serve at the same time as have Boxer, Feinstein, Feingold and Kohl. However, given its small Jewish population relative to other states that have had Jewish senators, it is unique that Minnesota has had three. Also unusual is each Jewish senator in Minnesota succeeded another Jew in that position. In 1978, Rudy Boschwitz became the first Jewish senator in Minnesota history. He was defeated twice by Paul Wellstone, in 1990 and 1996, in closely contested elections. Paul Wellstone and Norman Coleman were in a hotly contested race, which would have gone down to the wire, but for the tragic death of Wellstone in a plane crash a week before election day.

It is worth examining the characteristics of Minnesota voters and Minnesota's political culture that has led to the elections of these three. Two of them are conservative Republicans and one a liberal Democrat. Their backgrounds could not have been more different.

Rudy Boschwitz was born in Germany. He immigrated with

his family to the United States. Educated as a lawyer, he instead went into the plywood business with his brother in Wisconsin. He then settled with his wife and raised his family in Minnesota.

Paul Wellstone was a political scientist. He was educated in North Carolina before achieving a position as a political science teacher at Carleton College in Northfield.

Norm Coleman began in politics as a Democrat. His roots were in Brooklyn, New York. He grew up in a liberal Democratic family. He is a lawyer. He was a Democrat. He worked for Attorney General Skip Humphrey for 17 years before being elected Mayor of St. Paul. Coleman became a Republican. It was primarily over the claimed rigidity of the DFL Party endorsement and platform process in which a pro life adherent has little or no expectation of success in achieving endorsement for high statewide public office. Coleman married into a prominent Catholic family and is pro life. He realized, quite accurately, that he had no real future in the DFL endorsement process by holding pro life views. Boschwitz also holds pro life views. In the Minnesota Republican Party pro life views are as important in the endorsement process for state-wide office as are pro choice views in the DFL. Paul Wellstone held equally strong pro choice views.

Neither Boschwitz nor Wellstone held public office prior to their election to the senate. Coleman took a more traditional path. He first served successfully as St. Paul Mayor. His success as mayor was the launching pad to his GOP endorsement for the senate. Coleman's electoral success in St. Paul was achieved despite the fact that St. Paul has been a traditional DFL stronghold. St. Paul reverted to its traditional DFL voting habits with the 2005 defeat of incumbent Mayor Randy Kelly by Chris Coleman. That vote hinged on Kelly's 2004 endorsement of President George Bush's reelection.

Typically in Minnesota, mayors of Minneapolis and St. Paul have not achieved success in endorsement or election to statewide office. Arthur Naftalin was a successful mayor of Minneapolis with close ties to Hubert Humphrey. Yet he was unsuccessful in his quest for endorsement for lieutenant governor. Prior to his election as senator, Boschwitz was the Republican National Committeeman from Minnesota. He was, and remains, a prolific fund raiser for Republican candidates, particularly for Republican presidential candidates. Wellstone's route to the United States Senate was most unconventional. He did not hold any public office prior to his election. His skill at energizing and mobilizing young people with his progressive views served as his launching pad to the DFL endorsement and subsequent 1990 election over Boschwitz in a closely contested election.

The Boschwitz-Wellstone election results were narrow. Only 2.68 percent separated the candidates in the final election tally. Observers speculated that the decisive factor in Wellstone's victory was the letter signed by many Jewish supporters of Boschwitz challenging Wellstone's commitment as a Jew. Boschwitz is a member of Temple Israel. He also has been very supportive of the Lubovitchers, a very Orthodox Jewish group centered in St. Paul. His pro life views provoked considerable controversy within the Jewish community and particularly within Temple Israel. There was a dispute over whether Boschwitz, even though he was a U.S. Senator, should be invited to participate in the ceremony dedicating the renovation of Temple Israel. It was finally resolved that Boschwitz deserved to be recognized because of his official position. This was despite the fact that his pro life views were rejected by Temple Israel's Senior Rabbi Stephen Pinsky. Max Fallek, a Temple Israel leader with a history of civil rights activism dating back to the 1960 march on Washington, and I, finally prevailed in efforts to invite Boschwitz to the ceremony.

Despite his stands on certain controversial subjects, Boschwitz did an excellent job of constituent service. I particularly experienced his efforts on behalf of funding for childcare food programs in Minnesota. Boschwitz was also a strong proponent of small business. Fallek was an advisor to small business entrepreneurs.

Coleman is still in his first six year term. He was elected with strong support of the national Republican Party and President George W. Bush. He has been a faithful supporter of President Bush and his programs. Coleman is a very skillful politician with excellent instincts on issues. He has thus tried to walk a narrow line in his public positions and votes. He understands Minnesota voters have more moderate positions on most issues than he, President Bush, and the Senate Republican leadership.

Paul Wellstone was an unabashed populist. His outspoken views on issues earned him the love and great respect of many, while causing enmity on the part of those who held adverse positions. There was little, if any, middle ground in the opinions of people on Wellstone. You either loved or hated him. In his senate career he moderated his initially strident personal relationships with fellow senators. Wellstone became more comfortable in his role in the senate. However, he never moderated his views on the issues that were at the core of his beliefs. The spouses of Boschwitz and Coleman have taken a more traditional role as the spouses of high profile politicians. Sheila Wellstone, on the other hand, carved out an independent role as a strong advocate for her personal beliefs. This was particularly in the area of ending spousal abuse.

Chapter Thirty-five

Rudy Boschwitz

Rudolph Eli (Rudy) Boschwitz was born in Berlin, Germany on November 17, 1930. He attended John Hopkins University. In 1953 he graduated from New York University and from the New York University Law School. He was admitted to the New York Bar as an attorney in 1954, and to the Wisconsin Bar in 1959. In 1954-1955, Boschwitz served in the United States Army Signal Corps. He is the founder and chairman of a plywood manufacturing and home retailing firm.

Boschwitz was the Republican National Committeeman from Minnesota from 1971 to 1978. In November 1978, he was elected as a Republican to the United States Senate for a term commencing January 3, 1979. He was elected over Wendy Anderson in what is known as the "Minnesota Massacre." This was the election in which the Republicans swept Minnesota statewide in legislative offices. Boschwitz defeated Anderson, a popular governor, basically due to Anderson's "self appointment" to the senate seat vacated by Fritz Mondale when Mondale was elected vice president. Boschwitz won 56.57 percent of the vote.

After his election defeat Anderson resigned his senate seat early. He could have continued to serve in the senate until the end of his term on January 2, 1979. Anderson's resignation allowed the newly elected Boschwitz to be sworn in early. This early assumption of the senate seat allowed Boschwitz to have an advantage in senate seniority and to achieve better committee assignments.

Boschwitz was reelected in November 1984. He defeated Minnesota Secretary of State Joan Growe. With his second six year term ending in 1990, Boschwitz was defeated by Paul Wellstone in a close race. Boschwitz lost by 2.68 percent of the vote.

Boschwitz had a successful career in the senate. He served on the Agriculture, Foreign Relations, Veterans Affairs and Small Business and Budget committees. As a member of the budget committee, Boschwitz focused his efforts on reducing the federal deficit. In 1984, he offered what was characterized as the "Fair Play Budget." This was an attempt to slow the growth of the federal budget. Boschwitz was chairman of the national Republican Senatorial Campaign Committee from 1987 to 1988. The chair of that committee plays a key role in the Republican caucus in the senate. The committee is the major fundraising unit of senate Republican campaigns throughout the nation. The chair of the committee has a strong voice in allocating funds to senate GOP candidates. This enables the chair of the committee to build up equity with those who are ultimately elected.

As a senator Boschwitz was a strong supporter of the State of Israel. He thus earned the support of many in the Minnesota Jewish community. He received substantial campaign contributions, particularly from political action committees.

Political observers agree that the single item leading to Boschwitz's 1990 loss to Wellstone was a letter prepared and circulated late in the campaign. The letter was addressed "To our friends in the Minnesota Jewish community." It was a direct mail piece signed by 72 Jewish Boschwitz supporters. It included a number who were prominent in the Jewish community. Most of them were without visible Republican affiliation. The piece charged that Wellstone had "no connections whatsoever with the Jewish community or our communal life." Reference was made to Wellstone's spouse, Sheila Wellstone, who was raised as a Southern Baptist. The letter pointed out that the Wellstone "children were brought up as non-Jews." It went on to state that Wellstone had served as the state cochairman for the Jesse Jackson for President campaign. The letter concluded that this was all proof that "Wellstone is a disturbing element in American politics."

This letter is acknowledged to be one of the major political blunders in Minnesota electoral politics. It was as significant in Wellstone's defeat of Boschwitz as was Wendell Anderson's "self-appointment" in the first election of Boshcwitz. Many members of the Jewish community resented the attack by one Jew on another Jew notwithstanding Wellstone's intermarriage. There was no reason to inject the religion or religious commitment of either candidate or a spouse and children in the campaign. There were many substantive issues on which to disagree. It is unclear from whom or where the idea of the letter originated. Or who was the author of the text. However, as in all campaigns, the buck stops with the candidate. The candidate is responsible ultimately for the efforts of his/her supporters. Boschwitz really did not need to make such a move in an attempt to solidify his position in the Jewish community. While he was more conservative than most Minnesota Jews in his affiliations and votes in the senate, he was a very strong supporter of the government of Israel. He maintained a membership in Temple Israel. He had strong ties with the orthodox Jewish community. Religion did not appear to play a role in Boschwitz's 1978 defeat of Anderson. Nor did it in his 1984 reelection campaign. Thus, in 1990, it was unlikely that both he and Wellstone being Jewish would be of any real significance to most voters. The reference in the letter that "the Wellstone children were brought up as non-Jews" is likely to have raised questions in the minds of Christians as to whether Boschwitz believed that there was something inherently wrong if a person's children were raised as Christians.

The result of Boschwitz's defeat was the removal of a strong advocate for Israel from the senate, and from the key foreign relations committee. This was a result just the opposite of what Boschwitz's Minnesota Jewish supporters sought to achieve. At that point, Wellstone's views on Israel were largely unknown. He had no track record of involvement in the Minnesota Jewish community or with Israel. His support of Jesse Jackson for President raised questions of his commitment to Jewish causes and support of Israel.

Rudy Boschwitz was the first Jew to be elected to statewide office in Minnesota. Boschwitz's campaign manager was attorney James Rosenbaum. Boschwitz was instrumental in securing

Rosenbaum's appointment as U.S. Attorney for Minnesota. When a vacancy arose on the U.S. District Court bench, Boschwitz recommended, and the President appointed, Rosenbaum to that position. He has since become the Chief Judge of the U.S. District Court for Minnesota. Rosenbaum was the first Jew to serve as U.S. Attorney for Minnesota and as a U.S. District Court Judge for Minnesota. Attorney Marilyn Rosenbaum was appointed by Governor Arne Carlson as a Hennepin County District Court Judge. She continues to serve in that position.

In Boschwitz's 1996 unsuccessful effort to reclaim his senate seat from Wellstone, Boschwitz was subject to slanderous attacks by some anti Israel critics on the national scene. For example, former U.S. Senator James Abourezk, a South Dakotan of Lebanese ancestry, issued a blistering attack on Boschwitz's pro Israel efforts. Following his retirement from the senate Boschwitz has continued his prodigious fundraising efforts on behalf of Republican candidates and particularly on behalf of both Presidents Bush. He raised hundreds of thousands of dollars in both presidential campaigns. In 2005, as a reward for his ongoing and consistent fundraising efforts, service to the nation and to the Republican Party, President Bush appointed Boschwitz to become the U.S. Ambassador to the United Nations Human Rights Commission.

Norman Coleman

Norman "Norm" Coleman was born August 17, 1949, in Brooklyn, New York. He was raised in a Jewish home and continues to identify himself as Jewish. He is married to Laurie Casserly Coleman. She is a member of a prominent Twin Cities Catholic family. Norman and Laurie Coleman had four children. Two of them are deceased. Their children are now teenagers. They are a son Jacob and a daughter Sarah. In a profile in the Star Tribune, Coleman stated his hobbies as fishing, reading, juggling and music. He said his heroes are Robert Kennedy, Winston Churchill and his father Norman Coleman Sr. His favorite musicians are Joni Mitchell and Bob Dylan. In 1971, he received his B.A. in political science from Hofstra University. In 1976, he received his law degree from the University of Iowa College of Law.[1]

Coleman served under Minnesota Attorney General Skip Humphrey. For 17 years he was a criminal prosecutor, civil litigation supervisor and chief lobbyist. From 1986-1992, he served as chief prosecutor and as Solicitor General. As an Assistant Attorney General, Coleman was the chief strategist and directed the lobbying efforts for the successful Minnesota Drug Abuse Resistance Education Program better known as DARE. Ron Latz, as an Assistant Attorney General, worked closely with Coleman in lobbying for the DARE program.

During the entire 17 years of his service in the attorney general's office, Coleman identified himself as a Democrat and worked within the DFL Party. However, Coleman was identified as a more conservative Democrat. In 1993, running as a DFLer, Coleman was elected Mayor of St. Paul. In 1996, he served as the co-chair of the Minnesota Committee for the Reelection of President Clinton. In 1996, Coleman joined the Minnesota Republican Party. The differences between Coleman and the DFL were most evident on the issue of abortion politics. Coleman is pro life. It was clear that it was extremely unlikely that any professed pro life candidate could expect to be endorsed by the DFL Party for governor or U. S. Senator. In 1997, Coleman was reelected mayor. This made him St. Paul's first Republican mayor in more than 25 years. He polled almost sixty percent of the vote.

By most accounts Coleman's tenure as mayor was noteworthy for many accomplishments. He not only brought to the office significant intelligence, but also an indefatigable optimism and a hard work ethic. The enthusiasm he brought to the major projects he initiated was infectious. He had the ability to work together in partnership with Republican business interests in St. Paul. He was able to provide jobs and other forms of economic development. These included $1.7 billion worth of riverfront development. Coleman claimed success for not raising city taxes in eight years; in growing 18,000 jobs; and in achieving $3.5 billion worth of investments. St. Paul achieved its first triple-a-bond rating in its history.[2]

To sport's enthusiasts Coleman's most noteworthy feats were his leadership in securing a National Hockey League franchise for St. Paul, and the construction of a $175 million arena. He also helped create a $90 million Science Museum of Minnesota. He led the effort to bring Lawson Software to downtown St. Paul. Coleman also created what is being called a "national model for building public/private partnerships. He brought together the top twenty ceo's to create the Capital City Partnership. The Partnership is committed to promoting, marketing and developing St. Paul."[3]

As Mayor Coleman received several awards. They included the Award for Public Service from the Woodrow Wilson International Center for Scholars; the U.S. Conference of Mayors 2001 Award of Excellence in Public-Private Partnerships; the Mondale Award from the Pan America Society of Minnesota; and the 2001 Manhattan Institute Urban Innovator Award for Civic Innovation. Coleman has served on the boards of directors of the Minnesota DARE program; the National Jewish Fund; and the CQ Press, a division of Congressional Quarterly, Inc.[4]

In 1998, the Republican Party endorsed Coleman for Governor. Coleman ran in a three way race with the DFL endorsed candidate Attorney General Skip Humphrey, and the Independence Party candidate Jesse Ventura. Ventura took out a $300,000 loan to finance his campaign. Ventura was outspent three to one by Humphrey and five to one by Coleman. The vote was split three ways. Coleman ran ahead of Humphrey but lost to Ventura. Ventura won with a plurality of 37 percent of the vote. When a University of Kansas Professor of Political Science Burdett Loomis was asked why Ventura won, he replied, "Because of the Body's tremendous appeal to young males. They got out and voted. We want young people to take part in the electoral process," Loomis said. "Well, this time they did." When asked why the young people took part, his response was, "Because Jesse's a libertarian and so are many young people. They've got the live-and-let-live streak." When Loomis was asked "Why else did Ventura win?" he replied, "The opposition. Collectively the electorate isn't stupid. They saw this mayor of St. Paul, Coleman, who is an empty suit, a big smile kind of guy, they saw Skip Humphrey, a second generation politician, also a pretty gray guy. Oddly enough, Jesse, the former wrestler, with a boa, came across as the real human being in this race."[5]

Most Minnesota observers believe that part of the reason for the defeat of both Coleman and Humphrey was their refusal to take Ventura seriously. Thus, in joint television appearances, Coleman and Humphrey allowed Ventura, with his powerful persona, to dominate the exchanges. One of the other reasons for the Ventura victory was the very large turnout of young voters on election day. The Minnesota election law allows voters to register and vote at the polling place on election day. Following his defeat, Humphrey retired from public service and became a consultant.

Coleman was undeterred in his quest for higher political office. He began to work with the Republican Party organization in Minnesota and nationally. In 2000, he was the Minnesota chair

of Texas Governor George W. Bush's presidential campaign. This
was a rather remarkable turnaround from Coleman's co chairing
of Clinton's reelection campaign just four years earlier. Coleman
was obviously the favored son of the national Republican Party
leadership and of the Bush Whitehouse.

In 2002, there was a U.S. Senate seat up for election. House
Majority Leader State Representative Tim Pawlenty had his eye
on the senate seat along with Coleman. A call from the Bush
Whitehouse by Karl Rove, the president's political director, persuaded Pawlenty to remove himself from the senate race. This left
the field open for the GOP to endorse Coleman for the senate. At
the Republican state party convention Coleman was endorsed for
the senate and Pawlenty was endorsed for governor.

Coleman entered the race against the incumbent Democrat
Paul Wellstone. Coleman and Wellstone were locked in a very
tight race when Wellstone, his wife, daughter and other members of the campaign team, were killed in a plane crash a week
before the election. The Wellstone forces were convinced that with
a massive turnout of campaign workers in the last days leading up
to election they would have swung the vote in Wellstone's favor.
Unfortunately, that race ended prematurely.

The Minnesota DFL was left without a candidate. Former
Vice President and U.S. Senator Fritz Mondale, long retired from
elective office, stepped forward to fill the huge breach caused by
Wellstone's death. Democrats were encouraged by Mondale's willingness to run on short notice. However, their enthusiasm and
optimism were crushed by the occurrences at a public gathering
held to memorialize the Wellstones. In the presence of a huge
crowd, complete with Governor Ventura and many national per-
sonages of both parties, Rick Kahn, Wellstone's campaign treasurer and longtime friend, delivered an exceedingly partisan and
very emotional speech. The speech was such that Governor Ventura and his wife left in the middle of it. The speech was widely
televised with a very large viewing audience. Observers believed
that if there had been some way for television commentators to
cut off the speech when it became obvious that it was a very par-

tisan appeal, that they would have done so. The speech horrified many independents. It dismayed most Democrats. It energized the Republican faithful who had been largely silent following Wellstone's death. Observers questioned why Kahn's speech had not been vetted before it was delivered. However, this was somewhat understandable given the tumult following the events of the death of the Wellstone family and party. In the aftermath of the death and the rally, Coleman conducted himself very well.

What most Democrats had hoped would be a Mondale victory turned into an election night defeat. Coleman defeated Mondale by three percent of the vote. He received 50 percent to Mondale's 47 percent. There was a preelection television debate between Coleman and Mondale. While the long retired Mondale did show his expertise and continuing knowledge of politics, government, and current issues before Minnesotans and the nation, Coleman acquitted himself with decorum. He showed respect toward Mondale.

Coleman was coached in preparation for the debate by attorney Robert Weinstine of the firm Winthrop and Weinstine. Winthrop and Weinstine employed Coleman in an "of counsel" capacity during the election campaign. In 2005, Bob Weinstine served as the chair of a screening committee named to assist Senator Coleman in selecting a nominee for the U.S. District Court to replace Judge Richard Kyle.

By his election Coleman became Minnesota's junior senator. Minnesota's senior senator was DFLer Mark Dayton. However, with the Republicans in control of the U.S. Senate, Coleman was named to serve on the Senate Foreign Relations Committee. This committee is key to support for the state of Israel. According to the Minnesota unit of the American Israel Public Affairs Committee (AIPAC), "Senator Coleman has steadfastly supported resolutions and legislation in support of Israel."[6]

Coleman has angered some Minnesota Jews by his support for an experimental school voucher plan in Washington D.C. He opposed school vouchers in his campaign. Pro choice supporters criticized Coleman's strong support of a Bush sponsored bill signed into law that banned "so-called partial birth abortions." "Coleman was part of a Congress that drove up budget deficits to record levels. But he defended the President's economic record, saying that cutting taxes will lead to more jobs and ultimately reduce the national debt."[7] In the first two years of his term, Coleman "provided steady support to the war."(in Iraq).[8] Shortly after his election, Republican leaders in the Senate named Coleman to head two subcommittees including the influential Permanent Subcommittee on Investigations.

Coleman is up for reelection to the Senate in 2008. Therefore, it is unclear how his steady support of President Bush and the war in Iraq, together with his solidly conservative voting record, will affect his reelection chances. Will he suffer political consequences for his support of President Bush as did his successor St. Paul Mayor Randy Kelly? Or will the resourceful Coleman succeed in putting enough distance between himself and the increasingly unpopular Bush to win reelection against a DFL challenger?

Chapter Thirty-seven

Paul Wellstone

Of the three Jewish Minnesota U.S. Senators, none exemplified the biblical admonition to pursue justice better than the late Senator Paul Wellstone. From his days as a political science professor at Carleton College, through his tragic death in a plane crash, Wellstone was devoted to the cause of social justice. He had a passionate commitment to empower "...average citizens in using government to improve their lives..."[1] Whether it was encouraging college students to be politically active; organizing opposition to power lines in rural Minnesota; joining in picket lines of striking workers; or opposing the agendas of President Bush in the Congress, Wellstone exemplified a person with a deep social conscience coupled with the ability to articulate both his own views and those of the people he served. In a time when the conservative agenda seeks to achieve political debate around moral or family values, Wellstone stood for the most basic of human values: providing healthcare to those in need; protecting the environment; and raising issues of conscience even though they may have been unpopular or at a personal political cost.

Liberal causes have not had such an articulate spokesman since the early years of Hubert H. Humphrey's political career. While democrats nationally seek to find once again the middle ground enunciated by President Bill Clinton, Wellstone sought to restore the voice of liberals in and out of the Democratic Party. He often stated "I represent the Democratic wing of the Democratic party."[2]

There appears to be a growing cynicism among young people as to the role of government. It was evidenced by the libertarian attitude that propelled Jesse Ventura into the governorship.

Paul Wellstone had the ability to inspire young people to enter politics at the grassroots level and to work the long tedious hours necessary to mount successful political campaigns. These virtues propelled him to two successful elections to the U. S. Senate. They would likely have assured him a third six year term but for his death a week before the 2002 election. Few politicians of recent vintage in Minnesota or elsewhere had the same inspirational ability as Wellstone.

Paul Wellstone was the son of Jewish immigrants from the Soviet Union. He grew up in Arlington, Virginia. At age 19, he married Sheila Ison, a Baptist. Paul and Sheila had three children and six grandchildren. Wellstone earned a Ph.D. in political science at the University of North Carolina. A year after graduation, he secured a teaching position in the political science department of Carleton College. He had a rocky career at Carleton. His liberal beliefs expounded in the classroom earned him the support of his students. Along with that support came controversy when he sought tenure. It was only after a widespread uproar over efforts of the college's governing body to deny him tenure that he achieved tenure. With tenure came the free speech shield that comes with the security afforded a tenured college professor.

In 1990, after a flirtation with running as DFL candidate for State Auditor, Wellstone was endorsed to run for the U.S. Senate against incumbent Rudy Boschwitz. Wellstone was the underdog in that race. He ran a vigorous grassroots campaign. He traveled throughout the state in his trademark Green Bus. He invoked enthusiasm with his populist message. He was aided by humorous television ads. His campaign was underfunded in comparison to that of the incumbent Boschwitz.

Wellstone was fortunate to have met and inspired Sam and Sylvia Kaplan. The Kaplans became his longtime supporters. They were the predominant and successful fundraisers throughout his political career. As Sylvia Kaplan stated it, "At first nobody took him seriously. At first, we were very skeptical. But we were blown away by his energy and his enthusiasm. We became the first people who wore ties and suits - people who had some where-withal - to support Paul. In that sense, I think we gave him some legitimacy."[3]

The 1990 senatorial election was closely contested. In what was considered to be an upset, Wellstone defeated Boschwitz by 2.68 percent of the vote. Political observers agreed that the tipping point in that election was the direct mail piece signed by a number of Boschwitz's Jewish supporters that questioned Wellstone's marriage to a Baptist and inferred that there was something wrong with raising the Wellstone children in the Christian faith. Wellstone was the only Democrat to defeat an incumbent U.S. Senator in the 1990 election.

Wellstone had a rocky start in the tradition bound U.S. Senate. His cold reception there was likened to that of Hubert Humphrey on his entry to the Senate following his remarkable Democratic National Convention speech on civil rights. However, it was hard for even such conservative senators as Jesse Helms of North Carolina to withstand Wellstone's almost boyish enthusiasm for his populist causes and his friendly personal appeal. While moderating his personal relationships in the Senate, Paul Wellstone never deserted the liberal causes to which he was devoted. In 1991, he led a coalition that succeeded in defeating an energy bill that proposed opening the Alaska Arctic National Wildlife Refuge to oil drilling.[4] Wellstone joined with his wife Sheila in causes to end domestic spousal abuse.

In 1996, Wellstone won a reelection contest against Boschwitz. "Wellstone had been the only incumbent up for election to oppose welfare reform, saying it would take food out of the mouths of children and the elderly. When Boschwitz ran a series of ads calling him "Senator Welfare," Paul responded with T.V. spots saying his parents had taught him to stand up for what was right. "Senator Welfare" won a second term.[5] Adams described Wellstone's work as a "…lifetime of work supporting those whose voices would not otherwise be heard."[6]

When he first campaigned for the senate Wellstone pledged not to serve more than two six year terms. In 1995, he had a brief flirtation with running for president. However, in his campaign travels he saw that it would not be a successful race. He did believe that his work in the senate was unfinished. He and Sheila thus decided to campaign for a third term. He was engaged in the contest with Norm Coleman at the time of his death.

Few politicians will have lived a life that creates a lasting legacy. It was not simply the liberal views expressed in Wellstone's book *The Conscience of a Liberal.* Nor the determination or passion and devotion to principle that he expressed in his writings, his speeches and in his votes in the senate. He will be remembered as the sole senator facing a reelection fight who was willing to vote against President Bush's request that the congress authorize him to use force against Iraq just a month before election day. Americans and Minnesotans can learn from the public life of Paul Wellstone. It was his "...fierce commitment to justice that defined his life, and that shapes his enduring legacy."[7]

Perhaps a more enduring legacy is embodied in the Wellstone philosophy in how to win elections. It is in another book by Bill Lofy entitled *Politics: The Wellstone Way: How to Elect Progressive Candidates and Win on Issues.* (Wellstone Action.) Wellstone Action is the membership organization that carries on the work of Paul and Sheila Wellstone. It consists of action programs on behalf of such projects as strengthening the Violence Against Women Act. In Camp Wellstone, it trains young people to run for public office or work on campaigns. In 2005, Wellstone Action completed its eleventh Campus Camp Wellstone of the year. In 2005, they had 50 Campus Camp Wellstones. There is also a Camp Sheila Wellstone. It seeks to continue "...her work to end violence against women." Wellstone Action credits the work of Camp Wellstone in electing four new members to the Minneapolis City Council in 2005. "The goal of the Wellstone Action Network is to develop our large national network of supporters into an ongoing force for progressive social change."[8]

Chapter Thirty-eight

Political Genes

It would be a fitting subject for a psychologist to analyze the reasons why sons and daughters of political activists follow in the footsteps of a parent. For want of a better term, I would characterize it as "political genes". It would seem to have little to do with the genetic makeup of parent and child. Rather, it seems to be something which has developed within the family circle. It could well involve discussions within the family around the dinner table and at other times as it was in the Latz family. This occurred as I grew up. It was with my parents, and then with my immediate family. It could also involve the "father figure" image in which a child seeks to emulate, or even outdo, the parent who has been in the limelight and successful in public endeavors.

The examples of children following in the footsteps of a politically successful parent involve people at every level of the political process. One outstanding example is Kathleen Blatz, former Chief Justice of the Minnesota Supreme Court. Blatz, the daughter of former State Senator Jerry Blatz, was a successful member of the Minnesota House of Representatives. She then became an outstanding leader of Minnesota's judiciary.

Another example is the interesting saga of the Perpich brothers. They grew up in a struggling Iron Range family where the parents had little education. All three brothers, Rudy, George and Tony, became dentists. All three became state senators. Rudy became a two term governor. The fourth brother is a psychiatrist. The Perpiches, like the sons and daughters of other immigrants, sought the opportunity to be successful in their own right. They also valued the opportunity to use government to help improve the lives of others who were less successful or less able.

Political genealogy sometimes carries over into the third generation. An example is the Peterson family in the Minnesota House. The grandfather, Harry Peterson, a farmer from western Minnesota, served with me in the 1960's. His son, Doug Peterson, represented the same area in the house. Upon his retirement, his son, Harry's grandson, Aaron Peterson, was elected to the same seat.

Mike Freeman is the son of Jane and Orville Freeman. Mike Freeman served as a state senator. He was then elected and served as Hennepin County Attorney. Mike's principal ambition was to follow in the footsteps of Governor Orville Freeman and be endorsed and elected governor. His contest with Skip Humphrey for the DFL endorsement for that post caused anguish in the hearts and minds of those who had long histories with both families. Freeman received the DFL Party endorsement for governor. However, he was defeated in the primary election by Attorney General Skip Humphrey, and returned to private law practice. In 2006, he returned to the Hennepin County Attorney's post. He defeated attorney Andrew Lugar.

A third generation candidacy was that of Hubert H."Buck" Humphrey for Secretary of State in 2002. "Buck" Humphrey is the son of Skip Humphrey. He was the DFL endorsed candidate for that office. While that campaign was unsuccessful, Buck Humphrey did use an innovative website to keep in contact with his supporters. It was another move to the increasing use of the internet in the political process.

Ted Mondale is the son of Fritz and Joan Mondale. He served as a state senator from St. Louis Park and Hopkins. When he chose not to run for reelection, an incumbent house member, Steve Kelly, ran for and was elected to Mondale's seat. Kelly's race for the senate opened up the house seat to which Ron Latz was elected. Governor Jesse Ventura appointed Ted Mondale Chair of the Metropolitan Council. Ted did an outstanding job in providing leadership for the Met Council.

Former State Senator Julie Sabo is yet another family member who has followed in her father's footsteps in elective office. While still serving her first term in the Minnesota senate, she was selected by the DFL nominee for Governor Roger Moe to serve as Moe's running mate for lieutenant governor. Julie Sabo is the daughter of longtime and now retired Minnesota 5th Congressional District Congressman Martin Olav Sabo and Sylvia Sabo. State Senator Kathy Sheran is the daughter of former representative and later Minnesota Supreme Court Justice Robert Sheran. State Senator Katie Sieben is the daughter of former State Representative Michael Sieben.

Congressional Scholar Norman Ornstein traces his interest in government and politics to his maternal grandfather Rubin Latz. Our son, Ron Latz, serves as a state senator. A final example of political genealogy is our son Martin Latz. Marty, like Ron a Harvard educated lawyer, played a prominent role in the ill fated 1988 campaign for president of Massachusetts Governor Michael Dukakis. Marty served on the Dukakis national campaign staff headquartered in Washington. Marty, now a Phoenix, Arizona resident, later served President Clinton as a negotiator on the White House Advance Teams. He now runs the Latz Negotiation Institute, and is the author of *Gain the Edge!*, a book on negotiation strategy published by St. Martin's Press.

Chapter Thirty-nine

Franken, Friedman, and Ornstein

The suburb of St. Louis Park has sent forth to the world three prominent Jewish men each with a stellar reputation for achievement in public life. None of the three has held elective office. However, each has achieved high marks from numerous observers as to their intelligence, professional skills, and contributions to their chosen fields. They are, in alphabetical order, Al Franken, Thomas L. Friedman, and Norman J. Ornstein. All grew up in a Jewish community that consisted predominantly of Jews who originally settled in North Minneapolis and began their migration to St. Louis Park in the1950's and early 1960's. All three were raised in political and social traditions that placed a high value on education and contributions to the community. Each, through his writings and public appearances on television and radio, has left his mark on the public consciousness. But each has done so with a distinctive personality and approach.

Tom Friedman, author and *New York Times* columnist, has traveled the world. He has written extensively for the *Times*. In his books he has described the problems of the world, and he has suggested solutions.

Ornstein is a Congressional Scholar at the American Enterprise Institute, a conservative Washington think tank. He is considered an expert on the people, policies and practices of the Congress. Ornstein is often quoted in the news columns of the daily newspapers on Washington political and congressional activities. He is a frequent guest and analyst on public television's *The Newshour with Jim Lehrer*.

Franken's rise to prominence came from his talents as a comedian on the *Saturday Nite Live* television show. He has followed that stint as an author of three best selling books containing biting political satire. Franken was featured on his own show as a political commentator on the Air America Radio Network. He is a candidate for the DFL endorsement for the U.S. Senate seat now held by Norm Coleman.

The ties that bind them together, and their individual approaches to public life and public policy, are described in their respective profiles. Each has influenced public policy in a distinctly different manner. Franken, with his sardonic humor, has punctured the egos and inconsistencies of such conservative commentators as Rush Limbaugh. Friedman's insightful analysis of the world's problems, and particularly those of the Middle East, has helped to steer the U.S. on a more moderate course in troubled political and economic times. Ornstein, through his ability to explain complex legislative proposals and congressional personalities, rules and procedures, has helped both seasoned political observers and the public better understand what is happening in our nation's capitol.

Al Franken

Al Franken has earned the equivalent of a Ph.D. in political satire. But the question is can this intelligent and clever Minnesota born Jew earn an even more coveted degree, that of U.S. Senator? Can this successful comedian, prolific author, and political talk show host return to his home state of Minnesota and earn the endorsement of the DFL Party; the votes of Minnesota citizens; and become the fourth Minnesota Jew in 30 years to enter the hallowed chamber as a member of the U.S. Senate?

Franken's longtime friend Norman Ornstein believes he can. Ornstein told the *New York Times:* "Al is really a policy wonk. He has a nuanced sense of the issues and reads very widely. We've talked through foreign policy and defense issues and I can tell you he is able to deal with the substance of those better than a whole lot of members of the House and Senate I've dealt with."[1] While

Ornstein's observations were on Franken's ability on the issues rather than his electability, the comment answers an immediate question as to whether a comedian turned politician has the ability to come to grips with the major issues confronting a U.S. senator.

Franken does bring an unusual array of assets and considerable liabilities to the Minnesota political table.

In January 2006, Franken and his wife Franni moved back to Minnesota from New York City. They are empty nesters. Their two sons are grown. Franken's mother was a real estate agent. His father Joe was an immigrant. Franken said that his father was a Republican until he voted against Barry Goldwater over civil rights issues.[2] Franken is quoted in *Newsweek* as saying that, "... his father, a salesman and lifelong Republican switched parties. No Jew, he told young Al, could be for Jim Crow."[3]

Franken has the ability to produce and air his *The Al Franken Show* on the Air America Network from a Twin Cities base. He resigned from the show when he became a candidate. Radio gave Franken the opportunity to participate in Minnesota political events. It enables him to continue to raise funds for DFL candidates and causes, such as St. Paul Mayor Chris Coleman, Minneapolis Mayor R.T. Rybak, and other liberal and moderate candidates. It also gave him the opportunity to seek to enlist the support of major DFL political figures and fundraisers, and to attempt to secure the support of such political activists as Jeff Blodgett, and the participants in the Wellstone Action network.

The 54-year-old Franken has personal and family roots in St. Louis Park. He attended Blake School and went on to Harvard College. He first rose to prominence in 1975 with his political impressions and skits on the popular television show *Saturday Nite Live*. His character on that show, Stuart Smalley, is well remembered by students of political satire. His ability to "...make serious people laugh out loud – at him, at themselves, and at the Republicans..." has also expressed itself in three best selling books: 1996's *Rush Limbaugh is a Big Fat Idiot; Lies and the Lying Liars Who Tell Them*"(Dutton 2003); and, most recently, *The Truth (With Jokes)*.[4]

Franken's national radio program, *The Al Franken Show*, was heard in major markets throughout the U.S. This show, with regular guests and his commentaries on current political issues, was Franken's main current communication vehicle in Minnesota.

Questions remain as to whether Franken can make the transition from a successful comedian to a senatorial candidate who can be taken seriously and elected against an established and clever incumbent. Behind Franken's rapier-like wit and humorous commentary lies a bright mind. He has the apparent ability to reduce complex issues to a level easily understood by the politically sophisticated as well as by the average voter – whoever that may be. Norman Ornstein, while sometimes disagreeing with Franken's methods, "…said he believes Franken has developed true political clout,… Al is a genuine intellectual who knows about deficits and budgets and foreign policy, …while at the same time can be rubbing "people the wrong way."[5] It is questionable as to how his good humor and ever ready comments will hold up under the rigors of a statewide campaign and constant criticism, both personal and political. Former Congressman Vin Weber, who was also cochairman of President Bush's reelection campaign in Minnesota, said: "I've lost all regard for Al Franken… I think he has become a mirror image of the people he hates on the right."[6]

It used to be that there was a traditional pathway to a seat in the U.S. Senate. One must first be a governor, a member of congress, or at least have a track record of election wins and campaigns. Franken brings none of that to the political table. Perhaps all of these requirements have changed in an era of electronic media, computers and blogs. As Rudy Boschwitz showed in 1984, you do not have to have held prior public office to become a U.S. senator. To get elected, Boschwitz combined a folksy personality with a plaid shirt and the ability to raise huge dollars. Paul Wellstone had the ability to energize voters through populist principles. He struck a cord with disaffected voters. Each overcame the lack of the more traditional characteristics of a successful candidate.

Minnesota appears to be a more moderate state politically than in the days of Hubert Humphrey, Eugene McCarthy and Fritz Mondale. However, in the first tier of the Twin Cities suburbs, such as Minnetonka, Plymouth and Edina, and in the St. Cloud area, the quality of the candidates and the issues surrounding the Republicans nationally, can bring unexpected DFL victories. A Democrat, Amy Klobuchar, succeeded the retiring DFL senator Mark Dayton in the 2006 election. Franken has the name recognition – hopefully positive – to be an effective statewide candidate. But he must also convince grassroots political activists in the DFL, and delegates to the DFL state endorsing convention, that he has the gravitas and philosophical convictions to overcome other candidates and their supporters who have "paid their political dues" and believe that they are more entitled to the endorsement.

There is no doubt that a candidate must be an effective fundraiser, with the ability to raise the needed millions of dollars to run an effective statewide campaign. Otherwise one is unlikely to successfully combat an entrenched and well financed incumbent. It is expected that Franken has the connections and ability to raise the necessary resources. In 2008, Minnesota is expected to be a target state involving control of the U.S. Senate. As a senatorial candidate Franken will have to take positions on a host of controversial issues that are both national and local in scope. None of them have easy moral or political answers. Franken hopes to "win on values." He has called his political action committee (PAC) "Midwest Values PAC."[7] He will have to take positions on such controversial issues as the war in Iraq, abortion rights, gay marriage, gun control, healthcare, the environment and so on. Will people take him seriously on these issues? Or will he be perceived as just another big city liberal and stereotypical political comedian who is nothing more than an ambitious carpet- bagger who moved back to Minnesota simply to pursue his own political ambition?

Much can happen between now and 2008. Incumbent Senator Rudy Boschwitz and challenger Paul Wellstone faced off in the 1990 senatorial election. That was the first encounter between two Minnesota Jews for a U.S. Senate seat. Who would have expected that this state, with its very small Jewish population, would again witness a replay with the contestants this time incumbent senator Norm Coleman and senate aspirant Al Franken? It may yet happen.

Thomas L. Friedman

Three time Pulitzer Prize winning author; *New York Times* columnist; lecturer and television guest commentator, all describe St. Louis Park native Thomas L. Friedman. The major means of communicating ideas and political opinions have changed from the news and opinion columns of the world's newspapers and weekly newsmagazines to the electronic media: to television, computers, radio and blogs. With these changes one tends to overlook the importance of the written word in shaping ideas and discourse on local, national and international issues and events. Newspaper readership has shown a steady decline in circulation leading to sales and mergers. These include both the *St. Paul Pioneer Press* and the *Minneapolis Star Tribune.* Programs featuring personalities, such as Al Franken and Rush Limbaugh on radio, and Tim Russert and George Stephanopolis[1] on Sunday morning television, together with public television's *The Newshour with Jim Lehrer,*[2] and *Washington Week,* have become the principal sources of information and opinion on what is going on in the world. Local television newscasts have essentially been reduced to reports on robberies, homicides and the like in an ascending competition for viewership.

Tom Friedman is an example of a journalist who has used the print media, op-ed columns and books to achieve a reputation equaling, if not transcending, these other media personalities. His Pulitzer Prizes, newspaper commentary, and bestselling books led *Vanity Fair* magazine to call him "The country's best newspaper columnist."[3] Friedman has earned wide acclaim from his columns on the editorial-opinion page of the *New York Times.* He covered the Middle East for the *New York Times.*

After living in Beirut, Lebanon and Jerusalem, and reporting for the *Times*, Friedman wrote his first bestselling book, *From Beirut to Jerusalem.* This nonfiction work won him several awards,

including the 1989 National Book Award for nonfiction. Fried-
man was awarded two Pulitzer Prizes for his coverage of the
Middle East. They were the 1983 and 1988 Pulitzer Prizes for
International Reporting.

In the late 1980's and early 1990's, Friedman held several
assignments for the *New York Times*. They included posts as the
Times' Chief Diplomatic Correspondent working in Washington
D.C., and as the Chief White House Correspondent. In January
1994, Friedman's position and focus shifted to economics and for-
eign trade policies. He became the *Times'* International Economic
Correspondent. "In January 1995, Mr. Friedman became the *New
York Times'* Foreign Affairs Columnist." Friedman's third Pulitzer
Prize came in 2002. It was for "distinguished commentary" on "the
worldwide impact of the terrorist threat."[4]

A frequent lecturer, Friedman has spoken about "the war on
terrorism, attitudes regarding the United States and the Middle
East, and American foreign policy under the Bush admin-istra-
tion."[5] Tracing the roots of 9/11, Friedman was quoted as stating: "I wanted to know two things. First, what motivated those 19
young men, those hijackers, to board those planes and kill 3,000
of my brothers and sisters? And second, why did so many of their
fellow Arabs and Muslims applaud what they did?"[6]

Friedman has a "gift to translate complex things to the simple
people of the village."[7] That clarity of expression, and his diverse
background, has led to several television documentaries airing
on the Discovery Channel. They include one on "Straddling the
Fence." This was a documentary "…on the impact of the wall sepa-
rating Palestinians and Israelis."[8]

Friedman's other bestselling books, *The Lexus and the Olive
Tree*, and *The World Is Flat: A Brief History of the Twenty-first Century* have led to both acclaim and criticism. The *Kirkus Review*
called *The Lexus and the Olive Tree*, "simply the best book written on globalization." That book, together with *The World Is Flat*
on globalization and geopolitics, have drawn criticism from other
observers of the world scene.

One commentator, Jeff Faux, reviewing *The World Is Flat*,

states that "flattening the world" means "taking advantage of the new technologies that allow businesspeople to enter the global market from anywhere." However, Faux points out that there are economic casualties – lost jobs, lower wages, the proliferation of sweatshops - ..." that have mounted from this "flattening."[9] Faux observes that Friedman does not seem to have an understanding "...of the huge and growing U.S. trade deficit that has been the engine of growth for many of those export businesses in Asia that impress him [Friedman] so much."[10] He asserts that while it is true that the information age has drastically changed the world in which we live; that we ought to worry about the U.S. jobs that are being outsourced to India, China and other places around the globe; and that in "...the long run (we) should be fine"; so long as "...America maintains its ability to do cutting-edge innovation;" Faux charges that Friedman appears to overlook the dilemma that is caused when what we are doing across America is "cutting way back on educational availability and opportunity." As one commentator put it, "The one hand is promoting globalization of commerce while the other is doing its best to shut down the whole system of American public education. Together they are condemning an entire upcoming generation to a bleak future."[11] The controversy engendered by Friedman, and the effects at home and abroad of the "flattening," are likely to continue to be controversial for some time to come.

Friedman is married to Ann Friedman. They have two daughters. He is a 1975 graduate of Brandeis University. He graduated Summa Cum Laude with a degree in Mediterranean Studies. In 1978, he received a Masters Degree in Modern Middle East Studies from Oxford University. Friedman is a member of the Board of Trustees of Brandeis University and, "since 2005, the Board of the Pulitzer Prizes." Friedman has served as a Visiting Lecturer at Harvard University. He has been awarded numerous honorary degrees including one from the University of Minnesota. "In August 2004, he was awarded the honorary title Order of the British Empire (OBE), by Queen Elizabeth, II."[12] His columns continue to appear in the *New York Times*.

Norman J. Ornstein

Norman Ornstein's pathway from birth in Grand Rapids, Minnesota has been an extraordinary one. He grew up in St. Louis Park. He graduated from the University of Minnesota and the University of Michigan. His journey resulted in achieving a preeminent position as a Congressional Scholar and expert on the Congress and the presidency. Ornstein received his B.A. in Political Science from the University of Minnesota and his Ph.D. from the University of Michigan. While at Minnesota, Ornstein states that he was "...really inspired by one of my political science professors, Gene Eidenberg. He'd been a Congressional Fellow, and when he told us about that I decided that was something I wanted to do to."[1]

Coming to Washington in the 1970's, the now 58 year-old Ornstein worked in the office of Congressman Donald Fraser. He taught at Catholic University. He then became a Resident Scholar at the American Enterprise Institute for Public Policy Research. AEI is a conservative Washington think tank. From his base at AEI Ornstein has become one of the leading scholars and observers on the contemporary scene on Congress and the presidency. He writes for *U.S.A. Today*, and does a weekly column on Congress for *Roll Call* newspaper. Among the other major public publications for which Ornstein has written are the *New York Times*, *Washington Post*, *Foreign Affairs* and the *Wall Street Journal*. His cogent analysis of the personalities and policies of the Congress make him a regular contributor to television programs like Public Broadcasting's *The Newshour with Jim Lehrer*. He served as the editor and co-host for the widely acclaimed PBS documentary; "Congress: We The People."

Observers nationwide have called Ornstein "an icon of the press,"[2] and "the nation's hottest pundit."[3] Bob Garfield of National Public Radio's "*On The Media*" called Ornstein the "king of quotes." The *Houston Chronicle* stated Ornstein is "an expert on the presidency."[4]

As a student of, and an expert on Congress, Ornstein has

authored and coauthored numerous books and articles. His many books include *The Permanent Campaign and Its Future*; *Intensive Care: How Congress Shapes Health Policy*, both with Thomas E. Mann; and *Debt and Taxes: How America Got Into Its Budget Mess and What to Do About It*, with John H. Makin.[5]

His most recent book, with Thomas E. Mann, is *The Broken Branch: How Congress is Failing America, and How to Get It Back On Track*, Oxford University Press, 2006.

However, it is in two areas that Ornstein has made his most major contributions in the shaping of public policy. Following the 9/11 terrorist attacks it was Ornstein who began raising questions as to succession to leadership in the congressional, executive and judicial branches of the federal government. He questioned what if the terrorists were to be successful in killing or maiming a president and vice president; the members of the Supreme Court; or the hundreds of senators and members of Congress? Ornstein's writings and public concerns led to the creation of the Continuity of Government Commission. The Commission "…created largely because of Ornstein's efforts is composed of a who's who of American politics, including such notables as Newt Gingrich, Donna Shalala, Kweisi Mfume, and Leon Panetta."[6] The report of the Continuity of Government Commission recommended passage of a constitutional amendment. It made specific proposals for succession. Despite the seeming logic of its proposals, and the blue ribbon nature of the commission membership, the proposal became dead on arrival in Congress. Ornstein was "just stunned and disappointed" by the failure of such congressional leaders as Speaker of the House Dennis Hastert and Congressman David Dreier, Chair of the House Rules Committee, to support the proposal.[7] Ornstein stated that, "I thought the biggest problem we'd face would be overcoming inertia and the same kind of reluctance people feel about writing a will. Coming to grips with your own mortality. I've been taken aback by the strong opposition we've faced from some members of Congress."[8]

A similar proposal for continuity in Minnesota state government in the event of nuclear attack was passed in 1961, during the

Cold War with the Soviet Union. It passed with bipartisan support from Governor Orville Freeman and the Minnesota Legislature. I was the sponsor. The voters adopted the plan as an amendment to the Minnesota Constitution. The need for continuity of succession in the event of terrorist attack continues to be a serious problem. However, it probably will take a major change in the composition of both houses of the congress to provide impetus for its passage and submission to the states for ratification as an amendment to the U.S. Constitution.

Along with the frustration accompanying the proposal for continuity of government has come a major Ornstein success. Ornstein led a group that worked closely with Senators John McCain of Arizona and Russell Feingold of Wisconsin to enact the McCain-Feingold Act. That law represented a major reform in the system of financing political campaigns. The *Legal Times* referred to Ornstein as "a principal drafter of the law," and "his role in its design and enactment was profiled in the February 2004 issue of *Washington Lawyer*."[9]

Polling has risen from a behind the scenes activity to one in which politicians, political observers and commentators have placed more and more emphasis. More frequently than ever, elected officials from the president on down have based their initiatives and public statements on polling data. This is data that not only tells whether the public agrees or disagrees with or would vote for the official in the next election. It also reflects his/her attitudes on public policy issues in legislation submitted to or proposed for the Congress or the state legislatures.

Since 1987, Ornstein has served as a senior advisor to the *Pew Research Center for the People and the Press*. Since 1982, he has served as an election analyst for *CBS News*. Ornstein's service on boards and commissions includes membership on the board of the National Commission on Public Service (Volcker Commission).[10]

The lobbying scandal in Washington, involving lobbyists such as Jack Abramof, and the indictment of leaders in Congress, such as House Majority Leader Tom Delay, has led to calls in and out of Congress for reforms in the congressional rules and the laws governing lobbyists. Ornstein, along with his colleague Thomas E. Mann of the Brookings Institution, has added an important insight into the way the most recent Republican dominated Congress, and especially the House of Representatives, ran roughshod over the rules and traditions of that body.

In an op-ed piece for the *New York Times*, Ornstein and Mann point out, some of the abuses are straightforward breaches of the rules. The majority Republicans bypassed normal procedures and ignored objections that parliamentary rules have been violated. They then reframe substantive issues as procedural matters that demanded party discipline. Other abuses do not violate the rules, but they do transgress longstanding practice.[11]

Ornstein and Mann raised the rhetorical question, "What has all this got to do with corruption?" They go on to answer the question by stating, "If you can play fast and loose with the rules of the game in lawmaking, it becomes easier to consider playing fast and loose with everything else, including relations with lobbyists, acceptance of favors, the use of official resources and the discharge of governmental power." Mann and Ornstein point out specific rules reforms. They call for "Quick and decisive Congressional actions (that) could minimize the damage done by the explosion of scandals related to Mr. Abramof. But lobbying reform alone is a temporary solution. The real solution is for Congress to behave like the deliberative body it is supposed to be."[12]

Norman Ornstein is a member of the Board of Directors of the Public Broadcasting Service (PBS) and of the Board of Trustees of the U.S. Capitol Historical Society. In 2004, he was elected as a Fellow of the prestigious American Academy of Arts and Sciences.[14] Ornstein has not forsaken his Minnesota roots. He is a Distinguished Visiting Fellow with the Humphrey Institute's Center for the Study of Politics. In that capacity he returns frequently to lecture on political and governmental events to students, faculty and interested Minnesotans. Ornstein's sister Margaret Jaffe, and his brother Bloomington City Attorney David Ornstein, continue to reside in the Twin Cities. Norman Ornstein resides in a Washington D.C. suburb with his wife attorney Judith L. Harris. She is the managing partner of a leading Washington law firm. They have two sons Matthew and Daniel.

In May 2007, Ornstein was the commencement speaker at the Humphrey Institute. He was also awarded an Honorary Doctor of Laws Degree. (My personal interest and observations of Ornstein and his career are acknowledged. We share a common political heritage in what I describe as "political genes." Ornstein is my nephew. We share the political genealogy of my father and Ornstein's grandfather Rubin Latz. As Ornstein described it to Richard Broderick in an article in the March/April 2004 issue of *The University of Minnesota Alumni Association publication *In Minnesota* "... my maternal grandfather, Rubin Latz, was a major figure in the labor movement in Minneapolis and was part of Hubert Humphrey's Kitchen Cabinet that persuaded him to run for mayor and later for the Senate. My grandfather died before I was born, but I grew up hearing about Humphrey (B.A., 39) and even got to know him a little, so I guess that an interest in politics runs in my family.")

Chapter Forty

Scott Johnson

St. Paul Jewish attorney Scott W. Johnson is on the cutting edge of the latest use of the internet to gather information and opinions on political issues and personalities. The 54 year-old Johnson is married and father of three daughters. He is a member of Temple of Aaron congregation. He is a graduate of Dartmouth College and the University of Minnesota Law School. Johnson is Senior Vice President of TCF National Bank. TCF, the former Twin Cities Federal Savings and Loan, is led by William Cooper. Cooper is a former chair of the Minnesota Republican Party and a heavy contributor to conservative political causes.

Johnson's conservative politics represents an evolution from a political activist in high school supporting Eugene McCarthy in 1968, and interning for Walter Mondale in the summer of 1969, to a profoundly conservative writer and thinker. He shares his political philosophy with other Jewish neoconservatives. They include William Kristol, the founder and editor of the Weekly Standard, and the Jewish neoconservatives who have served in the Bush administration, such as Paul Wolfowitz.

Like the neoconservatives, Johnson is a strong supporter of the State of Israel. In a personal interview Johnson said, "Israel is the United States best friend, even more than England." The website of Power Line Blog contains a box showing the Star of David and the phrase "I'm a proud friend of Israel."

Johnson's academic history portrays his evolution from a liberal Democrat to a conservative Republican. While an undergraduate at Dartmouth College, he was impressed and "overwhelmed by a series of conservative philosophers including professors Jeffrey Hart, Jonathan Swift, Samuel Johnson and Edward Gilbain."

Further influencing Johnson was President Richard Nixon's willingness to help safeguard the survival of Israel by airlifting massive amounts of military material to Israel during the 1973 Arab effort to destroy Israel in the so called Yom Kippur War."

After graduating from the University of Minnesota Law School, Johnson clerked for 8th Circuit Court Judge Myron Bright. He then was an attorney at the Faegre and Benson law firm. While practicing at Faegre from 1981 to 1997, Johnson developed a friendship with John Hinderaker. In 1992, Johnson and Hinderaker started to coauthor newspaper and magazine articles on political subjects. Hinderaker is also a graduate of Dartmouth.

For more than ten years Johnson and Hinderaker have written on public policy issues. While their articles have appeared in many publications, including the conservative National Review, Johnson states that they found it increasingly difficult to write whatever they wanted to express without editor's revisions. This frustration led to the evolution and development of their blog "Power Line." "Blog" is short for an online journal, a log known as a "Weblog." A "blogger" is a person who writes an online journal or log. According to Johnson, a "blog" is a free site. A person can write whatever the person wants to write and submit it without editors changing the content.

The catalyst for the success of Power Line was the Paul Wellstone-Norm Coleman senate campaign. Johnson states that this campaign attracted thousands of readers to Power Line. The issue that propelled Power Line and Johnson and Hinderaker into national prominence was the controversy surrounding CBS news anchor Dan Rather. The Dan Rather CBS incident involved a fake letter alleging negatives about President Bush's National Guard record. Rather ran the story without sufficient verification of its authenticity. The Power Line blog received information that the letter was false and ran the information. The national media picked up the story. Ultimately, Rather was forced out after many years of service as primary anchor on CBS News.

Time Magazine named Power Line, www.powerlineblog.com "The Blog of the Year." Now, Johnson asserts, Power Line has an average of 150,000 readers per day. Johnson's party political activities have included service on the Minnesota Republican Party Platform Committee, and as the treasurer for Rudy Boschwitz in his 1996 loss to Paul Wellstone. However, Johnson says that he is not a politician. He is only a "writer and observer." While he says that he has no ambition to run for public office, his present role with Power Line makes him more successful in influencing politicians and public policy than service in all but the most significant of elective offices.

Chapter Forty-one

The 2004 Elections:
The National Scene

History will likely record the 2004 presidential election as representing a profound change in the tactics and dynamics of the election process. It also will likely be recorded as representing a significant change in how the federal government, through the President, the Congress and the Supreme Court, deals with the needs of Americans at all levels of the economic strata. Such changes will solidify the differences between the "haves" and the "have nots". It would likely also result in changes in the federal government's approach to social policies on such issues as the separation of church and state; the rights of homosexuals; abortion; and the stem cell research.

President Bush's posture on each of these issues proved decisive in winning his reelection bid for a second term. Bush, with increased majorities in both houses of Congress, has been able to implement his desire to make long term and significant changes in the membership of the U.S. Supreme Court.

Fundamental change is needed in the Democratic Party's approach to electing its candidates to office. One clear message delivered in most states is that voters placed their social and religious beliefs and values on a higher priority than on the "pocket book" issues and their economic self interest. The latter issues have been the mainstay of Democratic Party election policy since the New Deal of the depression era and the presidency of Franklin D. Roosevelt.

The Democratic Party nationally, and throughout most of the nation, has failed to respond positively to the message delivered by the success of President Clinton. Clinton moved governmental and Democratic party policies toward the center rather than being focused to the left. Except in isolated instances, being a political "liberal" is not the ticket to success in elective politics. It was in the days of my personal involvement in party and elective politics.

For all of the tactical and political policy considerations, and even the wars in Iraq and on terrorism, the 2004 presidential election boiled down to the question of which candidate and political party was more committed to the religious and social views of many Americans across the nation. Perhaps most decisive of all of these social/religious issues was that of gay marriage. The Republicans, and Karl Rove, their chief presidential campaign strategist, used with overwhelming success the so called "wedge" issues. These are issues designed to appeal to the strong religious and social values of Americans who were most likely to vote to support those views. "Gay marriage" was the most significant of these issues. Eleven states had ballot initiatives amending their state constitutions to prohibit gay marriage, and to define marriage as a union only between a man and a woman. In ten of these eleven states Bush out-polled Kerry and received those states electoral votes. The Republicans successfully blamed the problem on so called "liberal" judges. They claimed state legislatures could not be trusted on the issue. They argued that only through embedding a prohibition in the state constitutions could this historic definition of a legal union be protected.

The 2004 national election also saw a unique coalition and coincidence of religious and doctrinal views between evangelical Christians and conservative Catholics. They coalesced on the issues of abortion rights and stem cell research. Both issues involve opinions as to when life begins.

Effect on American Jews

How does the injection of the religious and social values of many American Christians into political issues effect American and Minnesota Jews? Despite the Republican hopes that they could slice off an additional percentage of American Jews from the Democratic Party and its candidates, this effort met with limited success in the 2004 election. According to the best estimate, in 2004, the Republicans hoped to increase their margin of support from American Jews from 19 percent to close to 30 percent. Exit polls, despite their limitations, showed that 24 percent of American Jews voted for President Bush in 2004 compared to 19 percent who supported him in 2002. This was despite a concerted effort by Jewish Republicans to exploit the President's strong support for Prime Minister Sharon and Israel.

Bush's attempts to appeal to American Jews, and particularly to the large Jewish population in South Florida, was evidenced by his announcement just before his arrival in West Palm Beach, that he had signed the Global Anti-Semitism Review Act of 2004. This act requires the State Department to document annually attacks on Jews worldwide.[1]

The increase in Jewish support for President Bush in the 2004 election appears to be based on several factors. One is that Orthodox Jewish groups' agendas differ from those of Conservative and Reform Jews. Orthodox Jewish groups are more likely to support an agenda that rejects abortion and promotes increased federal funding for religious institutions. Bush's faith based initiatives, and an effort to give federal Homeland Security funding to synagogues, churches, and other nonprofit organizations, collide with the traditional opposition of the organized Jewish community to any effort that breaches the separation of church and state.

Makeup of the 2005-2006 Congress appears to have made little difference to the agenda of most mainstream Jewish groups nationally. Congress consisted of eleven Jewish Senators and 26 Jewish Representatives.

The Minnesota Scene

The move of the Minnesota GOP to the right has left moderate Republican state legislators in a distinct minority in the 2004 and 2005 Sessions of the legislature. Among those moder-

ate Republicans serving in the 2004 Session were Representatives
Ron Abrams of Minnetonka and Jim Rhodes of St. Louis Park/
Hopkins. At the conservative end of the political spectrum was
Representative Eric Lipman. Lipman, a New York native, repre-
sented the Woodbury area.

Lipman was the one Jewish legislator who openly supported
the statements by Representative Arlen Lindner in the 2003 Session. Lindner introduced the bill to repeal the protection of gays
and lesbians in the Minnesota Human Rights Act. Lindner challenged the historical record that showed gays being persecuted and
killed in concentration camps during the Holocaust. While Lipman defended Lindner's statements as expressions of free speech,
Abrams condemned the statements on the floor of the House.
Throughout the debate, and in later sessions of the House Ethics
Committee, Representative Rhodes failed to condemn Lindner's
statements. His rationale was that he was an ex parte member of
the House Ethics Committee that would be called upon to consider charges of unethical conduct by Lindner. With Rhodes not
voting, the House Ethics Committee, after acrimonious hearings,
failed to act on the Lindner censure on a 2-2 tie vote. Representative Ron Latz was one of the two lead DFL members presenting
the case against Lindner before the Ethics Committee. The other
was an African American Representative from North Minneapolis attorney Keith Ellison.

The political effects of the Lindner statements were significant. To the credit of House Speaker Steve Sviggum, the House
Republican majority secured a credible candidate to run against
Lindner in the 2004 election. Lindner was denied the GOP Party
endorsement. He ran in the Primary as an independent and was
defeated. In that same election Steve Simon defeated Representative Rhodes. Rhodes' inaction in the Lindner controversy was a
major issue in that campaign.

In 2004, in Minnesota, where the Kerry-Edwards ticket won
by a margin of 54 percent to 46 percent, the DFL picked up 13
seats in the House of Representatives. Two new Jewish legislators
were elected. They were Steve Simon who defeated Jim Rhodes,

and Tina Liebling from Rochester. The net result is that there were six Jews in the House in the 2005-2006 sessions and three Jewish senators. The 2004 reelection of Phyllis Kahn made her one of the longest serving house members. With the conclusion of the term, Kahn will have served 34 years. Returned to the House, all with substantial margins of victory, were Frank Hornstein of Minneapolis; Michael Paymar of St. Paul and Ron Latz of St. Louis Park and Golden Valley. Ron Abrams of Minnetonka survived a closer than expected race to become the lone Jewish Republican serving in the house. The Minnesota Senate was not up for reelection in 2004. The 2005-2006 sessions saw three Jewish senators. Richard Cohen and Sandy Pappas of St. Paul were joined by Terri Bonoff of Minnetonka and Plymouth.

The 2005-2006 Sessions

For the 2005-2006 Sessions, Republicans controlled the Minnesota House with a margin of 68 to 66 votes. The senate remained in DFL control by a 35 to 31 margin. For the last 50 years there have been three occasions in which the house has been as closely divided as in the 2005-2006 Sessions. In 1955, the DFL controlled the house by a one vote margin. In 1978, the house was evenly split.

The result can be very interesting with ever shifting allegiances and alliances within the respective DFL and Republican caucuses. There is a substantial need for caucus-party unity when a party has only a two vote majority margin or less. It does require unity. But that unity comes at a price. The price is that an individual legislator in the majority can exact from the leadership and his/her caucus a price for casting the deciding vote on important issues.

There are still some self-designated "liberals" within the DFL group, although such labels are attached more by reason of voting records rather than self-designation. There are few moderates on the Republican side of the aisle. The lone remaining Jewish Republican, Ron Abrams, was a moderate. He is now a District Court Judge appointed by Governor Pawlenty. The only Jewish conservative, Eric Lipman, chose not to seek reelection in 2004.

In 1955, the DFL, then designated as "Liberals," exercised remarkable discipline in pushing their one vote margin into support for the initiatives of then first term Governor Orville Freeman. Despite control by the "Conservatives" in the Minnesota Senate, such initiatives as the Fair Employment Practices Act passed both houses and was signed into law.

The 1978 Session was much less successful. The results of that session are described in an interesting book by Rodney Searle. Searle served as Speaker of the House during that Session.[2]

The two vote margin in the house in the 2005-2006 sessions put unusual power in the hands of a few members of the majority in the same fashion that the one vote Liberal majority did in 1955. The most important vote that a legislator casts is for the person who aspires to be the Speaker of the House. The Speaker has great, although not unlimited, power to appoint chairs and members of the various legislative committees. In recent years the power has been shared with other leaders in the party caucus. In 1955, and prior, the Speaker's power of appointment of chairs and committee members was much more complete.

Term limits of chairs in the Minnesota House and Senate can have a tremendous effect on the power structure of the body. A prime example in 2005-2006 was Ron Abrams having to surrender his chairmanship of the House Tax Committee, because he served the maximum number of years under a caucus term limit plan. These term limits are caucus imposed rather than being required by statute or Constitution.

Chapter Forty-two

The 2006 National Election

The war in Iraq became the central focus of the 2006 elections nationally and in Minnesota. 2006 saw the end of Republican domination of the U.S. Congress. Since 1994, the GOP had control of the U.S. House of Representatives. It ruled with an iron hand. It trampled on the rights of minority Democrats, denying them the right to amend major bills on the floor, and refusing Democratic representation on conference committees where final decisions were made on legislation.

Benjamin Cardin, a long term Maryland congressman, was the only new Jewish addition to the U.S. Senate in 2006. Re-elected after a tough political contest, was long-term U.S. Senator and former vice presidential candidate Joseph Lieberman of Connecticut. Lieberman was a strong and unwavering supporter of the president and the war in Iraq. He lost the Democratic primary election to a millionaire businessman without political experience. However, his long record as a Connecticut senator was enough to result in his election as an Independent. As an Independent, Lieberman will still caucus with the Democrats. He thus retains his senate seniority and chairmanship of the Homeland Security Committee. His vote also helped secure the Democrats narrow 51-49 Senate majority.

The Year of the Woman in Politics

The 2006 election has been called the "Year of the Woman in Politics." Nancy Pelosi was chosen as the first Speaker of the U.S. House of Representatives. Amy Klobuchar's election made her the first female senator from Minnesota. Margaret Anderson Kelliher was chosen as the second woman in history to be chosen the Speaker of the Minnesota House. Lori Swanson is the first female attorney general in Minnesota. There were also three women, all Democrats, who were elected to state constitutional offices together with one Republican, the lieutenant governor. A Republican, Michelle Bachman was elected to congress from the 6th Congressional District over a woman DFL candidate.

In her inaugural speech, Speaker Pelosi looked out at a chamber still dominated by men. She said, "I marvel that the victory is not mine alone, but belongs to the women of this country. It's a moment for which we have waited more than 200 years."[1]

Senator Hillary Rodham Clinton's strong reelection victory in the State of New York, even in typical Republican areas, propelled her to the forefront of the Democratic candidates for election as President in 2008. If elected, she would be the first woman president.

A rising Democratic star is Illinois U.S. Senator Barak Obama. If Obama is nominated and elected he would the first Black president. Among the other possible Democratic candidates are Governor Bill Richardson of New Mexico. He would be the first president of Hispanic heritage. If Republican former Massachusetts Governor Mitt Romney is nominated and elected, he would be the first Mormon president. It is a sign of how far our country has come that these minority candidates can all be considered the strongest contenders for the presidential nomination.

In addition to Senator Lieberman there are eight Jewish members of the U.S. Senate. Seven of the eight are Democrats. The Democrats are Carl Levin of Michigan, Herbert Kohl and Russell Feingold of Wisconsin, Dianne Feinstein and Barbara Boxer of California, Ronald Widen of Oregon, and Charles Schumer of New York. Arlan Specter of Pennsylvania is the sole Republican Jewish U.S. Senator.

2006 Minnesota Elections

The 2006 statewide elections in Minnesota saw a DFL sweep comparable to that which took place nationally. The DFL elected all but one of the state constitutional officers. The only survivor was incumbent Governor Tim Pawlenty. In a close election Pawlenty defeated Attorney General Mike Hatch by a margin of 21,000 votes. This represented one percent of the vote.

The DFL also swept the races for the Minnesota House of Representatives. This vaulted the DFL into majority control of the house for the first time since 1998. Margaret Anderson Kelliher became the second woman in history to become Speaker of the House. Her one female predecessor, also from Minneapolis, was Dee Long.

All incumbent Jewish House members were reelected. They were joined by Jeremy Kalin of Lindstrom. Three of the Jewish legislators were named to chair important house committees. Frank Ornstein, who had achieved a solid reputation on transportation matters was named to chair the Transportation and Transit Policy Subcommittee. Michael Paymar was named chair of the Public Safety Finance Committee. Representative Phyllis Kahn, now the longest serving member of the house, was named to chair the State Government Finance Committee. Steve Simon was named an Assistant Majority Leader. Simon delivered the principle nominating speech for Kelliher's election as Speaker. Tina Liebling was also named an Assistant Majority Leader. The DFL now commands a membership of 85 representatives over the 50 GOP members in the 135 member Minnesota House.

The Minnesota Senate

In the senate, the DFL continued in the majority. Three incumbent DFL senators were reelected. One new senator was State Representative Ron Latz. Senator Richard Cohen of St. Paul retained his position as chair of the Senate Finance Committee. Sandra Pappas was returned as chair of the Higher Education Budget and Policy Division of the Finance Committee. Terri Bonoff of Minnetonka and Plymouth was elected over Mayor Judy Johnson of Plymouth. Bonoff will serve as the Vice Chair of the K-12 Education Budget Division of the Senate Finance Committee.

Ron Latz succeeded Senator Steve Kelley who unsuccessfully sought DFL nomination for governor and for the attorney general's post. Ron will serve as a Majority Whip as well as Vice Chair of the Public Safety Budget Division of the Finance Committee. Ron sought and was also named by Senate Majority Leader Larry Pogemiller to serve on the Higher Education Committee. This is the committee that passes on the selection of regents for the University of Minnesota. Ron Latz continued his four year effort as a house member to secure passage of a statewide anti-smoking law. He was a co-author of that measure in the senate.

The Ellison Controversy

There was substantial discord in the Jewish community over the efforts of Representative Keith Ellison to succeed retiring Congressman Martin Olav Sabo to the 5th Congressional District seat. There were several issues involving Ellison's failures to file campaign finance reports and traffic violations. The principal concern in the Jewish community was Ellison's background of support for Reverend Louis Farakahn and those associated with him. Both of those relationships took place years ago while Ellison was attending law school and participating in the million man march on Washington. During the campaign Ellison continued to receive support and money from those outside Minnesota with suspected anti-Semitic positions.

Congressman Sabo, a 26-year veteran of the Congress and in the legislature before then, had a long and secure record in support of human rights and of the Jewish community. The endorsement of Ellison by the 5th District DFL Convention, and in the primary election, over a strong field of prominent Democrats, assured him of an easy win over the GOP endorsed candidate Alan Fine. Fine is Jewish. Fine seemed to be conducting his campaign against Ellison right out of the GOP "playbook." His harsh and unfounded attacks on Ellison proved not only to be unsuccessful, they also served as an embarrassment to most Jewish residents of the 5th

District. The 5th District is composed of Minneapolis and most of the first ring suburbs.

Since his election Ellison has handled himself with patience and skill. This is particularly true in his responses to unfair criticism over his decision to be sworn into the Congress using the Qu'ran.

There is an interesting sidelight to the Ellison campaign. Two of Ellison's opponents in the DFL primary were Minneapolis First Ward councilmember Paul Ostrow and former Minnesota state senator and unsuccessful DFL candidate for attorney general Ember Reichgott Junge. At a candidate debate at Temple Israel, before a largely Jewish audience, Ostrow revealed that although he was a practicing Christian, he had a Jewish grandfather. On a previous occasion Reichgott Junge had revealed to Ron Latz that while she was a Christian, she had a Jewish father. Interestingly, Reichgott Junge did not mention that fact during the Temple Israel debate. Nor did she mention it at any other time during the primary election contest. The runnerup to Ellison in the DFL congressional primary election was Michael Erlandson. Erlandson was a former DFL state party chair and longtime aide to Congressman Sabo. Erlandson was endorsed by Sabo.

Chapter Forty-three

The Convergence of
Religion and Politics

Nomination by President Bush of the president's legal counsel to the U.S. Supreme Court focused clearly how there has been a convergence of religion and politics in this nation. "The injection of Miers' religious beliefs into the question of her qualifications for the nation's highest court brought into sharp focus the extent to which religion and religious beliefs have not only intruded into the political process, but the degree to which they have permeated the whole political process."[1]

Article VI of the U.S. Constitution provides that "no religious test shall ever be required as a qualification to any office." The Miers' nomination floundered on her apparent lack of experience and qualifications to pass judgment on such controversial issues as abortion rights and the right of privacy from which it was derived under *Roe v. Wade* and *Griswold v. Connecticut*.

Then President Bush and his cohorts among the religious conservatives sought to reassure Bush's base. This reassurance came in several direct and indirect ways. "President Bush told reporters that "People asked me why I picked Harriet Miers." He then proceeded to talk about the importance of religion in her life.

James Dobson, the founder of Focus on the Family, a conservative Christian group, told a radio audience that he had been reassured by Karl Rove, President Bush's top political advisor, that Ms. Miers is a member of "a very conservative church which is almost universally pro-life.""[2]

The Bush White House took the religious reassurance issue a step further by encouraging two judges in Texas who knew Miers "….to hold a conference call with evangelical leaders in which the judges said flat out that Miers would vote to overturn *Roe.* "[3] Dr. Dobson was reportedly enlisted by unnamed White House aides to participate in a conference call "...to explain their support for the nomination to uneasy conservatives around the country. Dr. Dobson assured them he was convinced she [Ms. Miers] was an opponent of abortion."[4] Dobson has stated repeatedly "...that he is supporting her [Ms. Miers] in part because he has received certain confidential information that he cannot divulge."[5]

The debate involves whether views on abortion have become a "litmus test" for nominees to the U.S. Supreme Court. However, the issues involved may also come before the nation's highest court on such divisive matters as gay rights and the constitutionality of the so-called "Defense of Marriage Act."

Before the 2004 presidential campaign some political observers were naïve enough to believe that the role of religion in politics had been put to rest with the 1961 election of John F. Kennedy. Kennedy was the second Roman Catholic candidate for president. The first was New York Governor Al Smith in 1928. He was resoundingly defeated. To reassure the nation's non-Catholics, Kennedy stated "I do not speak for my church on public matters, and the church does not speak for me."[6]

In the 2002 presidential campaign no issue arose as to the religion of Senator Joseph Lieberman as Al Gore's vice presidential running mate. By 2002, the selection of a Jew only a heartbeat from the Oval Office seemed to be a less risky step politically than selecting a woman as a vice presidential candidate. Walter Mondale did just that in selecting Geraldine Ferraro in 1984.

In 1960, Kennedy had to reassure Protestant voters that his religious faith would not govern his policies as president. In 2004, Democratic presidential nominee John Kerry, a practicing Catholic, had to reassure non Catholics that church teachings on abortion and related issues would not determine his political decisions as president. Thus, in the October 2004 presidential debate, Kerry stated, "I can't take what is an article of faith for me and legislate it for someone who doesn't share that article of faith."[7]

In 1960, Kennedy had nearly 80 percent of the vote of Catholics. In 2004, Kerry's support among U.S. Catholics who attended church regularly dropped precipitously. These voters gave Bush a 13 point lead over Kerry. Kerry led Bush among Catholics "who are not regular church goers" by only one point. The late Pope John Paul II "aggressively promoted church doctrine on social issues. In many cases that doctrine is conservative – and it divides Catholics. Abortion is one of those issues."[8]

In the 2004 campaign the Catholic Church hierarchy was itself as divided as Catholic voters. Several Catholic Bishops challenged Kerry's right to take communion. They also challenged other Catholics who have taken positions at odds with stated church positions on such issues as abortion. Archbishop Harry Flynn of the Minneapolis/St. Paul Archdiocese took a more moderate position. Flynn would leave it up to the individual Catholic and his/her priest to decide whether or not to offer communion.[9] Some have suggested that Catholics who vote for candidates who publicly disagree with the church's position on abortion should also be denied communion.[10]

Other Catholic clergy and Catholic laypersons state that there is much more to social justice in the teachings of the Catholic Church than about abortion. They state that "justice is about more than an abortion. Justice is about caring for children, homeless veterans and whether we should have sent our soldiers into Iraq."[11] Other social issues embedded in Catholic teaching include problems of poverty, the environment and immigration.

A Catholic priest in Chillicothe, Ohio highlighted the dilemma faced by practicing Catholics by noting that while the Catholic Church was steadfast in proclaiming that all life is sacred, that "too often the Church's proclamation is in conflict with its practice." The priest is also reported to have said that the Church ought to seek to persuade those who support abortion rights and otherwise oppose its teachings "by word and example" and not "ostracize them or treat them like lepers." The priest was a supporter of Senator Kerry and allowed Kerry to take communion.[12]

Some high ranking Roman Catholic Church prelates have stated that there was only one way for a faithful Catholic to vote in the 2004 presidential election, and that is for President Bush and against John Kerry. There are others who would not only deny communion to Kerry and other Catholics who support abortion rights, but they blanketed churches with guides identifying abortion, gay marriage, and the stem cell debate as among a handful of non negotiable issues.[13]

Senator Kerry was not the only prominent Democratic candidate for high national office who has clashed with some Catholic prelates over the abortion issue. Both former New York Governor Mario Cuomo, a one time presidential contender, and a fellow Catholic former Congresswoman Geraldine Ferraro sustained similar criticism. The dilemma faced by practicing Catholics of vast political experience, and as public office holders, is shown by that faced by my former legislative colleague Edward Gearty. As legislators, Gearty and I most often saw eye to eye on political issues. We differed on the issue of abortion. However, Gearty, now retired, told Lori Sturdevant, a *Star Tribune* editorial writer and columnist, that he weighed Bush's anti abortion views and claims of being a compassionate conservative with those things Gearty believed "are necessary for the living." Gearty said, "Good government is one of them. There are still the hungry, the homeless, the imprisoned, the lame. Helping them is also a moral imperative." What ultimately tipped Gearty to support Kerry "was the threat by some Catholic bishops to deny communion to Kerry and other politicians who share his views, and the bishops' declaration that the only "faithful Catholic vote in this election was for Bush." "This, Gearty stated, crossed an important line - the American demarcation between church and state."[14]

Bush's Faith Based Initiative

The injection of religion into the political scene nationally, and at the state and local levels, did not begin in 2004 with the reelection campaign of George W. Bush. Beginning with President Ronald Reagan, observers pointed out that "shrewd

Republicans figured out that the way to win in middle America is to convince people that the biggest threat to their way of life is not economic but moral. They set out to give the word "values" a distinctly partisan tinge as they claim[ed] that a candidate's faith and views on matters of personal moral conduct are what matter most, not his or her thinking about schools, roads and the rest of government's real work."[1]

President Bush and Republicans nationally have sought to galvanize support for Republican candidates at the national and local levels from ideological non Catholic Christians. President Bush's so called "faith based initiatives" were simply a beginning of the injection of religion into his administration and his campaign for a second term in office. It is not simply a question of support or opposition to such controversial public policy issues as abortion, gay marriage, embryonic stem cell research. Nor is it the use of public funds for school vouchers for private and parochial institutions. It is a more broad based strategy to inject the issue of so called "moral values" into the debates and campaigns at all levels of the political process in Minnesota and throughout the nation. The Republican Party nationally has gone so far as to warn residents of Arkansas and West Virginia, part of the so called "Bible Belt," that "liberals," i.e. the Democrats, seek to ban the Bible.[2] These Republican efforts use the issue of same sex marriage to induce the fear that some activist judges would allow both same sex marriages and remove the words "under God" from the pledge of allegiance. They claim this is evidence that conservative Christian voters of all denominations should be motivated to go to the polls and support Republican candidates for office.

In Minnesota, the issue of "moral values" has been used in an effort to induce voters to vote their Bibles rather than their economic interests. This was designed to divert attention from Republican legislative inaction on such issues as education, transportation, budgets and taxes.[3]

The issue of a woman's right to choose an abortion remains a fundamental issue in politics. It divides Americans along religious and gender lines. However, it has been transcended by the injection of religion on a much broader base than the so called "choice" issue. Perceptive observers have pointed to what has been characterized as President Bush's "political fundamentalism."[4]

David Domke, an Associate Professor of Communication at the University of Washington, is the author of "God Willing? Political Fundamentalism in the White House, The War on Terror and the Echoing Press." Domke writes of Bush's "fusion of faith in politics." He states that while "key political leaders long have emphasized religious symbols and language in their addresses, the Bush administration has done something altogether different: *it has converged a religious fundamentalist world view with a political agenda – wrapped in the mantle of national interest, but crafted by and for those who share its outlook. It is a moderate form of political fundamentalism – the adaptation of a self-proclaimed conservative Christian rectitude into political policies.*" (Emphasis added.)

This wrapping of the mantle of religion into political policy and rhetoric is not simply an expression of President Bush's religiosity. There is evidence that the national Republican Party has played the religious card in several other ways in the 2004 campaign at all levels throughout the nation. The Republican Party and their allies sought to motivate conservative Christian voters to support Bush and other Republican candidates by emphasizing such issues as opposition to abortion into same sex marriage, support of school prayer, and stopping efforts to remove the words "under God" from the Pledge of Allegiance.

Should Jews Be Concerned?

Should the nation's and Minnesota's Jews be concerned over the increasing injection of Christian religious doctrine into politics? Will any Jew who seeks statewide office in Minnesota be subject to an implicit if not explicit religious test of his/her qualifications or fitness for such public office? These questions cannot be answered definitively. They were not in the forefront at the time that Rudy Boschwitz was endorsed by the Minnesota Republican Party and elected to the U.S. Senate. While the issue of who was a "better Jew" was injected by Boschwitz into his campaign against Paul Wellstone, it did not surface in the endorsement by the Republican Party of Norm Coleman in his quest for the United States Senate seat held by Wellstone. It may have been because Coleman is married to a Catholic and has taken a pro life stance. We have yet to see whether a pro choice Democrat of any religious faith can be elected governor of Minnesota. Certainly a pro choice Republican has no greater chance of being endorsed for high statewide office than does a pro life candidate in the DFL.

An example of campaigning based on religion is a Republican legislative candidate in rural Minnesota. He not only campaigned that he would do whatever he could to ensure that same sex couples could not legally marry in Minnesota, something Minnesota law already prevents. He also campaigned door to door with a little gold cross in his lapel. He "revealed to potential voters that he had prayed about the possibility that gay marriage could take place in Minnesota."[1]

A similar use of religion in 2004 was the appeal to Jewish voters by Bush's evangelical Christian supporters and Jewish Republicans. They argued that American Jews should vote for Bush because of his acknowledged strong support for the Sharon government in Israel. Jewish voters with whom I discussed the subject in the 2004 campaign took Bush's commitment at face value. None questioned why Bush would be a strong supporter of Israel. They did not understand that evangelical Christians, such as Bush, are strong supporters of Israel because they believe that the return of the Jews to the Holy Land is foretold in the Scriptures and heralds the return of Jesus Christ as the Messiah. What the return of the Messiah would mean to the existence of Israel as a uniquely Jewish state and its Jewish inhabitants is not discussed.

This appeal by Republicans, hoping that Bush support for Israel would wean traditional Jewish support from the Democrats, has not been met with notable success nationally. Exit polls taken in the 2004 election reflected a 5 percentage point increase in Jewish vote for Bush over his vote in 2000. The vote went from 19 to 24 percent.

It is not simply right wing evangelical Christians who have engaged in ongoing and divisive battles over the rights of gays and lesbians. The issue of performing legal marriage ceremonies for same sex couples has divided mainstream religious bodies. So has the question of the ordination of gay and lesbian clergy. "Black Protestants, who have a long history of championing many civil rights and other liberal positions have become among America's most ardent opponents of gay marriage and related causes."[2] A Fall, 2003 survey by the Pew Research Center for the People and the Press found that 67 percent of black Protestants polled stated they opposed allowing gays to legally marry. This was the largest percentage behind white evangelicals. At the national meeting of the African American Episcopal Church, one of the largest African American denominations, they voted unanimously to prohibit any minister from presiding over a marriage for same sex couples.[3]

Another issue of religious significance is embryonic stem cell research. Pro life supporters equate stem cell research with abortion. President Bush has sought to have it both ways. He has allowed limited federal government funding for research on a small number of stem cells. Senator Kerry would have imposed no such limitations. Stem cell research is such a significant issue that it has divided the sons of late President Ronald Reagan. One spoke at the 2004 Democratic National Convention in support of public funding of stem cell research. His half brother took the opposite view at the Republican National Convention. Inherent in the situations of abortion and stem cell research is the question of when one believes that life begins.

Placement of replicas of the Ten Commandments in public places has divided communities in such diverse places as the state capitol of Alabama and the city of Duluth. It also has divided the U.S. Supreme Court.

Religious issues have significantly changed the complexion of both the Republican and DFL parties in Minnesota. In prior years there were many contentious caucases and convention battles in the DFL over a woman's right to choose versus legal bans on abortion. After pro choice DFLers were successful in adopting "pro choice" platform planks, and endorsing candidates for statewide office who have been almost uniformly pro choice, most pro life supporters left the DFL. The exodus of pro life DFLers has led to a significant shift in the traditional DFL Party base. At the time of the 1944 merger of the Democratic and Farmer Labor parties, the Democrats were traditionally Irish Catholic. Their geographic base was in St. Paul. In recent years there has been a loss of support for statewide and national DFL and Democratic Party candidates in those parts of Minnesota with predominantly Catholic populations. The abortion issue, coupled with fights over gun control, and the more conservative bent of some labor union members, has weakened DFL support in such formerly DFL bastions as St. Louis County, the Iron Range and Anoka County.

The polarization of the two major political parties in Minnesota over these issues has left little room for moderates in either party. Former Republican governors, such as the late Elmer L. Andersen and Arnie Carlson, no longer supported the right wing conservative dominated Minnesota Republican Party and its support of a no tax pledge for state budget purposes. Several prominent DFLers have either left the DFL or have moved to more conservative ideological positions. Longtime DFL Party officer and former University of Minnesota Regent David Lebedoff no longer calls himself a Democrat. He is quoted as saying he "leans independent."[4] Lebedoff, businessman and former University Regent Lawrence Perlman, and former Lieutenant Governor A. M. "Sandy" Keith have all served at one time or another as board members of the staunchly conservative Center for the American Experience headed by Republican Mitchell Pearlstein. In 2006, Keith announced his support for the reelection of Governor Tim Pawlenty.

The imposition of religious tests as qualification for public office at any level, and the appeals to voters to judge candidates solely by their views on so called "moral value" issues, has inevitably led to a polarized and divided nation. It is the kind of religious conflict which many fear will return the United States to a country in which any majority, be it the "moral majority," or a like group, can take control of the governance of our nation at all levels.

Is the Separation of Church and State Eroding?

The U. S. Supreme Court has in the past been something of a bulwark in keeping church and state separate as required by the U.S. Constitution. However, a divided Supreme Court on issues such as the presence of Ten Commandment monuments on the grounds of the Texas State Capitol, and on court house walls or other public places, raises concern as to whether the separation of church and state has been eroded. Do the display of these items on government property amount to an unconstitutional "establish-ment" of religion in violation of the Constitution? Does government accommodate the religious needs of prison inmates as required by a recently enacted federal law? Does the recitation of the Pledge of Allegiance in a public school classroom violate the Constitution? This latter challenge by the father of a young female public school student was decided inconclusively when five U.S. Supreme Court Justices decided that the father lacked standing to pursue the case before the high court. Will the selection of new Chief Justice John Roberts swing the Court to overrule *Roe. v. Wade*? Or will it shift the abortion rights battleground to each of the 50 states? In the last campaign Senator John Kerry stated flatly that he would not appoint any Supreme Court Justice who voted to overturn *Roe. v. Wade*. While President Bush stated he would not impose any "litmus test" on prospective nominees, it is clear from the battle over the Miers' nomination that he was not being honest with the American public. Fundamental changes are taking place in American politics. How they evolve will do much to affect our lives and those of our children and grandchildren.

Chapter forty-four

The Changing Political Allegiance of American and Minnesota Jews

There has been an evolution in the political allegiance of Jews to major political parties both nationally and in Minnesota. American Jews have become more conservative in their voting behavior. For those who are politically active, this shift is reflected in a switch from the Democratic to the Republican Party, or from Democratic Party to becoming an "Independent." The shift is shown in the voting behavior of American Jews. Yet when American Jews are asked explicitly about the qualities that most strongly define their own Jewish identity, they are four times as likely to mention a commitment to social equality as they are to choose either support for Israel or religious involvement.[1]

Greenberg and Wald state: "The attachment to liberal values and candidates is just one of the traits that make American Jewry such an interesting phenomenon in American public life. Jewish Americans represent an extremely small percentage of the population – two to three per cent - depending on how Judaism is defined: yet, as voters, donors, activists, leaders and thinkers, they have had a profound impact on American political debate and the political process. The extent to which liberalism defines Jews' political attitudes is remarkable because it violates all the assumptions we make about the effect of upward mobility and dissimulation on political behavior. Most immigrant groups move politically to the right as they become more integrated in American society. By contrast, American Jewry has retained a distinct political identity and a liberal ideology despite rapid social advancement and acceptance. We find relatively little political differentiation based on their economic or educational attainment."[2]

I believe that upward mobility and increasing affluence, coupled with the move to the suburbs and assimilation caused by intermarriage, have had a more profound effect on the thinking and voting behavior of Minnesota Jews than is reflected in the studies referred to by Greenberg and Wald. What Greenberg and Wald have described as "Jewish political cohesion," that is, support for progressive social values that lead to identification with the national Democratic Party, is, in my opinion, eroding.

I discussed the subject with a number of affluent Minnesota Jews during the 2004 presidential campaign. With them support for the State of Israel was the predominant factor influencing support for President Bush over Senator Kerry. In social conversations, and in more pointed questioning as to why an affluent Minnesota Jew would support President Bush, the consistent rejoinder was because of Bush's strong support for the State of Israel. When I questioned the basis for the Bush support, most replied, "His support for the Sharon government in Israel and the War in Iraq which deposed Saddam Hussein." Saddam Hussein was viewed as a threat to neighboring Israel.

When the question was pursued further with a question as to why would Bush, an evangelical Christian, be such a strong supporter of Israel, considering Bush's close family ties to Saudi Arabia and its oil interests, most were not able to give a specific response. When they were asked if the support for Israel by evangelical Christians was based principally on Israel being in existence for the return of Jesus Christ, the Messiah, to occur, rather than specific support for Jews or Israel as such, there was also no specific response. No one had thought to question Bush's motives on the subject. The same respondents had little if any interest in, or knowledge of, Senator Kerry's long Senate record in support of Israel. This lack of knowledge may be mainly attributed to the ineffectiveness of the Kerry campaign. It was too sensitive to broach in a social setting the question as to whether these affluent Jewish suburbanites were more likely to have been influenced by their having personally benefited from the Bush sponsored tax cuts. While extrapolation into general conclusions from these limited conversations is not appropriate, this informal poll does provide some insight into the thinking of some affluent Minnesota Jews.

The support for the continued strength and existence of the State of Israel continues to be an important issue influencing American Jews. However, that commitment may be overshadowed by the commitment of American Jews to social justice. The 2004 Survey of American Jewish Opinion by the American Jewish Committee asked the question: "Which one of the following qualities do you consider most important to your Jewish identity?" Twenty per cent responded that it was a commitment to social justice." Support for Israel achieved only a six per cent response among those polled.[3]

This poll was taken before the November 2004 presidential election. On such hot button political issues as the rights of gay couples, forty nine per cent favored allowing gay couples to legally marry. Thirty six per cent stated that gay couples should be allowed to form civil unions but not legally marry. Only thirteen per cent responded that there should be no legal recognition. Two per cent were not sure. Twenty four per cent of those responding stated they would favor an amendment to the United States Constitution that defined marriage as a union only between a man and a woman and make same sex marriages unconstitutional. Seventy four per cent were opposed. Two per cent were not sure.

On the issue of whether those Jews surveyed favored or opposed government aid to parochial or other religious schools, twenty five per cent favored such aid. Seventy two per cent were opposed. Three per cent were not sure. In 2003, by identical margins of seventy three per cent to twenty five per cent, the American Jews polled by the American Jewish Committee opposed government aid to parochial or other religious schools. They also objected to Bush's faith based initiatives which would provide taxpayer funds for social service programs run by religious institutions.

In my informal poll during the 2004 campaign, the limited

number of Minnesota Jews whom I questioned expressed support for such causes as the right to choose an abortion; embryonic stem cell research; government supporting the affordability of medical care for those who are economically disadvantaged; protection of the environment; and support for public education.

There are a number of dynamics which have historically influenced how Minnesota Jews have voted and supported liberal causes and the Democratic Party. The combination of vicious anti-Semitism experienced by immigrant Jews in Europe, and repeated in Minnesota in the 1938 gubernatorial campaign, made Minnesota Jews reluctant to support the Minnesota Republican Party and its causes. Right wing isolationism at the time of World War II and beyond, coupled with the Holocaust, made Jews concerned over its replication in America. The allegiance to the Democratic Party nationally was reinforced by Democratic President Harry Truman in his 1947 prompt recognition of the State of Israel. The perception that the Democratic Party was "a more natural political home for Jews" was reinforced by the nomination of Connecticut Senator Joseph Lieberman as the Democratic candidate for Vice President in 2000.[4]

These considerations have been counterbalanced by the increasing affluence of Minnesota and American Jews; rising rates of intermarriage and assimilation; and the ease with which Jews were able to achieve success in business and the professions beginning in the late 1950s. The civil rights measures adopted in Minnesota in the mid 1950s and early 1960s eliminated legal employment and housing barriers for Minnesota Jews. The removal of quotas in professional schools opened up opportunities for the generation of Minnesota Jews that came of age in the 1980s and 1990s. However, the allegiance of their parents and grandparents to liberal principles and the Democratic Party, are for some, simply history. Some believe that only their skills and ambitions can limit their opportunities for social and economic advancement. How they rose to the position where they could take advantage of these opportunities, is irrelevant to a rising number. Since they had not personally experienced the struggle to achieve these opportunities, they feel little or no allegiance to those political activists and political parties that struggled to achieve these goals.

The decline in synagogue affiliation, coupled with higher rates of intermarriage and assimilation, have weakened the commitment of American and Minnesota Jewry to the social causes, that are based upon the principle of Tikkun Olam – social justice causes and the biblical principle found in Deuteronomy, "Justice, justice shall you pursue." The synagogue has traditionally been the source of teaching religious and social values. While these commitments to social activism are evidenced by such Minnesota organizations as Jewish Community Action, the Four Squared Program of the Minnesota Jewish Community Relations Council, and the Joint Religious Legislative Coalition, there is simply not enough participation to stem the flow to non involvement or to more conservative political causes.[5]

There has also been weakening of support for the Minnesota DFL Party among Minnesota Jews. The litmus test of pro choice views imposed by the DFL on those ambitious to run for statewide office has driven some politically ambitious Jews, such as now U.S. Senator Norman Coleman, into the arms of the Republicans. Even at the rank and file level, those who do not share the DFL liberal agenda have been made to feel unwelcome. The reforms adopted by the Democratic Party nationally and the Minnesota DFL, to enhance the opportunities for all to take part in the party processes, has served to fractionalize participation at the grassroots level into single issue allegiances. Thus, instead of there being an overarching unifying element in party participation, the DFL has become only a collection of special interest groups and their advocates.

Prior to the 1950's, there were only a handful of publicly identified and prominent Jewish Republicans in Minnesota. The trend toward Jewish Republican political involvement in Minnesota began quietly in the 1940's with the election of Luther Youngdahl as governor. It continued into the 1950's with the election of President Dwight D. Eisenhower. The few prominent and visible Republican activists, such as Buddy Ruvelson, quietly raised sub-

stantial sums of money from affluent Minnesota Jewish businessmen on behalf of Republican candidates. On the national level
Michigan industrialist Max Fisher became a prominent and successful fundraiser for Republican candidates and causes. The emergence of moderate Republicans representing Minneapolis' suburbs
provided an avenue for more successful Jews, who had become
more conservative in their views on tax and other economic issues,
to support Republican state legislators and congressmen such as
William Frenzel. Several successful Jewish business people of my
acquaintance, while not prominently or publicly identified with
the Republican Party, were consistent supporters of Frenzel in his
long tenure in Congress representing the suburban Third Congressional District.

The election of Rudy Boschwitz to a U.S. Senate seat in 1978
highlighted the emergence of Minnesota Jews to prominence in
the Minnesota Republican Party and the nation. That same year
Jewish Republican Elliot Rothenberg defeated a DFL incumbent. Rothenberg was elected to the Minnesota House from St.
Louis Park. He served for two two-year terms before his 1982
unsuccessful candidacy as the Republican endorsed candidate for
attorney general. The change in political attitudes on the part of
some Minnesota suburban Jews was presented pointedly in 2002,
in Ron Latz's campaign for election to the House.

I was calling district residents whom I knew personally in an
attempt to secure their votes for Ron. One call was made to a household with a name familiar to me as an acquaintance from North
Minneapolis. The family ran a small suburban retail business. The
recipient of the call turned out to be the son of the acquaintance. I
described Ron's background and experience. I expressed the hope
that he would vote for Ron, a DFLer. I received a cold and perfunc-
tory response. There was a rather clear indication that the person
would not vote for Ron. I was taken aback by the response. I then
called the person's father with the same request for his support and
vote. It was readily given. The father laughed when he was told of
the conversation with his son. He said that his son was financially
successful and did not consider himself a supporter of the DFL

or its candidates. He said that his children and grandchildren had no memory of the struggles that his parents and grandparents had endured to achieve social and economic success through the efforts of such Democrats as Hubert H. Humphrey. He stated that to this younger generation it was simply a part of history to which they had little reason to personally relate.

This kind of response was rarely encountered. It was certainly not indicative of the overwhelming majority of the residents of District 44B in St. Louis Park and Golden Valley. Ron was overwhelmingly elected. It is, however, indicative of the kinds of issues DFL Jewish candidates in the suburbs can face. The response of this successful younger Jewish voter had something of a parallel in the decision of Ron's opponent in that race, Lisa Lebedoff Peilen, to run as the Republican endorsed candidate. She ran despite her family's significant roots as supporters of liberal causes, and her brother David Lebedoff's long history of involvement with and support for the DFL and its candidates.

Chapter Forty-five

Is There a Jewish Vote?

In Minnesota Jewish legislative candidates have been, with some recent exceptions, elected only from districts that had significant numbers of Jewish voters. Sam Bellman was elected to the Legislature from North Minneapolis in 1934, at the height of the popularity of Governor Floyd B. Olson. He served one two year term. Some 50 years later I was elected from a heavily Jewish district in North Minneapolis and served four two year terms. Gloria Segal and Irving Stern, Elliot Rothenberg, Jim Rhodes, Ron Latz and Steve Simon were all elected from suburban St. Louis Park, Golden Valley and Hopkins where many Jews reside. In St. Paul, Jews such as Senators Dick Cohen and Sandy Pappas and Representative Michael Paymar have been elected from the Highland Park area. Milton Rosen and Len Levine were elected citywide and served on the St. Paul City Council. Ron Abrams served for 18 years representing the suburban Minnetonka area with a limited Jewish population. In 2005, Terri Bonoff of Minnetonka was elected to the Senate. Eric Lipman served in the Minnesota House from a decidedly non Jewish area in Woodbury. In 2004, Tina Liebling, a DFLer, was narrowly elected to a House seat from a district encompassing Rochester and Olmsted County.

In 2006, Bonoff and Liebling were reelected. With this kind of an elective history the question is legitimately raised as to whether there is, in fact, what could be termed a "Jewish vote?" Greenberg and Wald put the question in more sociological terms. They asked the question, "Are Jews more politically cohesive than non-Jews?"[1] Put another way, do Jews actually vote as a bloc? The polls reflected in the Study of Jewish Public Opinion cited by Greenberg and Wald are from exit polls conducted of a sample of

1498 Jews each in 1990, 1992, 1994, 1996 and 1998. The results stated that there were "...enduring differences between Jews and non Jews on school prayer and religion in public life, abortion and the death penalty, but fewer divisions around race and affirmative action." The polls found that "Jews strongly support the separation of church and state, abortion rights, the women's movement, gun control, civil rights and environmental protection."[2] While Jewish Americans respond to the Democratic Party's appeal to the disadvantaged and support a social welfare state, they do not think of themselves as opposing business interests. They are, however, more likely to support intervention in international conflicts. This dates back to Nazi Germany, the Holocaust, and the fight for the survival of a Jewish State of Israel surrounded by its enemies.

According to the Jewish Public Opinion Study, thirty five per cent of Jews call themselves "liberal," compared to eighteen per cent of non Jews. Eight per cent of Jews call themselves "conservative," compared to twenty six per cent of non-Jews. Nearly an equal number of both groups call themselves "moderate." (Fifty per cent of Jews compared to forty four per cent of non Jews.) Jewish Americans support the women's movement more than non Jews. They are therefore more likely to call themselves pro choice than pro life.[3]

We can compare the results of the Jewish Public Opinion Study with the more recent 2003 and 2004 Annual Surveys of American Jewish Opinion conducted by the American Jewish Committee. In 2003, forty per cent of American Jews considered themselves "a liberal." This may be compared to twenty seven per cent who defined themselves as "conservative." Thirty three per cent of American Jews identified themselves as being "moderate, middle of the road."

The 2004 American Jewish Committee Survey respondents to the identical question identified themselves as follows: "liberals" forty five per cent. This is compared to twenty three per cent who considered themselves to be "conservative." Between the two surveys, those expressing moderate, middle of the road views decreased by three percentage points from 2003 to 2004, while those defining themselves as "liberal" increased by five percentage points from forty per cent to forty five per cent. Those with a conservative self definition declined from twenty seven per cent in 2003 to twenty three per cent in 2004.

While there has been some shifting in Jewish support for the Democratic Party and its presidential candidates in the last forty years, Jewish Americans gave Democratic presidential candidates two thirds of their votes in the 1980's. Despite his ongoing problems, Bill Clinton received eighty per cent of the votes of Jewish Americans in 1992, and seventy eight per cent of their votes in 1996. Even in the weak campaign conducted by Al Gore in 2000, seventy nine per cent of Jewish voters supported him. In a forty year period only Jimmy Carter received weaker support from Jewish Americans. In the 1990's, only African Americans supported the Democrats with more constancy than American Jews. This was during the period when Catholics and white southerners were deserting the Democratic Party.

The "family values" of the "Christian right" and the Republican Party have not typically had support from Jewish voters. This division is reflected in disagreement over such issues as abortion, school prayer and the rights of gays and lesbians. The conclusion of the study cited by Greenberg and Wald is that "Jewish Americans believe the Democrats better represent Jewish values" and the "interests of Jewish Americans" than those associated with the Republican Party."[4]

Before the 2004 elections there were differences of opinion as to whether American Jewish voters would vote in larger numbers for the Republican presidential candidate. Following the 2000 presidential election, the American Jewish Committee Poll questioned respondents as to whether they voted for Al Gore or for George W. Bush? Sixty-six per cent responded that they had voted for Al Gore and twenty four per cent for George W. Bush. Three per cent volunteered they had voted for "other"; three per cent said that they "did not vote"; and four per cent were "not sure."

The AJC 2003 poll resulted in fifty nine per cent of respondents stating that they expected to vote for John Kerry. Thirty one per cent said that they expected to vote for George W. Bush. Ten per cent were "not sure." A pre election article in Twin Cities Jewish Life referred to the 2003 American Jewish Committee Survey. It concluded that if Bush were to receive the thirty one per cent of the vote counted in the actual 2004 election results, "...it could be the largest Jewish vote in the history for a Republican presidential candidate."

The 2004 annual Survey of American Jewish Opinion, taken before the election, posed the question "suppose the next general election for president were being held today and you had to choose between George W. Bush, a Republican, John Kerry, the Democrat, or Ralph Nader, the Independent – for whom would you vote? The response was George W. Bush, twenty four per cent; John Kerry, sixty nine per cent; Ralph Nader, three per cent; "not sure", five per cent. Thus, Bush's percentage of the Jewish vote was expected to remain constant with the results of the 2003 survey, with Kerry increasing his support by three percentage points.

While there are no post election survey results available from any national Jewish organization, the 2004 vote, based on an average of exit polls from CNN, AP, and Frank Luntz, showed President Bush increasing his margin of victory over the 2000 election results by five percentage points. The exit poll results in the 2004 election showed Kerry with seventy six per cent of the Jewish vote; Bush with twenty four per cent of the Jewish vote; and Nader with less than one per cent. The Bush margin was remarkably the same as the result of the 2004 American Jewish Committee Survey. The survey results showing support of Ralph Nader at three per cent and undecided – "not sure" at five per cent, indicates that those possible Nader voters and those undecided swung to Kerry in the polling places.[5]

While the George W. Bush victory in 2004 did represent a substantial increase in the Republican presidential vote over the 2000 results, it did not represent the largest number of Jewish voters historically for a Republican presidential candidate. In the 1980 presidential election, Ronald Reagan received thirty nine per cent of the Jewish vote. Jimmy Carter received forty-five per cent, and the Independent candidate John Anderson received fourteen per cent.[6]

There are, however, some trends that appear to be evident in the election results, and in the surveys of Jewish public opinion. Greenberg and Wald found "affluent and well-educated Jews exhibit more Republican tendencies than their poor compatriots."

Increasingly, American Jews who have become suburbanites have begun to mirror the voting habits of their non Jewish suburban neighbors. American and Minnesota Jews in the 21st century are becoming more and more like their non Jewish neighbors. The second and third generations have little or no memory of the struggles that brought their parents and grandparents to their present economic and social levels. There is a greater tendency to vote for candidates based on the voters' personal economic status rather than judging candidates and party platforms based on their compassion toward the disadvantaged and their willingness to protect individual rights.

Greenberg and Wald found that younger Jews are less committed to the Democratic Party than their elders. This, however, does not mean that younger Jews have moved into the Republican Party. They are simply now calling themselves politically "independent." Greenberg and Wald found that while only ten per cent of Jews under the age of 35 call themselves Republicans, forty nine per cent in that age bracket identified themselves as Democrats. Forty two per cent called themselves politically independent.[7] The future seems to be that as the younger Jewish voters become more successful, they are becoming more conservative in their political behavior.

One of the problems facing the Democrats nationally and in Minnesota is how do they reconstruct their platforms and appeal to offset the lessening of feelings of compassion towards the disadvantaged and the importance of protecting individual rights? These have been the traditional values central to Jewish support for the Democratic Party and its candidates since Floyd B. Olson, Hubert H, Humphrey and Franklin D. Roosevelt. Education, age, gender and economic status are all issues to be considered when trying to discern the attitude of voters, both Jewish and non Jewish, on various social issues such as abortion, gay marriage, gun control, and the death penalty.

On the issue of separation of church and state, the Jewish community is distinctly at odds with those comprising the religious right. As Greenberg and Wald observed, "when the state promotes religion, the beneficiary is likely to be the faith of the majority at the expense of minorities."[8] The only issue that erodes the strong Jewish support for separation of church and state is the issue of school vouchers. In a school voucher program the state could use its tax revenues to fund attendance at private and religious schools. The Jewish day school movement has grown primarily because of reports that fifty per cent of Jews are now marrying out of their faith.[9] That study provided evidence that Jews who experienced a Jewish day school education were more likely to marry within their religion. Others in the Jewish community argue that diverting limited tax dollars would cause significant harm to the public schools while at the same time eroding the wall of separation between church and state. Jews nationally comprise three to four per cent of the total population.[10] The Jewish Virtual Library statistics estimate a Minnesota Jewish population of 42,000 out of a total of 4,931,000 Minnesotans. Jews thus would comprise 0.9 per cent of the total population in Minnesota.

There are expected to be profound divisions in the Minnesota Jewish community over the subject of school vouchers. While the number of adherents to the Jewish day school movement are unknown, the national survey in 2004 by the American Jewish Committee puts the number of those Jews who consider themselves to be Orthodox at seven per cent. Thirty one per cent of American Jews surveyed responded that they considered themselves as "conservative"; twenty nine per cent as "reform"; thirty per cent as "just Jewish"; and two per cent as "reconstructionist".

Chapter Forty-six

Where Are We and Where Do We Go from Here

We have described the Jewish political experience in Minnesota in the last half century. We have explored the lessons that may be learned from that experience as to Minnesota politics in general and as to Minnesota Jews in particular. Senator Joseph Lieberman has said that his inspiration to enter politics was guided by the examples of those who came before him. Lieberman expressed the hope that "this volume will help to inspire a new generation of American Jews ...to dedicate themselves to public life and public office."[1] The portraits of Jews in Minnesota politics and public life recited hopefully will serve as role models and motivate others to participate in politics and public life in Minnesota or elsewhere in the United States. We have also sought to highlight those aspects of uniqueness to Jewish religion and culture that call for a dedicated involvement in improving the life of communities in which Minnesota Jews live and work.

Reflecting on the last years of involvement of Minnesota Jews in their communities, public institutions, politics and public life leads inevitably to the conclusion that they have much for which to be thankful. Anti-Semitism is no longer overt and publicly accepted. Accomplished Jews are accepted in the institutions from which they were previously excluded. Minnesota Jews are now included on boards of prominent Minnesota, national and international corporations. Previously their religious counterparts were excluded solely because of their religion.

In Minnesota, Jews have been elected to high public office, such as U.S. Senator, regardless of their political party affiliation.

Jews have served as presidents of the University of Minnesota and on prestigious boards such as the University of Minnesota Board of Regents. While numerous Jews have served as trial court judges, Minnesota Jewish lawyers and judges have yet to be appointed to the Minnesota Court of Appeals. In the Minnesota Legislature, Jews of both major political party affiliations have been elected in districts with few Jewish voters.

While there has not yet been a Jewish candidate for President nominated by a major political party, Senator Lieberman was a Democratic candidate for Vice President. The administrations of presidents from both parties have had major policy advisors at the presidential, vice presidential and cabinet levels. There is a Jewish presence on the U.S. Supreme Court. Jews in Minnesota and nationally have now entered the mainstream of politics and public life.

While there are still gains to be made, and pockets of overt and covert prejudice remaining, one can proudly cite the strides we have made and the accomplishments that have occurred individually and collectively. As we have seen, the path to acceptability, socially and politically, has not been an easy one. Hopefully, the lessons learned will help guide those who seek careers, acceptance and success in their dedicated efforts to affect public policy in institutions of all kinds.

The phrase that one who does not learn the lessons of history is bound to repeat them still rings true. The Minnesota and national Jewish communities have changed economically and politically. Failure to recognize these changes is perilous for those involved in the political process. One thing that is quite clear is that the characterization by Professor Daniel Elazar of Minnesota as a state with liberal roots and philosophy is correct historically but incorrect presently. While some Jewish office seekers still characterize themselves as "Humphrey Democrats," as has Al Franken, Minnesota voters generally, and in the Jewish community have become increasingly conservative politically and unaffiliated with the Minnesota DFL.[2] Increasing numbers of voters appear to have accepted what Hubert Humphrey and Minnesota economist Walter Heller described as "trickle down economics." These are tax policies which favor directing wealth toward the few in the expectation that eventually the benefits will trickle down to the masses thereby stimulating purchasing power.

The agrarian liberalism which flourished in Minnesota and the Dakotas in the 1930's and 1940's no longer exists. Minnesota's role as a leader in the "grain belt" of America has significantly diminished. The exodus from the farms and small towns in Minnesota to the central cities and suburbs has lessened the influence of rural Minnesotans and rural legislators. With that exodus has come congressional and legislative redistricting which has transferred legislative and political power to the suburbs. That shift is evidencing itself in how members of the Minnesota Legislature distribute state revenues to institutions in the cities and suburbs as compared to what is now known as "Greater Minnesota." Massive plant closures and job losses on Minnesota's Iron Range, and the diminished influence of labor unions there and throughout Minnesota, has led to changes in voting power and election in the battles between the Minnesota GOP and the DFL.

However, the demographic and economic changes in the Minnesota political landscape are already overshadowed by two major changes. One already evident is the injection of religion and so called "religious values" into the political process. "Single-issue politics" is not a new phenomenon. The war in Viet Nam energized young people in opposition to presidents Lyndon B. Johnson and Richard Nixon. It created the candidacy for president of Eugene McCarthy. The failed effort to free and democratize Iraq is energizing young and old alike in opposition to the policies of President George W. Bush. However, it is the increasing entry of organized religious groups, churches and their religious leaders into the battles over abortion and gay marriage that has led to polarization of the public, religious bodies and the political parties nationally and in Minnesota. Notwithstanding the strict prohibitions of the Internal Revenue Code on direct political endorsements and participation by religious institutions in politics, there is a disturbing increase in their direct political participation. It is centered on such controversial issues as a woman's right to abortion and prohibitions by constitutional amendment on so called gay marriage.[3]

Abortion politics in Minnesota has resulted in a litmus test being applied to candidates for endorsement by both the DFL and Republican parties. If you are not "pro life" you stand little if any chance of being endorsed for statewide political office by the Republican Party. If you are not "pro choice" you are simply not going to be endorsed for statewide office by the DFL. This focus on these religious issues has had a significant effect. It has reduced the importance of debate and discussion by candidates and the political parties on other very important social and economic issues. If a candidate for endorsement does not have what a majority of delegates view as the "right position" on these religious issues, the candidate's opinions on economics and tax policy, healthcare, education, labor and the environment become of much reduced relevance.

I do not pretend to have the answers to this Rubik's Cube puzzle. Given the militancy of those Minnesotans committed to the injection of so called "religious values" or "social values" into the political election process, and the ability of religious leaders to turn out these single issue voters to the polls, the return of the DFL to majority party status at <u>both</u> the gubernatorial and legislative level remains doubtful. Most Minnesota Jews holding elective office, Democrats and Republicans alike, are pro choice and profess moderation in their allegiances. This focus on single issue politics with strong religious overtones will remain significant impediments to election to higher public office. Of course, overarching issues, such as the war in Iraq, may motivate voters, particularly younger voters, to support or oppose a candidate of either political party. They did this in the 2006 election. That, and the emergence of the "cult of personality" evidenced by the election of Jesse Ventura in Minnesota and Arnold Schwarzenegger in California, show that personal characteristics, personalities and charisma may overshadow the records and experience of their political opponents.

What does all of this have to do with Jews in Minnesota politics? Second and third generation Jewish voters, like their counterparts in traditional DFL areas as Anoka County and the Iron Range, have little memory of the struggles of their parents and grandparents to organize and support labor unions and the candidacies of the Hubert Humphreys and Fritz Mondales. To them the Humphrey's and Mondale's elections were the result of politics and economics of another generation. What interests them is what is happening to them and their families today. As a rule they do not get their information from newspapers. They get it from blogs, television and computer web sites. They look down on the so called "professional politicians."

Young Jewish voters in the suburbs are less likely to be influenced by the commitments to social justice of the candidates than they are to the candidate's views on policies that affect their pocketbooks. I found this specifically in soliciting votes for Ron Latz's reelection in 2004. Children of my longtime political supporters were more conservative in their political views. The fact of the Jewish candidate's religion and commitment to Jewish religious and social values was less important than the candidate's views on economic and tax policies. President Bush's and the Republican Party's supported tax cuts at the federal level overrode any concerns about the intrusion of religious and social values into the political marketplace. This happened too often to believe that this was just a blip on the political horizon. It was a generational change. It indicated that these generations of Jewish voters in the suburbs had entered, or believed that they had entered, the economic mainstream.

However, it is unwise to translate these changes into conclusions that there have been massive changes on the part of Jewish voters in Minnesota and nationally toward a Republican president and the Republican Party. Despite President Bush's and the Republicans' tax cuts, and the support of Republican oriented evangelical Christians for Israel in the Middle East conflict, President Bush garnered only a five percent gain nationally in the votes of Jewish voters in the 2004 presidential election. Bush garnered the votes of 24 percent of Jewish voters compared to 19 percent four years previously.

The unanswered question nationally and in Minnesota is what will result from the large influx of immigrants into the United States and our state. While the national issues surround Hispanic immigrants predominantly in the Western states, there have been large numbers of Hispanic, Asian and African immigrants to Minnesota. There is a large scale social, economic and religious battle taking place in Congress and at the national level as this text is written. It is clear that what *Newsweek* has described as "the Immigration War" will, regardless of the current battles, have a significant effect socially, economically and politically in those states directly affected and in the nation.[4]

Some of the rhetoric on the issues fuels ethnic and religious biases. It is reminiscent of the attitudes expressed toward Irish Catholic and Jewish immigrants around the beginning of the 20th century. It is downright scary that some would seek to criminalize with harsh felony penalties those who employ or grant support and sanctuary to immigrants. Hopefully, wiser heads will prevail in resolving these significant social and economic issues.

The changing political scene affects the ability to be endorsed and elected to public office for those Minnesota Jews of either major political party. However, there are important areas other than elective office remaining open to those with a social conscience and a willingness to serve both the Jewish community and the community at large. Minnesota Jews can put into the practice the injunction of Tikkun Olam, the "duty to repair the world," through participation in non political, religious and social institutions and organizations. For all the Rudy Boschwitz's, Paul Wellstone's, Norm Coleman's and Arthur Naftalin's who have achieved high elective and appointive office, and have left lasting legacies, there are the many referred to in this text, and others left unnamed, who have made an imprint on our state and on the Jewish and general communities. They too, along with those who have served in public offices who have participated actively in the political process, have had a significant influence in shaping public policies that have affected all of our lives. This is as it should be in a democracy. This book is principally dedicated to all those here named, and to the countless others, who have helped make the Minnesota Jewish community, our state and our nation, places of which we are all justly proud.

Minnesota Jews who have been first persons elected or appointed to very significant public office or community organizations.

- U.S. Senator, Rudy Boschwitz
- U.S. Ambassador – to the Netherlands, Geri Joseph
- U.S. District Court Judge, James Rosenbaum
- Minnesota Supreme Court Justice, Lee Loevinger
- President, University of Minnesota, Kenneth Keller
- Chancellor, Minnesota State College Systems, G. Theodore Mitau
- Regent, University of Minnesota, George B. Leonard
- Mayor, City of Minneapolis, Arthur Naftalin
- Mayor, City of St. Paul, Lawrence Cohen, Chief Judge Ramsey County District Court, Chair Ramsey County Board
- Endorsed Candidate by Minnesota Political Party (DFL) for State-wide Constitutional Office – Attorney General, Robert Latz, 1966
- President Pro Tem, Minnesota State Senate, Allan Spear
- Speaker Pro Tem, Minnesota House of Representatives, Ron Abrams
- Minnesota State Senator, Jack Kleinbaum (St. Cloud)
- Woman State Representative, Esther Fieldman (Park Rapids)
- State Representative, Emmet Z. Mark, 1901-1905
- Hennepin County Commissioner, Nancy Olkon
- Mayor of St. Louis Park, Irv Stern
- Hennepin County District Court Judge, Irving Brand
- Ramsey County District Judge, Gustavus Loevinger
- St. Louis County District Judge, Sidney Kaner
- Isaac N. Cardozo, Federal Commissioner – Deputy to U.S. District Court Judge, 1870

- Charles Bechhofer, District Court Judge
- Jacob Jackson Noah, Federal Magistrate – before
  Minnesota became a state in 1858
- President, Minnesota State Bar Association, Sidney
  Feinberg
- President, Minneapolis Chamber of Commerce, Jay Phillips
- Member – Minneapolis Club, Jay Phillips
- Partner, Major Twin Cities Law Firm
  Arthur Weisberg – Dorsey Law Firm, 1952
  Mitchell Goldstein – Faegre & Benson
- Minneapolis School Board Member, Viola Hymes
- President, Rotunda Club – Spouses of Minnesota State
  Representatives, Carolyn Latz, 1963
- Chief Executive Officer, I.E. Dupont, Irving Shapiro
- Chairman, U.S. Business Round Table, C.E.O.s of Major
  U.S. Corporations, Irving Shapiro
- President, Anti-Defamation League (ADL), Burton Joseph
- President, National Council of Jewish Women, Fanny Brin
- President (interim), Wellesley College, Luella Goldberg
- Chairman, Committee on Jewish Law and Standards,
  United Synagogues of Conservative Judaism, Rabbi
  Kassel Abelson
- First Jewish woman Regent, University of Minnesota,
  Linda Cohen
- Fanny Fligelman Brin, President of the National Council of
  Jewish Women, 1932-1938*
- St. Paul City Attorney, Louis Frankel*
- Faculty Member, University Minnesota Law School,
  Robert Kolliner, 1896**

---

* *The Jews in Minnesota, The First 75 Years*, Rabbi Gunther
Plaut
**University of Minnesota Alumni Association, *Minnesota
Magazine*, 1/11/2007 - Tim Brady

OTHER JEWS INVOLVED IN
MINNESOTA POLITICS

(The following represents a list of Jews involved at various
levels of Minnesota Politics. Omitted are those who are
otherwise referred to in the text. It is not meant to be exclusive.
The names are listed alphabetically.)

- Jay Benanav. Member St. Paul City Council, 1998 and
  continuing. Unsuccessful candidate for Mayor of St.
  Paul losing to Randy Kelly by 403 votes.

- Benjamin Berger. Minneapolis theater owner and
  philanthropist. Republican. Member of the Minneapolis
  Park Board, 1963-1976.

- Frank Berman. University of Minnesota Regent,
  2001-2007.

- Michael Berman. Native of Duluth. Assistant to
  Senator and Vice President Walter F. Mondale. Author
  of Capitol Hill newsletter. Acknowledged expert on
  campaign finance matters.

- Lois Binder. Assistant to Minneapolis Mayor Donald
  Fraser.

- Aviva Breen. Director of Minnesota Legislative
  Commission on the Economic Status of Women, 1984-
  2001. Active in feminist movement.

- Aaron Brown. Former CNN anchor and commentator.

- Dan Cohen. Republican member of the Minneapolis
  City Council, 1965 to 1969. Unsuccessful candidate for
  Minneapolis Mayor in 1969. Cohen worked as a public
  relations person during the unsuccessful candidacy of
  Wheelock Whitney for Governor. Cohen was revealed
  as the source of information published in the Twin Cities
  newspapers about the alleged shoplifting conviction of
  Marlene Johnson. Johnson was the DFL candidate for
  Lieutenant Governor with gubernatorial candidate Rudy
  Perpich. Cohen waged a successful libel suit growing out
  of the newspapers' revelation attributing to him personally
  these charges about Johnson after Cohen had been
  granted assurance of "off the record" confidentiality to his
  information. In 1995, Cohen's book about his experiences
  was published by Oliver Press. It is entitled *Anonymous
  Source – At War Against the Media.* Cohen's story is
  especially interesting in view of the 2006 controversy
  regarding the confidentiality of sources of an alleged leak
  to several media persons of the information that Valerie
  Plame was an undercover CIA operative. Allegations
  of a "leak" of Ms. Plame's CIA identity involved high
  officials in the Bush administration including "Scooter"
  Libby, top aide to Vice President Cheney and Karl Rove,
  the architect of President Bush's successful political
  strategies. In 2007 Libbey was convicted of lying under
  oath in the Plame incident.

- Gary Cohen. Candidate for Minneapolis City Council,
  1981.

- Philip Cohen. Mayor of Brooklyn Center, 1966 to
  1977. Active in metropolitan suburban affairs. Served
  on Metropolitan Council's Housing and Redevelopment

Advisory Committee for a record 24 years. (1974-1998).

- Pearl Cole. Assistant to Senator Walter F. Mondale. Ran Mondale's Minnesota office. Named as a DFL Woman of Distinction.

- Morris Dickel. Attorney, Crookston, Minnesota, Member of the Minnesota Board of Law Examiners.

- Gail Dorfman. Served on St. Louis Park City Council 1991 to 1995. Mayor of St. Louis Park from 1996 to 1999. Elected to Hennepin Country Board of Commissioners in 1999 and continues to serve. Strong advocate of smoking ban for Hennepin County.

- Robert "Bob" Fine. Serves as member and President of Minneapolis Park Board, 1997 and continuing.

- Philip Finkelstein. Member of St. Louis Park City Council, 2004 and continuing.

- Lisa Goodman. Represents 7th Ward on Minneapolis City Council, 1997 and continuing.

- Scott Grayson. Member of Golden Valley City Council, 2002 through 2006. (Elected 11/2001.)

- Zollie Green. Member of Minneapolis City Council, 1971 to 1979.

- Michael Held. Republican Party Chairman, St. Louis Park, Hopkins, Golden Valley 15 years and continuing.

- Frank Hornstein. State Representative for South Minneapolis District including areas of Lake Calhoun and Lake Harriet, 2002 and continuing.

- Samuel Hunegs. Farmer Labor Party activist in the 1930's and 1940's. Grandfather of Steve Hunegs who gave up a successful law practice with his father Richard Hunegs to fill the vacant post of Executive Director of the Jewish Community Relations Council of Minnesota-Dakotas in 2006. Steve Hunegs is a past president of the JCRC.

- Morris Kaplan. Mayor of Bemidji, Minnesota.

- Jack Kleinbaum. Served as State Representative from St. Cloud area 1967 through 1972. Served in Minnesota Senate from 1973 to 1980.

- Harry Lerner. Candidate for Minneapolis Library Board, 1960.

- Leonard Levine. Served on St. Paul City Council for 13 years. Chair, Metropolitan Transit Commission. Commissioner Minnesota Department of Transportation and Commissioner Minnesota Welfare Department under Governor Rudy Perpich.

- Andrew Lugar. Candidate for Hennepin County Attorney in 2006.

- Paula Macabee. Member St. Paul City Council.

- Hiram Mendow. Attorney. Handled lawsuit before

Minnesota Supreme Court that broke the restrictive covenants on real estate ownership in the Homewood area of North Minneapolis. Justice of the Peace in Columbia Heights in 1930's. Also known as "Capone lawyer" for his representation of Al Capone and/or his allies.

- Alan Miller. Radio and television talk show host. Program is *Access to Democracy.*

- Jerry Miller. Mayor, City of Winona, 1997 and continuing.

- Iric Nathanson. Assistant to Congressman Donald Fraser. Author on history of Minneapolis Jewish community.

- David Ornstein. Bloomington City Attorney. Instrumental in shaping successful policies for development of the Mall of America.

- Howard Orenstein. Former member of the Minnesota House of Representatives from St. Paul.

- Solly Robins. Noted trial lawyer. Successfully represented plaintiff in establishing landmark product liability law. Founder of what is now the firm of Robins, Kaplan, Miller and Ciresi.

- Michael Rothman. Chair, DFL State Constitution Committee. Elected Finance Chair, Minnesota DFL Party, 2007.

- Susan Sanger. Member of St. Louis Park City Council, 1995 and continuing.

- Gloria Segal. Served in Minnesota House of Representatives from St. Louis Park, from 1983 to 1992. Leader in efforts to assist the mentally ill.

- Yvonne Selcer. Member of District 270 – Hopkins/ Golden Valley School Board, 2004 and continuing.

- Norman Sherman. Press Secretary to Senator and then Vice President Hubert Humphrey.

- Alan Sherr. Candidate for Minneapolis School Board, 1960.

- Alan Silver. Member St. Louis Park School Board. President of Jewish Community Relations Council, 2006 and continuing. Treasurer Ron Latz Campaign Committee prior to 2006.

- Beverly Smerling. Candidate for Minneapolis Park Commissioner, 1960.

- Irving "Irv" Stern. Mayor of St. Louis Park, 1977 to 1979. Served in Minnesota State Senate, 1979-1982.

- Judy Traub. Elected 1991. Served one term in Minnesota Senate from Minnetonka area.

- Alan Weinblatt. Legal Counsel - Minnesota DFL Party. Past President of Jewish Community Relations Council.

NOTES

INTRODUCTION (pgs. xiii-xx)

1. *Jews in Minnesota-A People of Minnesota*, Hyman Berman and Linda Mack Schloff, Minnesota Historical Society Press, 2002
2. David Tibbles
3. *Children of the Gilded Ghetto*, Kramer and Leventman, Yale University Press, 1961
4. *Jews in American Politics,* Maisel and Forman, Rowman and Littlefield Publishers, 2001
5. *Minnesota – The Epitome of the Moralistic Political Culture.* The *Jerusalem Center for Public Affairs,* Daniel Elazar, www.jcpa.org.
6. Elazar, p. 10
7. Elazar, p. 5
8. Elazar, p.6
9. Elazar, p.7

CHAPTER ONE (pgs. 1-14)

1. The seminal article about political anti-Semitism in Minnesota was written by Professor Hyman Berman. It is entitled "Political anti-Semitism in Minnesota during the Great Depression." *Jewish Social Studies, Vol. XXXVIII,* Summer-Fall 1976. See also Arthur Naftalin, "History of the Farmer Labor Party in Minnesota." Ph.D. thesis, University of Minnesota, and John Earl Haynes. "Dubious Alliance – The Making of Minnesota's DFL Party," University of Minnesota Press, 1984.
2. Jews in Minnesota, Hyman Berman and Linda Mack Schloff, Minnesota Historical Society Press, 2002, p. 51
3. 1912 history.ohio-stateedu/debs.htm
4. Berman, Schloff, p. 72
5. *Henry Ford and the Jews,* Neil Baldwin, Harper Collins, 2001
6. Berman, p. 262
7. Historian Robert Rockaway, The Journal of the American Jewish Historical Society
8. Rockaway, ibid

9. Berman, pp 255-257

10. Naftalin, p. 29

11. Vince A. Day Papers, Box 3, Folder 22, Minnesota Historical Society, quoted by Berman, p. 219

12. Naftalin, p. 42

13. Berman, p. 259

14. Haynes, pp. 17-21

15. Naftalin, p. 204

16. See interview with Sander Genis, available at the Minnesota Historical Society, quoted in Naftalin, p.122. For a more complete description of the battle between the national Communist Party and the CIO, see Max Kampelman, *The Communist Party vs. The CIO*, New York, Prager, 1957

18-28. Berman, p. 250-262

29. Mitau, p.23, *Minnesota Politics*, University of Minnesota Press, 1970

CHAPTER TWO (pgs 15-31)

1. Minneapolis: Curious Twin, Common Ground, 1946

2. T'kiah, The Voice of Jewish Community Action, Summer 2004

3. T'kiah, Winter 2004

CHAPTER THREE (pgs 32-76)

1. Nellie Stone Johnson – The Life of an Activist, Ruminator Books Press, 1999

2. Johnson, p. 135

3. 38 Minnesota Law Review 730 (1954)

4. Minneapolis Tribune, Daniel J. Hafrey

CHAPTER FOUR (pgs 77-82)

1. Minneapolis Star, February 27, 1959

2. Minneapolis Star, April 15, 1959

3. Minneapolis Star, ibid

4. Minneapolis Star, February 10, 1959, Wallace Mitchell

5. Minneapolis Star, Richard P. Kleeman

CHAPTER FIVE (pgs 83-92)

1. *Minnesota-The Magazine of the University of Minnesota Alumni Association* – March – April 2004, Richard Broderick
2. ibid
3. ibid

CHAPTER SIX (pgs 93-102)

1. Author's interview with Alan, better known as "Buddy" Ruvelson on September 16, 2003
2. Interview with Ruvelson in *Ramsey County History*, a publication of the Ramsey County Historical Society, winter 2003, Vol. 37, No. 4
3. Samuel L. Hayes, III, an investment banking specialist at Harvard University, quoted in the Money and Business Section of the *New York Times* on April 16, 2002
4. *Inc. Magazine*, ibid
5. ibid
6. Ramsey County Historical Society Interview reported in *Ramsey County History*, winter 2003, Vol. 37, No. 4
7. 1997 Annual Report, St. Thomas Academy
8. ibid

CHAPTER SEVEN (pgs 103-113)

1. Mitau, p. 28

CHAPTER EIGHT (pgs. 114-120)

1. Author interview conducted November 29, 2003

CHAPTER NINE (pgs 121-128)

1. Mitau, p. 31
2. ibid
3. Mitau, pp. 31-32
4. *Recount*, Charles Backstrom and Ronald Stinnett, National Document Publishers, Inc. 1964
5. *Recount*, p. 1
6. *Recount*, p. 21
7. *Recount*, p. 34
8. *Recount*, p. 73

9. *Recount*, pp. 265-281
10. *Recount*, p. 89
11. ibid
12. *Recount*, p. 94
13. *Recount*, pp. 95-96
14. *Recount*, p. 154
15. *Recount*, p. 190

CHAPTER TWELVE (pgs 138-144)
1. Minnesota Legislative Manual 1967-1968
2. ibid
3. Mitau, p. 52

CHAPTER FOURTEEN (pgs 148-150)
1. *Minnesota Standoff – Politics of Deadlock*, Rodney Searle,Alton
   Press,1990

CHAPTER SIXTEEN (pgs 154-169)
1. Author Interviews conducted on October 16, and December 3, 2003
2. *Minnesota Daily* on-line, 4/19/1996
3. University of Minnesota Department of American Indian Studies
   Heritage page. www.cla.umn.edu/amerind/heritage
4. Minnesota Historical Society Press, 2002
5. Jewish Social Studies 38, No. 34, Summer-Fall, 1976
6. American Jewish Historical Quarterly, Vol. LII (52), No. 2
   (December, 1962) Berman's Ph.D. 1956 dissertation at Columbia
   University was entitled *"Era of the Protocol: A Chapter in the
   History of the International Ladies Garment Workers Union,
   1910-1916."*
7. Berman, ibid
8. Berman interview, 12/3/2003
9. Berman, ibid
10. Berman, ibid
11. www.hhh.umn.edu/assets/1840/case pdf
12. *Rudy! The People's Governor*, Betty Wilson, Nodin Press, 2005,
    Chapter 19
13. Wilson, ibid

CHAPTER SEVENTEEN (pgs 170-175)
1. Author Interview conducted September 12, 2003.

CHAPTER EIGHTEEN (pgs 176-190)
1. Author Interview conducted September 12, 2003.

CHAPTER NINETEEN (pgs 191-193)
1. A Tribute to Eric Severeid, homepage of the Minnesota News Council, www.mnc net/Norway/severeid
2. University of Minnesota, 1948, unpublished

CHAPTER TWENTY-TWO (pgs 1995-211)
1. Subcommittee Final Report of January 13, 1975, p. 2, hereafter "Report".
2. ibid, p. 2
3. ibid, p. 7
4. ibid
5. ibid, p. 8
6. ibid
7. ibid
8. ibid
9. ibid, emphasis added
10. Report, p. 9, emphasis added
11. Report, pp. 9-10
12. Report, p. 10
13. ibid
14. ibid
15. ibid
16. Report, pp. 12-13
17. Report, p. 13
18. Report, p. 14
19. ibid
20. Report, p. 15
21. Report, p. 19
22. Report, p. 16
23. Report, p. 19
24. Report, p. 20
25. Report, p. 23

26. Report, p. 24
27. Report, p. 25, emphasis added
28. Report, pp. 25-26
29. Report, p. 27, emphasis added
30. Report, p. 26
31. Report, p. 30
32. Report, p. 31, emphasis added
33. Report, p. 32
34. Report, p. 23
35. *Minnesota Daily*, 10-16-74
36. *Minnesota Daily*, 10-17-74
37. ibid
38. Lehmberg and Pflaum, *The University of Minnesota, 1945-2000*, University of Minnesota Press, 2001, pp. 135-136

CHAPTER TWENTY-FOUR (pgs 219-221)
1. *Minnesota Daily*, January 7, 1974
2. *Minnesota Daily*, ibid

CHAPTER TWENTY-FIVE (pgs 222-226)
1. *Star Tribune,* 4/6/05, A12.
2. *Miranda v. Arizona*, 348 U.S. 436 (1966)
3. Lehmberg and Pflaum, *The University of Minnesota, 1945-2000*, University of Minnesota Press, 2001, pp. 236-237
4. Lehmberg and Pflaum, p. 230
5. www.ineas.org/article/zollissue2
6. History of Medicine//National Institute of Health/ www.nlmnihgov/ hmd/ manuscript/dad/rigler
7. ada.org/prof/resources/pubs/adanews/adanenewsarticlesap
8. Star Tribune, 2/21/2007
9. Lehmberg and Pflaum, pp. 213, 277

CHAPTER TWENTY-SIX (pgs 227-228)
1. website of the Jay Phillips' Center for Jewish-Christian Learning
2. ibid

CHAPTER TWENTY-EIGHT (pgs 236-245)

1. www.littleindia.com/archive/DEC02
2. www.membersclabar.ca.gov/search/ memberdetail
3. *Rajender v. University of Minnesota,* 563 F. Supp. 401, (D. Minn. 1983)
4. Rajender Consent Decree at 3-4
5. *Nancy Kobrin v. University of Minnesota; the Regents of the University of Minnesota,* March 10, 1997, www.caselaw.in.findlaw. com/scripts, U.S. Court of Appeals for the Eighth Circuit, No. 96-2674
6. *Kobrin,* ibid
7. Personal communication to author by Judge Parker. Parker left the panel in November, 1983 for a seat on the Minnesota Court of Appeals. As an assistant attorney general under Miles Lord, Parker assisted me in the prosecution of the *Carl Carter v. McCarthy's Café* race discrimination proceedings
8. www.1.umn.edu/women/ history. The website for the University of Minnesota Office of University Women.
9. Office of University Women website, id. See this website for a historical overview 1960-2004 of the University's efforts on behalf of its women faculty and staff.
10. Lehmberg and Pflaum, p. 177

CHAPTER TWENTY-NINE (pgs 245-252)

1. 719 F. 2d at 280
2. ibid
3. ibid
4. ibid
5. 719 F. 2d at 281
6. 719 F. 2d at 283
7. ibid
8. ibid
9. ibid
10. ibid
11. 719 F. 2d at 285
12. 719 F. 2d at 283
13. ibid
14. 719 F. 2d at 284

15. 719 F. 2d. at 285
16. ibid
17. Lehmberg and Pflaum, p. 138

CHAPTER THIRTY (pgs 253-255)

1. Lehmberg and Pflaum, *The University of Minnesota, 1945-2000,* pp.197, 199, University of Minnesota Press, 2001
2. ibid
3. ibid, fn. 53, p. 370
4. ibid, p.204
5. ibid, p 257, emphasis added

CHAPTER THIRTY-ONE (pgs 256-260)

1. Rose v. Koch, 278 Minn. 235, 154 N.W.2d 409 (1967)
2. 154 N.W.2d 409, 417
3. ibid
4. ibid
5. 154 N.W. 2d. 418, fn 15
6. 154 N.W.2d 418
7. 376 U.S. 254, 84 S. Ct. 710, 11 L. Ed. 2d 686, 95 A.L.R. 2d 1412
8. 154 N.W. 2d 422

CHAPTER THIRTY-TWO (pgs 261-266)

1. Naftalin, *"A History of the Farmer-Labor Party in Minnesota", p.* 93
2. *"Ethical Considerations for a Lawyer-Lobbyist," Hennepin Lawyer, Robert Latz, (March-April 1982)*
3. Star Tribune, ibid

CHAPTER THIRTY-THREE (pgs 267-273)

1. Star Tribune, 8/24/03, Rob Hotakainen
2. Star Tribune, ibid
3. Crystal/Robbinsdale/New Hope/Golden Valley Sun Post/December 15, 2005, Sue Weber
4. Minneapolis/St. Paul Magazine, February 2, 2004
5. See 1982 article on the ethics of the lawyer-lobbyist in Minnesota,supra
6. In re Gillard, 260 NW 2d 562 (Minn. 1977), and *In re Gillard*, 271 NW 2d 785 (Minn. 1978)

CHAPTER THIRTY-SIX (pgs 282-287)

1. www.startribune.com/stories/587 11/9/03; profile published 10/16/02
2. www.newsmax.com/archives/articles/2003/10/21/ 172212.shtml
3. newsmax, ibid
4. www.csd.cl.com/ election/Winners/Coleman.html, 11/9/03
5. News release University of Kansas Office of University Relations. www.ur.ku.edu/News/ 98/N/Nov/News/Nov6,1998/thebody.html
6. AIPAC invitation to a Twin Cities community annual event, May 2, 2004.
7. *Star Tribune* 1/5/04 Rob Hotakainen
8. ibid

CHAPTER THIRTY-SEVEN (pgs 288-291)

1. Remembering Paul Wellstone, David Moberg, www.linkerusadr.com/paul
2. www.wikiquote org/wiki/PaulWellstone
3. Sylvia Kaplan, City Pages; www.citypages.com/databank/23/1143/article10826.asp
4. www.cnn.allpolitics.com/Wellstone/SeanLoughlin/10/ 25/02
5. Remembering Paul Wellstone, Scott Adams, Salon.com News, 10/29/02
6. Adams, ibid
7. U.S. Senator Russ Feingold in describing the vibrant spirit of my friend Paul Wellstone…" in comment on *Paul Wellstone: The Life of A Passionate Progressive*, Bill Lofy, University of Michigan Press (August 29, 2005.) Wellstone lives on in his own words in *The Conscience of a Liberal: Reclaiming the Compassionate Agenda*, University of Minnesota Press.
8. www.wellstone.org/11/20/05

CHAPTER THIRTY-NINE (pgs 295-307)

1. Ornstein on Franken, *Minneapolis/St. Paul Magazine*, January 2006, William Swanson

2. Franken interview with members of the *Minneapolis Star Tribune Editorial Board*, December 11, 2005
3. *Newsweek*, 3/29/04
4. All have appeared on the *New York Times Bestseller List*. [*Minneapolis/St. Paul Magazine*, January 2006, William Swanson.]
5. *Star Tribune*, Franken interview with members of the *Minneapolis Star Editorial Board*, December 11, 2005
6. ibid
7. Franken, *Minneapolis Star Tribune Editorial Board* interview, ibid.

Thomas L. Friedman
1. Minneapolis native Aaron Brown, relieved of his position as host of *CNN Newshour*, and Ted Koppel recently retired as host of his own network news and commentary program, are two recent examples of the ever changing television scene where personality may overshadow experience and lucid commentary
2. Duluth native Lester Crystal was the Executive Producer of Public Television's *The Newshour*. Crystal is a former President of NBC News.)
3. www.roycecarlton.com
4. Royce Carlton, ibid
5. www.diplomacv.shu.evu/friedman.html. Inaugural Lecture of the Philip and Mary Shannon Seton Hall Speaker Series, October 16, 2002
6. Seton Hall Lecture, ibid
7. Audience comments from a lecture Friedman delivered at Purdue University, Royce Carlton, ibid
8. Royce Carlton, ibid
9. www.workinglife.org/Descend-friedman.pbf
10. Faux, ibid, (Jeff Faux was the founding president and is now Distinguished Fellow of the Economic Policy Institute. He has written *The Global Class War,* Wiley, January, 2006.)
11. www.snowcrest.net/reltl/reason.html
12. Royce Carlton, ibid

Norman J. Ornstein

1. *In Minnesota*-Richard Broderick, March/April 2004
2. *The National Journal*
3. *Columbia Journalism Review*
4. *Houston Chronicle*, May 1, 2003
5. www.aei.org/scholars
6. *In Minnesota*, Broderick, ibid, p. 25 - Gingrich is a former Speaker of the House of Representatives; Shalala was Secretary of Health and Human Services in the Clinton administration; Mfume is a former member of Congress and then led the National Association for the Advancement of Colored People (NAACP); Panetta served in the Congress from California and was Chief of Staff to the President during the Clinton administration.
7. *In Minnesota*, Broderick, ibid, pp. 26-27
8. *In Minnesota*, Broderick, ibid, p. 26
9. www.aei.org/scholars
10. ibid
11. *New York Times,* nytims.com,1/19/06
12. www.aei.org/scholars

CHAPTER FORTY-ONE (pgs 311-316)

1. *Star Tribune*, October 17, 2004, based on a New York Times report by Richard Stevenson
2. *Minnesota Stand-off; The Politics of Deadlock*, Rodney Searle, Alton Press, (1990.) See also *Tribune of the People: The Minnesota Legislature and Its Leadership,* Royce Hanson, University of Minnesota Press (1990.)

CHAPTER FORTY-TWO (pgs 317-322)

1. Newsweekonline, www.msnbc.msn.com/id/ 16472057/1/2007

CHAPTER FORTY-THREE (pgs 322-331)

1. *Star Tribune* editorial, 10/21/05
2. *New York Times* editorial, 10/18/05, nytimes.com
3. ibid
4. *New York Times*, 10/09/05

5. ibid
6. The Role of Catholic Voters, 4/8/05, CNN.com, William Schneider
7. CNN.com, 4/8/05, ibid
8. ibid
9. *Star Tribune*, 10/16/04, "The Spiritual, Political Worlds Come to a Crossroads" Chuck Haga
10. ibid
11. Mary Ann Bryndal, a Catholic who supported John Kerry, *Star Tribune*, 10/16/04, ibid
12. *Star Tribune*, 10/17/04, reporting on a *New York Times* article by David M Halbfinger
13. *New York Times*,10/12/04 "Group of Bishops Using Influence to Oppose Kerry."
14. *Star Tribune*, 10/24/04, AA2

Bush's Faith-Based Initiative

1. *Star Tribune*, 10/10/04, Lori Sturdevant quoting from the book "What's the Matter with Kansas? How Conservatives Won the Heart of America" by Thomas Frank, Henry Holt & Co., 2004
2. *Star Tribune*, 9/24/04, quoting the *New York Times*
3. *Star Tribune*, 10/10/04, Sturdevant
4. *Star Tribune*, 9/22/04, David Domke

Should Jews be Concerned

1. *Star Tribune*, 9/22/04, David Domke
2. *Star Tribune*, 9/11/04, B. 7
3. ibid
4. *Twin Cities Jewish Life*, September/October 2004, Stacy Gallop

CHAPTER FORTY-FOUR (pgs 332-338)

1. Greenberg and Wald, "Still Liberal After All Those Years?", *Jews in American Politics, 2001,* p.162
2. ibid
3. www.theamericanjewishcommittee.com
4. Greenberg and Wald, p. 166
5. Greenberg and Wald, p.167

CHAPTER FORTY-FIVE (pgs 339-344)

1. Greenberg and Wald, p.169
2. Greenberg and Wald, p.170
3. ibid
4. Greenberg and Wald, pp.171-173, citing data from the Voters News Service Exit Poll Data, 1998
5. www.jewishvirtuallibrary, adivisionoftheamerican-israelicooperativeenterprise.com
6. ibid
7. Greenberg and Wald, p.175
8. Greenberg and Wald, p.179
9. The National Jewish Population Study of 1990 cited by Greenberg and Wald at p.181
10. Greenberg and Wald state that Jews comprise less than three per cent of the U.S. population. Greenberg and Wald, p.192. Other surveys put the number at 2.2 per cent. Jewish Virtual Library

CHAPTER FORTY-SIX (pgs 345-360)

1. *Jews in American Politics*, Maisel & Forman, Roman & Littlefield, 2001
2. Franken interview with Tim Russert, CNBC, 9/27/03
3. *New York Times*, nytimes.com, 3/21/06, David D. Kirkpatrick
4. *Newsweek*, 4/3/06

INDEX

Borman, Marvin, 19, 19, 230

Boschwitz, Ellen, 275

Boschwitz, Rudy, xii, 23, 93, 136, 149, 165, 268, 269, 271, 274-281, 289, 290, 298, 299, 310, 327, 328, 337, 350, 352

Boxer, Barbara, 274, 318

Brady, Tim, 354

Brand, Irving, 126, 352

Breen, Aviva, 354

Breen, Stanley, 23

Bright, Joseph, 49

Bright, Myron, 49, 309

Brill, Josiah, Sr., 2

Brin, Fanny, 353

Brooks, Ronnie, 165

Brown, Aaron, 355

Brown, David, 226

Bruninks, Robert, 255

Buchwald, Henry, 225

Bumpers, Dale, 195-196

Burnquist, J.A.A., 12, 32, 38-39

Burton, Richard, 197

Bush, George W., Jr., 229, 275-277, 281, 285-288, 291, 298, 301, 308, 309, 311-313, 322, 324-329, 331, 333, 334, 341, 342, 347, 349, 355

Bush, George, Sr., 96, 281

Cardin, Benjamin, 317

Cardozo, Isaac N., 352

Carle, Norman, 54, 55

Carlson, Arne, 127, 166, 167, 281, 330

Carman, Harry, 167

Carter, Carl L, 44-49

Carter, Jimmy, 104, 147, 163, 195,

341, 342

Carty, Denzil A., 44, 47

Casey, 249

Chambers, Clark, 162

Chase, Ray T., 11, 12

Chavez, Cesar, 243, 244

Cheit, Earl, 192

Chilgren, Ed, xx, 67

Choper, Jesse, 224

Christenson, Gerald, 142

Churchill, Winston, 282

Cina, Fred, 67, 71, 134

Cleveland, Harlan, 190

Clinton, Bill, xvi, 130, 285, 288, 294, 312, 341

Clinton, Hillary, 318

Coates, John, 56

Coffman, Lotus, 154

Cohen, Burton, 19, 217

Cohen, Dan, 79, 355

Cohen, Gary, 356

Cohen, Jay, 226

Cohen, Lawrence "Larry", xii, 135, 148, 217, 352

Cohen, Linda, 157, 353

Cohen, Philip, 356

Cohen, Richard, 151, 315, 319, 339

Cohen, Sidney R., 228

Cole, Pearl, 356

Coleman, Chris, 275, 297

Coleman, Jacob, 282

Coleman, Laurie Casserly, 282

Coleman, Nicholas, 165, 200, 206, 209, 211, 214- 216, 219

Coleman, Norman, xii, 269, 271, 274-277, 282-287, 291, 296, 300, 309, 328, 336, 350